The
LYLE

Price Guide to Collectibles and Memorabilia
Memorabilia
#2

The LYLE

Price Guide to Collectibles and Memorabilia
#2

compiled by Anthony Curtis

A Perigee Book

Perigee Books
are published by
The Putnam Publishing Group
200 Madison Avenue
New York, NY 10016

Firefighter's hat on front cover courtesy of CIGNA Museum
and Art Collection.
Other items on front cover are public domain or courtesy
of Hake's Americana and Collectibles, York, PA, auction
catalogue.

Library of Congress Cataloging-in-Publication Data

The Lyle price guide to collectibles and memorabilia #2 /
    edited by Anthony Curtis.

        p.   cm.
     "A Perigee book."
     Includes index.
     ISBN 0-399-51515-1
     1. Antiques—Catalogs.   I. Curtis, Tony.
NK1125.L79   1990   89-3695 CIP
745.1′075—dc19

Cover design copyright © 1990 by Jack Ribik
Front cover: Photograph of firefighter's hat courtesy CIGNA Museum and
Art Collection; photographs of other items are in the public domain or courtesy
Hake's Americana and Collectibles, York, PA, auction catalogue.

Printed in the United States of America
           5   6   7   8   9   10

This book is printed on acid-free paper.

PRICE GUIDE TO COLLECTIBLES AND MEMORABILIA

Collecting is a world governed by uncommon rules, which allow everyone to participate in the fascinating game at any chosen level from attractive yet inexpensive home furnishings to big money investments.

It is a passion that can become a way of life. The lure of the chase, the search for the elusive treasure, the fascination of knowing almost, but not quite, everything about some out-of-the-ordinary subject is what makes the collector's adrenalin surge. They thrive most of all on the teasing certainty that fortunes can be made and that just around the corner they could find the one thing that will make their collection complete and unique.

When bitten by 'the bug', men and women of all ages and all walks of life have become collectors and their specialities range from Art Pottery to Wristwatches, from Anchovy Pot Lids to Zeppelin Memorabilia. Everything and anything can be collected, from 18th century Meissen china to today's Coca-Cola signs.

If nobody collected golfing books, then the first edition of 'The Golf' written in 1743 wouldn't be worth $25,000 and for the same reason an old wine bottle wouldn't be worth $5,000 and Marilyn Monroe's autograph wouldn't be worth over $1,000.

Whilst scarcity value can take even the most commonplace artefacts of a past age into a high price range, it is still possible to build a fascinating collection for a minimal outlay and, of course, with many items being newly collectable, valuable pieces can still be found for a few dollars. Rarity however, does not always herald instant wealth, for one of the most important rules of the game is supply and demand. The bigger the collecting field – the bigger the market therefore, the greater the chance of a rare item being fully appreciated – and that means money. With a little of the right knowledge there is always the real possibility of turning a modest investment into a considerable nest egg.

Obviously condition is of great importance when establishing value. The prices quoted here are based on collectables which are in fair and average condition. There is still a rich source of material available and an example which has survived in good condition will prove to be a better investment than one damaged or showing signs of wear and tear.

This book is specifically designed to aid both the busy specialist and the enthusiastic beginner by creating an awareness of the vast scope of this fascinating field and by providing a guide to the sometimes surprising current market value of thousands of items.

The sky really is the limit for successful collectors, so – join the treasure hunt.

Acknowledgements

Abridge Auction Rooms, Market Place Abridge, Essex RM4 1UA
Helen Anderson, Page Galleries, 29 High Street, Kington
Aviation Antiques, 369 Croydon Road, Caterham, Surrey
Bearnes, Rainbow, Avenue Road, Torquay, Devon TQ2 5TG
Bermondsey Antique Market, Tower Bridge Road, London
J. J. Binns, Alpha Antiques, High Street, Kington, Hereford
Border Bygones, The Vallets, Forge Crossing, Lyonshall, Kington HR5 3JQ
British Antique Exporters, School Close, Queen Elizabeth Avenue, Burgess Hill, West Sussex
R. Brocklesby, 8 Whites Road, Bitterne, Southampton SO2 7NQ (Cigarette Packets)
Brown & Merry, 41 High Street, Tring, Herts HP23 5AB
Shirley Butler, Oddiquities, 61 Waldram Park Road, Forest Hill, London (Fire Irons)
Capes Dunn & Co., The Auction Galleries, 38 Charles Street, Manchester M1 7DB
Chancellors Hollingsworth, 31 High Street, Ascot, Berkshire SL5 7HG
The Chicago Sound Company, Northmoor House, Colesbrook, Gillingham, Dorset (Jukeboxes)
Christie's, 8 King Street, St James's, London SW1Y 6QT
Christie's South Kensington Ltd., 85 Old Brompton Road, London SW7 3LD
Nic Costa & Brian Bates, 10 Madeley Street, Tunstall, Stoke on Trent ST6 5AT (Amusement Machines)
Courts Miscellany, (George Court), 48 Bridge Street, Leominster
Dacre, Son & Hartley, 1-5 The Grove, Ilkley, West Yorkshire LS29 8HS
Dreweatt Neate, Donnington Priory, Donnington, Newbury, Berks RG13 2JE
Du Mouchelles Art Galleries Co., 409 E. Jefferson Avenue, Detroit, Michigan 48226 USA
The Enchanted Aviary, 63 Hall Street, Long Melford, Sudbury, Suffolk (Taxidermy)
Judith Gardener, The Childrens Bookshop, Hay on Wye
Gorringes, Auction Galleries, 15 North Street, Lewes, East Sussex
Goss & Crested China Ltd., 62 Murray Road, Horndean, Hants PO8 9JL (Bairnsfatherware)
W. R. J. Greenslade & Co., 13 Hammet Street, Taunton, Somerset TA1 1RN
Gerald N. Gurney, Guildhall Orchard, Gt Bromley, Colchester, Essex CO7 7TU (Racketana)
Mark Harrison, Middlesex (Telephone)
Hat Pin Society of Great Britain, 26 Fulwell Road, Bozeat, Wellingborough, Northants NN9 7LY
Giles Haywood, The Auction House, St John's Road, Stourbridge DY8 1EW
Heathcote Ball & Co., 47 New Walk, Leicester
Hobbs & Chambers, 'At the Sign of the Bell', Market Place, Cirencester, Gloucestershire
Hobbs Parker, Romney House, Ashford Market, Ashford, Kent TN23 1PG
Paul Jones, Hereford Alternative Arts Centre, Dilwyn, Hereford (Stained Glass, Taps)
G. A. Key, Aylsham Salerooms, Palmers Lane, Aylsham, Norfolk NR11 6EH
Kingsland Auction Services, Kingsland, Leominster
Bob Krasey, 134 Lansdowne Avenue, Winnipeg, Canada R2W 0GY (Coca Cola)
Lalonde Fine Art, 71 Oakfield Road, Clifton, Bristol, Avon BS8 2BE
Lawrence Fine Art, South Street, Crewkerne, Somerset TA18 8AB
David Lay, The Penzance Auction House, Alverton, Penzance, Cornwall TR18 4RE
Min Lewis, The Vine, St Davids Street, Presteigne, Powys (Pianola Rolls)
Tim Lewis, Woonton, Herefordshire
Locke & England, Walton House, 11 The Parade, Leamington Spa
Lots Road Chelsea Auction Galleries, 71 Lots Road, Chelsea, London SW10 0RN
R. K. Lucas & Son, 9 Victoria Place, Haverfordwest SA61 2JX
Lynn Private Collection, Tyne & Wear (Childrens Books)
Duncan McAlpine, Flat 4, 55 Lordship Road, Stoke Newington, London N16 0QJ (American Comics)
Miller & Co., Lemon Quay Auction Rooms, Truro, Cornwall TR1 2LW
Onslow's Auctioneers, Metrostore, Townmead Road, London SW6 2RZ
Osmond Tricks, Regent Street, Auction Rooms, Clifton, Bristol, Avon BS8 4HG
Phillips, Blenstock House, 7 Blenheim Street, New Bond Street, London W1Y 0AS
Geoff & Linda Price, 37 Camberford Drive, Tiffany Green, Wednesbury WS10 0UA (Model Buses)
Prudential Fine Art Auctioneers, 5 Woodcote Close, Kingston upon Thames, Surrey KT2 5LZ
Reeds Rains Prudential, Trinity House, 114 Northenden Road, Manchester M33 3HD
Record Collector, 45 St Marys Road, Ealing, London W5 5RQ
Brenda Riley, Kaleidescope, London House, Presteigne, Powys (Ladies Underwear)
Russell, Baldwin & Bright, The Fine Art Saleroom, Rylands Road, Leominster HR6 8JG
The Peter Savage Antique Bottle Museum, Cambrook House, Nr Warwick CV35 9HP
Lacy Scott (Fine Art Dept), 10 Risbygate Street, Bury St Edmunds, Suffolk IP33 3AA
Robt. W. Skinner Inc., Bolton Gallery, Route 117, Bolton, Massachusetts, USA
David Stanley Auctions, Stordan Grange, Osgathorpe, Leicester LE12 9SR
Street Jewellery, 16 Eastcliffe Avenue, Newcastle on Tyne NE3 4SN
Louis Taylor & Sons, Percy Street, Hanley, Stoke on Trent, Staffordshire ST1 1NF
Trench Enterprizes, Kevin Holmes, Three Cow Green, Bacton, Stowmarket, Suffolk (Jigsaw Puzzles)
M. Veissid & Co., Hobsley House, Frodesley, Shrewsbury SY5 7ND
Trevor Vennett-Smith, 11 Nottingham Road, Gotham, Nottingham NG11 0HE (Signed Photographs)
Wallis & Wallis, West Street Auction Galleries, West Street, Lewes, East Sussex BN7 2NJ
Peter Wilson Fine Art Auctioneers, Victoria Gallery, Market Street, Nantwich, Cheshire
Woolley & Wallis, The Castle Auction Mart, Salisbury, Wiltshire SP1 3SU
Worsfolds Auction Galleries, 40 Station Road West, Canterbury, Kent
Yesterday's News, 43 Dundonald Road, Colwyn Bay, Clwyd LL29 7RD
Yesterday's Paper, 40 Southview, Holcombe Rogus, Wellington, Somerset TA21 0PP

Contents

CONTENTS

ADVERTISING SIGNS

From the Victorian age till the mid 20th century, mass market advertising had to catch the passing public's eye. Large metal or card signs in shop windows or stuck on walls were a favourite way. They were designed to make an immediate impact and so most were at least one metre square, brightly colored and bearing a trade emblem or figure. The most valuable signs today are enamel on metal from the Art Nouveau or Art Deco periods though cardboard ones in good condition are also popular. Famous artists like McKnight Kauffer, Nerman and Harry Rountree designed signs for brand name firms like Oxo, Fry's, Nestle's, Rowntree's, petrol and oil companies. Car manufacturers' signs are very collectable − especially those for Lagonda, Bentley, Rolls Royce and Bugatti.

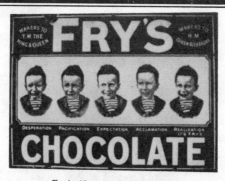

Fry's Chocolate. (Street Jewellery) $187

Martini. (Street Jewellery) $160

Player's 'Drumhead' cigarettes. (Street Jewellery) $185

Lucas 'Ace of Spades'. (Street Jewellery) $275

Belga Vander Elst. (Street Jewellery) $120

Singer Sewing Machines, 11 x 7½in. (Street Jewellery) $175

Coleman's Mustard Cabinet, a printed tin facsimile packet, 46cm. high. (Onslow's) $363

Lazenby's Specialities, show-card, 74 x 92cm., in original frame. (Onslow's) $830

A jeweller's shop sign, America, late 19th century, wood and metal in the form of a pocket watch with a gilt painted frame, 20in. high. (Robt. W. Skinner Inc) $550

Gilbert Rae's High Class Aera-ted Waters Dunfermline, prin-ted tin sign, embossed, 71 x 51cm. (Onslow's) $743

Brasso The New Metal Polish, enamel advertising sign, pictorial, 61 x 38cm. (Onslow's) $190

C.W.S. Crumpsall A Lucky Dip Crumpsall Cream Crackers, prin-ted tin sign, 61 x 46cm. (Onslow's) $1,522

R. Fry & Co's High Class Table Waters, showcard, 51 x 38cm. (Onslow's) $709

A polychrome zinc trade sign, America, early 20th century, in form of a hip-roofed house with projecting porch, 32in. high. (Robt. W. Skinner Inc.) $800

Olympic Ale, showcard, pub-lished Brussels 1937, 46 x 31cm. (Onslow's) $27

This Is The Union Label of The Felt Hatters and Trimmers Unions of Gt. Britain, showcard, laminated, 23 x 31cm. (Onslow's) $34

A polychromed cast zinc cigar store Indian Princess, attributed to W. Demuth & Co., New York, circa 1870, 54½in. high. (Robt. W. Skinner Inc.) $16,000

Bluebell Metal Polish, showcard, 38 x 53cm. (Onslow's) $20

Brasso Metal Polish, showcard, 51 x 33cm. (Onslow's) $311

Jones Sewing Machines, enamel advertising sign, pictorial, 81 x 87cm. (Onslow's) $346

Cherry Blossom Boot Polish Is The Best, enamel advertising sign, shaped pictorial, 175cm. high. (Onslow's) $4,152

Parkinson's Sugar Coated Blood and Stomach Pills, showcard, 48 x 38cm. (Onslow's) $112

Bassett's Liquorice Allsorts shop dispenser, tin. (Onslow's) $86

Robin Starch, showcard, 38 x 26cm. (Onslow's) $553

ALBUMS

The age of photography opened all sorts of possibilities for record-keeping, but early daguerreotypes were expensive, and it was not until the later 19th century that the art became generally affordable. It was then that the photograph album came into its own as a prized Victorian family possession. Often of richly tooled leather, gold-embossed with heavy clasps, their bindings rivalled those of the family Bible. Fascinating collectables, they are usually worth more if the pictures are identified or identifiable.

Late 19th century Japanese photographic album with a finely painted frontispiece. $175

A small, fine quality embossed leather album with plated mounts and gilt decoration. $50

Late Victorian photographic album with finely printed mounts. $105

Late 19th century black lacquered album decorated with mother of pearl and ivory. $105

Early 20th century black leather album with finely cut silver plated mounts. $130

Late 19th century embossed brown leather album with floral decoration and gilt brass clasp, complete with photographs. $125

Edwardian tooled red leather album with gilded brass clasp, containing family photographs. $140

AMERICAN INDIANWARE

The American Indian has for long been a figure of romance and many collectors are interested in amassing anything connected with them. These range from "Cigar Store Indians", wooden figures carved in the likeness of Red Indians wearing feather headdresses that used to stand outside cigar stores in America, to pieces of their costume, head-dresses or bead necklaces. Buffalo hide was used by Indian tribes for making their clothes to their tents and they painted the hide in colourful patterns. Collectors also vie to possess Indian totem poles, carved and painted in characteristic ways. Tribespeople used bone, ivory, quills, corn husks, willow twigs and beads in making their artefacts and the beadwork is particularly interesting because it was first introduced among southern tribes in the 16th century by the white man as a kind of currency and spread north and east during the 18th and 19th centuries. Certain types of beads provide clues about the extent of contact between Indian tribes and white settlers.

Plains pony beaded and fringed hide dress, 19th century, formed of two skins, 51in. long. (Robt. W. Skinner Inc.) $7,200

Classic Navajo chief's blanket, woven in single strand home-spun and ravelled yarn, 82 x 62in. (Robt. W. Skinner Inc.) $30,000

Plains beaded hide boot moccasins, Southern Cheyenne/Arapaho, 1880's, 15in. high. (Robt. W. Skinner Inc.) $1,800

Navajo pictorial weaving, woven on a burgundy ground in white, green, brown, black and pink, 43 x 57in. (Robt. W. Skinner Inc.) $900

Eskimo/Northwest Coast polychrome wood mask, 19th century, cedar, 8½in. long. (Robt. W. Skinner Inc.) $2,200

A Verneh horse blanket, the blue field with rows of stylised animals, 5ft.5in. x 4ft.7in. (Christie's) $1,163

Southern Plains painted buffalo fur robe, 92in. long, 67in. wide. (Robt. W. Skinner Inc.) $500

Plain beaded hide cradle cover, Sioux, 1880s, 19in. long. (Robt. W. Skinner Inc.) $1,500

Nez Perce twined cornhusk bag, 13½ x 18in. (Robt. W. Skinner Inc.) $475

Tlingit twined spruce root rattle top basket, 5¼in. diam. (Robt. W. Skinner Inc.) $500

Hopi polychrome wood Kachina doll, possibly the clown figure, 'Piptuka', early 20th century, 8½in. high. (Robt. W. Skinner Inc.) $900

Northwest coast polychrome wood face mask, carved and incised cedar, 9½in. high. (Robt. W. Skinner Inc.) $2,500

Great Lakes loom beaded cloth bandolier bag, late 19th century, 36in. long. (Robt. W. Skinner Inc.) $850

Southwestern polychrome pottery jar, Zia, 14in. diam. (Robt. W. Skinner Inc.) $2,100

Plains beaded and fringed hide cradleboard, Ute Reservation Period, 39in. high. (Robt. W. Skinner Inc.) $650

A Hopi polychrome pottery canteen, painted over a creamy yellow slip in dark brown linear and 'Koshare' figural decoration, 3¼in. high. (Robt. W. Skinner Inc.) $200

Southwestern pottery dough bowl, Cochiti, the interior painted over a cream slip in black foliate motifs, 14in. diam. (Robt. W. Skinner Inc.) $1,200

Pacific Northwest Coast Attu circular basket with cover, 4in. high. (Christie's) $1,980

Woodlands husk face mask, composed of bands of braided cornhusks, 11½in. high. (Robt. W. Skinner Inc.) $1,000

Navajo fringed Germantown rug, woven on a bright red ground in navy-blue, dark red, pink, white and green, 76 x 83in. (Robt. W. Skinner Inc.) $7,750

A Southwestern polychrome storage jar, San Ildefonso, of tall rounded form, 12½in. high. (Robt. W. Skinner Inc.) $700

A Southwestern polychrome basketry tray, Yavapai, woven in red and dark brown designs on a golden field, 14½in. diam. (Robt. W. Skinner Inc.) $950

Late 19th century Hopi polychrome wood Kachina doll, possibly 'Qoia', a Navajo singer, 16½in. high. (Robt. W. Skinner Inc.) $4,000

Northwest coast mask, Bella/ Bella Coola, of polychrome cedar wood, 12.5/8in. high. (Robt. W. Skinner Inc.) $49,000

AMUSEMENT MACHINES

The delights of Victorian seaside holidays always included a stroll along the pier and several attempts at the amusement machines lined up there. They ranged from the naughty "What the Butler Saw" — nothing very much it turned out — to fortune telling machines, weighing machines that announced your weight in a loud voice and Test-Your-Strength punch balls. Now that amusement machines have been herded together in arcades and powered by electronics, Victorian pieces look out of date and old fashioned — except to collectors of course. They seek out pin-ball machines like the Genco ones that were popular in the 1930's and grip-test machines that used to stand on railway platforms or seaside boulevards around the turn of the century. Some machines had miniature grabs inside and when pennies were put in the slot they would reach down for a packet of sweets. Others showed two football teams valiantly kicking balls at each other.Today the price for some of these machines can be in excess of $1,000

The Clown by Jentsch & Meerz, Leipzig, circa 1915. (Brian Bates) $480

The Misers Dream, working model by Bolland, circa 1950. (Brian Bates) $1,300

Conveyor, manufactured by Stevenson & Lovett, 1947. (Nic Costa) $260

Try Your Grip, by the Mechanical Trading Company, circa 1895. (Brian Bates) $1,750

1930's Aeroplane Allwin. (Nic Costa) $300

1930's Mills Century One Arm Bandit, U.S.A. origin. (Nic Costa) $480

AMUSEMENT MACHINES

1950's All Sport two-player game by Bryans. (Nic Costa) $300

Sapphire, Allwin type 'reserve' machine of French manufacture, 1920's. (Brian Bates) $300

Gipsy Fortune by Bolland, 1950's. (Nic Costa) $260

Personality 'Love Test Meter' manufactured by Oliver Whales, Redcar, circa 1950. (Brian Bates) $245

Mid 1930's, Mutoscope 'Adam & Eve', manufactured in the U.S.A. (Nic Costa) $875

1930's, Allwin nine cup. (Nic Costa) $300

Fruit Bowl by Bryans, circa 1963. (Nic Costa) $200

Reel 21 gaming machine by Groetchen, U.S.A., 1930's. (Brian Bates) $350

Matrimonial Bureau, 'Correct photo of your future husband, wife or baby,' by Bolland, 1930's. (Brian Bates) $435

ANCHOVY POT LIDS

Anchovy paste with its salty taste is not everyone's idea of a tasty tea time snack but the Victorians loved it and consumed it on toast in vast quantities. To attract customers, paste manufacturers put their products in eye-catching tins or jars with brightly patterned lids. Those that have survived provide a rich field of interest for collectors. The most sought after are made of Prattware and decorated with transfer printed designs. Patriotic themes were especially popular and Royal coats of arms or pictures of Queen Victoria were very common — inferring that the paste was as popular with the Royals as with their subjects. The best known makers of anchovy paste were Burgess, Osborn and Thorne who made a brand called Thorne's Inimitable Anchovy Paste which came in a pot with a flag decorated lid.

Small lid by E. Lazenby & Son 6 Edwards Street, Portman Square, London. $25

Gorgona anchovy paste lid by R.T.N., printed in black on a white background. $45

Small lid by E. Lazenby & Son of London, bearing the word 'Manufactory'. $30

Anchovy paste lid by Morel Bro' Cobbett & Son Ltd., 18 Pall Mall, London. $25

Rare lid by J. N. Osborn with the design in pastel shades of blue and red on a white background. $435

Anchovy paste lid by G. F. Sutton & Co., 100 High Holborn, London. $18

Hannell's Real Gorgona anchovy paste lid, 35 Davies Street, Berkeley Square, London. $25

Real Gorgona anchovy paste lid by Manfield's, 20 Poland St., Oxford Street, London. $35

Large size Burgess's genuine anchovy paste lid, '107 Strand, corner of the Savoy steps'. $20

ANCHOVY POT LIDS

Edward VII lid by Burgess's, Hythe Rd., Willesden, London. $14

Anchovy paste lid referred to as 'London Lid', with no maker's name. $55

Anchovy paste lid by Burgess's 'The Original Fish Sauce Warehouse'. $10

Early 1860's lid by Cross & Blackwell, 21 Soho Square and Ilking St., Soho. $55

E. Lazenby & Son lid, Edward Street, Portman Square, London. $45

Small lid by G. F. Sutton, Sons & Co., Osborne Works, Brandon Road, King's Cross. $14

Crosse & Blackwell lid, 21 Soho Square, London, established 1706. $14

Real Gorgona anchovy paste lid by Harry Peck's, Snow Hill, London. $20

A pictorial lid by Crosse & Blackwell, in sepia on a white background. $60

Anchovy paste lid by G. F. Sutton & Co., Osborne Works, King's Cross, W.C. $18

'London' lid printed in black on a white background. $35

George V anchovy paste lid by Burgess's, Hythe Road, Willesden, N.W. $20

ANIMAL FIGURES

Animals have figured in decorative arts from the earliest cave paintings, and man has always found their depiction irresistible. Even the Moorish sculptor of the Plaza de los Leones in the Alhambra defied the edicts of his religion to carve stone lions round the fountain. (By not giving them eyes he probably kept his!) This fascination has found a ready outlet in china and pottery — examples exist from every age and culture, from priceless Chinese tigers to the two-a-penny cats and dogs found in any seaside souvenir shop. The Victorians had a passion for introducing 'wild life' into their ordered homes, as the stuffed figures of their favourite pets or wild animals bear witness, and just about every pottery of the time had its range of animal figures.

Collectors can concentrate on one animal type, one pottery or even one designer. They form a superb range of collectables to suit all pockets.

A large Royal Doulton Flambe model of a fox, glazed in black and red, 23.6cm. high, c.m.l. & c., signed Noke. (Phillips)
$171

A Ralph Wood figure of a recumbent ram, on an oval green rockwork base moulded with foliage, circa 1770, 18.5cm. wide. (Christie's)
$3,801

A 19th century painted chalkware cat, America, 10¾in. high. (Robt. W. Skinner Inc.)
$850

A Staffordshire saltglaze agateware cat, with irregular blue markings and brown striations, circa 1750, 13.5cm.high. (Christie's)
$2,692

Pair of Kakiemon cockerels standing on rockwork bases, circa 1680, 28cm. high. (Christie's)
$35,200

'Dog Begging with Lump of Sugar on nose', produced 1929, probably a prototype, 8in. high. (Louis Taylor)
$759

ANIMAL FIGURES

One of a pair of 17th century Arita standing puppies, 24cm. long. (Christie's) $37,400

A Staffordshire seated dog, circa 1790, 3½in. high. (Christie's) $240

A Zsolnay Pecs lustre group, modelled as two polar bears on a large rock in a green and blue golden lustre, 4½in. high. (Christie's) $400

A Minton 'majolica' garden seat modelled as a crouching monkey, circa 1870, 47cm. high. (Christie's) $12,512

Seated Bulldog with Union Jack, hat and cigar, 7.5in. high. (Louis Taylor) $858

A 19th century Arita model of a tiger climbing on rocks among dwarf bamboo, 71cm. high. (Christie's) $5,610

A 19th century Coalport porcelain peacock in gold and white on a rococo base, 6in. high. (G. A. Key) $222

'The Bull', a Poole pottery stone-ware figure, designed by Harold and Phoebe Stabler, 33.5cm. high. (Christie's) $252

Royal Doulton china model of a Siamese cat, 5½in. high, HN1655. (Prudential Fine Art) $33

ANIMAL FIGURES

An Art Deco Wedgwood animal figure, modelled as a fallow deer, designed by J. Skeaping, 21.5cm. high. (Phillips) $230

A Portobello cow creamer, with milkmaid on a stool, 16cm. wide. (Phillips) $734

A late Wemyss small model of a pig, 15.5cm. high, painted mark Wemyss, printed mark Made in England. (Phillips) $1,337

Late 19th century German figure of a monkey, decorated in grey and yellow glazes, 46cm. high. (Christie's) $638

A Doulton mouse group moulded with three minstrels on a green mound, by George Tinworth, circa 1885, 3¾in. high. (Abridge Auctions) $1,275

An attractive small Derby model of a Pug, modelled and coloured with a gold studded collar around its neck, 6cm. high. (Phillips) $699

A Staffordshire figure of an Alcibiades hound, on a black marbled base edged in green and turquoise, circa 1810, 42cm. high. (Christie's) $2,059

Late 17th century model of a Kakiemon seated tiger, 18.5cm. high. (Christie's) $35,530

Late 19th century painted chalkware horse, 10in. high. (Christie's) $286

ART NOUVEAU
POSTCARDS

Of all types, Art Nouveau postcards are the most prestigious and can fetch hundreds and even thousands of pounds. Many were originally designs for posters by such artists as Alphonse Mucha or Jules Cheret (worth $75-$500 each). Look out for the Collection des Cent, a series of 100 cards published in 1901, or Editions Cino (1898) a series of 35 cards including work by Toulouse Lautrec, which can be worth $75-$750 each.

Art Nouveau postcard embossed and overlaid with silver, by Raphael Tuck.
$12

'Autumn', an Art Nouveau study by A. K. Macdonald.
$25

'Mikado', an Oriental study by Raphael Kirschner, Series 600. $35

Velkonocni Pozdrav, an Art Nouveau Easter postcard printed in Czechoslovakia.
$10

'In the Eventide', a study by A. K. Macdonald. $25

'Der Verrufene Weiher', by M. Webenwein, Viennese artist. $10

An embroidered Continental study by Hans Volkert. $14

ART NOUVEAU POSTCARDS

Art Nouveau study of a girl with a goblet, printed in black. $9

Art Nouveau study of a girl with a cigarette, by S. Hilderscheimer. $18

An Art Nouveau Easter card printed in Czechoslovakia by Velkonocni Pozdrau. $10

'Cartolina Postale', a set of four cards by Raphael Kirchner. $210

'Femme a L'Eventail' by Brunelleschi, printed in France. $105

'My hope and heart is with thee', a series postcard by Raphael Tuck, No. 3571. $30

'Peacock Feathers' by Raphael Kirschner, series 660. $35

ART POTTERY

Art pottery is the work of an individual potter which shows that person's artistry, style and originality. It is not mass produced. From earliest times artist/potters have made one-off items of beauty and in the 19th century there was a great demand for individually created pieces. The Martin brothers were art potters par excellence. One of the first big pottery concerns to encourage and provide facilities for art potters was Doulton's for, from the 1860's onwards, Henry Doulton invited students from the nearby Lambeth College of Art to work in his Studio which was financed by the more prosaic side of his business. He never attempted to impose an "house style" on his protégés who were encouraged to give their art full expression. Among many who worked at Doulton's were George Tinworth, the Barlows, William Rix, who discovered ways of producing marbling effects in pottery glazes, and Charles J. Noke who invented the famous Flambe and Chang glazes.

A faience vase decorated with entwined leaves and fruit, 8½in. high, circa 1877. $150

A large Royal Doulton Burslem Holbein Ware jardiniere decorated with four cavaliers playing cards, 13¼in. high, signed W. Nunn. $785

Royal Doulton vase painted by Ethel Beard, 13in. high.$210

A Doulton Lambeth coffee pot painted with a purple iris, circa 1879. $385

A pair of Doulton Lambeth faience oil lamp bases decorated by Esther Lewis, 10¼in. high.
                                    $785

Royal Doulton Chang vase by Noke and Moore, 7½in. high, circa 1935. $960

Royal Doulton Sung vase by
Charles Noke and Fred Moore,
10¼in. high, circa 1930.
$455

Royal Doulton Chinese jade
two-handled bowl in white and
green, 3½in. high. $560

A Doulton Lambeth Silicon
ware oviform vase, by Edith
D. Lupton and Ada Dennis,
20.5cm. high, dated 1885.
$330

Doulton Lambeth faience vase
decorated with daffodils and
narcissi, 10½in. high. $140

A large Royal Doulton Sung
vase by Arthur Eaton, decorated with dragons amongst
clouds, 13in. high, circa 1930.
$1,400

A Royal Doulton jug decorated
with a maiden wearing a flowing
dress, 10½in. high. $260

A Royal Doulton earthenware
globular vase, 21.8cm. high.
$95

A Royal Doulton Titanian ware
teapot, 6½in. high, circa 1920.
$55

Royal Doulton Chang vase by
C. J. Noke and Harry Nixon,
7½in. high, circa 1930.
$2,100

Doulton Lambeth faience vase with the artist's monogram for Mary Butterton, circa 1880. $315

A Royal Doulton Sung vase by Charles Noke and Fred Moore, 7in. high, circa 1930.$260

A Royal Doulton Sung vase by Noke, 6¾in. high, circa 1928. $700

Royal Doulton faience vase by John H. McLennan, decorated with panels representing Earth and Water, 13½in. high. $315

Doulton Art Pottery jardiniere with a blue ground and applied flowers, 8¾in. high. $105

A Doulton Burslem baluster vase painted with an Edwardian lady, by H. G. Theaker, 10¼in. high. $575

A Doulton Lambeth faience vase painted with stylised flowers, by Emily Gillman, 9¼in. high. $150

A Doulton Burslem Morrisian ware teapot decorated with a band of dancing maidens, 7¾in. high, circa 1899. $140

An oviform pate-sur-pate vase decorated with birds by Florence Barlow, 15in. high. $610

AUTOGRAPH LETTERS & DOCUMENTS

Libraries and museums all over the world avidly collect the letters and holograph writings of famous people which are prized not only because they are the raw material of history but for the insights they give into notable lives and events. There is a peculiar thrill at seeing at the signature of Queen Elizabeth the First written by her own hand or reading a note penned by Charles Dickens. The identity of the writer is of paramount importance when collecting autograph manuscripts and so is rarity because some people were more generous in signing their name than others. It is the rare ones that are most valuable.

Some artists like Edward Lear, Picasso and Chagall were often generous when signing their names or writing letters because they would frequently add a little drawing as well. These make the value soar.

The content of a note or letter is very significant. If something of interest is being recounted, the value of the manuscript is higher than if the writer was only refusing an invitation to dinner. Condition of autograph letters is also important and so is provenance because if authenticity can be proved that is a bonus. Some famous people did not sign their own letters but had a secretary copy their signatures and there is a brisk trade in forged Churchill letters for example.

Official documents concerning the lives of famous people can be valuable. Thomas Chippendale's 1748 marriage certificate was sold for $1,000 and a 1940 cheque from Bernard Shaw changed hands at $275. Even documents relating to the lives of lesser people are eagerly collected – records of Victorian hospitals or lunatic asylums; boxes of old legal deeds or wills are all the stuff of history.

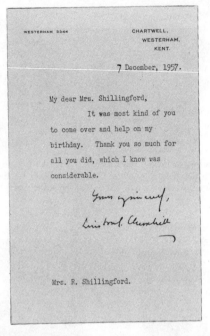

Sir Winston Churchill, Typewritten Letter signed, 1957. $775

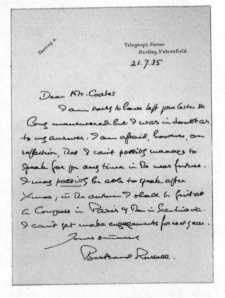

Bertrand Russell, Autograph Letter signed, 1935. $260

(John Wilson)

30

AUTOGRAPH LETTERS & DOCUMENTS

J. M. Keynes, Typewritten Letter signed, 1932.
$260

Franz Liszt, Autograph Letter signed in French,
17th May, no year. $850

Augustus John, Autograph Letter signed, 1933.
$115

Robert Browning, Autograph Letter signed
accepting an invitation, undated. $650

(John Wilson)

Sir Arthur Conan Doyle, Autograph Letter
signed mentioning Holmes, undated. $675

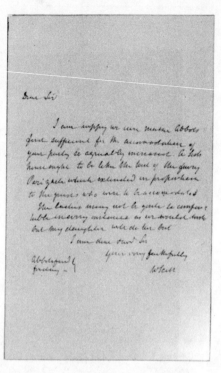

Sir Walter Scott, Autograph Letter signed,
undated. $850

Charles Dickens, Cheque completed and signed,
1866. $600

William Ewart Gladstone, Autograph Letter
signed to John Murray, 1863. $100

Alfred, Lord Tennyson, Cheque signed, 1871.
                                           $130

(John Wilson)

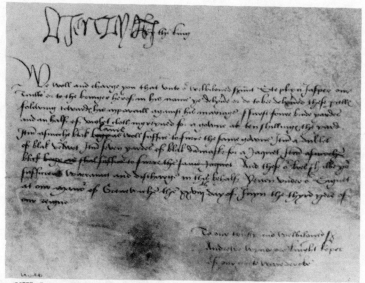

Henry VIII, Letter signed to the keeper of the great wardrobe ordering materials for the wedding apparel of Stephen Jasper, 6 x 7½in. on vellum, 1512. $15,000

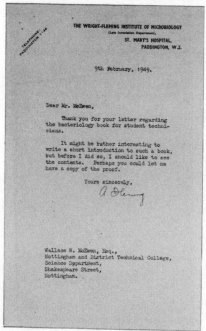

Sir Alexander Fleming, Typewritten Letter signed, 1949. $775

David Livingstone, Autograph Letter signed, 1864. $575

(John Wilson)

AUTOGRAPH LETTERS & DOCUMENTS

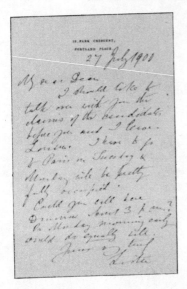

Joseph Lister, Autograph Letter signed, 1900.
$425

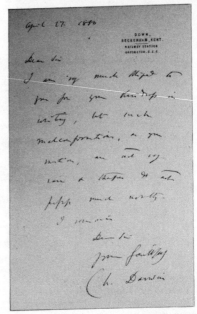

Charles Darwin, Autograph Letter signed, 1880.
$2,200

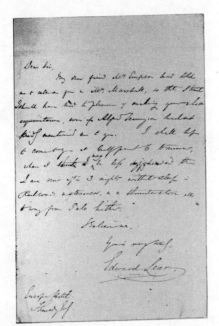

Edward Lear, Autograph Letter signed,
'Thursday evening'. $600

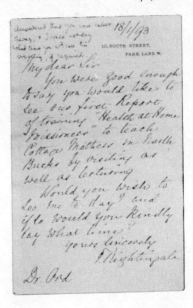

Florence Nightingale, Autograph Letter to Dr
Ord, 1893. $600

(John Wilson)

AUTOMATONS

The Victorian age was the hey-day of the automaton for not only were hundreds of ingenious mechanical toys produced but there was a huge demand for automatons for adults as well — automatic writers, piano players, shoe cleaners, music makers and pier-end machines figured among the hundreds of them.

The earliest automatons were devised in the 18th century by a Swiss family called Jacquet-Droz and they were the wonder of the sophisticated world at that time. Some early automatons were made in the form of animal orchestras with monkeys in powdered wigs and silken jackets playing instruments with musical accompaniments, or elegant singing birds in gilded cages, opening their beaks and turning their heads as they poured out their songs. The first automatons were, like watches, powered by ingeniously coiled springs but other inventors propelled their machines with compressed air, water, sand, mercury or steam. It was the spring however that proved to be the most popular and most efficient.

Early automatons by such famous names as Vaucanson, Robertson or Rechsteiner, particularly the writing and drawing machines, are worth thousands of dollars today. Talking dolls developed by Von Kempelen are in the same price bracket.

In the 19th century German manufacturers saw the possibility of mass producing automatic toys for children and their tin plate industry began to boom around the 1870's. These toys were not so sophisticated as the earlier automatons for they were pressed out by machines and their works were rudimentary but they were cheap and popular and were exported widely, especially to England.

Mid 19th century Swiss musical automaton of singing birds, on oval base, 60cm. high. (Christie's) $1,980

Mid 19th century automaton of a singing bird in a cage, the movement signed Bontems, Paris, 21½in. high. (Christie's) $1,760

A French musical clock diorama, signed Hy Marc, 37¾ x 26¾in. (Lawrence Fine Arts) $2,774

Late 19th century 'Boy Feeding Pig' automaton, the bisque head marked Jumeau SGDG 4, 18¾in. high. (Robt. W. Skinner Inc.) $2,600

A musical automaton of a bisque headed doll beside a dressing table, marked Simon & Halbig S & H 6, the doll 15in. high. (Christie's) $3 000

AUTOMATONS

Late 19th century Continental singing bird automaton in repousse sterling silver gilt casket, 4¼in. wide. (Reeds Rains) $769

A 19th century clockwork lady knitting automaton, Germany, 21in. high. (Robt. W. Skinner Inc.) $1,800

A varicoloured gold musical fob seal with commemorative portraits of Napoleon I and Josephine and an erotic automaton, Swiss, early 19th century, 42mm. high. (Christie's) $17,600

A singing bird automaton with clock, Swiss, probably by Jacquet Droz, circa 1785, 20in. high. (Christie's) $44,000

A clockwork fur covered rabbit automaton, emerging from a green cotton covered cabbage, 7½in. high, French, circa 1900. (Christie's) $544

A mid 19th century German portable barrel organ automaton, 52cm. wide. (Phillips) $9,000

A composition headed automaton modelled as a standing Chinese man, 30in. high, French 1880. (Christie's) $9,000

A French automaton dancing couple by Theroude, on velvet lined circular base, 12in. high. (Lawrence Fine Art) $1,700

A Leopold Lambert musical automaton doll, 'The Flower Seller', the Jumeau bisque head impressed 4, 19½in. high. (Lawrence Fine Art) $6,265

AVON BOTTLES

Most women will remember at least some of the pretty and imaginative containers in which the Avon company have marketed their products since their launch on the market in the early 60s, and it seems somehow obvious that these should now be a subject for collection. To attract top prices, bottles should be in pristine condition, accompanied by original boxes where these existed. Full bottles, however, do not attract a premium, so the contents of your Christmas gift can be used with impunity!

Hud Aftershave, Viking Discoverer bottle. $45

Avon Nexus Aftershave, orange car. $12

Sweet Honesty perfume teddy bear. $7

Blue Racing Car Aftershave. $15

Tai Winds Aftershave, bloodhound pipe bottle. $14

Aftershave motor bike bottle. $25

Stanley Steamer mug, handpainted in Brazil for Avon, 1982. $35

Wild Country aftershave in blue train bottle. $20

Tai Winds Aftershave, Dutch pipe bottle. $25

Moonwind eau de cologne, black cat bottle. $9

AVON BOTTLES

Avon Moonwind Pierot bottle. $10

Moonwind eau de cologne, gold telephone bottle. $9

Occur eau de cologne, gramophone bottle. $7

Tai Winds Aftershave, veteran car bottle. $18

Wild Country Aftershave, siege cannon bottle. $12

Tai Winds Aftershave, pointer dog bottle. $10

Andy Cap Blue Blazer body powder, 1969. $175

Exclusive Bath Oil in green marbled jug. $7

Nexus Aftershave, footballer bottle. $35

Xmas decoration bubble bath oil. $15

Elegance, blue bell bottle. $10

Moonwind bath oil, orange teapot. $14

BABY PLATES

With the increasing use of plastic in infant feeding, any baby plate made of china or pottery is a potential collectable – including such modern ones as Beatrix Potter, Walt Disney and even Kermit the Frog. Look out for German plates brought over between 1880-1900, which were sold as baby plates but had illustrations aimed firmly at the adult market – an interesting piece of subtle marketing policy.

German baby plate decorated with a country scene, 7in. diam. $32

Royal Doulton bone china 'Bunnykins' $14

Royal Doulton baby plate. $10

Doulton 'Bunnykins' bowl. $10

Rockwood pottery dish, Cincinnati, Ohio, 1882, signed by Nathaniel J. Hirschfield, diam. 6½in. (Robt. W. Skinner Inc.) $125

'Painted Feelings' rack plate, Behind the Painted Masque Series, 9in. diam., 1982. $18

Saturday Evening Girls pottery motto plate, Mass., 1914, signed S.G. for Sara Galner, 7½in. diam. (Robt. W. Skinner Inc.) $3,700

Wedgwood Beatrix Potter's 'Peter Rabbit'. $9

Royal Doulton bone china 'Bunnykins'. $14

Carrigatine Pottery, 'Winnie the Pooh'. $5

BADEN POWELL ITEMS

Although Robert Stephenson Smyth Baden-Powell is remembered today as the founder of the Scouting movement, he was a hero before that. The people of Victorian Britain lauded him as the defender of Mafeking during the Boer War because he held the town against the besieging Boers for many months in 1900 and when it was relieved, the general populace rejoiced wildly up and down the country. Baden-Powell became a popular hero and pieces of commemorative pottery, statuettes, biscuit tins, cigarette cards, badges and Vesta cases were decorated with his image. It was not until 1908 that he started the Boy Scout movement and its worldwide success has provided Baden-Powell collectors with a second string of possibilities. Not only can they look for relics and mementoes of the military hero but they also seek out early Scouting items which range from copies of his book "Scouting for Boys", to early badges, photographs, pieces of uniform and other mementoes of the great jamborees of the movement.

Staffordshire cup depicting Major General R. S. S. Baden Powell. $45

Colourful biscuit tin with 'View of Mafeking and Baden Powell', in brown and blue. $35

Small Staffordshire fluted cream jug with portrait of Baden Powell. $35

Wooden butter dish with Staffordshire centre depicting Baden Powell in sepia, 7in. diam. $45

Brass bust of Baden Powell on a marble plinth, 3in. high. $70

Nicely shaped Staffordshire jug with a portrait of Baden Powell. $35

Two-handled loving cup with the portrait of Lieut-Col. R. S. S. Baden Powell. $35

Unusual clay pipe in good condition, the bowl formed in the image of Baden Powell. $45

German made teapot of pale orange ground with sepia image of Baden Powell and gilt decoration. $55

BAIRNSFATHERWARE

If ever a war needed a leavening of humour to help men survive its horrors, it was the Great War of 1914-18. Not surprisingly humour was rather short at the time however and when the cartoons of Bruce Bairnsfather made their first appearance in a military newspaper, featuring the character of "Ol' Bill" the long suffering Tommy, they were greeted with enthusiasm. Perhaps the best known of Bairnsfather's cartoons shows two Tommies sharing a shell hole and one saying to the other who is obviously grumbling . . . "Well, if you knows a better 'ole, go to it".

Ol' Bill became a cult figure, a sort of pro-war propaganda to divert attention from the reality of the carnage. He was reproduced in hundreds of different ways — not only in Bairnsfather's own "Fragments from France" cartoons but also in pottery figures including one made by Carlton Ware showing Ol' Bill with the arms of the City of London stamped over his greatcoat. There were Ol' Bill mugs, car mascots, ashtrays and badges. His image was printed onto handkerchiefs, scarves, posters, postcards and magazines. There were films and plays about him and Bairnsfather's cartoons were made into jig saw puzzles and prints. More than 50 different ones were available.

There is now an illustrated catalogue of Bairnsfatherware called "In Search of the Better 'Ole" published by Milestone Publications, 62 Murray Road, Horndean, ENGLAND, PO8 9JL.

Beswick 'Old Bill' coloured mug, tooth brush moustache. $105

Grimwade shaving mug, 'Where did that one go to?' with Margate Coat of Arms. $105

Grimwade vase, 'Where did that one go to?' 33cm. high. $114

Old Bill 'Humpty Dumpty' shape cloth doll with no arms, 18cm. high. $140

St Dunstans Collecting Box with 'Three Happy Men of St Dunstans' and 'Old Bills' Appeal', tin, 14cm. high. $105

41

Grimwade vase depicting 'Old Bill', 'At present we are staying at a farm'. $85

Grimwade pottery plate with decorative edging 'Where did that one go to?' $85

Grimwade vase 'Well if you knows of a better 'ole, go to it'. $85

'Old Bill' pottery head in white. $85

Bystander 'Fragments' Playing Cards, by Chas. Goodall & Son Ltd. $50

Carlton ware standing figure of 'Old Bill', with coloured face and balaclava, 'Yours to a cinder Old Bill'. $190

Grimwade vase 'Well Alfred, 'ow are the cakes'. $105

Shaped pottery plate with decorative border in relief 'What time do they feed the sea lions Alf?' $80

'Old Bill' brass car mascot. $263

BAKELITE

Hailed as a miracle medium when it was invented in 1909 by L. H. Baekeland, bakelite was put to a million different uses before it was superseded by plastics in the 1960's. Baekeland's material was a synthetic resin which could be moulded into any shape and its only drawback was a tendency to crack which is where plastic proved superior. Because it would not melt or burn, bakelite was originally devised for use in the ignition systems of aeroplanes but it was quickly realised that it could be used for many other things as well. Manufacturers began turning out cheap and cheerful ashtrays, dishes, ornaments and toys and bakelite was used for everything from the cases of radio sets or heavy domestic equipment to   jewelry or small decorative objects. Artists, realising the possibility of creating fluid-looking figures with bakelite seized on it and made some very sophisticated Art Deco pieces with the material which are quite valuable today.

An Allcocks Aerialite Cadet reel made out of bakelite in its makers box, circa 1950. $18

A Lalique red bakelite box and . cover, of square section, the cover moulded and carved, with carved signature R. Lalique, 7.5cm. x 7.5cm. (Christie's) $1,394

Black bakelite stand, made in Hong Kong. $3.50

'Ekco' AC Mains model A22 round, bakelite, 1938. $175

An Art Deco bakelite comb, brush and mirror set, by R. Amerith, France, 1920's. (Robt. W. Skinner Inc.) $444

'Ekco' Mains AC Radio model 830A bakelite 1932. $150

1930's bakelite cigarette case. $3.50

1940's bakelite pen tray. $7

Bakelite dolls house settee, 3in. long. $9

BANKNOTES

The oldest surviving paper money dates from the Chinese Ming dynasty of the 14th century when 12 inch long bank notes were printed on mulberry paper bark. Though the notes were worth a small fortune in their time, today they can be bought for around $650 each. More valuable are Scottish notes issued by banks which crashed spectacularly. The first to go was Douglas Heron's bank in Ayr which had a three year life span in the 1770's but more sought after by collectors are notes issued by the City of Glasgow Bank which closed in 1878. One of its £5 notes is today worth around $2,000.

Collectors of bank notes seek out notes issued by transitory regimes – French Revolution notes, American Confederate notes, notes made as currency in concentration camps and notes issued by dictators like Idi Amin or governments like the Sandinista regime in Nicaragua. Even more desirable are notes with mistakes or one of the very rare million pound notes issued by the Bank of England in 1948 but quickly withdrawn. Condition is an important factor in the pricing of old bank notes so they should be handled as little as possible.

Portugal: 1910 100 milreis. (Phillips)
$284

J. G. Nairne Bank of England Note £5
21 September 1916 issued at Hull. (Phillips)
$783

Great Britain: Cruikshank Anti-Hanging note.
(Phillips) $302

Ireland: Ulster Bank: £100 1941. (Phillips)
$284

United States of America: 1890 $20 National Currency for 1st National Bank of San Francisco. (Phillips) $284

J. B. Page Bank of England Note £10 1971-75 error with most of reverse image appearing on front of note. $640

New Zealand: 1916 Band of New Zealand £1 uniface colour trial in green, yellow and multicolour. (Phillips) $445

Henry Hase Bank of England Note £2 13 April 1811, tears in body of note and damaged upper right. (Phillips) $356

Ireland: Central Bank: £100 1949. (Phillips) $231

St Kitts: 1938 Royal Bank of Canada $5. (Phillips) $462

Ireland: Provincial Bank: £1 July 1924, 10mm tear bottom of centre crease. (Phillips) $106

K. O. Peppiatt Bank of England Note £20 16 December 1939. (Phillips) $605

Trinidad: 1940 $100. (Phillips)$462

C. P. Mahon Bank of England Note 10/-
1928 A01 prefix. (Phillips) $302

Australia: 1870 Bukkulla Vineyards £1.
(Phillips) $320

1914 Banque Industrielle de Chine $1.
(Phillips) $133

Isle of Man: Manx Bank £1 1919. (Phillips)
$605

Russia: 1811 25 roubles Assignat. (Phillips)
$462

1871-72 Bank of South Australia unissued
set of £1, £5, £10, £20 and £50. (Phillips)
$4,628

China: 1918 Yokohama Specie Bank $1
issued at Tientsin. (Phillips) $302

BANKNOTES

J. Bradbury Treasury Note £1 August 1914,
(Phillips) $516

British Guiana: 1929 Government £1.
(Phillips) $249

Devon and Cornwall Banking Company: £5
proof on card for Exeter. (Phillips) $462

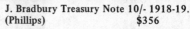

J. Bradbury Treasury Note 10/- 1918-19.
(Phillips) $356

China: 1939 British Municipal Council
(Tientsin) note "Will Pay to Bearer on
Demand, Twenty Cents Local Currency".
(Phillips) $160

New Zealand: £10 uniface colour trial in
dark blue, mauve and multicolour. (Phillips)
                                              $515

United States of America: 1872 $1 National
Currency for The Pomeroy National Bank
(Ohio). (Phillips) $587

Belgian Congo: 1921 5 francs uniface
colour trials, front in blue and green for
Stanleyvill and back in brown for Kinshasa.
(Phillips) $267

BAROMETERS

The principle of the barometer was invented in 1643 by a Florentine mathematician called Evangelista Torricelli and in 1660 British born Robert Boyle adapted the technique to the production of a weather glass. The earliest barometers were produced by famous horologists like Tompion, Quare, John Patrick, Henry Jones and Charles Orme and examples of their craftsmanship that survive today are exorbitantly expensive. However the possibility of being able to forecast the weather appealed to people in every walk of life and soon cheaper barometers were produced in large numbers. By the end of the 18th century, the banjo shaped barometer made its appearance and the Victorians bought them as essential pieces of decoration for their halls. The finest examples were made in mahogany or satinwood frames with boxwood stringing round the edges and silvered dials. Some incorporated thermometers, hygrometers, spirit levels or clocks and the more dials there were, the more expensive the barometer was and still is.

A grande sonnerie calendar carriage clock cum barometer, the barometer inscribed R. W. Inglis 1897, 6½in. high.
$4,375

Brass ship's barometer, circa 1860. (British Antique Exporters) $130

A walnut cased combined time-piece, barograph, aneroid barometer and thermometer, signed Chadburn & Son, 26¾ x 14in. (Lawrence Fine Arts)
$800

A brass and nickel plated yacht barometer modelled as a turret with simulated cannons, 4½in. high. $125

A George I walnut signal barometer, the brass plate inscribed Made by John Patrick in the Old Bailey London, 36¼ x 29½in. (Christie's)
$12,250

A late 19th century oxodised brass surveying aneroid barometer, by Pidduck & Sons, Hanley, 6in. diam. $260

BAROMETERS

A large Victorian oak wheel barometer, inscribed Fletcher and Sons, London, 46½in. high. (Christie's) $569

A late 17th century walnut stick barometer, the engraved brass plates for Summer and Winter, 48in. high. (Christie's) $2,499

A Sheraton period wheel barometer, by J. B. Roncheti. (Woolley & Wallis) $5,904

A late 17th century walnut stick barometer, unsigned, 39½in. high. (Christie's) $3,234

A large 19th century rosewood wheel clock barometer, signed J. Amadio, 128cm. high, circa 1835. (Phillips) $3,620

A late 19th century oak American Forecast or Royal Polytechnic bulb Cistern barometer, 107cm. high. (Phillips) $536

A mid Victorian papier-mache barometer, 38in. high. (Christie's) $471

An early 19th century mahogany Sheraton shell wheel barometer, 8in. diam. silver dial signed Lione, Somalvico & Co., 100cm. high. (Phillips) $457

BARREL TAPS

Among the most attractive artefacts of the old time pub were barrel taps, often made of brass and proudly polished. The advent of keg beer made them unnecessary and if they are now found in pubs today, they have been kept for decorative reasons only. They were fitted to beer kegs, wine and cider barrels and collectors seek them out in rubbish dumps and old stores. The ones that are most highly prized are stamped with a brewer's and a maker's name and among the most attractive specimens are those of porcelain though the most common material was wood, closely followed by brass, silver plate, chrome or nickel plate. Some barrel taps were fitted with locks to prevent pilfering and later versions had a thumbturn tap on top that featured a locking lever and padlock.

Victorian brass barrel tap with integral key and hammering pin. $18

Early 20th century wooden barrel tap.
$9

Early 19th century barrel tap,
9in. long. $18

A large Victorian brass barrel tap. $14

Brass tap with swivel lever and locking plate, late 19th century. $14

Late Victorian brass tap, 3in. high. $9

Small early 19th century brass barrel tap, 5in. long. $10

A William IV silver barrel spigot, by Wm. Wheatcroft, London, 1830, 6¼in. long, 16oz.10dwt. (Christie's) $880

BARRELS

Barrels have been used for storing everything from biscuits to beer, from gunpowder to gin, and the shape is so pleasing that it has been reproduced for decorative purposes where it has no practical application, eg. tiny silver sewing cases made to hang on a chatelaine.

While beer barrels and so on are strong wooden constructions, more decorative and infinitely more expensive examples are the beautiful spirit barrels made of china or glass.

A Westerwald grey stoneware spirit barrel, 33.5cm. high. (Christie's) $1,093

A brass bound oak rum barrel inscribed 'HMS Victory No. 3', 16½in. high. (Christie's) $3,162

A German porcelain wine barrel supported on a wood stand, circa 1880, the barrel 30cm. wide. (Christie's) $1,512

One of a pair of blue and white late 18th century hexagonal barrel-shaped garden seats, 49cm. high. (Christie's) $4,847

Saltglaze water barrel, circa 1880. (British Antique Exporters) $130

Pair of Staffordshire pottery spirit barrels with metal taps, 12in. high. (G. A. Key) $272

Royal Doulton 'Ginger Wine' barrel made for Rawlings, complete with tap, 10in. high. (Abridge Auctions) $180

BASKETS

Perhaps the best documented basket is the one in which Moses found himself in the bulrushes. They have been around for a long time and have served a multitude of purposes in the everyday life of the ages. 19th century baskets were an indispensible part of a genteel lady's equipment, whether of the lidded variety to carry jellies and cordials to ailing cottagers, or the flat, wooden slatted Sussex trugs in which she could carry her cut flowers. Attractive in themselves, they are eminently collectable today.

California coiled basketry bowl, Pomo, diam. 12in., 5¾in. high. (Robt. W. Skinner Inc.) $500

A Cascade/Plateau imbricated coiled basket, Klikitat, 19th century, 10¼in. high. (Robt. W. Skinner Inc.) $700

An Indian-style covered woven basket, 1916, 8¼in. high, 10½in. diam. (Robt. W. Skinner Inc.)$450

A mahogany octagonal waste paper basket with tapering fretwork sides and bracket feet, 11½in. wide. (Christie's) $4,329

A Gustav Stickley slat sided wastebasket, circa 1905, no. 94, signed, 11¾in. diam. (Robt. W. Skinner Inc.) $2,500

A 19th century American large polychrome woven splint market basket, 19in. wide. (Christie's) $286

One of a pair of Edwardian giltwood baskets, on rope moulded bases, lined interiors, 41cm. and 36cm. (Phillips)   Two $748

BEADWORK BAGS

Beadwork bags became popular in the 19th century, and the beads could be made from various materials, such as glass, steel, jade, leather, etc. Some were made of 'crochet' beadwork (worked outward in circles from the centre) or were knitted in rows. 20th century beadwork was often embroidered on a patterned canvas, while loom beadwork was used for more commerical bags. Look out for rare large bags with good landscapes or animal subjects worked on silk or satin.

Beadwork evening bag circa 1910, with chain link strap. $18

19th century beadwork bag with tortoiseshell fittings and chain. $60

19th century beadwork 'Dolly' bag with steel beads and tassel, satin lined. $105

1920's black jet beaded evening bag with chain strap. $30

1940's beadwork bag decorated with sequins, foreign made, with mirror inside. $20

Early 1920's beadwork bag of black beads and sequins with satin lining. $40

Late 19th century beadwork bag with gilded fittings and gold beads. $95

BELLS

In the days before electric alarms, bells were essential items of life. They were in churches, on doors, in servants' halls and drawing room tables or hung round animals' necks. Basically there are two kinds of bell — the open church bell shape with a clapper swinging inside and the closed variety with a loose clapper moving freely inside the globe of the bell.

Bells were and still are used for a myriad different purposes from alerting people to fires to calling children to school or people to worship. Shepherds kept track of their flock with bells and tradesmen alerted customers to their approach by ringing a handbell. Collectors are fond of little bells that were used for summoning servants. They were made in a variety of materials ranging from china and glass to brass or silver. Favourites are in Cranberry, Bristol, Nailsea or Tiffany glass or the delicately carved Oriental bells that travellers brought home from India or Burma.

A table bell by Godert Van Ysseldijk, 14.5cm. high, maker's mark, The Hague, 1767, 306gr. $742

An archaic bronze bell, nao, mid-1st Millenium B.C., 40cm. high, fitted box, wood stand and bell striker. (Christie's) $3,146

A 19th century clear and cranberry glass bell, 13in. high, complete with clapper. (Robt. W. Skinner Inc.)
$245

20th century Welsh brass souvenir bell with lion handle, 7in. high. $9

A small bronze ship's bell, almost certainly of European origin, circa 1750, 10.5cm. high. (Christie's)
$3,004

A French table bell, 10.2cm. high, maker's mark J.D., Paris, 1761, 138gr.
$5,009

BICYCLES

The first bicycle recorded in history is depicted in a stained glass window in a Stoke Poges church. It shows a figure seated on a wheeled instrument using his feet to propel himself along the ground. A better bicycle was exhibited before the court of Louis XVI and Marie Antionette in 1779 and in 1816 came the invention of the hobby horse, a simple device of two wheels and a cross bar on which the feet were again used for propulsion. The first real bicycle however was invented in Scotland in 1840 by Kirkpatrick MacMillan of Dumfries. Riding his machine, the inventor was fined for 'furious driving'. The first crank driven bicycle was the velocipede or 'bone shaker' of the 1860's and after that a wave of interest in bicycling swept both Britain and America. Even the lowest paid workers were able to achieve independence and mobility at a low cost. Today early bicycles, especially those made in the mid 19th century by the Coventry Sewing Machine Co or the Swift Cycle Co Ltd fetch high prices and examples from the early years of the 20th century are also rising in value.

A 1930's baker's iron framed delivery tricycle with original wooden boxed front and rear wheel brake, 85in. long. (Andrew Hartley) $743

Dursley-Pedersen pedal cycle, circa 1905, with three-speed gearing. $1,435

A James Starley Coventry lever tricycle built by Haynes & Jeffy s, 1877.
                                    $3,500

Nickel plated steel high wheel bicycle, the 'Expert Columbia' model, by The Pope Manufacturing Co., wheel diam. 52in. (Robt. W. Skinner Inc.) $1,800

A wood velocipede with canvas covered wheels, straight backbone and turned handlebars, 26in. diam., probably French, circa 1880. (Christie's) $1,821

A fine, wooden framed Pedestrian Hobby Horse bicycle. (Phillips) $3,500

Swift pedal tricycle with steering by twin hand grips, circa 1880. $3,250

English BSA safety bicycle, circa 1885. $3,850

A late 19th century child's bicycle with 16in. detachable driving wheel. (Christie's) $665

A Royal Mail pennyfarthing bicycle painted in black with red coachline, with original leather seat. (Anderson & Garland) $1,662

BILL HEADS

The introduction of the penny post in 1840 ushered in a boom in communication. People who rarely wrote letters started putting pen to paper. As with all booms, it sparked off subsidiary industries like printing because enterprising merchants and manufacturers wanted to put across their firms by eye-catching letter heads. Engravers produced designs for butchers, bakers, candlestick makers, mill owners and hotels to name only a few.

Some of the designs, especially the early black and white ones before the introduction of color printing,   are a delight to the eye. Mill chimneys belch smoke; inn yards are full of bustling ostlers and coaches; butchers' billheads show woolly sheep or ferocious looking bulls. As cheaper printing became available the vogue even passed to private householders who commissioned letter heads with elegant script and pretty flourishes.

The Billy Mayerl School, Modern Syncopation for the Pianoforte, 1939. $5

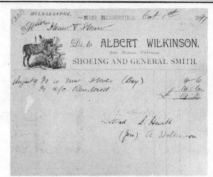

Albert Wilkinson, Shoeing and General Smith, 1897. $3.50

Dr. to William Shaw & Sons, Grove Mills, 1893. $7

The Hammond Typewriter Company Ltd., 1916. $3.50

Tom Norton, the Automobile Palace, 1910.
$12

Horner, Son & Co., Manufacturing
Clothiers, 1917. $9

R. A. Harding, Manufacturer of Invalid
Carriages & Motors. $2

J. & E. Dalton Ltd., Emery Manufacturer,
1894. $9

Dr. to John Bragg & Son, Motor Haulage and
Carting Contractors, 1922. $3.50

BIRDCAGES

The keeping of a caged bird as a toy and a diversion has been common in every country since very early times. Indian Rajput paintings and Roman friezes show birds in cages, caged birds are referred to in poetry and their popularity has persisted to the present day. In the Middle Ages people kept jays and magpies — which often talked — in cages as pets while larks and goldfinches were popular because of their song, especially in Italy.

The cage was often as prized as its inhabitant and these to be found by collectors can range from a 1930's Art Deco type of cage in chrome on a tall stand for the family budgie to tiny jewelled cages of gold which were made for the finches of the rich in Renaissance Italy. Sometimes these exotic cages were inhabited by stuffed birds because they were less trouble to keep.

Cages can vary enormously in size, shape and in the materials used for their manufacture. The earliest ones, of which few survive, were made of basket work with turf on the floor. In the 18th and early 19th centuries bird cages were made in wood and designed like houses. Parrots and cockatoos became popular during this period because they were brought home by travellers to distant countries, and they were housed in miniature mansions with make-believe doors and dome shaped roofs. Later brass cages for parrots became more popular though these were always expensive and cheaper versions in metal could be bought. Some of the most interesting bird cages are miniature aviaries modelled on the Crystal Palace which was built in 1851.

Mid 19th century red-painted birdcage of Gothic design with sloping roof, 14½in. wide. $875

An architectural wire birdcage with a mahogany base, circa 1900, 2ft.9in. wide. $1,750

A wooden framed wire birdcage. (Worsfolds) $268

19th century ormolu birdcage with ogee top, 24in. high. $3,500

A late Georgian birdcage, complete with its contemporary glass feeder. $700

A Dutch mahogany birdcage, the stepped front with four compartments, late 18th century, 41in. wide. (Christie's) $30,525

BISCUIT BARRELS

Biscuit barrels are popular with collectors perhaps because of the infinite variety of decorative designs, makers, and the many different materials from which they can be made, such as wood, pottery, metal, fine china, or cut glass. The most highly esteemed potteries, such as Wedgwood, included them in their production lines, and set their best designers, such as Hannah Barlow to work on their conception.

The rim mounts and handles, too, were subjects for endless imaginative variations, and these could range from simple cane to the most intricately crafted and engraved precious metalwork.

A conception perhaps of a more gracious and elegant age, biscuit barrels are above all practical as well as ornamental, and even today make a most attractive addition to a dinner party table.

Victorian oak biscuit barrel with plated mounts, 1870. (British Antique Exporters) $45

A Clarice Cliff Bizarre biscuit barrel with wicker handle, 16cm. (Osmond Tricks) $252

1950's hand painted wooden biscuit barrel. $9

A Doulton Lambeth stoneware biscuit barrel, by Florence and Lucy Barlow, 20cm. high, r.m. 1883. (Phillips) $686

An English cameo glass biscuit barrel with plated mount, swing handle and cover, 17cm. diam. (Phillips) $1,337

Victorian biscuit barrel with plated top. (British Antique Exporters) $85

BISCUIT TINS

Towards the end of the 18th century a technique was devised for printing onto metal sheets. Because metal could not absorb ink as paper does, the development of lithography made printing on metal a possibility but it was not till 1837 that a system of chromolithography was developed by Godefroye Engelmann in Paris and some beautiful results were obtained. In the 1860's mass production started because Benjamin George worked out the earliest form of off-set printing in Britain using rubber cylinders to effect the transfer of the design directly onto metal. From that date the manufacture of colourful tins, especially for the Christmas market, became a booming industry. They were made in every shape and form − some in simple shapes with pretty designs on the lids and others in the shape of houses, jewel caskets, treasure chests, trains or motor cars. Biscuit manufacturers, in particular Huntley & Palmer, made the design of their tins a speciality and produced a catalogue listing the dozens of types available.

Huntley & Palmers 'Mirror' circa 1914, with detachable lid and handle which becomes a hand held mirror. (Phillips) $109

W.R. Jacob & Co. 'Houseboat' circa 1923, fair to good condition. (Phillips) $169

1953 Coronation Queen Elizabeth souvenir biscuit tin. (Border Bygones) $14

Huntly & Palmers Assorted Cocktail Biscuits tin. (Border Bygones) $3.50 £2

A pair of Huntley & Palmer 'Statuary' tins, circa 1910, with hinged lids. (Phillips) $210

Huntley & Palmers 'Literature' circa 1901, very good condition. (Phillips) $321

McVitie & Price 'Bluebird' tin, circa 1911. (Phillips) $175

A Mettoy 'OK Biscuits' spring drive tin delivery van, brightly coloured in yellow and red, 10cm. x 24cm. (Phillips) $118

Huntley & Palmers 'Bookstand' circa 1905, very good condition. (Phillips) $143

BISCUIT TINS

Peek Frean & Co. book tin with a portrait of a woman on the front, 20.5 x 16cm. (Phillips) $85

W. & R. Jacob & Co. 'Coronation Coach' circa 1936, lacking box, very good condition. (Phillips) $304

Victoria Biscuit Co. book tin of Dordrecht – Holland 'Gourmets Delight', 24.5x17cm. (Phillips) $85

Huntley & Palmers 'Oval Basket' circa 1905, basket work and tin in good condition, lacking basket lid. (Phillips) $84

1950's Tally Ho biscuit tin by Scribbens Bakeries. $9

Huntley & Palmers 'Scallop' shell shaped tin with a hinged lid, 8.5cm. high. (Phillips) $175

John Buchanan & Bros. Ltd., two dark blue urn shaped confectionery tins decorated in the Art Nouveau style, 31cm. x 13cm. (Phillips) $338

Crawfords Biscuits Bus OK 3852, with original box, 25.5cm. (Phillips) $4,488

The Queen's Silver Jubilee, 1952-1977 biscuit tin. (Border $2

Huntley & Palmers 'Books' circa 1909, very good condition. (Phillips) $270

1937 Coronation of George V and Queen Elizabeth souvenir biscuit tin. (Border Bygones) $18

Huntley & Palmers 'Arcadian' circa 1902, very good condition. (Phillips) $270

BONDS & SHARE CERTIFICATES

"Busted bonds" are stock or share certificates which have no longer any value – though there are sometimes surprises. The collecting of them is called scripophily and it was almost unknown until the 1970's. There has been a strong American interest since the 1980's however and more people are becoming attracted to it because of the decorative appearance of the certificates which are often highly colored and beautifully designed. Bonds and shares have been issued since the 17th century. Early examples were printed on vellum but printers like Waterlow, Bradbury Wilkinson and the American Banknote Co produced some very attractive certificates. Often they were signed by famous people who were associated with the companies.

The fall of kings and the rise of revolutions has always caused an avalanche of busted bonds and some of the most common relate to Russian and Chinese companies. A couple of years ago the Russian government suggested that some recompense would be made to the holders of stocks and shares in Tsarist companies and families who retained their certificates did indeed reap some return from those old holdings. Some of the most interesting certificates relate to American railway companies and banks which often had an ephemeral existence and other collectors pick a theme – like steamship companies or Egyptian cotton mills and stick to that. In the United Kingdom, a share or bond certificate is legally the property of the person named on it but in Canada and America shares were often made out "to the bearer" so if the company is still in existence, the certificate could be worth serious money.

Mexico, El Buen Tono, Cia Manufacturera del Cigarro Sin Pegamento, $50 share, 1912, good vignette of cigar making machine, ornate border. $35

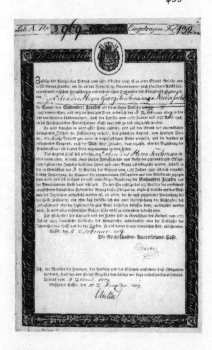

Germany, Kingdom of Westphalia, 1808 Loan, 100 frank bond, dated 1809, ornate border, black, with numerous coupons. $435

(M. Veissid & Co.)

63

Victor Gold Mining Co. Ltd., Cripple Creek, Colorado, 5 shares of $5, 1895, vignette of miners, ornate border, red and black. $40

Columbus Gold Mining Company of the Black Hills, $10 shares, 1880, 2 vignettes of miners, black. $45

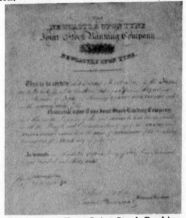

Canterbury Navigation & Sandwich Harbour Co., £25 share, 1826, large vignette of coats of arms, cathedral and proposed canal, black on thick paper. $435

Newcastle Upon Tyne Joint Stock Banking Company, £25 shares, 1836, black, on vellum. The Company was formed during the boom period of 1836. $300

Farmers & General Fire & Life Insurance & Loan & Annuity Co., £10 shares, 1848, vignette of wheatsheaf at top and plough at bottom. $60

Lamport & Holt Limited, 6% preference shares of £1, 1913, vignette of steam ship, ornate border, black, pink underprint. $25

(M. Veissid & Co.)

Brooklyn & Brighton Beach Railroad Co.,
5% consolidated mortgage bond, $1,000, 1896,
steam train at top, ornate border. $60

Roumania, Monopolies Institute, Stabilisation
and Development Loan, 1929, £100 bond,
vignette of castle, ornate border. $45

Andover National Bank, Massachusetts, $100
shares, 1896, lovely vignette of Government
building at top, gentleman at lower left, ornate
border. $30

Ilex Mill Co. Ltd., £5 share, 1876, vignette of
mill at left, printed in Rochdale, black. $60

Exchequer receipt, 1707, printed with
manuscript insertions, for 3 months interest
on £300, subscribed in 1693 under the Act
of that year, signed by John, Lord
Colepepper. $175

(M. Veissid & Co.)

Russia, Riazan-Uralsk Railway Co., 4½% loan,
1893, bond for 5000 roubles, mauve
(D/H 1107d), lacks coupons. $210

East Kent Light Railways Co., £1 shares,
1921, 2 vignettes of a steaming train and
colliery buildings at Tilmanstone, blue.
$100

Tuolumne County Water Company, $250 share,
Columbia 1862 over 185-, lovely vignette of
miners sluicing for gold in the mountains, black.
$50

South Sea Company, printed form of power
of attorney, 1714, empowering Joseph Chitty,
a London Merchant, to deal with stock
belonging to Sir Joseph Hodges, Baronet,
signed and sealed by Hodges and witnessed
by two others, 3 embossed revenue stamps.
$1,000

Snowdown Colliery Ltd., group of 3
certificates for founders' shares, 1908;
ordinary shares, 1913 and preferred shares,
1908, all with good vignette of mine at top.
$70

(M. Veissid & Co.)

BONDS & SHARE CERTIFICATES

Spain, Sociedad General de Automoviles S.A., 500 pesetas share, Barcelona 1911, vignette of early motor car, black, with coupons, only 1,000 issued. $80

Elder Dempster & Co. Ltd., 6% preference shares of £1, 1914, vignette of steam ship, ornate border, green and pink. $25

India, Apollo Mills Ltd., 100 rupee shares, 1920, large vignette of Apollo at left, black and brown. $25

India, Mahalakshmi Woollen & Silk Mills Co. Ltd., 10 rupee shares, 1923, extremely ornate border with vignettes of factory, shepherd, elephants & peacocks, blue and green. $25

Spain, Compania de los Ferrocarriles Economicos de Villena a Alcoy y Yecla, bond for 475 pesetas, Barcelona 1902, lovely Art Nouveau design. $30

New Centaur Cycle Co. Ltd., 10/- ordinary shares, 1906, vignette of Centaurs and other figures, green. $55

(M. Veissid & Co.)

BOOKMARKS

Bookmarks are making a come-back today after a long time in the doldrums. They used to be used as a means of advertising and modern bookshops are adopting this method again but in the 19th and early 20th centuries, the bookmark promoted all kinds of goods ranging from chocolate bars to insurance policies. Walter Crane, the illustrator of children's books, designed a lovely bookmark for the Scottish Widows' Fund and there were also attractive shaped marks like the cricket bat which promoted Wisden and a hand advertising Fry's chocolate creams. Bookmarks were also often given as gifts by skilled needlewomen who made them for their friends and these were particularly popular with the Victorians. Bookmarks of woven silk were sold in their thousands, particularly Stevengraphs and others made of embroidered French ribbon.

Hoyts German Cologne bookmark, Lowell, Mass. $10

Cherry Blossom, bookmark, Perfume Toilet Powder and Soap, 1890. $20

Wisden's Exceller Bat bookmark, from the 1936 Wisden's. $3.50

Fry's Cocoa and Chocolates, the best line of all is Fry's. $9

Wright's Coal Tar Soap, the seal of health and purity. $3.50

Kleen-eze Brush Co. Ltd., Royal Silver Jubilee souvenir bookmark, 1935. $3.50

Sons of the Empire, with compliments Dr Lovelace's Soap. $7

Singer's bookmark with portrait of Lt. Col. R.S.S. Baden-Powell. $7

Yesterday's Paper

BOOKMARKS

Air France, Fastest to 4 Continents. $1

Lloyd's Weekly News, the Best Family Paper. $13

Theatre Royal, Manchester, Little Women with Katharine Hepburn. $5

St Ivel Cheese, the Pride of the West Countrie. $4

Allenbury's Foods for Infants, the Milky Way to Health. $4

Scottish Widows' Fund, the largest British Mutual Life office. $2

The Studio bookmark for a carol, 'Good King Wenceslas'. $2.50

Silk bookmark, 'In loving memory of Private James Brodie', 1918. $7

Fry's Milk Chocolate, Pull up his head. $21

Brown & Polson's Cornflour, nearly 40 years world wide reputation. $5

Yesterday's Paper

BOOKS

For centuries books have been a favorite item for collection and more love has been lavished on them than on any other kind of collectable. They are treasured for their content as well as for their appearance. Book collecting is one of the more specialised areas of the market, one much practised by millionaires, and books are regarded as a safe resort for money against inflation. It is now rare for a box of mixed books with a first edition tucked away among them to be picked up in a local auction house for a few cents because each sale is attended by knowledgeable dealers.

Since books deal with every aspect of the world and life, a serious collector must specialise. Among the most highly sought after areas is topography because of the magnificent plates that illustrate many books — however they are expensive. Similarly "blue chip" are books on wild life, flowers and horticulture. Single plates of Redoute's roses or lilies fetch enormous prices. Victorian travel books and sporting books are also highly desirable.

Children's books, especially if illustrated by artists like Shepherd, Tenniel, Jessie M. King, Kay Neilsen or Kate Greenaway are very sought after as are Victorian children's books with attractive embossed covers. There is a strong market too in modern first editions with the ebb and flow of fashion and favour flowing from one author to another. Anniversaries of a certain author tend to put up their price. Even paperback books are collected — first edition Penguins, especially "Ariel", the first of them all, fetch hundreds of dollars. Modern first editions must have their dust covers and be in good condition to fetch premium prices.

Combe (William): The English Dance of Death, 2 vol.s, hand-col. front, and vig. title, 72 hand-col. plates by Rowlandson, 1 cover detached. (Phillips) $1,337

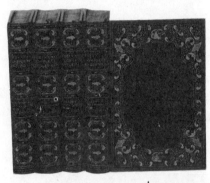

Walton (I.) and Cotton (C.): The Complete Angler, ed Sir H. Nicolas, extended to 4 vols with specially printed titles. (Phillips) $3,490

Combe (W.): The Tour(s) of Doctor Syntax. (Phillips) $930

BOOKS

Sydenham Edwards: The new Flora Britannica, 61 hand-coloured plates, quarto, 1812. (Phillips) $1,680

Lunardi (Vincent): An Account of the First Aerial Voyage in England, 2nd Edn., small 4to, 1784. (Phillips) $264

The Bible bound with Book of Common Prayer, engraved title dated 1672, printed title 1679. (Phillips) $3,200

Omar Khayyam, Rubaiyat, trans. E. Fitzgerald, 16 colour plates, by W. Pogany, g.e. by Riviere, circa 1930. (Phillips) $987

George Adams, Essays On The Microscope, with atlas of plates, First Edition, London 1787, 2 vols., 4to and oblong 4to (the atlas). (Christie's) $1,100

Philippes (Henry: The Advancement of the Art of Navigation, First Edn., 3 parts in 1 vol., illus. in text, 4to, 1657. (Phillips) $1,764

Koch and Kellermeistern von Allen Speison Getrenken, title printed in red and black woodcuts, Frankfurt, 1554. (Phillips) $4,160

Irish Binding: Book of Common Prayer, contemporary red morocco, lined case, Cambridge, John Baskerville, 1760. (Phillips) $1,434

Doves Press, Alfred Lord Tennyson, Seven Poems and two Translations, Limited Edition, by Cobden-Sanderson, signed and dated 1903. (Phillips) $1,128

BOOKS

 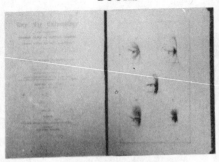 

John Watson Stewart, The Gentleman's and Citizen's Almanack, g.e., Dublin, T. and J. W. Stewart, 1755. (Phillips) $1,015

Halford (F. M.): Dry Fly Entomology, 2 vols., No. 22 of 75 copies signed by the author, 1897. (Phillips)
$1,249

Orwell (G.): Nineteen Eight-Four, First Edn., 1949. (Phillips) $750

 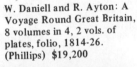

Gianutio (Horatio): Libro nel Quale si tratta della Maniera di Giuocara Scacchi, modern vellum, Turin, A. de Bianchi, 1597. (Phillips) $3,200

Greco Gioachino, 1600-c.1634, Manuscript entitled 'The Royall Game of Chess', comprising 95 games executed in pen, ink and green wash. (Phillips)
$1,408

W. Daniell and R. Ayton: A Voyage Round Great Britain, 8 volumes in 4, 2 vols. of plates, folio, 1814-26. (Phillips) $19,200

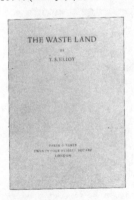  

T. S. Eliot: The Waste Land, Ltd. Edn., No. 92 of 300, Officina Bodoni, 1961. (Phillips) $992

James Scott of Edinburgh Binding, The Holy Bible containing the Old and New Testaments, London, J. Baskett, 1741 bound with Psalms of David, Edinburgh, A. Kincaid, 1772. (Phillips) $1,762

James Scott of Edinburgh Binding, The Holy Bible bound with Psalms of David, dark blue morocco gilt, g.e., Edinburgh, A. Kincaid, 1772. (Phillips) $1,410

BOOKS

Vale Press, R. Browning, Dramatic Romances and Lyrics, Limited Edition of 210, 1899. (Phillips) $958

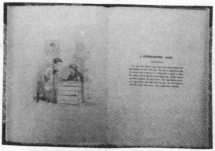

Bridges (R): Sketches Illustrative of the Manners and Costumes of France, Switzerland and Italy, 49 col. plates, 4to, 1821. (Phillips) $447

Fowles (J.): The Collector, First Edn., 1963. (Phillips) $135

E. Dodwell: Views in Greece, 30 hand-coloured views, folio, 1821. (Phillips) $6,400

A 17th century miniature Book of Psalms with embroidered cover, England, 2 x 3¼in. (Robt. W. Skinner Inc.) $2,000

Capt. Robert Melville Grindlay: Scenery Costume and Architecture on the Western Side of India, folio, R. Ackermann, 1826. (Phillips) $2,880

'The Story of a Passion", by Irving Bacheller, published by Roycrofters, 1901, hand-illuminated by Abby Blackmar, suede cover. (Robt. W. Skinner Inc.) $150

C. Dickens: Great Expectations, 3 vols., 1st Edn., 32pp. of advertisements, original cloth gilt, 1861. (Phillips) $19,200

Eragny Press, R. Browning, Some Poems, Limited Edition of 215 col. woodcut front, by L. Pissarro, 1904. (Phillips) $846

BOTTLES

Four categories of bottles are most popular with collectors — mineral water, beer and beverage bottles; quack medicine bottles; glass and stone ink bottles; poison bottles. The most popular mineral water bottles are Hiram Codd's marble stoppered lemonade bottles, preferably with the marble intact. Sometimes unfortunately the necks of these bottles were broken off by children wanting to get at the marbles. The best are the colored ones, some of which fetch over $200 each especially the cobalt blue variety. They are followed in the popularity stakes by transfer printed stone ginger beer bottles which can be found in rubbish dumps over the entire country.

Quack cure bottles often carried fascinating labels or had slogans printed on the glass and one of the most valuable is Warners Safe Cure which is green in colour and can be priced at around $75. The most common ink bottles are made of glass and are octagonal in shape but the ones made of stone and shaped like little cottages with embossed doors and windows have a strong following. Overseas collectors will pay up to $500 for a good specimen.

Poison bottles are also often found by treasure hunters in rubbish dumps. They were usually colored a bright color — blue, purple or viridian green — to alert users to the danger of their contents and they were also often made in peculiar shapes for the same reason. There was even one shaped like a coffin and others were marked with embossed skulls and crossbones which could be felt by the fingers if picked up in the dark.

Early stoneware ginger beer bottle with applied seal, circa 1840. $350

Cobalt blue Prices Patent candle bottle. $85

Black glass shaft and globe shaped, small size (6in. high) wine bottle with applied glass seal, circa 1650.
$5,250

Stoneware Reform flask for gin, circa 1840.
$700

Martin's Patent medicine bottle. $260

Roman flask with handle, circa 4th century A.D.
$2,600

(Peter Savage Antique Bottle Museum)

BOTTLES

Fire Extinguisher bottle. $70

Submarine shaped, cobalt blue poison bottles. $435

Stoneware ginger beer bottle with picture transfer on body, circa 1890. $45

Black glass soda water bottle with pontilled base, circa 1830. $3,500

Black glass wine bottle with applied glass seal, circa 1760. $875

Black glass bear shaped bottle for liqueurs, circa 1880. $105

Cobalt blue marble stoppered pop bottle. $1,800

English, black glass, straight sided onion shaped bottle, circa 1720. $600

Stoneware ink bottle in the shape of Mr Punch. $875

(Peter Savage Antique Bottle Museum)

75

BOTTLES

Roman flask with handle, circa 4th century A.D. $2,600

Aqua colour glass figural bottles in shape of a bird and a fish, circa 1870. $40

English onion shaped wine bottle, circa 1695. $700

Black glass Dutch embossed gin bottle, circa 1860.$260

Black glass square wine bottle with applied glass seal, circa 1780. $260

Amber bitters bottle dated 1872. $85

Stoneware Reform flask for gin, circa 1840. $700

T-kettle shaped inkwell inside very ornate gilt cage. $875

Black glass shaft and globe shaped wine bottle, circa 1665. $1,750

(Peter Savage Antique Bottle Museum)

76

BOTTLES

Patent medicine bottle 'True Daffy's Elixir', dark green glass, circa 1830. $1,400

Stoneware egg ended mineral water bottle, circa 1840. $350

Black glass, quarter size, wine bottle with applied glass seal, dated 1791. $600

Very rare shaped pop bottle with glass marble stopper. $435

English, black glass, mallet shaped wine bottle, circa 1740. $600

Dutch black glass wine bottle with long stretched neck, circa 1760. $175

Early stoneware stout bottle made by Stephen Green's Pottery, circa 1840. $350

English, black glass, onion shaped wine bottle, circa 1700. $600

Rare shape pop bottle with one flat side and glass marble stopper. $260

(Peter Savage Antique Bottle Museum)

BOXES

A box as a place of safe keeping was an essential item in homes from earliest times. Even Egyptian tombs and sparsely furnished castles contained boxes in which clothes and precious items could be securely locked. They range from tiny ones for keeping items of jewelry to large dower chests that young girls filled with items for their dowry. The Victorians loved boxes and bought them in vast quantities for a myriad of purposes ranging from travelling medicine chests to snuff, pill or tobacco boxes. They can be found in almost any material — Tunbridge ware, wood, ivory, silver, gold, china, cardboard, papier maché . . . . Specialist collectors often concentrate on the boxes used by specific professions like the ones full of fearsome looking instruments carried by surgeons or boxes with cupping bowls used by bloodletters. There are also barber's boxes, picnic boxes, writing boxes and needlework boxes — all have their devotees.

Late 16th century Momo-yama period Christian host box or pyx, 9cm. diam. (Christie's) $38,720

One of a pair of Federal mahogany and mahogany veneer inlaid knife boxes, America or England, circa 1790, 14½in. high. (Robt. W. Skinner Inc.) $950

A 17th century Flemish ebony and ivory table cabinet, on later bun feet, 21in. wide. (Christie's) $1,995

A wooden, painted gesso and gilded casket, by W. Cayley-Robinson, 35cm. wide. (Phillips) $1,224

A Spanish 17th century rose-wood and ivory inlaid table cabinet, 40cm. wide. (Phillips) $2,624

A 19th century French gold mounted tortoiseshell jewel casket, 5in. high. (Christie's) $8,250

BOXES

A 19th century leather covered document box, the dome top with brass bail handle, 11½in. wide. (Christie's) $242

Bird's-eye maple Academy painted polychrome box, circa 1820, 12¼in. long. (Robt. W. Skinner Inc.) $3,600

A 19th century leather covered document box, with brass bail handle and brass stud trim, 5¾in. high, 14in. wide. (Christie's) $275

Early 19th century wallpaper hat box, 'A Peep at the Moon', America, 12½in. high, 17in. wide. (Robt. W. Skinner Inc.) $200

A George III satinwood travelling necessaire box, the hinged lid enclosing a well-fitted interior, with leather label inscribed 'Manufactured by Bayley & Blew, 5 Cockspur Street, London', 15½in. wide. (Christie's) $2,645

A 19th century cylindrical cosmetic box with an inner tray and three small containers, 9.3cm. diam., 8.8cm. high. (Christie's) $15,895

A French straw-work workbox worked in a three-coloured diapered pattern, pink, gold and green, 7½ x 5½ x 4in., circa 1750. (Christie's) $1,443

A 19th century English Colonial camphorwood and ebony chest, 32½in. wide. (Parsons, Welch & Cowell) $1,771

Late 18th century document box (bunko), decorated in gold and silver hiramakie, takamakie and hirame on a nashiji ground, 40 x 30 x 15cm. (Christie's) $9,350

A mid Victorian black and gilt japanned papier-mache cigar box with hinged lid, 7¾in. wide. (Christie's) $125

Late 16th century Momo-yama period small domed travelling casket, 21 x 12 x 10.5cm. (Christie's) $748

A 19th century pine Scandinavian bride's box, 11½in. high, 21½in. wide. (Christie's) $495

A 19th century rounded rectangular suzuribako, 23 x 19.8cm. (Christie's) $3,366

An Anglo-French silver and silver mounted dressing table set contained in a brass inlaid rosewood case, by C. Rawlings, 1821, and P. Blazuiere, Paris, 1819-38. (Christie's) $25,740

Late 16th/early 17th century gourd-shaped roironuri suzuribako, 25.5cm. long. (Christie's) $11,220

Mid 19th century Victorian rosewood and mother-of-pearl inlaid sewing box with fitted interior. (G. A. Key) $462

One of a pair of George III mahogany vase-shaped cutlery boxes, 26in. high. (Christie's) $3,888

A travelling dressing set with silver mounts, dated 1901, Birmingham, in an alligator skin case. (Lots Road Chelsea Auction Galleries) $680

BREWERIANA

Breweriana, as its name suggests, involves the collecting of all items related to beer and brewing. Beer mats and beer bottles are perhaps the most popular of the related specialist collections and are dealt with as such elsewhere. Other highly collectable items, however include counter displays, pump handles and heads, trays, ashtrays, advertising signs, posters – the list is endless. Some counter displays in the form of china figurines, for example the Guinness Toucan or Younger's 'Father William', can be small works of art in their own right.

Beer badges form another specialist subject. Some of these go back 60 years or more, and used to be worn by workers in various breweries, some of which may be no longer in existence. They can be very colourful and show a wide range of emblems, from the Fremlin elephant to the Guinness Toucan. Rare ones can fetch up to $50.

A brown and stone coloured ½ pint water jug for Watkins Brewers Dublin Stout, by Thos. Watkins of Llandovery, 1927. $50

Advertising figure 'Brewmaster', brewed by Flowers. $85

A white 1 pint mug for Thos. Dutton Brewery, produced for Henry Milner Ltd., Stoke-on-Trent, 1962. $25

A Royal Doulton figural bottle for Sandiman's Port, 10¼in. high, circa 1920.1956. $70

Black & White Scotch Whisky tray. $50

A whisky bottle made for Bell's Old Scotch Whisky, 7¾in. high, circa 1950. $35

BREWERIANA

Doulton Lambeth stoneware match-holder and striker for John Dewar & Sons. $60

'Schlitz Brewery' tin sign, circa 1915, 24in. diam. (Robt. W. Skinner Inc.) $375

My Goodness, My Guinness statuette, 4in. high. $60

Whisky flask in the form of a crow made for National Distillers of Kentucky, circa 1954. $200

Card advertisement for Coronation 'Cheerio'. $35

A water jug made for William Younger & Co., circa 1920. $52

Younger's Tartan Beer plaster advertising sign, 'Get Younger every day'. $45

1950's printed metal sign for Fremlins Ale, in the form of an elephant, 9in. high. $175

A small Johnnie Walker advertising figure. $52

BRONZE

The malleability of bronze makes it an ideal medium for sculptors and in the 19th century there was a great upsurge in the manufacture of decorative items made from the material. Animals were favourite subjects and sculptors like P. J. Mene, Isidore Bonheur, Jules Moigniez and Christophe Fratin followed the lead of Antoine-Louis Bayre in creating lifelike bronze figures of animals. Bayre created a sensation at the Paris Salon of 1831 when he exhibited a vibrant bronze of a tiger devouring a gavial which inspired a school of sculptors known as "les animaliers" whose aim was realism. Bonheur, for example, was highly regarded among connoisseurs for the realistic way he created galloping horses. During the 19th century there was a great upsurge of interest in Japanese bronzes, especially figures and vases with metal work and enamel decoration. The best ones date from the Meiji period of 1868-1912. Bronze was also used along with ivory by figure sculptors like Chiparus and Preiss.

Early 20th century bronze bust of Woman, signed Wigglesworth, stamped Gorham Co. Founders, 13¾in. high. (Robt. W. Skinner Inc.) $800

Huntress, a silvered bronze figure cast from a model by G. None, Paris, 34cm. high. (Christie's) $1,887

A 19th century bronze bust of a bearded 16th century scholar, his cloak cast with allegorical figures, 28cm. high. (Phillips) $1,304

A French bronze figure of a Neapolitan mandolin player, bearing the inscription Duret, 55cm. high. (Phillips) $1,222

A 19th century French bronze group of a python attacking an Arab horseman, cast from a model by Antoine Louis Barye, circa 1835-40, 22 x 29cm. (Christie's) $23,595

Egyptian Dancer, a gilt bronze and ivory figure cast and carved from a model by C. J. Roberte Colinet, 42.5cm. high. (Christie's) $28,512

BRONZE

A late 19th century French bronze statuette of Diana, signed Denecheau, 60cm. high overall. (Christie's) $6,380

A 16th/17th century late Ming bronze group cast as Budai, 32.5cm. wide. (Christie's) $2,831

A Viennese cold painted bronze of a seated Indian brave, bearing the inscription C. Kauba and stamped Geschutzt 5806, 17cm. high. (Phillips) $1,271

Late 19th century bronze lobed koro on karashishi mask and scroll tripod feet, 61cm. high. (Christie's) $1,405

Pair of 19th century French bronze, copper and silver plated busts of 'La Juive d'Alger' and the 'Cheik Arabe de Caire', by Charles-Henri-Joseph Cordier, 86cm. high. (Christie's) $161,656

A 19th century French bronze head of a child, 'Bebe Endormi', cast from a model by Aime-Jules Dalou, 19cm. high. (Christie's) $3,993

A late 19th/early 20th century bronze memorial relief, attributed to Sir Alfred Gilbert, 25cm. high. (Christie's) $551

Morning Walk, a parcel gilt bronze and ivory group cast and carved after a model by A. Becquerel, 26.8cm. high. (Christie's) $1,900

A 19th century French bronze statue of Cupid, after Denis-Antoine Chaudet, 60cm. high. (Christie's) $3,122

Europa and the Bull, a bronze figure cast from a model by H. Muller, 25.4cm. high. (Christie's) $1,022

An Art Deco bronze group of a male and female nude, 65cm. high. (Christie's) $3,304

A 19th century bronze group of a mounted African Hunter, incised P. J. Mene, 46cm. high. (Phillips) $3,423

A 19th century French bronze group of Hebe and the Eagle of Jupiter, inspired by Rude, the base inscribed E. Drouot, 78cm. high. (Phillips) $4,564

A pair of French 19th century bronze busts of a Nubian man and woman, also known as 'Venus Africaine', both signed Cordier, 83cm.and 79cm. high. (Christie's) $166,980

Bear Hug, a bronze figure cast after a model by F. Rieder, 30.8cm. high. (Christie's) $2,044

An early 19th century French romantic bronze portrait plaque of Albert Bertin, cast from a model by A. Etex, 43 x 32cm. (Christie's) $1,514

A 19th century bronze of Actaeon kneeling on a wounded stag, incised Holme. Cardwell Fect. Roma 1857, 83cm. high. (Christie's) $14,520

Bronze bust of 'Dalila', by E. Villanis, circa 1890, seal of Societe des Bronzes de Paris. (Worsfolds) $1,440

BUCKETS

Buckets in bygone times could be quite upmarket items designed for very specific purposes. One such was the plate pail, used in 18th and 19th century homes for preheating plates and fetching them to and from the table. These were usually made in pairs, and a pair is worth much more than a single. A voiding pail is another specialised example; its uses include catching table crumbs or even transporting ice for the wine cooler.

A George III mahogany brass bound peat bucket with brass liner, 11¾in. high. (Christie's) $1,730

A Georgian mahogany caned plate bucket with brass liner and loop handle, 14in. (Worsfolds) $3,520

An 18th century Dutch peat bucket on triple ball supports with metal liner. (Greenslades) $630

1st World War water carrier of kidney section, painted red and bearing crest, rope carrying handles, 21in. high. (Peter Wilson) $70

A fine painted leather ceremonial parade fire bucket, branded by John Fenno, Boston, circa 1790, with enclosed leather swing handle, 13½in. high. (Christie's) $1,980

A pair of George III Irish brass mounted mahogany plate buckets of large size, 40cm. high. (Phillips) $7,200

A painted leather fire bucket, America, 1822, 12½in. high. (Robt. W. Skinner Inc.) $8,500

CADDY SPOONS

Tea was first imported into England in the early 17th century but it was not in general use until the 1650's when it was bought only by the rich for it cost around $20 a pound. Little wonder that tea caddies were provided with a lock and key and the precious leaves were measured out with a special spoon! Caddy spoons can be made of a wide variety of materials ranging through horn, ivory, tortoiseshell, silver, pewter, mother of pearl, treen and porcelain. The most sought after are early and have seal tops. Apostle spoons which have a cast finial joined to the flattened stem with a V joint are also highly prized. Some caddie spoons were called mote spoons for scooping floating leaves off the top of the tea in the cup and others were moustache spoons with a barrier on the leading edge. The most valuable spoons have large ornate bowls and short handles. Those with handles in the shape of eagles can be worth around $2,000.

A Victorian caddy spoon with scalloped bowl, the openwork handle of vine leaf, tendril and grape bunch design, by George Unite, Birmingham, 1869. (Phillips) $193

A George III caddy spoon, with heart-shaped bowl and bifurcated 'mushroom' handle by Josiah Snatt, 1808. (Phillips) $211

A rare William IV die-stamped eagle's wing caddy spoon, the bowl chased with overlapping feathers, by Joseph Willmore, Birmingham, 1832. (Phillips) $1,408

A good and realistic George III caddy spoon with acorn bowl, the bifurcated handle ending in an octagonal 'fiddle' terminal, by Hart & Co., Birmingham, 1806. (Phillips) $774

An unmarked George III filigree jockey cap caddy spoon, the corrugated cap with wide filigree peak, circa 1800. (Phillips) $457

A good George III caddy spoon with acorn bowl engraved with diaperwork, the shaped handle with central oval panel, by Elizabeth Morley, 1809. (Phillips) $457

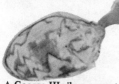

A George III silver-mounted natural shell caddy spoon, the bifurcated octagonal handle with double-thread edge, by Matthew Linwood, of Birmingham, circa 1800. (Phillips) $616

A George III die-stamped caddy spoon, chased with overlapping stylised feathers enclosing an oval centre, by Wardell & Kempson, Birmingham, 1818. (Phillips) $228

A George IV caddy spoon, with plain scallop-shaped bowl and ovoid handle, by Joseph Willmore, Birmingham, 1822. (Phillips) $193

CADDY SPOONS

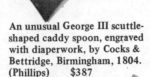

A George III caddy spoon with octagonal bowl, the sides with ribs separated by bands of chevrons, by Samuel Pemberton, Birmingham, 1806. (Phillips) $440

An unusual George III scuttle-shaped caddy spoon, engraved with diaperwork, by Cocks & Bettridge, Birmingham, 1804. (Phillips) $387

A George III caddy spoon with gilt oval fluted bowl and oval filigree central panel, by Samuel Pemberton, Birmingham, 1807. (Phillips) $422

A George III filigree caddy spoon, the bowl of near anthemion shape, each flute terminating in a disc motif, unmarked, circa 1800. (Phillips) $211

A George III right-hand caddy spoon, the flat handle with curved top and incurved sides, by Josiah Snatt, 1805. (Phillips) $616

A George III silver-mounted natural shell caddy spoon, the bifurcated octagonal handle with double-thread edge, by Matthew Linwood, of Birmingham, circa 1800. (Phillips) $598

A George III shovel caddy spoon, engraved with wrigglework on a hatched background, by William Pugh, Birmingham, 1808. (Phillips) $281

A George III jockey cap caddy spoon, of ribbed design with reeded surfaces, by Joseph Taylor, Birmingham, 1798. (Phillips) $387

A rare George III cast caddy spoon, decorated in relief with a Chinese Mandarin holding a tea plant, by Edward Farrell, 1816. (Phillips) $2,200

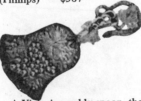

A George III caddy spoon, the feather-shaped bowl chased with stylised overlapping feathers, by William Pugh, Birmingham, 1808. (Phillips) $739

A Victorian caddy spoon, the thistle or bellshaped bowl parcel gilt and embossed with grapes and vine leaves, by Hilliard & Thomason, Birmingham, 1862. (Phillips) $176

A George III 'frying pan' caddy spoon. the circular, engine-turned bowl with central rosette, by Matthew Linwood, Birmingham, 1807. (Phillips) $352

CALENDARS

For many years it has been a practice for friends to send each other calendars at Christmas. They have always been brightly coloured and though today they usually have a page for each month, earlier ones had a square picture with a little booklet containing a leaf a month hanging beneath them. Favourite calendars were cherished for years and some from the 1930's are very collectable especially those that offer a nostalgic view of the past and the countryside. The same kind of pictures appeared on calendars as on jig-saw puzzles – gardens full of flowers; ladies in crinolines gathering blossoms and, a great favourite, a black dog and a white one surrounded by sprigs of heather and in a Highland background. The firm of Duttons made some of the most popular. Other trade calendars were given away as gifts for customers and they range from superbly engraved calendars gifted by Victorian merchants to the super-photography of the Pirelli calendar which is the most eagerly collected of all.

Varga Calendar, 1948, with verses by Earl Wilson.
$50

The Pirelli Pin-up Calendar, 1973.
$210

Calendar for 1900 by E. P. Dutton & Co., with a
moving ship operated with a string. $45

Playboy 'Playmate Calendar', 1978.
$7

CAMERAS

Cameras for the common man began being produced in considerable numbers towards the end of the 19th century and late 19th century wood and brass cameras are very popular with today's collectors. The majority of wooden cameras found today were produced after the introduction of dry plates in the 1880's and maker's names to look for include Meagher, Ross, Dallmeyer, Hare and Sands Hunter. British cameras are reckoned to be the best for the early period and in the early 20th century popular makers were Lancaster, Thornton-Pickard, Underwood, Lizars and Sanderson, Sinclair and Newman & Guardia.

In the 1920's however the German Leica camera appeared and dominated the quality market. Even the Japanese are today eager collectors of Leicas. Those made before about 1960 all have screw thread lenses and the ones manufactured afterwards have bayonet fitting lenses. Before 1931, Leica also made cameras with fixed lenses — the Leica 1 (model A) and Compur-Leica. Almost any Leica will sell at auction or to a collector. Other cameras to look out for include the early Kodak camera by George Eastman which appeared in 1888 — one of those will sell for over $2,000 today. A 1915 Kodak box Brownie is a fairly common item still and should not make much more than $20. Other cameras that turn up for sale include Rolleiflex T twin lens reflex cameras which were popular in the 1950's and their successors, the Tele-Rolleiflex twin lens which actually sells for a higher price because it was a special purpose camera and not so many were sold.

An Eastman Kodak Co. rare Cine Kodak Special II camera with a Kodak Cine Ektar 25mm. f 1.4 lens. (Christie's) $935

A Nippon Kogaku, 325 mm. Nikon SP camera, with a Nippon Kogaku Nikkor-S f 1.4 5cm. lens. (Christie's) $1,247

A half plate brass and mahogany studio camera with revolving carte de visite back, Tessar f 4.5 210mm. lens. (Christie's) $156

CAMERAS

A Fabrik Fotografische Apparate, Germany, rare sub-miniature Fotal camera with an E. Rau, Wetzlar lens. (Christie's) $1,143

Eastman Kodak Co., Rochester, NY, 5 x 4 in. No. 4 Folding Kodak camera No. 465 with a Bausch and Lomb pneumatic shutter. (Christie's) $415

A Le Coultre Co., Switzerland, Compass camera, with a CCL3B f 3.5 35mm. anastigmat lens. (Christie's) $935

Kodak, Stuttgart, a very rare new type Retina IIIC camera No. 94058 with a Schneider Retina-Xenon f 2.0 50mm. lens. (Christie's) $540

A good brown Vanity Kodak camera No. 98343 with catch 'Vest Pocket Kodak Series III', a Kodak Anastigmat f 6.3 83mm. lens No. 48988. (Christie's) $228

A Ihagee, Dresden, Original Kine Exakta camera, with a Dallmeyer super-six anastigmat f 19 2in. lens. (Christie's) $1,039

An Adams & Co., London, 5 x 4in. Idento camera No. 3192 with a Ross, London, Homocentric 6in. F 6.3 lens. (Christie's) $124

A Voigtlander, Braunschweig, pre-war Prominant camera, with a Voigtlander Heliar f 4.5 10.5cm. lens. (Christie's) $790

A rare and important Original Kodak camera No. 1127 with winding key, barrel shutter and film holder, stamped 'Pat May 5, 1885'. (Christie's) $3,308

A blue Girl Guide Kodak camera with matching blue leather case stamped with the Girl Guide insignia. (Christie's) $249

An E. Lorenz, Berlin, 4½ x 6cm. rigid bodied Clarissa camera, with a Meyer and Co. Plasmat f 2 9cm. lens. (Christie's) $2,702

A Houghton-Butcher Mfg. Co. Ltd., tropical model Ensign roll-film reflex camera No. E1053. (Christie's) $500

A Kodak Suprema camera No. 189646K with a Schneider Xenar f 3.5 8cm. lens No. 1182748 in maker's leather case, (Christie's) $374

A Kleinbild-Plasmat Roland camera No. S1137 with a Rudolph 70mm. f 2.7 lens, set into a rim-set Compur shutter. (Christie's) $831

An Arthur S. Newman, London, rare and important prototype 9.5mm. cinematographic hand camera with polished aluminium casing. (Christie's) $2,702

A rare Super Kodak Six-20 camera No. 2209 with a Kodak Anastigmat special f 3.5 100mm. lens No. 622. (Christie's) $1,247

An Eastman Kodak Co., No. 1 Brownie camera with winding key in maker's canvas case and an EKC Brownie finder. (Christie's) $52

A green Boy Scout Kodak camera with maker's leather case. (Christie's) $177

CAR MASCOTS

Around 1905 the first mascots appeared perched on the sleek bonnets of cars. The earliest examples were made of cast metal but later they appeared in carved wood or glass. The most famous car mascot is perhaps the Rolls Royce Spirit of Ecstasy which the company adopted as their trademark and the American Lincoln company followed by adopting a greyhound as their symbol. Mascots can be found — but at a price — in a large variety of shapes; skiers, nude goddesses, eagles, horses, swallows and flying spirits, rabbits, policemen, leaping deer or herons and they were designed by some of the most accomplished artists of the time. The most famous mascots of all however are those made in glass by Rene Lalique who produced 46 different designs in clear, colored or frosted crystal between the late 1920's and the late '30's. Any one of them is worth several thousand dollars today.

'Sir Kreemy Knut', chrome plated mascot of Sir Kreemy was the trade mark and Company mascot of Sharp's Toffee Co. $260

'Spirit of the Wind', a red-ashay car mascot on chromium plated metal mount, 11.5cm. high. (Christie's) $1,353

'Punch', British made, chrome plated mascot, early 1930's, no markings or indication of the manufacturer. $175

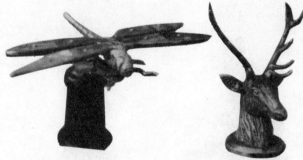

'Coq Nain', a coloured car mascot, the topaz and satin finished glass moulded as a cockerel, 20.2cm. high. (Christie's) $4,510

'Dragonfly', chrome plate with mother of pearl wings by Desmo, 1930's. $910

'Stag's Head', an accessory mascot, produced in the 1920's by A. E. L., nickel plated brass. $210

'Touch Wud', a good luck mascot with a leather head, glass eyes and a brass body, circa 1908. $290

'Girl on a Goose', British made mascot signed L.L. for Louis Lejaune. $785

A brass car mascot of Minerva, inscribed 'Minerva P. de Soete', 6in. high. (Christie's) $403

'Sanglier', a Lalique car mascot in clear and satin finished glass, moulded as a boar, 6.5cm. high. (Christie's) $1,022

'Lady Skater', chrome plated Desmo mascot from the 1930's was for skating enthusiasts. $260

'Tete de Coq', a Lalique car mascot, in clear and satin finished glass, 18cm. high. (Christie's) $2,044

A chromium plated car mascot figure of 'Puss in Boots', 6in. high. (Christie's) $465

A rosewood and ivory toucan radiator cap, inscribed Howett, London, 5in. high. (Christie's) $248

'Pharaoh', a Red-Ashay, car mascot in clear and satin finished glass, 11.5cm. high. (Christie's) $1,321

CAR MASCOTS

A brass stylised car mascot bust of Minerva, inscribed P. de Soete, 5½in. high. (Christie's) $589

'The Dummy Teat', nickel plated mascot manufactured by J. Grose & Co., 1926, for the Austin 7 fondly known as the Baby Austin. $525

'Tete de Belier', a Lalique car mascot, moulded as a ram's head, 9.5cm. high. (Christie's) $27,060

A Lalique clear and frosted glass car mascot of 'Victoire — Spirit of the Wind', 10in. long. (Prudential Fine Art) $9,454

An early 20th century cold painted metal car mascot of a dragonfly golfer seated on a composition golf ball, 6in. high. (Woolley & Wallis) $693

'Grand Libellule', a Lalique car mascot in clear and satin finished glass, 21cm. high. (Christie's) $5,783

A Lalique car mascot, Long-champs, in clear and satin-finished glass, 13cm. high. (Christie's) $12,672

'Vitesse', a Lalique car mascot moulded as a naked female, 18.5cm. high. (Christie's) $9,020

'Archer', a Lalique car mascot in clear and satin finished glass, 12cm. high. (Christie's) $2,044

CARDS

Greeting cards for birthdays, Christmases and especially Valentine's Day really took popular hold in the 19th century with the advent of cheap postal services. Valentine cards had been exchanged by lovers since the end of the 18th century but by 1835 the Post Office reported mailings of 60,000 on February 13th and after the introduction of the penny post in 1840, the number increased even more. At the same time the Victorian popularisation of Christmas started a vogue for Christmas cards. Over the years many famous artists have designed greetings cards and if the artist can be identified, the card's value is enhanced. Rarer greetings cards are those which were produced for Hallowe'en, the Jewish New Year and Krampus, a name little heard today. While Santa Claus rewarded good children at Christmas, Krampus punished naughty ones. Among the more accessible cards for collectors are deckle edged cards dating from between 1918 and 1945 and photographically reproduced cards with hand colored pictures. Many attractive examples were produced in the Beagle and Rotary series.

46th Infantry Division Christmas greetings, Austria, 1946. $3

Pleasant Hours, 'May all the Joys and Mirths of Christmas be Yours'. $5

'From over the sea to greet you, a Happy Christmas'. $1

'Oh lead me, holy dove to rest', by Ernest Nister, printed in Bavaria. $3.50

'Wishing you a joyous Christmas'. $3.50

Valentine's Greetings, 1914-18. $7

Wireless Greetings, received by M.V. Landaura from London. $7

Good Wishes, 'Here's my pug and little kitty'. $5

Happy Tune record Christmas Card, 'Hark the Herald Angels Sing'. $5

CARDS

'May nothing floor your happiness this Christmas', Davidson Bros., London. $5

A Birthday Greeting, 'Many Happy Returns'. $7

'To Greet You, with loving Christmas greetings'. $7

'Hearty Greetings, A happy New Year to you'. $5

'A New Year Greeting with love', Faulkner. $3.50

'Hurrah for dear old Christmas Day, May you be happy blithe and gay', $3.50

Conveying Good Wishes, Christmas, 1934. $2

'May your Christmas be Happy'. $9

'Christmas Greetings, Come what may', 1940. $2.50

The first Christmas card sent to Henry Cole by William Makepeace Thakeray. (Phillips) $4,775

Happy Birthday, 1957, Emmett artwork. $1

'Like merry robin redbreasts, we ring our roundelay'. $2.50

CARLTON WARE

The name Carlton Ware was given to pottery produced by Wiltshaw and Robinson of Stoke on Trent from 1890 till 1957. After that date the firm was renamed Carlton Ware Ltd. The firm's usual mark is a circle enclosing a swallow and topped by a crown and some pieces are marked Carlton Ware. The most popular lines were porcelain vases decorated with bright enamelling and gilded decorations in flower or fan motifs often on black backgrounds which were turned out in large numbers in the 1920's. The firm also made pieces in Art Deco styles with designs of lustrous trees in unusual colors or decorated with Kate Greenaway style fairies, mythical birds or chinoiserie designs.

Carlton Ware
Handpainted
MADE in ENGLAND
"TRADE MARK"

Carlton Ware
ENGLAND

Carlton Ware

Oviform vase with dark grey ground simulating nightfall, signed by E. F. Paul, with Kate Greenaway style fairies design, 230mm. high. (Goss & Crested China) $950

Carlton Ware lustre jug with gilt loop handle, the body painted and gilded with stylised floral and fan decoration, 5in. high. (Prudential Fine Art) $189

A Carlton Ware ginger jar and cover, the oviform body painted with clusters of stylised flowerheads, 10¾in. high. (Christie's) $801

A Carltonware plaque painted in gilt, orange, blue, green and white with wisteria and exotic plants, 15½in. diam. (Christie's) $308

A Carlton Ware service decorated in polychrome enamels, coffee pot 20.4cm. high. (Christie's) $1,174

Vibrant lustrous red 'Rouge Royale' leaf, one of a series introduced after 1930, 220mm. long. (Goss & Crested China) $18

CARTES DE VISITE

The carte de visite consisted of a small portrait, usually full length but occasionally only head and shoulders, measuring about two and a half by three and a half inches and mounted on a visiting card. It was first mentioned in the French magazine "La Lumiere" in 1854 which said it had been invented by two anonymous Frenchmen but the idea was patented by the photographer Disderi who promoted the cards with the public and sold so many that he is reputed to have earned as much as $75,000 a year. It soon became the fashion to have one's portrait on a carte de visite and society photographers did a roaring trade turning them out. Everyone who was anyone in society wanted a carte de visite and even the Princess of Wales sat for a photographer called W. Downey in 1867. The card with her likeness sold 300,000 copies. Photographers to look out for include Downey and Disderi; C. Silvy who had a sophisticated clientele in London; Saroni and Claudet.

Study of three Welsh ladies taking tea, circa 1880, by Charles Allen Photographic Artist, Tenby and Haverford West. $7

Envelope containing two cartes de visite posted from David Rees, Clapham Road, London, Certified Artist and Photographer — Prize Medal Awarded, 1872, bearing penny red stamp. $9

Full length portrait study of a girl by M. Boak, Driffield and Pickering. 'This portrait can be enlarged to life size', on reverse. $3.50

Portrait study of a bearded gentleman by W. J. Welsted and Son, 'Photographers of the Prince and Princess of Wales'. $2

Pair of cartes 'Joy' and 'Sorrow', Girl holding Punch puppet, by 'Dicksee', circa 1877. $7

Portrait study of lady, circa 1880, by J. R. Dowdall, Great Western Studio, Swansea. $2

CARTES DE VISITE

A fine portrait study of the Duke of Edinburgh. $10

Australian carte de visite portrait study of a man in a bowler hat by A. Lomer and Co., Brisbane. $2

H.R.H. The Prince of Wales, later Edward VII. $12

A fine portrait study of Queen Victoria in the 1890's. $9

Portrait study of a country gentleman, with a typical pictorial reverse back, by M. Boak, Bridlington. $3.50

'Fun' type carte de visite of Matrimony and Courtship by Perry and Co., London. $14

Twelve views of Shrewsbury, circa 1893. $20

His Grace the Archbishop of Canterbury, Dr Tait, by the London Stereoscopic and Photographic Co. (Prize medal for portraiture Vienna Exhibition 1873.) $10

Portrait study of The Duke of Connaught. $9

(Border Bygones)

100

CARVED STONE

Carved stone is one of the earliest forms of artistic expression and one which, because of its very nature, can survive indefinitely, as the prehistoric stones of Easter Island, and elsewhere bear witness. Age, indeed does not seem to play a great part in determining value, since an ancient Sumerian tablet, for example, can be picked up for $200 or so, while modern examples, by such practitioners as Henry Moore and Barbara Hepworth, sell for huge sums.

A pair of carved stone putti the plump figures standing, one holding a bird, the other a basket of fruit, 38in. high. (Christie's) $3,300

A carved stone figure of Hercules, partly draped with lion's skin, holding golden apples of the Hesperides, 40in. high. (Robt. W. Skinner Inc.) $800

A Sumerian brick fragment impressed with four lines of cuneiform —'Ur Namma, King of Ur, who built the temple of Namma', 27 x 29cm. overall. (Phillips) $290

Late 17th century English stone figure of 'Prometheus Bound', in the manner of Cibber, 175cm. high. (Phillips) $15,750

Late 17th century Buddhist stone stela of typical form, dated Genroku 5 (1692), with a later inscription and date Meiji 34 (1901), 77.5cm. high. (Christie's) $1,389

Contemporary Eskimo carving of a wrestling man and bear in mottled greenish-grey stone, 18in. high. (Robt. W. Skinner Inc.) $700

A greenish-grey and black stone figure of a seated roaring lion, Tang Dynasty, 13cm. high. (Christie's) $1,746

One of a pair of carved granite Foo dogs and stands; China, 19th century, 28½in. high. (Robt. W. Skinner Inc.) $4,200

A dark stone figure of Guanyin, seated in dhyanasana, Tang Dynasty, 39.5cm. high, mounted on black marble stand. (Christie's) $14,157

A naturalistically coloured stone carving of a chimpanzee, 53.5cm. high. (Phillips) $460

A sandstone head of rounded form, on a long cylindrical neck, 27cm. high, perhaps Romano-Celtic. (Phillips) $229

A stone horse's head, Han Dynasty, 12.9cm. high. (Christie's) $13,500

One of a pair of 5th century A.D. large stone figures of chimera, heavily carved from a matt grey material of limestone type, approx. 55.5cm. high. (Christie's) $157,300

A Northern Qi stele with two figures of Buddha seated side by side, dated Tianbao 6th year, tenth month, tenth day, corresponding to AD555, 29cm. high. (Christie's) $15,000

A carved limestone sculpture of Mother and Child, by W. Edmondson, circa 1934/39, 15in. high. (Christie's) $9,900

A Buddhist stone stele, dated to the 2nd year of Zheng Guan of the N. Wei Dynasty, 36cm. high. (Christie's) $943

CARVED WOOD

Wood carving is one of the most ancient and universal arts, found in a multitude of objects from altars to nutcrackers. Many early toys were of wood—a Charles II carved wooden doll sold recently for over £70,000. Carved furniture demands a book on its own, while another interesting speciality field consists of tribal arts—weapons, figures and utensils.

Wood carving is perhaps at its finest when applied to religious subjects, as the many glorious carvings in Christian and other places of worship bear ample witness.

A stained wood smoker's compendium in the form of a motor car, 6½ x 11½in. (Christie's) $322

A Shinto wood sculpture of a seated deity wearing Heian/Kamakura style robes and hat, Edo period, 58.8cm. high. (Christie's) $2,400

A pair of Chinese painted carved wooden figures, late 18th/early 19th century, the gentleman 46¼in. high, the lady 21¼in. high. (Christie's) $17,820

A carved walnut figure of St. Lucy, traces of original polychrome, the reverse hollowed, 44.5cm. high, probably S. German. (Phillips) $720

A 19th century carved walnut panel with a coat-of-arms and motto Le Main Tiendrai, 46in. wide. (Christie's) $2,478

A stylised figure of a carved wooden horse, America, 23in. high, 23in. long. (Robt. W. Skinner Inc.) $1,200

A late 16th century polychromed and carved lime-wood relief panel of a bearded saint, possibly St. Christopher, 37cm. high. (Phillips) $652

CARVED WOOD

A carved oak panel depicting the martyrdom of St. Lawrence, 1764, 96cm. high. (Phillips) $2,100

A gilt bronze and carved wood figure of a Spanish flamenco dancer cast and carved from a model by Hagenauer, 23.9cm. high. (Christie's) $939

A 19th century Japanese carved hardwood okimono of humorous deity, 5½in. high. (Hobbs & Chambers) $264

A 16th century Flemish oak relief carved group of a moustachioed soldier and his female companion, 42cm. high. (Phillips) $5,542

One of a pair of giltwood jardinieres with overhanging reeded lips, 11in. wide. (Christie's) $1,837

A painted wooden hollow standing horse, American, circa 1850/90, 49in. long, possibly used as a harness-maker's sign. (Christie's) $3,520

A 19th century boxwood wrist-rest, unsigned, 5.5cm. long. (Christie's) $880

A Charles X period carved walnut cradle on foliate scroll dolphin supports. (Phillips) $7,000

An Egyptian Anthropoid wood mask, 18cm. high, Ptolemaic Period. (Phillips) $254

A 19th century wooden model of a seated camel, 50in. wide, 27½in. high. (Christie's)
$20,358

A Netherlandish oak panel carved in relief with the Adoration of the Magi, 17th/18th century, 71 x 81cm. (Phillips) $2,934

A 19th century lacquered wood mask of Ayagiri, 4.6cm. high. (Christie's)
$1,487

A 16th/17th century carved and polychromed limewood group of the Madonna and Child, 52cm. high. (Phillips)
$1,630

A North Italian late 18th/early 19th century walnut panel. (Parsons, Welch & Cowell) $1,087

Late 18th century carved hard pine spoon rack with chip carved decoration, New Jersey, 21in. high. (Robt. W. Skinner Inc.) $1,800

A Continental carved wooden tankard with hinged cover, 8in. high. (Prudential Fine Art) $2,184

A Momoyama period Christian folding lectern (shokendai), decorated in aogai and hira-makie, circa 1600, 50.5cm. high. (Christie's)
$38,880

A 19th century American carved wooden rooster, 12½in. high. (Robt. W. Skinner Inc.)
$1,500

CHAIRS

Since man gave up squatting on the floor, the chair has become one of the most essential items of household furniture and it can range from the strictly utilitarian to the positively luxurious. As far as style goes, the buyer has a huge range from which to pick — what about a Tudor chair with a high wooden back and deep carving? Or if a softer seat is required, a nice deeply padded Victorian ladies' chair with short cabriole legs might do very well. The Georgian arm chair with its lug eared sides and lion's paw feet fits in with most people's idea of a comfortable seat while others may prefer a round armed 1930's fireside chair reminiscent of nights spent listening to the wireless.

Sets of dining table chairs have soared in price over the past few years and those specially sought after are Georgian chairs with sabre legs or in Chinoiserie designs. Victorian dining room chairs tend to be heavier and more stolid than the Georgian but they too fetch high sums. Sets of twelve including two carvers are at a premium. Kitchen chairs are selling well, especially those with ladder or spar backs; bedroom chairs are lighter and more frivolous but are also popular and bentwood chairs, chairs with basket work seats or bergere backs and sides do well. There is a growing vogue for chairs dating from the 1940's and 1950's, especially those made of chromium and leather. On the Continent, buyers are especially keen on chairs dating from the 1930's and the bizarre chairs made by the designer Bugatti.

Two of a set of twelve Regency simulated rosewood and parcel gilt dining chairs comprising six armchairs and six side chairs. (Christie's)   Twelve $28,512

Two of a set of six Federal painted fancy chairs, N.Y., 1800-15, 33¾in. high. (Christie's)   Six $3,850

A Federal carved mahogany side chair and armchair, possibly by John Carlile Jr., Rhode Island. (Christie's) $3,080

CHAIRS

An Italian Directoire white painted and parcel gilt elbow chair. (Phillips) $2,592

One of a pair of walnut bergeres upholstered in green velvet, on moulded cabriole legs and scrolled toes. (Christie's) $1,633

An early Victorian oak open armchair attributed to A. W. N. Pugin, the back and seat upholstered in contemporary foliate cut velvet. (Christie's) $8,910

A Regency mahogany armchair with cane-filled back and seat with red leather squab cushion. (Christie's) $1,262

One of a pair of Finimar laminated birchwood open armchairs designed by Alvar Alto. (Christie's) $2,044

One of a pair of Regency blue-painted and parcel gilt armchairs with padded arm rests and seats, both stamped T. Gray. (Christie's)$19,057

A mid Victorian open armchair of Gothic style with drop-in seat. (Christie's) $1,473

A George III mahogany 'cockpen' open armchair with pierced trelliswork back and arms. (Christie's) $1,982

A Regency mahogany library armchair, the cane filled back and seat with red leather squab cushions. (Christie's) $3,406

A blue PVC inflatable armchair. (Christie's)
$578

One of a pair of upholstered easy armchairs by Howard & Sons. (Christie's)
$3,306

A wicker patio chair designed by Terence Conran. (Christie's) $134

A George III mahogany Windsor armchair with comb-back and yoke-shaped arms. (Christie's)
$10,692

A late Regency mahogany hall porter's chair with arched hooded back and seat covered in brown leather, 61½in. high. (Christie's)
$4,303

A Chippendale mahogany corner chair, Newport, Rhode Island, 1750-70, 32½in. high. (Christie's)
$27,500

An inlaid rosewood curule-type armchair, attributed to Pottier and Stymus, circa 1870, 34in. high, 31in. wide. (Robt. W. Skinner Inc.)
$1,100

Early 20th century wicker arm rocker, 31in. wide. (Robt. W. Skinner Inc.)
$200

One of a pair of early Victorian rosewood armchairs, each with a spoon-shaped back and serpentine seat, on cabriole legs. (Christie's) $4,712

CHAMBER POTS

The "po", a name which derived from the French 'pot de chambre' was an essential in bedrooms in the days before modern plumbing. They were usually part of a set consisting of a jug, a basin, slop pail and soap dish and these ranged from coarse pottery to lovely porcelain. Chamber pots have even been made from silver and gold. Every major pottery company made those sets and they can be found by Wemyss Ware, Masons Ironstone, Wedgwood pottery or even from Limoges, decorated with elegant painting and gilding. Some chamber pots were vulgarly crude in their designs, bearing rude inscriptions and pictures inside. Some held a crouching pottery frog within the bowl while others were decorated with the face of Napoleon or a watching eye.

A blue and white chamber pot painted with peony and bamboo issuing from rockwork, circa 1750, 18.5cm. diam. (Christie's) $2,293

A late Victorian chamber pot, with a scroll handle. (Woolley & Wallis) $619

An English china chamber pot by Brown-Westhead, Moore & Co., circa 1870, with polychrome rhododendron decoration on cream ground. $80

20th century white enamel chamber pot with blue rim. $9

Sunderland lustre pottery chamber pot with an applied frog and cartoon face in the interior. $700

One of two chamber pots, circa 1750, 15.5cm. wide, 12.5cm. diam. (Christie's) $3,754

A Royal Doulton Aubrey chamber pot decorated with Art Nouveau designs. $85

Staffordshire floral china chamber pot. $70

Early 19th century pewter chamber pot. $175

CHEESE DISHES

In the days before health scares about food, milk, butter and cheese were bought from the town dairy where there was often a cow tethered in the back and the cheese was cut with a cheese wire off a huge slab that lay on the marble counter. There were all sorts of pieces of equipment and domestic ware associated with the preparing and keeping of dairy products – butter moulds, paddles for making butter balls, lidded dishes, strainers and particularly cheese dishes which range in size from small ones for a special little titbit of cheese to huge ones big enough to accommodate an entire Stilton. Those which were going to be presented on the dining table were often beautifully painted, and the blue and white ones are especially attractive to collectors, but the ones that were used for storing cheese in the kitchen were made of fine china and plain white, in order to give a feeling of cleanliness and freshness perhaps.

A majolica glazed Stilton cheese dish and cover, probably by George Jones & Sons, late 19th century. (G. A. Key) $140

Stilton cheese dish and cover in the style of Wedgwood, circa 1900, 12in. high. (Lots Road Galleries) $160

A George Jones 'majolica' circular cheese dish and cover, circa 1880, 28cm. diam. (Christie's) $577

Wilkinson Ltd. 'bizarre' cheese dish and cover, 1930. $130

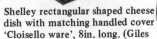

Shelley rectangular shaped cheese dish with matching handled cover 'Cloisello ware', 8in. long. (Giles Haywood) $106

Staffordshire pottery cheese dish with floral decoration. $25

A Minton majolica cheese dish and cover with reclining bull finial, 29cm. high. (Christie's) $1,285

A Cheese dish in the form of a bull's head. (Worsfolds) $184

A George Jones majolica cheese dome and stand. (Dreweatts) $604

CHELSEA

The most famous British porcelain factory is Chelsea which is thought to have started around 1745 when a series of small, well moulded cream or milk jugs called "goat and bee jugs" were made. The earliest pieces bore an incised triangle mark and were usually made of white porcelain. Chelsea porcelain was always marked with an anchor in various colors and shapes but it was much faked and marks should not be taken at their face value. Later examples of Chelsea became more richly decorated and followed Meissen or Oriental patterns. The Chelsea factory produced a large range of different forms — tea, dessert and dinner services as well as ornaments, figures and groups. It always catered for a higher class of client and no earthenware was produced. After 1784 it is usually referred to as Chelsea-Derby because it was taken over by a Derby manufacturer called William Duesbury.

A Chelsea 'Hans Sloane' botanical plate, red anchor and 43 mark, circa 1755, 23.5cm. diam. (Christie's)
$6,463

A Chelsea group of two goats, painted in the workshop of Wm. Duesbury, raised red anchor mark, circa 1751, 16.5cm. wide. (Christie's)
$14,256

A Chelsea-Derby Jardiniere of 'U' shape, Chelsea style with fabulous birds on rockwork and in the branches of leafy trees, 17cm. high. (Phillips)
$1,485

A Chelsea acanthus leaf moulded cream jug with bamboo styled handle, crown and trident mark in blue, circa 1749, 8.4cm. high. (Christie's) $6,336

A pair of Chelsea masqueraders, gold anchor marks at back, circa 1765, 30cm. high. (Christie's) $2,059

A Chelsea apple tureen and cover naturally modelled and coloured in green and russet, the base with red 3 mark, circa 1755, 10.5cm. high. (Christie's)
$6,134

A Chelsea fluted oviform teapot and cover painted in the Kakiemon palette, circa 1752, 12.6cm. high. (Christie's) $5,214

A Chelsea group of two children, naked except for a white and gold drapery, seated on a rocky mound, 17.5cm. high. (Lawrence Fine Art) $1,539

A Chelsea fluted teabowl painted in a vivid Kakiemon palette with birds perched and in flight, 1750-52, 5cm. high. (Christie's) $1,900

A Chelsea double scent bottle modelled as a parrot and a rooster, circa 1755, 7cm. high. (Christie's) $2,692

Pair of Chelsea Derby candlestick figures of a gallant and his companion, 6½in. and 6in. high, no nozzles. (Graves Son & Pilcher) $830

A Chelsea acanthus leaf moulded white chocolate pot on four feet, 1745-49, 24cm. high overall. (Christie's) $1,346

A Chelsea octagonal dish, painted in the Kakiemon palette with pheasants, circa 1750, 20.5cm. wide. (Christie's) $1,925

A Chelsea group of two children, naked except for a pink drapery, with large fish, 24cm. high. (Lawrence Fine Art) $1,458

A Chelsea silver shaped plate painted in the Kakiemon palette with The Red Tiger Pattern, 1750-52, 23cm. diam. (Christie's) $6,336

CHILDREN'S BOOKS

When buying children's books it is important to remember that condition is of paramount importance. A child's book in pristine condition is hard to find and when they do turn up, they are invariably expensive. The earliest children's hornbooks or chapbooks are usually bought for high prices by libraries or museums and ordinary collectors stick to more recent books, sometimes specialising in those they read themselves when children. The nostalgia factor plays a large part in this collecting field.

Illustrated books are the most highly prized and those with plates by artists like Arthur Rackham, Kay Neilsen, E.H. Detmold or Jessie M. King are always eagerly sought after. There are artists whose work sells a book — Edward Lear for example, but also Cruikshank, Tenniel and Ernest Shepherd who illustrated A.A. Milne's Winnie the Pooh books. Arthur Lang's fairy tale books make good prices if they are illustrated by Austen Dobson, Linley Sanbourne, Kate Greenaway, T. Bowick or Randolph Caldecott.

Another good selling point is an attractive cover, especially for Victorian children's books which tend to be on the stuffy, righteous side as far as content is concerned. The colorful covers of Henty's adventure stories however are more refreshing. Some collectors tend to buy all the books by one author or about a special character. For example Arthur Ransome's books or Richmal Crompton's William books. A battered "William" second edition might change hands at $5 while a first edition with its dust cover will cost $40. Alphabet books, Mabel Lucie Attwell books; the novels of Enid Blyton, W.E. Johns, creator of Biggles; and Frank Richards who dreamed up Bunter of Greyfriars are also highly prized.

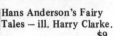

Hans Anderson's Fairy Tales — ill. Harry Clarke. $9

The Children's Treasury. $9

Grand Jubilee Volume of Little Folks 1921. $18

Gulliver's Travels — ill. John Hassall. $25

Infants Magazine 1903. $20

Blackie's Girls' Annual 1930. $12

(Lynn Private Collection, Tyne & Wear)

113

CHILDREN'S BOOKS

Child's Companion Annual
1934. $18

Cassell's Children's Annual
1920 — illustrations include
Anne Anderson, Harry Rountree and C. E. Brock. $25

Hotspur Book for Boys 1937.
$20

Blackie's Granny's Old Stories
— ill. Hassall 1939. $25

Modern Boy's Book of True
Adventure. $18

Aldine Robin Hood Library.
$2

Madge Williams Children's
Annual. $12

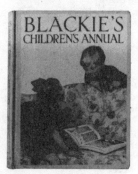

Blackie's Children's Annual
1922 — illustrations include
Honor Appleton, H. M. Brock,
Ruth Cobb, A. E. Jackson.
$25

The Jolly Book 1919. $25

(Lynn Private Collection, Tyne & Wear)

114

CHILDREN'S BOOKS

Teddy Tail's Annual 1937.
$20

Peek-a-Boo Japs — ill. Chloe
Preston 1916. $35

School Girl's Annual volume 3.
$15

Les Vacances de Nane 1924.
— ill. Henry Morin. $14

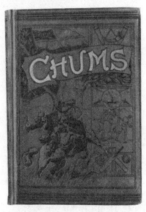

Chums Volume 1, 1892. $70

Noah's Ark Annual 1935.
$14

Pets and Playmates. $20

Tiny Tot's Picture Book 1934
— 80 pages of pictures including
Rountree, Beaman and Gordon
Robinson. $25

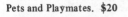

Make Believe Story Book 1924.
$35

(Lynn Private Collection, Tyne & Wear)

CHILDREN'S BOOKS

Lawson Wood's Merry Monkeys.
$20

Master Charlie 1899. $25

Nister's Holiday Annual.
$45

Lawson Wood Nursery Rhyme
Book. $20

The Bunty Book — published
by G. Heath Robinson & J.
Birch Ltd. Illustrations include
Louis Wain and Gordon Browne.
$45

Sunbeam Annual 1933.
$20

Musical Box Annual. $12

Boys Illustrated Book of the
War 1917. $14

Cicely Mary Barker's Flower
Fairy Picture Book. 40 illustrations. $14

(Lynn Private Collection, Tyne & Wear)

CHILDREN'S BOOKS

Wilfred's Annual 1936. $20

Sunbeam's Picture Book 1926.
$9

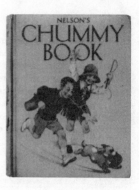

Nelson's Chummy Book 1933.
$25

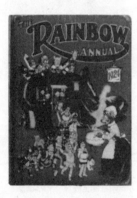

Rainbow Annual 1924. $25

Adventure Land 1938. $20

Book of Great Adventurers.
$14

Mrs Strang's Annual for Children 1914. $35

The Prize for Boys and Girls
Volume 66. $12

Children's Stories from the
Poets 1940 – ill. Frank Adams.
$20

(Lynn Private Collection, Tyne & Wear)

117

CHINA

China is a truly enormous subject, and countless books have been written on every type and aspect of it. Porcelain was introduced into Europe from China in the 16th century and became an instant collectable for moneyed classes. The secrets of its manufacture were discovered in France and Germany in the early 18th century, and during the next few decades the Sevres, Meissen and Dresden factories produced most of the cabinet ware of the period. England at this time lacked the ingredients and skills for making fine porcelain, and it was not until the 19th century that such factories as Worcester, Swansea and Derby began manufacturing in any quantities.

During the Victorian times, fine porcelain became affordable for the middle classes also, and its popularity has persisted to the present day.

A model of a roistering Dutchman astride a Dutch gin cask, 37.5cm. high. (Christie's)
$52,360

A Frankenthal group of chess players modelled by J. F. Luck, blue crowned Carl Theodor mark, circa 1765, 17cm. high. (Christie's)
$11,583

A Whieldon tortoiseshell coffee pot and cover, of baluster shape with domed cover, circa 1760. (Phillips)
$8,010

A Berlin two-handled campana vase painted in the neo-classical taste, 1803-1810, 45cm. high. (Christie's) $13,365

A Wiener Keramik figure of a putto, designed by M. Powolny, 40.5cm. high. (Christie's) $3,304

A Wedgwood solid pale-blue and white jasper cylindrical sugar bowl and cover, circa 1785, 10.5cm. diam. (Christie's) $673

A stoneware 'spade-form' vase by Hans Coper, circa 1972, 23.4cm. high. (Christie's) $16,720

One of a pair of Yorkshire models of cows, one with a gardener, the other with a woman, 14.5cm. long. (Phillips) $4,676

A Ralph Wood Vicar and Moses group, circa 1780, 24.5cm. high. (Christie's) $866

An inscribed Liverpool delft puzzle jug, the rim with three spouts and hollow handle, circa 1750, 8in. high. (Dreweatts) $3,190

A Derby baluster jug, painted by Richard Dodson, 17cm. high, crown, crossed batons and D mark in red. (Phillips) $2,865

A Maw & Co. pottery vase, the body painted in a ruby red lustre with large flowers and foliage all on a yellow ground, 13in. high. (Christie's) $644

A Doulton Lambeth style stoneware conservatory planter in the form of a weathered tree trunk. (Locke & England) $978

A Nymphenburg oil and vinegar stand with two bottles and hinged covers, circa 1765, the bottles 18cm. high. (Christie's) $12,571

A glazed ceramic grotesque face jug, by H. B. Craig, N. Carolina, ovoid with two applied strap handles, 16½in. high. (Christie's) $330

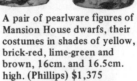

A Minton majolica-ware Neptune shell dish, 17cm. high, impressed Minton, shape no. 903 and date code for 1861. (Phillips) $462

A pair of pearlware figures of Mansion House dwarfs, their costumes in shades of yellow, brick-red, lime-green and brown, 16cm. and 16.5cm. high. (Phillips) $1,375

Royal Worcester Hadley-style footed vase, designed as a jardiniere, 1906, 5in. high. (Giles Haywood) $458

A Pilkington Lancastrian pottery vase by Richard Joyce, impressed Bee mark and date code for 1909, 11¾in. high. (Christie's) $1,006

A Linthorpe earthenware vase moulded on each side with grotesque fish faces, 17.9cm. high. (Christie's) $589

A pearlware puzzle jug, the serpent handle with three spouts, circa 1820, 29cm. high. (Christie's) $689

Shaped Canton shrimp dish, 19th century, typical Canton scene, diam. 10¼in. (Robt. W. Skinner Inc.) $275

A mid 19th century Japanese Imari goldfish bowl. (Miller & Co.) $787

Late 19th century German porcelain table centrepiece, underglazed blue 'R' mark, 11½in. high. (Peter Wilson) $704

CHINA

A pair of large Sancai standing figures of Court Dignitaries, Tang Dynasty, approx. 85cm. high. (Christie's) $29,887

Late 17th century large Arita blue and white baluster vase and cover, 47cm. high. (Christie's) $8,800

A pair of Derby figures of a sailor and his lass, Wm. Duesbury & Co., circa 1765, approx. 24cm. high. (Christie's) $1,996

An Urbino maiolica wet drug or syrup jar, workshop of Orazio Fontana, 1565-70, 34cm. high. (Phillips) $22,920

Pair of Royal Dux figurines, signed F. Otto, pink triangle to base, 17in. high. (Giles Haywood) $574

A Rookwood pottery standard glaze portrait vase, decorated with portrait of a black African with a cap, 1897, 12in. high. (Robt. W. Skinner Inc.) $2,500

A 19th century Liverpool transfer-printed pitcher of baluster form with pulled spout and applied C-scroll handle. (Christie's) $1,100

Royal Copenhagen poly-chromed porcelain fairytale group, marked June 10, 1955, 8in. high. (Robt. W. Skinner Inc.) $850

A Jervis Art pottery motto mug, 1906, 5¾in. high, 4in. diam. (Robt. W. Skinner Inc.) $200

CHIPARUS FIGURES

Of all the practitioners of bronze and ivory Art Deco models, the Rumanian born Dmitri Chiparus is perhaps the most familiar to the public at large, if only because such modern personalities as Paul McCartney and Elton John are known collectors. Chiparus' figures range from nudes and women in everyday clothes, through pierrots to theatrical and exotic dancers (many of which show the Egyptian influence engendered by the discovery of Tutenkhamun's tomb), often in amazing, gravity-defying postures.

A gilt bronze and ivory group of three young girls, signed Chiparus, 6in. high. $2,600

An Art Deco period figure in bronze and ivory of a lady holding a muff, signed D. H. Chiparus, 12½in. high. (R. H. Ellis & Sons) $2,743

A bronze and ivory figure cast and carved after a model by D. H. Chiparus, 16in. high. (Christie's) $6,930

'Actress', a bronze figure cast from a model by D. H. Chiparus, of a maiden standing on tip-toe, 29.5cm. high. (Christie's) $2,431

'Young Girl', a bronze figure cast from a model by Demetre Chiparus, of a maiden standing on tip-toe with one foot held before her, signed in the onyx Chiparus, 29.5cm. high. (Christie's) $2,244

'Les Amis de Toujours', a bronze and ivory figure by Demetre Chiparus, of a standing lady, flanked by two borzois, on a rectangular amber coloured onyx base, 63cm. high. (Christie's) $22,440

'Dancer', a bronze and ivory figure cast and carved from a model by D. H. Chiparus, of a young woman dancing with one foot pointing outwards and arms outstretched, signed in the marble D. Chiparus, 41.5cm. high. (Christie's) $8,415

A painted bronze and ivory figure, 'Hush', 42cm. high, inscribed D. H. Chiparus. (Phillips) $3,888

Lioness, a bronze figure cast after a model by Demetre Chiparus, 57.8cm. long. (Christie's) $1,494

A painted bronze and ivory figure, 'Oriental Dancer', 40.20cm. high, inscribed on the marble Chiparus. (Phillips) $6,624

'Priestess', a gilt bronze and ivory figure cast and carved from a model by D. Chiparus, 43cm. high. (Christie's) $4,384

'The Fan Dancer', a bronze and ivory figure by Chiparus, on marble and onyx base, 15in. high. (Christie's) $6,615

An ivory figure of a girl, 'Invocation', carved from a model by D. Chiparus, 24.5cm. high. (Phillips) $1,584

'Apres la lecture', a bronze and ivory figure cast and carved from a model by D. Chiparus, 36.5cm. high. (Christie's) $10,824

'Sheltering from the Rain', a bronze and ivory group cast and carved from a model by D. Chiparus, 26cm. high. (Christie's) $2,534

'Nubian Dancer', a bronze and ivory dancing girl, cast and carved after a model by D. H. Chiparus, 15½in. high. (Christie's) $18,120

The trappings of Christmas as we know them became popular in the Victorian period – everyone knows how Prince Albert introduced the Christmas tree to Britain, and such items as crackers (or bon-bons as they were known, because they always contained sweets) already have a devoted following of collectors. Early ornaments were produced by leading china factories such as Dresden, and were really exquisite – a far cry from the mass-produced baubles on sale today.

Late 19th century Dresden Christmas ornament, white poodle with red silk ribbon, 3¼in. long. (Robt. W. Skinner Inc.)
$280

Late 19th century Dresden Christmas ornament of a three-masted ship, 4½in. high, 4.7/8in. long. (Robt. W. Skinner Inc.) $235

Late 19th century Dresden Christmas ornament of a silver champagne bottle candy container, 3.5/16in. high. (Robt. W. Skinner Inc.)
$130

Late 19th century Dresden Christmas ornament of a rooster, brown wash over gold, 3.1/8in. high. (Robt. W. Skinner Inc.) $175

Late 19th century Dresden Christmas ornament of a sitting silver retriever, 2¾in. high. (Robt. W. Skinner Inc.)
$400

Late 19th century Dresden Christmas ornament of a gold and rose iridescent cockatoo in a hoop, 3.3/8in. high. (Robt. W. Skinner Inc.)
$230

Late 19th century Dresden Christmas ornament of a silver three-quarter flat jockey on horse, 2in. high. (Robt. W. Skinner Inc.)
$210

CHROMIUM PLATE

From its introduction chromium plating was used for many high quality items such as early auto lamps and cycle fittings, and even some wristwatches and Art Deco jewelry.

Older chrome plate is quite easy to spot, and is usually a delight to handle. Some Art Deco chrome statuettes can be worth many hundreds of pounds and even quality chromed household fittings are becoming harder to find.

A Hagenauer chromium-plated stylised figure of a polar bear, 20cm. long. (Christie's)
$1,301

An Austrian chromium-plated ashtray and matchbox-holder, the circular tray with vertical sides and pierced grid decoration, 21cm. wide. (Christie's)
$523

A Hagenauer wood and chromium plated figure of a cockerel on a round metal base, stamped marks wHw, Austria, 44.6cm. high. (Christie's)
$836

A large Art Deco white metal and bakelite urn, the flared form on four disc-shaped feet, 27.5cm. high. (Christie's)
$1,115

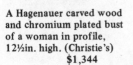

A Hagenauer carved wood and chromium plated bust of a woman in profile, 12½in. high. (Christie's)
$1,344

A Hagenauer figure of a javelin thrower, the stylised male figure with a javelin in hand, stamped marks wHw, Franz Hagenauer, Wien, Made in Austria 1218, 31.6cm. high. (Christie's)
$1,159

A Ronson 'Touch-Tip' petrol-fuelled table-lighter, shaped as a bar with a negro barman, partially chromium-plated and enamel painted, circa 1935, 15.3cm. long. (Christie's)
$836

CIGARETTE CARDS

Cigarette cards were first used as stiffeners in packages of cigarettes in the days before slide packets. They probably made their first appearance in the 1860's in the United States. The oldest card known to exist is in the Metropolitan Museum in New York and dates from 1878. W.D. & H.O. Wills were the first British firm to give away cards with their cigarettes in 1885. Between then and the end of the Second World War more than 5,000 sets of cards were produced and they range over every aspect of life as their theme. Royalty, railway trains , wild flowers and footballers, film stars and circus clowns, gardening and how to swim all made their appearance on cigarette cards.

The earliest cards had blank reverses or were used as advertising space but towards the end of the 19th century, informative text began to fill the empty space. The golden age of the cigarette card is from the last decade of the 19th century until about 1910. In the main the cards and their information was extremely accurate and they have been used by film companies researching period backgrounds. The texts are regarded as some of the best examples of pared down prose.

TADDY'S CLOWN

When the production of cigarette cards began to dwindle from 1950 onwards, the collecting mania began and today a set of Taddy's "Clowns and Circus Artistes" cards featuring circus clowns are the "penny blacks" of the card world. A set of them has been sold for over $25,000. As in the case of all paper items and ephemera, condition is very important. Thumbed and bent edged cards will sell for much less than those in good condition.

Hignetts Pilot Cigarettes, 'Cabinet' 1900, set of 20. $1,750

Ogden's, 'Owners racing colours and jockeys' 1906, set of 50. $130

Players, 'Gallery of Beauty Series' 1896, 50 in set. $1,500

British American Tobacco Co. Ltd., 'Butterflies' 1928, set of 50. $125

Salmon and Gluckstein, 'Wireless Explained' 1923, set of 25. $110

W. A. Churchman, 'Sporting Celebrities' 1931, set of 50. $90

(Border Bygones)

CIGARETTE CARDS

Ogden's, 'Soldiers of the King' 1909, set of 50. $260

Rothmans Ltd., 'Beauties of the Cinema' 1939, set of 24. $60

Woods Purple Heather Cigarettes, 'Yeomanry' 1902, set of 25. $700

Wills Scissors Cigarettes, 'Drum Horses' 1909, set of 32. $300

Carreras, 'Alice in Wonderland' 1930, set of 48. $35

Nicolas Sarony & Co., 'Origin of Games' 1923, set of 15. $45

Ogdens, 'Flags and Funnels' 1906, set of 50. $225

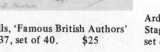

Wills, 'Famous British Authors' 1937, set of 40. $25

Ardath Tobacco Co., 'Film, Stage & Radio Stars', 1935, set of 50. $35

(Border Bygones)

127

CIGARETTE CARDS

Cohen Weenen Co., 'Famous Boxers' 1912, set of 25. $260

Stephen Mitchell & Son, 'Village Models' 1925, set of 25. $90

W. A. Churchman, 'Wonderful Railway Travel' 1937, set of 50. $14

Forcasta 'Racing Greyhounds' 1939, set of 25. $18

Wills, 'Old Furniture' 1923, set of 25. $60

Salmon & Gluckstein, 'Army and Navy Traditions' 1917, 25 in set. $260

Ardath Ltd., 'Famous Film Stars' 1935, set of 50. $35

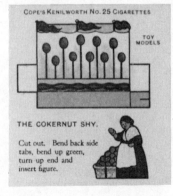

Copes, 'Toy Models' 1925, set of 25. $7

Hignetts, 'Modern Statesmen' 1906, set of 25. $160

(Border Bygones)

CIGARETTE CARDS

Taddys, 'Royalty Series' 1903, set of 25. $525

J. Wix & Son Ltd., 'Kensitas Flowers' 1933, set of 60. $160

B. Morris & Sons, 'Golf Strokes' 1923, set of 25. $70

Morris & Sons, 'Measurement of Time' 1924, set of 25. $26

Sunstripe Cigarettes, 'Wireless Telephony' 1923, set of 20. $55

Races of Mankind, F. & J. Smith's, Series of 40, 1900. $1,250

Carreras, 'Birds' 1939, set of 50. $26

Wills, 'Old Silver' 1924, set of 25. $60

Hignett Bros., 'Dogs' 1936, set of 50. $55

(Border Bygones)

129

CIGARETTE CASES

Early cigarette cases were meant to be carried by men so they usually have a more solid and weighty appearance than those made later for the use of women when the cigarette smoking habit became accepted in both sexes and all classes of society. These cases can be made of a variety of materials from gold and silver downwards through tortoiseshell, papier maché or mother of pearl to base metal. Some of the most attractive cases are those made for women in the 1920's which were decorated with brightly colored enamels in bold Modernist designs. A few of the more expensive cases were designed as evening bags and incorporated cigarette lighters and lipsticks. The best cigarette cases are often works of art, displaying the skill of the silversmith and the engraver. Interesting collections can still be built up for modest outlays.

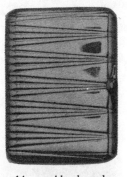

A jewelled two-colour gold cigarette case, the reeded body set with diamonds, St. Petersburg, 1908-17, 9.8cm. $3,395

A Continental cigarette case, cover enamelled with a nude lying on the edge of the shore, with English import marks for 1906. (Phillips) $528

An oblong gold coloured cigarette case with cabochon bluestone pushpiece, with Swedish control marks, 3¼in. long. (Christie's) $1,166

A Portuguese enamel cigarette case, the cover depicting a bare-breasted Classical girl, circa 1900. (Phillips) $573

A Victorian cheroot case, by Yapp & Woodward, Birmingham, 1854, 12.7cm. high, 4.75oz. (Phillips) $271

Late 19th century Austrian enamel cigarette case, the cover enamelled with an Ancient Egyptian scene, circa 1895. (Phillips) $906

An Austrian cigarette case applied with two-colour gold and gem set monograms and facsimile signatures, circa 1895. (Phillips) $774

A Victorian cigarette case, the cover enamelled with a nude girl lying beside a stream, Birmingham, 1887. (Phillips) $588

An Austrian white metal and enamel eight-sided cigarette case, the enamel by F. Zwichl, depicting a Samson car in black, red and cream. (Christie's) $783

A Continental plated cigarette case enamelled with a collie dog on a sky background, circa 1910. (Phillips) $223

An Edwardian gilt lined cigarette case, polychrome-enamelled with a picture of a lady, R.C., Birmingham, 1905. (Christie's) $284

A German cigarette case enamelled on cover with a spaniel carrying a dead duck in its mouth, circa 1900. (Phillips) $367

An Austrian enamel cigarette case, signed 'Schleiertanz', circa 1895. (Phillips) $735

A white metal and enamel cigarette case, the enamel by F. Zwichl, circa 1920. (Christie's) $2,818

A late Victorian gilt lined cigarette case, enamelled with a scene from R. Kipling's poem 'Absent minded beggar', C.S. & F.S., Birmingham, 1899. (Christie's) $372

CIGARETTE CASES

A late Victorian cigarette case enamelled on cover with a coaching scene, by J. Wilmot, Birmingham, 1896. (Phillips) $509

A good 19th century Russian niello cigarette case, cover depicting a despatch carrier being driven by a peasant in a horse-drawn carriage, Gustav Klingert, Moscow, 1888, 8.5cm. long. (Phillips) $618

A Russian cigarette case with separate hinged vesta compartment, probably by Dmitri Nikolaiev, Moscow, circa 1890. (Phillips) $402

An enamelled silver cigarette case, probably German, circa 1910, thumbpiece missing, 3½in. high. $502

An Omar Ramsden 9ct. beaten gold cigarette case with cut steel relief decoration, gold mark for 1922, 11.3 x 8.8cm. (Christie's) $950

An enamelled cigarette case, German, circa 1905, 9cm. high. $401

A 1930's cigarette case, silver and two-colour gold coloured metal, with stripes of black lacquer, 11.75cm. wide. $451

An Omar Ramsden silver cigarette case, with gilt interior, 1923, 9.5cm. $170

An Art Deco sterling silver cigarette case with black and silver ground in a crackle pattern with red enamel zigeraut decoration on one side. (Robt. W. Skinner Inc.) $200

132

CIGARETTE LIGHTERS

Cigarette lighters first made their appearance about 1900 and the most widely collected are those made by Dunhill some of which are highly decorative objects in the form of hunting horns or dancing maidens. Lighters made before 1920 worked on the flint principle and a well known maker was Orlik. In the 1920's table lighters became popular – some of them working by flint as well. They can be found incorporated in figures of birds or dancers. Others had a torch drawn from a fuel tank and struck on a strip of cerium to produce a flame. Wheeled pocket lighters made by Dunhill became popular in the 1930's and they were also made by Howitt, Parker Beacon, Polo, Thorens Oriflame, Imco and Beney. During both World Wars servicemen turned out lighters from scraps of shell or bullet cases and battered out coins. These lighters, known as Trench Art, sell today for between $10 and $50 each. Lighters are a good area for investment because they can still be found at reasonable cost.

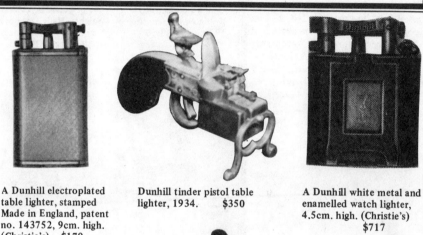

A Dunhill electroplated table lighter, stamped Made in England, patent no. 143752, 9cm. high. (Christie's) $179

Dunhill tinder pistol table lighter, 1934. $350

A Dunhill white metal and enamelled watch lighter, 4.5cm. high. (Christie's) $717

1920's plated metal table lighter in the form of a dancing nude. $85

Chromium plated table lighter in the form of an aeroplane. $130

A large 1930's gilt plaster table lighter. $260

CIGARETTE PACKETS

Cigarettes began being sold in Britain in 1851. Initially they were sold in wrappers, but soon after, the cigarette packet was developed and since trade marks were first registered in 1876 over 30,000 different brands have appeared.

The hull and side packet came into use around 1890, and the flip-top, though it was invented in the USA in 1927, was not introduced into Britain until 1956, when it was first used for Churchman's No. 1. The collecting of cigarette packets is a fairly recent enthusiasm but there is infinite potential for exploration, and finds range from pretty Passing Clouds packets to the striking red packaging used for Du Maurier.

Many collectors specialise in themes, for example sports, or maritime, or perhaps restrict themselves to Players or Wills items only. Flip top or crushproof packs, mainly from the pre-Health Warning era, are also collected, while soft packs seem more popular with overseas collectors.

Condition plays an important part in assessing the value of cigarette packets, and if they come complete with cigarettes this also attracts a premium.

Ogden's packet of 10 Robin cigarettes, circa 1920. $3.50

The original Player's Weights, Made from pure Virginia Tobacco, packet of 10, circa 1920. $2

Premier's packet of 10 Navy Cut medium cigarettes, made in England, circa 1930. $5

Gunboat high class Virginia cigarettes, Lambert & Butler, England, circa 1920. $5

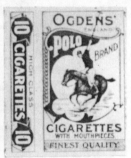

Polo brand, 10 packet Ogdens' finest quality cigarettes with mouthpieces, circa 1915. $7

Beechwood, packet of 10 cigarettes, C.W.S. Ltd., Manchester, circa 1930. $5

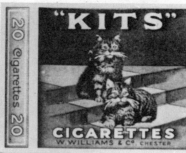

The Clown Cigarettes, packet of 10, Ardath, circa 1915. $9

Kits, packet of 20 cigarettes, W. Williams & Co. Chester, circa 1915. $20

John Player & Sons, Anchor packet of 10 Virginia tipped cigarettes, circa 1958. $3.50

Little Sweetheart cigarettes — A dainty whiff, fresh and sweet — manufactured by The American Cigarette Co. Ltd., circa 1900. $26

Campaign '88, Bush for President, soft pack, 20 cigarettes, circa 1988. $1

A. & M. Wix packet of Clock cigarettes, manufactured in England, circa 1930. $5

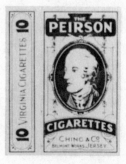

Air Mail, packet of 10 Golden Honeydew cigarettes, R. & J. Hill, circa 1925. $5

Dandy Fifth cigarettes, 'We called them the Kid Gloves Dandy Fifth', packet of 10, Salmon & Gluckstein Ltd — Ever cigarette bears our name as a guarantee of quality — circa 1900. $26

The Peirson Cigarettes, packet of 10, Ching & Co., Belmont Works, Jersey, circa 1915. $7

CIGARETTE PACKETS

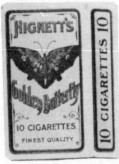

Hignett's Golden Butterfly, 10 finest quality cigarettes, circa 1920. $5

Twin Screw, special straight cut Virginia cigarettes, Themens, circa 1915. $9

United Service cigarettes, packet of 10, W. D. & H. O. Wills, Bristol & London, circa 1910. $18

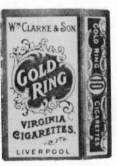

Darts, packet of 5, Gallaher Ltd., Virginia House, London & Belfast, circa 1930. $3.50

Sweethearts cigarettes, tipped with Papier Ambre, Do not stick to lips, Salmon & Gluckstein Ltd., Largest tobacconists in the world, circa 1904. $20

Gold Ring, packet of 10 Virginia cigarettes, Wm. Clarke & Son, Liverpool, circa 1900. $20

Motor cigarettes, W. D. & H. O. Wills, Bristol & London, circa 1920. $10

Russian Lauka, (first dog in space), 20 cigarettes. $1

Rugger cigarettes, packet of 10, The United Tobacco Companies (South) Ltd., Cape Town, circa 1920. $9

CLARET JUGS

Claret jugs, as their name suggests, were designed to hold wine at table. Usually pear-shaped, and with a handle, English jugs from the early 19th century were often of silver with corked necks, while later glass examples favored silver mountings with hinged lids.

Claret jugs were designed by such leading practitioners as Christopher Dresser, while George Fox in the mid 19th century produced animal and other shapes as novelties.

A pair of French silver gilt mounted clear glass claret jugs, by Risler & Carre, Paris, circa 1870, 11¾in. high. (Christie's) $4,924

A Victorian claret jug, by Marshall & Sons, Edinburgh, 1865, 35cm. high, 30oz. (Christie's) $1,110

A late Victorian mounted glass claret jug in the form of a cockatoo, by Alex. Crichton, 1882, 27cm. high. (Phillips) $3,450

A Victorian silver mounted glass claret jug, by Elkington & Co., Birmingham, 1878, 10½in. high. (Reeds Rains) $1,512

A Hukin & Heath EPNS mounted large cut glass claret jug, 12in. high. (Hetheringtons Nationwide) $304

A George IV claret jug, maker's mark probably that of Joseph Angell, 1829, 29cm. high, 31oz. (Lawrence Fine Art) $2,392

An ovoid glass claret jug with a star design, the plain mount with bracket handle, 7¾in. high. (Christie's) $144

CLARICE CLIFF

The woman who set the style for the crockery of the 1920's and 30's was Clarice Cliff who began work as a painter at A.J. Wilkinson Ltd and went on to become art director at the Royal Staffordshire Pottery and Newport Pottery. Her work is distinguished by brilliant color and clean lines. The pottery she painted in vibrant combinations of yellow, orange, red, purple, green and blue, was cheap and cheerful and was sold at Woolworths as well as at more prestigious stores. She had a refreshing way of combining avant garde styles with old fashioned almost childish themes — cottages tucked away on hillsides with smoke rising from their chimneys for example. The crockery she painted with crocuses brought life and color to many a kitchen. Clarice Cliff was an innovator and her self portrait plaque and the designs she made inspired by Diaghilev's Ballet Russe which made its debut in London in the 1920's , now fetch high prices. Her most collected patterns are Bizarre, Crocus and Fantasque.

A Clarice Cliff 'Isis' shaped vase, painted with a central frieze of stylised leaves, 24.6cm. high. (Phillips) $1,169

A Clarice Cliff Bizarre cubist breakfast set painted with geometric designs in red, blue, green and ochre, circa 1931. (Christie's) $835

A Clarice Cliff vase, painted in blue, yellow, orange and green, with stylised leaf and triangular panels, 20.5cm high. (Phillips) $1,215

A Clarice Cliff Bizarre Latona vase of lotus shape with single handle, 30cm. high. (Osmond Tricks) $1,140

A Clarice Cliff 'Bizarre' 17-piece tea-set painted in green, yellow, red and brown, with flowerbed, comprising; a teapot, milk jug, sugar bowl, honey pot, large plate, six side-plates and six teacups and saucers. (Christie's) $1,496

A Clarice Cliff Fantasque lotus jug, 25cm. high, printed factory marks. (Phillips) $648

A Clarice Cliff 'Bizarre' bowl, standing on four disc-shaped feet, painted in black, yellow, orange and green with climbing flowers on a geometric design, 12cm. high. (Christie's) $841

A Clarice Cliff wall pocket in the form of a pair of budgerigars, 23cm. high. (Osmond Tricks) $93

An early Clarice Cliff bowl, painted in green, orange and amber, with painted inscription and signature, *Bon Dieu, I think that I shall never see a form so lovely as a tree, Clarice Cliff, 1932,* 14cm. high. (Christie's) $743

A Clarice Cliff 'Bizarre' circular charger, painted with a central house in yellow with a vivid orange roof, 42cm. diam., factory marks. (Phillips) $2,580

A Clarice Cliff Fantasque pottery vase, painted in brown, black green, yellow and orange with a cottage and trees, 20.3cm. high. (Phillips) $216

A large Clarice Cliff wall charger, painted with a band of acorns and acorn leaves in green red and black on a yellow and brown streaked ground, 45.7cm. diam. (Christie's) $1,481

A Clarice Cliff Bizarre pottery mask, kite-shaped, 28cm. long. (Christie's) $1,793

A Clarice Cliff 'Inspiration' charger, 'The Knight Errant', 45.5cm. high. (Phillips) $1,728

A Clarice Cliff 'Bizarre' small two handled tureen and cover designed by Dame Laura Knight, the cover with a clown in full relief, 6in. high. (Christie's) $370

CLOISONNE

In cloisonne enamelling, every detail of the design is defined with narrow bands of metal, gold, silver or copper, in such a way as to cover the whole surface to be decorated. These are then filled with the appropriate enamel colors, ground to a fine powder, moistened and fired. After firing, the wires remain visible and become an integral part of the design. The method differs from Champleve enamelling in which depressions are cut into a metal base and filled with enamel paste before firing. It is thought that the Chinese adopted cloisonne techniques from the West, particularly from Byzantium, but it became very popular again in Europe during the 19th century when Alexis Falize, a French silversmith, began importing and selling articles of Chinese cloisonne as well as adopting the technique for his own products.

A cloisonne enamel candle holder formed as a standing elephant, late Qing Dynasty, overall 33cm. wide. (Christie's) $3,775

Two 18th century cloisonne enamel and gilt bronze Ruyi sceptres, 31cm. long. (Christie's) $3,000

A cloisonne enamel circular box and flat cover, Qianlong, 32.7cm. diam., wood stand. (Christie's) $3,460

Late 19th century cloisonne cabinet decorated in various coloured enamels, 14.5 x 9 x 12cm. (Christie's) $1,110

A Namikawa compressed globular tripod censer and domed cover, circa 1900, 10.3cm. diam. (Christie's) $3,124

A cloisonne enamel and gilt bronze tripod censer and domed cover, Qianlong/ Jiaqing, 39cm. high. (Christie's) $2,516

A 16th century Ming cloisonne enamel globular tripod censer, 12.8cm. diam. (Christie's) $2,831

One of a pair of cloisonne enamel vases and covers, 6in. high. (Lawrence Fine Art) $446

A 16th century cloisonne enamel shallow tripod dish on three short feet, 16.5cm. diam. (Christie's) $1,125

Late 19th century cloisonne enamel oviform vase with flaring neck, 61.5cm. high. (Christie's) $4,440

A pair of 19th century cloisonne enamel and gilt bronze cockerels, 17½in. high. (Bermondsey) $2,100

Late 19th century large cloisonne enamel hexagonal vase with flaring neck and spreading foot, 66.4cm. high. (Christie's) $4,440

Late 19th century cloisonne lacquer on porcelain covered jar, Japan, 18in. high. (Robt. W. Skinner Inc.) $875

A cloisonne enamel barrel shaped bowl on three small gilt metal lingzhi feet, 10cm. diam. (Christie's) $820

An early 19th century cloisonne enamel vase with ring handles, 15¼in. high. (Bermondsey) $1,250

CLOTHES

It is not surprising that few clothes from very early times have survived but those that do generally find their way into museums where they make eye catching displays. The clothes that are more available to collectors date from Victorian times and baby dresses, christening robes, nightdresses and fur lined tippets from that period can be fairly easily found. More discriminating collectors however tend to prefer the clothes from the early part of the 20th century, from an age of ease and elegance which has perhaps never been surpassed. Rich women bought enormous wardrobes and changed their clothes frequently so that those which have survived often show little sign of wear. Shabby or damaged items do not fetch high prices but those in good condition certainly do. Clothes by well known dressmakers like Nina Ricci or Fortuny and, from a later date, by Dior, Jacques Patou or even early Mary Quant are eagerly sought after. As well as glamorous dresses and wrappers, hats, bags, shoes, shawls and even underclothes from the period are also fetching high prices.

An embroidered vest and pair of embroidered shoes, 18th century, the vest with floral sprays on ivory silk. (Robt. W. Skinner Inc.) $800

A late 19th century bridal veil of tamboured net designed with flower sprays and sprigs, 2 x 2m. (Phillips) $320

A late 18th century gentleman's double-breasted waistcoat of yellow silk brocade. (Phillips) $119

A late 19th century two-piece gown of mauve, grey and orange silk brocade of striped design, circa 1880. (Phillips) $241

A gentleman's banyan of printed worsted, circa 1820's. (Phillips) $1,057

A mid 19th century dress of cream and brown wool printed in mainly red, green and orange. (Phillips) $253

CLOTHES

A 1920's dress of black crepe, the skirt designed with grey and cream crepe insertions and ivory silk embroidery. (Phillips) $309

A 1920's dress of brown chiffon embroidered in chain stitch with green and crimson silks, maker's label Gabrielle Chanel, Paris. (Phillips) $5,642

A 1920's dress of black and pink chiffon and silk with silvered bead decoration to the hips and side bodice. (Phillips) $837

A 1930's dress of cream crepe, having bias cut skirt and pleated attached scarf, bearing the maker's label Molyneux, 48 Grosvenor Street, London. (Phillips) $509

A 1920's dress of dusty-pink velvet with full back bodice and bow trim, bearing the maker's label, Chanel. (Phillips) $2,002

A 1910's dress of white net, having bauble trim, the bodice and upper skirt with cotton cutwork and filet lace overlay. (Phillips) $728

A 1920's dress of black chiffon and silk with tie to the waistline, bearing the maker's label Molyneux, 5 Rue Royale, No.35767. (Phillips) $982

A 1920's dress of black silk and gold thread brocade of striped design, the divided hem looped up to the back shoulder. (Phillips) $1,001

A 1920's coat of burnt-orange silk with gold thread brocade, having deep cuffs and collar. (Phillips) $200

A 1920's dress of midnight-blue chiffon and silk, the lower skirt of tiered petal design, bearing the maker's label, Chanel. (Phillips) $1,638

A 1920's dress of sea-green and blue chiffon, having paprika chiffon and gold thread trim, after Poiret. (Phillips) $1,001

A 1910's dress of ivory silk, having ivory chiffon and lace overlay of tiered design. (Phillips) $1,001

COAL BOXES

The coal box was a product of the age when designers turned their attention to the fireplace as the focal point of the room, rather than just a functional feature. 'Purdoniums', named after their inventor, Purdon, became part of the standard accoutrements of the fireside, and were often richly decorated and ornamented. Some can fetch several hundred pounds at auction today, which is surprising, bearing in mind their humble function.

Victorian mahogany coal box, 1860. (British Antique Exporters) $130

A Regency black and gilt japanned coal box with rounded rectangular domed lid, and another, 19in. wide. (Christie's) $6,350

A late Victorian brass coal box with domed lid and pierced finial, 17in. wide. (Christie's) $551

A late Victorian black and gilt japanned papier-mache purdonium, on later rose-wood bracket feet, 18¾in. wide. (Christie's) $1,573

A mid Victorian black, gilt and mother-of-pearl japanned papier-mache purdonium, 20in. wide, and another. (Christie's) $1,573

Late 19th century Art Nouveau style brass coal box. (British Antique Exporters) $130

An early Victorian walnut coal bin of sarcophagus form with coffered top and hinged front with metal liner, 21in. wide. (Christie's) $1,533

COCA-COLA

Coca-Cola was originally sold from the back of a quack doctor's wagon as a cure-all. Nowadays you will find the ubiquitous Coke advert from Taiwan to Timbuctoo, and Coca Cola items are major collectables.

The classic waisted Coke bottle made its appearance in 1916 – hitherto, from about 1886 Coca Cola was sold in cylindrical bottles with sloping shoulders. A bottle with its name embossed in red or yellow dates from after 1933.

Enamel sign 'Drink Coca-Cola here'. $175

Red, white and blue rhinestone brooch in the form of the American flag centrally set with a mini glass Coca-Cola bottle, dated 1976. (Robt. W. Skinner Inc.)　$360

An assortment of Coca-Cola badges with pin clasps. $1

Coca Cola advertising tip tray, oval, America, circa 1907. (Robt. W. Skinner Inc.)　$200

Small red backed Coca-Cola sign.　　　　$35

Enamel sign 'Refresh yourself! Coca-Cola sold here ice cold'.　$210

Enamel sign 'Drink Coca-Cola Strike Matches Here'. $75

Enamel sign with thermometer 'Drink Coca-Cola, Thirst knows no season'.　$350

COMICS, AMERICAN

Collecting American comics has boomed in the last few years owing to the popularity of films like "Star Wars" and "Superman" and the most recent screen outing for the now cult character Batman. Indeed both Superman and Batman have enjoyed their 50th anniversaries which has added to their historical and financial value.

Prices vary widely from a mint copy of "Action Comics" number 1 featuring the first appearance of Superman at $31,500 to dozens of titles at no more than 50c. In all cases condition is of the utmost importance, lesser condition bringing lesser values. Marvel comics from the 1960's featuring such characters as Spiderman and The Hulk are commanding high prices and for further reading another wise investment would be the Overstreet Comic Book Price Guide which concentrates on golden age comics (1930's to 1950's) and the Official Comic Book Price Guide for Great Britain which concentrates on selected British Comics and a complete listing of American Comics from when they were officially distributed in the U.K. from November 1959.

Detective Comics, No. 28, June 1939, 'Batman'. $4,900

Action Comics, No. 1, June 1938, 'Superman'. $31,500

New Book of Comics, No. 2, 1938. $1,300

All Star Comics, No. 1, Summer Issue, 1940. $3,500

The Big Book of Fun Comics. $2,600

All-American Comics, No. 16, July 1940, 'Green Lantern'. $6,500

(Duncan McAlpine)

Tillie Toiler, No. 184.
$26

New Fun, No. 1.
$4,900

Yellowjacket Comics,
No. 2. $60

Movie Comics, No. 1,
April 1939. $1,000

Action Comics, No. 15,
August 1939. $1,450

The Purple Claw, No. 1.
$70

New Adventure Comics,
No. 27, June 1938.
$300

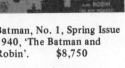

Batman, No. 1, Spring Issue
1940, 'The Batman and
Robin'. $8,750

Adventure Comics, No. 72,
March 1942, 'Sandman'.
$1,150

(Duncan McAlpine)

Walt Disney's No. 1.
$3,000

Comics on Parade, 'Li'l
Abner', No. 45. $45

Billy the Kid and Oscar,
No. 1. $25

Action Comics, No. 5,
October 1938.
$3,500

More Fun, No. 8, 1938,
D. C. Comics. $1,300

More Fun Comics, No.
55, May 1940.
$2,100

All-American Comics, No. 1,
April 1939. $1,000

All-American Comics, No. 2,
July 1938, 'Superman'.
$4,900

Spysmasher, No. 2. $350

(Duncan McAlpine)

COMICS, BRITISH

The most valuable British comic is the first edition of the Beano, published by D.C. Thomson of Dundee, on 30th July, 1938 at the price of twopence. Today a copy in good condition could demand anything up to $4,000. Comics were often considered as waste paper the moment they were read and the waste paper drives of the Second World War swept them away in their thousands so early copies are valuable. The most sought after comics are the Beano, the Dandy, Film Fun, Radio Fun, Eagle and Knockout. Running them close are Magnet, Gem, Adventure, Hotspur, Rover, Skipper and Wizard. Most have now disappeared with the exception of the Beano and the Dandy which will keep alive memories of Desperate Dan and Lord Snooty, both creations of artist Dudley Watkins.

Other artists of note are Eric Parker and Frank Hampson who drew Dan Dare for the Eagle. Comics from more recent times are now achieving collecting status and one of the most highly regarded is 2000 AD, a science fiction comic strip which, though less than ten years old, commands over $5 a copy.

The Triumph, May 27th, 1933, 'The Boys Best Story Paper'. $4

The Beano Comic, No. 1, July 30th, 1938, complete with it's free Whoopee Mask and in pristine condition. $3,500

Detective Weekly, February 18th, 1939, The Big Smash. $5

Giggle, 30th September, 1967, Adventure and Fun for Everyone. $1.50

The Magnet, May 13th, 1939, Billy Bunters Own Paper. $4

The Popular, May 12th, 1923, The Story Book for Boys. $2.50

Dandy, March 31st, 1951, with Korky the Cat. $9

Chips, November 3rd, 1951, Weary Willie and Tired Tim. $2.50

The Ranger, September 7th, 1935, Thrill Stories of the Week. $2.50

Fantastic, 18th March, 1967, A Power Comic. $1.50

The Hornet, October 26th, 1963, The Wakefield Kicker. $1.50

No. 1 Radio Fun, October 15th, 1938. $130

151

The Rover, August 12th, 1950.
$2.50

Sun, December 18th, 1954,
Billy the Kid. $2.50

Young Britain, May 21, 1920,
Prime of the Pictures. $4

Knockout, May 14th, 1955,
The Happy Family Fun Paper.
$2.50

The Champion, August 30th,
1947, '2 Brand New Thrillers
Inside'. $2.50

The Beano, July 31st, 1954,
Biffo the Bear. $11

The Union Jack, Xmas Number,
December 22nd, 1923. $4

Wonder, September 4th, 1948,
The Comic Full of Laughter.
$2.50

Boys Cinema, The Lost City,
1923. $5

COMMEMORATIVE CHINA

The arrival of Queen Victoria on the throne opened the floodgates for the manufacture of commemorative china. Her predecessors as rulers were more often lampooned than venerated, but Victoria changed the popular attitude towards royalty. China commemorating events in the reigns of William and Mary, George III, George IV and William IV are rare but pieces with pictures of Victoria and Albert were made in their thousands and enjoyed pride of place on the walls and mantlepieces of rich and poor up and down the land. Plates, tobacco jars, mugs, vases, pipes, teapots, doorstops and spill jars marked every event in the royal life. The china cost little to buy and proved so popular that the range spread to include political happenings, military displays, exhibitions and even famous crimes and criminals. One of the most rare items are mugs celebrating Victoria's coronation — before the commemorative china boom really took off — which can be worth around $1,000 today if in good condition. Her Jubilee mugs were produced in such vast numbers that their value is much less.

A Staffordshire blue and white cylindrical mug printed with equestrian figures of The Duke of Wellington and Lord Hill, 4¾in. high. (Christie's) $260

An oviform vase made to commemorate the Coronation of Edward VII and Queen Alexandra in 1902, 27.5cm. high. $225

An 18th century blue and white pottery jug with loop handle, 7.75in. high. (Prudential Fine Art) $214

A 19th century Liverpool transfer-printed pitcher of baluster form with pulled spout and applied C-scroll handle. (Christie's) $1,100

An Obadiah Sherratt group of Polito's menagerie, circa 1830, 29.5cm. high. (Christie's) $21,546

A Liverpool creamware inscribed and dated armorial oviform jug with loop handle, 1792, 14.5cm. high. (Christie's) $766

A black glazed terracotta teapot and cover, printed in yellow and decorated in enamels and gilt, 16cm. high. (Phillips) $80

A Doulton stoneware three handled mug commemorating the hoisting of the flag at Pretoria, 6½in. high. $127

A Staffordshire jug depicting Wellington at Salamanca, 5½in. high. (Christie's) $117

A creamware tall cylindrical mug, circa 1785, 12.5cm. high. (Christie's) $726

Pair of mid 19th century copper lustre jugs with blue band decoration and painted figures of Queen Victoria and Prince Albert, 5½in. high. (Reeds Rains) $372

A vase with a grey Doulton & Slater lace ground with an applied white bust of the Prince of Wales, circa 1885, 6¼in. high. $195

A Staffordshire brown and white part glazed Parian jug with portraits of Wellington and Blucher, inscribed Jane Roberte, 7½in. high. (Christie's) $247

Queen Caroline: a small lustre pottery cream jug, printed in black with portrait and national flora, 8cm. high. (Phillips) $480

A Liverpool creamware jug, 21cm. high. (Phillips) $1,252

A tankard designed by John Broad commemorating the 1897 Jubilee, circa 1897, 6½in. high. $135

A Staffordshire saltglaze tartan ground Royalist teapot and cover with loop handle, circa 1750, 14cm. high. (Christie's) $15,336

A jug with a portrait of H.M. Stanley below the inscription 'Emin Pasha Relief Expedition 1887-1889', 7½in. high. $120

A Liverpool creamware oviform jug, inscribed in black script W.B., 6¾in. high, circa 1800. (Christie's) $209

A Royal Doulton two-handled loving cup commemorating King George V silver jubilee, 10in. high, No. 584 of a limited edition of 1,000. (Christie's) $338

A Worcester small cylindrical mug transfer-printed in black by R. Hancock with The King of Prussia, date 1757, 9cm. high. (Christie's) $1,185

A jug commemorating the hoisting of the flag at Pretoria, circa 1900, 8¼in. high. $165

A Doulton stoneware double handled tankard commemorating War in the Sudan, 1883, 6in. high. $127

A coronation jug commemorating the accession of Edward VII and Queen Alexandra, circa 1902, 7½in. high. $142

CONVERSATION PIECES

The essential criteria for these is that they must be either bizarre or not immediately recognisable. The category covers everything from a bath chair to a painted refrigerator, and a number of antiques, such as a mid-Victorian chicken drumstick holder could easily fit the bill. They may or may not be valuable — it's really beside the point. Basically, they're fun things to collect.

Thirteen Star American flag, circa 1810, 28 x 45in. (Robt. W. Skinner Inc.) $450

A Spanish Colonial dress saddle with white leather seat and pommel, also a pair of 'Botas' leggings, 30in. long. (Robt. W. Skinner Inc.) $925

A decorative cartridge display board, arranged geometrically in stylised floral motif, 43in. square. $4,323

A pair of fireside companions painted with a boy and a girl in 18th century costume, 42in. and 45in. high. (Christie's) $4,347

One of two sheets of Chinese wallpaper painted in fresh colours, 18th century, 92 x 38in. (Christie's) $1,749

A Dutch oak birdcage of architectural design, the seven compartments with black-painted metal bars and refuse-trays, basically 18th century, 44½in. wide. (Christie's) $10,120

Mid 19th century North Italian parcel gilt and painted sedan chair, 30½in. wide, 69in. high. (Christie's) $14,696

A wooden artist's palette, belonging to Pierre Matisse, circa 1907, a label on reverse bears the inscription 'Matisse Palette of 1907 – (Blue Still Life),' 9½ x 14in. (Christie's) $13,200

A Victorian three-wheeled bath chair, with metal rimmed wooden wheels, painted olive green with maroon and yellow lining, 78in. overall. (Lawrence Fine Arts) $597

A papier mache lacquer match case holder, the top painted with a peasant woman seated and eating, by the Lukutin Factory, 19th century. (Christie's) $446

Two fragments of early George III printed wallpaper, after C. N. Cochin the Younger, 44½ x 22½in. and 47½ x 22¾in. (Christie's) $482

A pair of Nancy pate de verre bookends fashioned as dolphins, signed X Momillon, 6½in. high. (Lots Road Chelsea Auction Galleries) $4,550

An Art Deco glass cocktail shaker with silver mounts, Birmingham, 1936, 8in. high. (Dreweatt Neate) $748

A refrigerator decorated by Piero Fornasetti, on black painted tubular steel framed base, 70cm. wide. (Christie's) $861

Early 19th century cabinet of geological specimens, by M. le Prof. Jurine et M. Brard. (Christie's) $1,320

An alabaster peep egg with three scenes of the Crystal Palace, 4½in. high. (Christie's) $175

Late 19th century Oriental carved coral figural group, 8in. long. (Robt. W. Skinner Inc.) $296

An American 19th century papercut picture, depicting two eagles with flags, 5¾ x 7½in. (Christie's)
$1,100

Cast zinc St. Bernard dog figure, probably Mass., circa 1880, 45in. wide. (Robt. W. Skinner Inc.) $2,600

One of twenty sheets of Chinese wallpaper painted in fresh colours.(Christie's)
$78,408

Two plate glass Royal Warrant Holder's display signs, bearing the coat of arms of H.M. Queen Alexandra, 18½ x 18in. (Christie's) $393

An Eley 'Sporting and Military' cartridge board, including brass rifle and pistol cartridge cases and tins of primers etc., in its oak frame. (Christie's)
$205

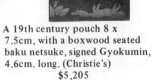

A lead winged cherub with dolphin fountain, 26in. high. (Lots Road Chelsea Auction Galleries)
$992

A WMF plated corkholder, each cork surmounted by a sculptural figure, 15.5cm. high. (Christie's) $896

A 19th century pouch 8 x 7.5cm, with a boxwood seated baku netsuke, signed Gyokumin, 4.6cm. long. (Christie's)
$5,205

CONVERSATION PIECES

President Chester A. Arthur's Parade flag, red wool field of several sections, American, circa 1883, 69 x 45in. (Robt. W. Skinner Inc.)
$1,400

'Hires' syrup dispenser, Phila., patented 1920, 14¼in. high. (Robt. W. Skinner Inc.) $340

Edwardian novelty desk clip and pen brush in the form of a muzzled bear, Birmingham, 1908. (Prudential Fine Art) $462

'The Tap Dancer', a life-size metal figure of a young negro, 185cm. high. (Christie's) $3,608

A pair of 19th century glass specie jars enamelled in white on the inside and enamelled colours with the Royal Arms, 18.1/8in. high. (Christie's) $844

An Egyptian mummified hawk, 22cm. long, Late Dynastic Period. (Phillips) $473

A group of yacht 'Gore' sail design books, by the Ratseys and Lapthorn sailmaking firm, New York, 1902-60. (Christie's) $8,250

A Victorian child's sledge, painted red on shaped metal runners. (Lots Road Chelsea Auction Galleries) $486

A circular, gilt lined love token box, probably French, 2½in. diam. (Christie's) $492

159

COPPER & BRASS

Brass is an alloy made basically from copper and zinc. In early times it was sparingly used but from the Middle Ages on it became popular for ornamental metal work like the chandeliers which were made in Holland, Norway and Sweden in the 16th and 17th centuries, many of which still hang in churches in Britain. It was also used for smaller objects in churches and private homes where it was turned into candlesticks, firedogs, warming pans, fenders and clock dials. The Victorians were very fond of brass ornaments and they were engraved or cast with a design in relief and the lines of the design filled in with enamel. Copper goes back to much earlier times because it was used in Egypt and Ancient Greece but its most common use today is in pots and pans for the kitchen which are still being made. The best ones from a collecting point of view are those produced during the 18th and 19th centuries but look out for signs of damage.

A 17th century brass candlestick engraved 'For the use of ye Company of Joyners and Carpenters', dated 1690, 9in. high. (Gorringes) $7,920

A George III brass and steel basket grate, 34¼in. wide, 30½in. high. (Christie's) $7,047

A copper and brass 'Bell Resonator' ear trumpet, English, mid 19th century, 6in. long. $227

An early 17th century South German gilt brass and copper miniature casket, signed Michel Mann, 7.3cm. wide. (Phillips) $4,608

A fine pair of 20th century brass candlesticks, 8½in. high. (Robt. W. Skinner Inc.) $375

An oval brass planter with gadroon embossed decoration, 13in. high. (Peter Wilson) $300

Early 19th century copper coal helmet, also a matching shovel, 17½in. high. (Peter Wilson) $616

A brass pen tray in the form of a roaring hippopotamus with hinged back, 12½in. wide. (Christie's) $5,808

An urn-shaped lidded coal bin fitted with two lion mask ring handles, 18in. high. (Peter Wilson) $189

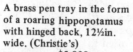

Benedict Art Studios hammered copper wall plaque, N.Y., circa 1907, 15in. diam. (Robt. W. Skinner Inc.) $800

Copper milk churn with cover. (Ball & Percival) $95

A Nara period copper gilt square plaque decorated in repousse with Amida, 7th/8th century, 11.3 x 11.3cm. (Christie's) $13,992

A copper and brass diver's helmet, date 8.29.41, with clamp screws, valves, plate glass windows and guards, 20in. high. (Christie's) $2,032

A hammered copper chamberstick, by Gustav Stickley, circa 1913, 9¼in. high. (Robt. W. Skinner Inc.) $700

An enamelled hammered copper humidor, by R. Cauman, Boston, circa 1925, 6½in. high. (Robt. W. Skinner Inc.) $425

CORKSCREWS

The corkscrew is a fine example of a simple gadget which has undergone much elaboration. A screw device with a simple steel spiral fixed to a wooden handle for pulling corks out of bottles was in common use in the 17th century — before that wine was sold in flagons or kegs and there was no need for corkscrews. By 1850 however, the Victorian love for elaboration and invention meant that the corkscrew was embellished and prettified with handles made of inlaid or engraved silver, brass, ivory or horn often carved in the shape of animals or birds. Sometimes various gadgets, including a brush for dusting the necks of bottles, was added to the basic corkscrew and collectors prize the more fantastic and complicated examples most highly. Miniature corkscrews in silver were made for the use of ladies drawing tiny corks out of necks of perfume bottles and other tiny ones were to be found included in the gadgets hanging from a Victorian housekeeper's chatelaine or ornamental bunch of keys, pencils and scissors that swung from the waist. Some corkscrews inscribed with messages were given as gifts from house guests to their hosts.

A Dutch silver cork-
screw, struck with
date letter for
1895, 4in. high.
(Christie's) $880

A silver corkscrew
by John Reilly.
$3,500

Late 18th century
silver corkscrew by
Cocks & Bettridge of
Birmingham, 3in. high.
(Christie's) $255

A Dutch silver and
mother-of- pearl cork-
screw, apparently un-
marked, circa 1775,
3in. high. (Christie's)
$770

Early 19th century
variant of Thomason's
double action cork-
screw with elliptical
brass turning handle
and helical worm.
(Christie's) $1,540

A cast iron bar cork-
screw, black painted
with gold decoration,
origin unknown.
(Christie's) $1,100

Early 19th century Thomason-type double action corkscrew with open frame, turned bone handle and helical worm. (Christie's) $528

A German 'folding lady' corkscrew, circa 1900, height closed 2.5/8in. (Christie's) $605

Early 19th century Thomason-type double action corkscrew, with turned bone handle and helical worm. (Christie's) $825

A Dutch silver and mother-of-pearl corkscrew, struck with indistinct maker's mark, circa 1780, 3.1/8in. high. (Christie's) $880

A Dutch silver corkscrew, by Johannes Van Geelen, Gouda, 1799, the handle cast in the form of a lion passant on a scroll base, 3¾in. high. (Christie's) $1,320

A Dutch silver corkscrew, by L. Olfers, Groningen, the handle cast as a galloping horse on a scroll base, 3¾in. high. (Christie's) $935

A George II silver combination corkscrew and nutmeg grater, apparently unmarked, circa 1750, 3½in. long. (Christie's) $1,540

Late 19th century silver 'lady's legs' folding corkscrew, probably American, marked Sterling, height closed 2in. high. (Christie's) $418

A 19th century Dutch silver corkscrew, the curled platform handle with the cast figure of a cow, 3½in. high. (Christie's) $605

CORKSCREWS

A Dutch silver corkscrew by J. J. Koen of Amsterdam, 3¼in. high. (Christie's) $305

A rotary eclipse bar corkscrew, in brass, with steel helical worm and wood side handle. (Christie's) $770

A Dutch silver and mother-of-pearl corkscrew, circa 1800, maker's mark apparently DP with vase of flowers between, 3¼in. high. (Christie's) $1,100

A 19th century Dutch silver corkscrew, the platform handle with the cast figures of a man in 18th century dress and two rearing horses, 4in. high. (Christie's) $880

Late 19th century American silver mounted and mother-of-pearl corkscrew, stamped Sterling, 4¼in. wide. (Christie's) $528

A Dutch silver corkscrew, struck with date letter for 1908, 4in. high. (Christie's) $935

Early 19th century King's screw double action corkscrew, with turned bone handle and helical worm, nickel side handle. (Christie's) $462

'Amor', a German figural folding corkscrew, formed as a Bakelite soldier and his lady, circa 1900, height closed 2¾in. (Christie's) $572

Hull's 'Royal Club' side lever corkscrew, with helical worm. (Christie's) $880

CRESTED CHINA

The greatest name in crested china was Goss but there were some 200 other makers who copied the lead set by William Henry Goss and his enterprising son Adolphus. The names of their British rivals include Arcadian, Carlton, Foley, Fords China, Grafton China, Macintyre, Melba, Nautilus, Podmore, Savoy, Shelley, Tuscan and Victoria. There were also foreign competitors who often made mistakes with British coats of arms.

Crested china boomed as a result of the enthusiasm for day trips and holidays that overtook the British public at the end of the 19th century. Trippers wanted a souvenir of their trip away from home and the perfect solution was a cheap little piece of china with the holiday town's coat of arms on it. Several subjects dominate the china manufacturers' output — the Great War — one of the more unusual items was a figure of Old Bill produced by Shelley; animals and birds; transport; memorials including the Cenotaph; statues; cartoon and comedy characters; sport and musical instruments. A cup and saucer was one of the most common items sold and, as a result today the price for such an item would be considerably less than for an Old Bill or a model of the Cenotaph. The rivals to Goss never took such fastidious care about their products as the trail blazers and their china is never as fine. However when buying crested china it is important to remember that imperfections of manufacture do not affect the price so much as subsequent damage. Cracks or chips can affect the value of a piece considerably.

Arcadian Black Cat sailing yacht. (Goss & Crested China Ltd) $107

Arcadian plump lady on weighing scales, inscribed 'Adding Weight'. (Goss & Crested China Ltd) $59

Carlton Jenny Jones. (Goss & Crested China Ltd) $63

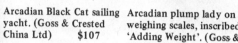

Carlton Monoplane with moveable propellor. (Goss & Crested China Ltd) $100

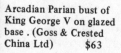

Arcadian Parian bust of King George V on glazed base . (Goss & Crested China Ltd) $63

Arcadian Banjo. (Goss & Crested China Ltd) $16

CRESTED CHINA

Arcadian ball vase with cartoon. (Goss & Crested China Ltd) $18

Corona Renault Tank. (Goss & Crested China Ltd) $116

Grafton Monkey wearing coat. (Goss & Crested China Ltd) $23

Arcadian Traffic Policeman on point duty. (Goss & Crested China Ltd) $45

Cyclone Cenotaph. (Goss & Crested China Ltd) $11

Willow Art Burns and Highland Mary. (Goss & Crested China Ltd) $54

Willow Art Guildford Castle. (Goss & Crested China Ltd) $54

Carlton Drunkard leaning on lamppost, ashtray, striker and holder, lustre. (Goss & Crested China Ltd) $107

Alexandra Westminster Abbey, West Front. (Goss & Crested China Ltd) $39

CRYSTAL SETS

With the commencement of commercial radio broadcasting in the early 20's, the crystal set arrived on the scene. The earliest commercially made ones were primitive, consisting usually of a hardwood base with headphones. More elaborate cabinet design, whether of bakelite or hardwood, followed, as did 'home-made' versions. Early crystal sets were taken to the Post Office, and the licence stamp actually stuck on the set! Many home-made sets therefore remained unregistered.

The Curry Super Low Loss crystal set coil. $5

Brownie Wireless Co. of Great Britain, No. 2 Model, crystal set, patent no. 9117/25, in a bakelite case. $175

Brownie Wireless Co., No. 3 Model crystal set with built in coil in a bakelite case. $175

Ivalek crystal set, in the shape of a radio, early 1950's. $45

Home-made kit form crystal set on a bakelite baseplate. $35

T.M.C. crystal set No. 351, wave length 300–500 metres and 1580 to 1680 in a red mahogany case with brass fittings. $235

British Thompson Houston Co. Ltd., Rugby, England, Radiola 'Bijou' crystal receiver Form B, G.P.O. Reg. No. 861, mahogany boxed. $260

CUCKOO CLOCKS

Cuckoo clocks originated in the Black Forest, when local farmers used their woodworking skills to supplement their income in winter. Early movements were of wood apart from lantern pinions and some use of wire. The theme of the cuckoo is said to have been introduced by Franz Ketterer around 1730. Trumpeter clocks have a trumpeter sounding instead of a cuckoo. These date from around 1857 and are choice collectors' pieces.

Black Forest shelf mounted German cuckoo clock with spring driven movement, striking on a gong and cuckoos. $525

A fine Black Forest clock with two train movement striking in a wire gong and with cuckoo, 48in. high. $3,000

A small 1950's decorated carved wood clock with two cuckoos and a weight driven movement. $45

Combined cuckoo and weather clock, complete with thermometer. $35

German Black Forest carved cuckoo clock. $50

A small 1980's Black Forest cuckoo clock with weight driven movement. $25

A finely carved Black Forest cuckoo clock decorated with a stag and dead game. $1,225

CUPS & SAUCERS

Collecting cups and saucers is an excellent way to begin a lifelong fascination with antiques. There was no need for cups and saucers until tea drinking became fashionable and the earliest examples have saucers without wells for resting the cup and the cups themselves have no handles but look like large mouthed bowls. Many of these were products of the Worcester factory from around 1750 and were often painted with variations of Chinese designs. From that date, the manufacturing of tea services boomed and every pottery produced them. A tea set has been a traditional wedding gift for many years and the recipients often proudly displayed their best sets in glass fronted cabinets. It is possible to trace the development of artistic trends through the tea sets that have survived. The Victorians loved ornate cups and saucers with flourishes on the handles and embossed gilding round the rims.

Bizarre
by
Clarice Cliff

The designs they preferred were flowery and one of the most popular manufacturers was Rockingham. In the 20th century, cups and saucers often took on an angular look and among the best examples are those painted by Clarice Cliff in her Bizarre range especially the Summer House pattern which had sharp wedge handles sticking out of the sides of the cup without a hole for the fingers. Collectors tend to stick to cups and saucers by the same pottery, from the same period or in the same style — blue and white is very popular for example. Others collect moustache cups with a little draining ledge for wet moustaches. They were popular gifts in Victorian times.

Derby handled cup and saucer, white ground with floral and gilded decoration, red mark to base, circa 1815. (Giles Haywood) $70

A Sevres hard-paste cup and saucer, blue crowned interlaced L mark enclosing date letter U for 1773. (Christie's) $675

A Chelsea flared and fluted coffee cup with scroll handle, circa 1750, 7.5cm. high. (Christie's) $3,250

A Minton pink-ground cabinet cup and saucer, circa 1825. (Christie's) $272

A Wedgwood blue jasper dip cylindrical coffee cup and deep saucer, impressed mark. (Christie's) $444

A Paris (Nast) green-ground cabinet cup and saucer, gilt marks, circa 1810. (Christie's) $220

A Berlin cylindrical coffee-cup and saucer with garlands of flowers between blue bands gilt with foliage, blue sceptre mark and gilt dot circa 1795. (Christie's) $1,260

A Berlin Celadon ground Tasse D'Amitie the saucer inscribed Le tems s'envole; votre amour est bien plus constant, circa 1805. (Christie's)$2,468

A Sevres bleu nouveau cylindrical coffee cup and saucer, blue interlaced L marks enclosing the date letters EE for 1782. (Christie's) $766

An early Worcester reeded coffee cup with a scroll handle, painted in Kakiemon style, circa 1753-55. (Phillips) $1,302

A jewelled Sevres cylindrical cup and saucer, gilt interlaced L marks and painter's marks LG of Le Guay, circa 1783. (Christie's) $12,150

A Paris (Jacob Petit) two-handled cup, cover and trembleuse-stand, blue JP marks, circa 1840, the stand 16.5cm. diam. (Christie's) $580

CURTAINS

When rummaging around among the bundles of old curtains in salerooms or at jumble sales, keep an eye open for old curtaining for some can be worth fair sums of money. The Victorians tended to favour dull colored, heavy curtains to keep out the cold, but a new interest in interior decoration was created by William Morris who revolutionised the art of furnishing and house decorating in Britain. With the co-operation of fellow artists from the Pre-Raphaelite Brotherhood, he opened his first decoration company which was to become Morris & Co in 1861. They designed everything for the home from cutlery, wallpapers, curtaining and furniture to carpets. Due to Morris, the old clutter beloved by the Victorians became unfashionable and was replaced by more simple, less cluttered rooms based on Morris' idealised ideas about Mediaeval life. The furnishing fabrics that he designed matched many of his wallpapers and had stylised, flowing plant and animal bird patterns which still fit in very well with modern furnishing schemes.

One of two pairs of Morris & Co. printed cotton curtains, designed by Wm. Morris, 'Corncockle' design, 1880's, 216 x 139cm. $340

One of a pair of crewelwork curtains, one signed Mary Fincher 1703, 65 x 86in., another pair 41 x 52in. and two pelmets. (Christie's) $2,887

One of a pair of Morris & Co. wool curtains and matching pelmet, designed by Wm. Morris, 1880's, 'Bird' pattern, 250 x 240cm. $3,547

One of a set of three wool and silk Templeton's curtains, designed by Bruce Talbert, circa 1880, together with two pelmets. $3,121

A printed velvet curtain designed by C. A. Voysey, 262 x 239.5cm. (Christie's) $3,965

One of a set of four Jacobean crewel-work bed hangings, embroidered in coloured wools, 3ft.1in. wide. (Lawrence Fine Art) $4,250

CUSHIONS

Worked cushions were popular in the 19th century with Berlin woolwork finding favour between the 1820's and 1870's. This was similar in concept to the modern painting by numbers kit with designs first painted on squared paper and then transferred to the canvas by the needlewoman. By the 1830's designs were being printed directly onto the canvas and 14,000 patterns were available for the British market alone by 1840. Many such cushions can still be found for a few dollars in second hand charity shops.

A Berlin woolwork cushion with a large central medallion and sprays of flowers, 18in. square. (Christie's) $1,409

A Berlin woolwork cushion, the central medallion worked with raised plush roses, circa 1860, 18in. square. (Christie's) $2,035

One of a set of five cushions worked in coloured wools with sprays of flowers and edged with pink and yellow wool fringe. (Christie's) $3,132

A feather cushion covered in purple and gold brocade woven with a displayed eagle, 15¼in. square. (Christie's) $1,250

A 17th century needlework cushion, silk and metallic yarns in a variety of stitches, England, 8 x 10in. (Robt. W. Skinner Inc.) $3,000

A rectangular needlework cushion with summer flowers on a brown ground, 18in. wide. (Christie's) $311

A tapestry cushion cover woven with a classical scene, Dutch, 17th century, 12 x 23in. (Christie's) $982

DAUM

In 1875 Jean Daum started a glassworks at Nancy in France and it was continued by his two sons Jean-Louis and Jean-Antonin who made Art Nouveau glass in the style of Emile Galle. The glassworks has continued in the hands of the Daum family ever since and their products have been distinguished by exquisite quality and style. Much of their output was colored glass with etched floral decorations and also cased glass but they also created new shapes including the long necked Berluze vase. Since 1966, th firm has made a great deal of Pate de Verre glass with designs by artists like Salvador Dali. All wares produced by the factory since its inception carry the Daum signature which has changed in form many times over the years.

A Daum overlaid and acid-etched table lamp with wrought-iron mount, 60cm. high. (Christie's) $11,088

A Daum limited edition pate-de-verre and fibre glass surrealist sculpture by Salvador Dali, depicting a soft clock slumped on a coat hanger. (Christie's) $2,975

A Daum Art Deco acid etched vase, the smoky-blue glass deeply etched with oval and circular panels, 33.5cm. high. (Christie's) $2,345

One of two Daum Cameo glass rosebowls, crimped ruffled rim decorated with cameo-cut sprays of violets, signed 'Daum/Nancy', diam. 7in. (Robt. W. Skinner Inc.) $800

A Daum cameo landscape vase, the tapering cylindrical body with swollen collar, 27cm. high. (Christie's) $783

A large Daum cameo glass hanging lampshade of shallow domed form, 46cm. diam., signed. (Phillips) $3,024

A Daum enamelled and acid etched vase of rounded cube form, 11.5cm. high. (Christie's) $2,345

Daum Cameo and enamelled glass perfume bottle with conforming stopper, signature 'Daum/Nancy', height 4½in. (Robt. W. Skinner Inc.) $1,400

A small Daum rectangular section cameo glass jug, circa 1900, 11cm. long. (Christie's) $380

A Daum Nancy acid etched glass table lamp, France, circa 1900, 14in. high. (Robt. W. Skinner Inc.) $2,000

A Daum Art Deco acid etched vase, bell-shaped, 28cm. high. (Christie's) $992

A Daum cameo table lamp with wrought-iron, three-branch neck mount, 44.1cm. high. (Christie's) $8,712

A Daum acid textured two-handled vase, engraved signature Daum Nancy with the Cross of Lorraine, France, 25.5cm. high. (Christie's) $1,443

A Daum cameo and engraved martele baluster vase, engraved Daum Nancy with Cross of Lorraine, 25.4cm. high. (Christie's) $2,674

A Daum bowl, the white, green and red mottled glass acid-etched with primroses and foliage, 13.9cm. high. (Christie's) $865

In the days when many decanters were made of opaque or colored glass it was the custom to hang a label round the necks telling what was inside. Some of the labels were very beautifully made in silver, enamel, porcelain or Sheffield plate and could be finely chased or decorated. They were used in wealthy homes from around 1730 onwards and until the mid 19th century most of them were individually made by craftsmen. Later however they were mass produced. After 1860, they dropped out of general use because the Grocers' Licences Act of that year made it possible for wine to be sold in single bottles with paper labels indicating the contents.

Old labels can be valuable, especially the ones made of Battersea enamel and dating from between 1753-56. They were quite large with a wavy outline and could be worth several hundreds of dollars today. Other valuable labels are those which were originally printed with the name Madeira but later overprinted with titles like brandy or whisky. There are many die-stamped reproduction labels on the market but they can usually be distinguished from the genuine ones which are heavier.

An early 19th century wine label of cast openwork fruiting vine design, possibly Irish, circa 1820. (Phillips) $422

A Victorian stamped-out hunting horn wine label, incised 'Port', by G. Unite, Birmingham, 1857. (Phillips) $474

A Victorian cast wine label, title scroll incised 'Red Constantia', by Rawlings & Sumner, 1843. (Phillips) $573

A George IV Irish wine label, incised 'St. Peray', by L. Nolan, Dublin, 1825. (Phillips) $474

A George III cast openwork wine label with a reclining satyr beside a barrel, by Phipps & Robinson, probably 1817. (Phillips) $210

One of a pair of George IV Irish oval wine labels, by James Scott, Dublin, circa 1825. (Phillips) $560

A Victorian Provincial escutcheon wine label, possibly by Thomas Wheatley of Newcastle, circa 1850. (Phillips) $113

A pair of George III wine labels of shell and fruiting vine design, by Richard Turner, 1819. (Phillips) $402

A Victorian silver bottle ticket for Sherry, in the form of a bat, English or Indian Colonial, circa 1880, 4¼in. wide. (Christie's) $880

A George IV armorial wine label of openwork ribbed disc form, by Riley & Storer, 1829. (Phillips) $630

A set of four Victorian wine labels, each engraved with a crest, by Rawlings & Sumner, London, 1859 and 1860. (Christie's) $281

One of three George III silver gilt wine labels for Port, Claret and Champagne, by Benjamin Smith, 1808, 3in. high, 7oz.5dwt. (Christie's) $3,676

A George III wine label modelled as a putto, by Peter, Anne and William Bateman, 1799. (Phillips) $1,435

A George II Provincial wine label, formed as two putti, by Isaac Cookson, Newcastle, circa 1750. (Phillips) $367

A George III Provincial rectangular thread-edge wine label, by Hampston & Prince, York, 1784/5. (Phillips) $122

A Victorian wine label of fruiting vine and leafy scroll design, circa 1840. (Phillips) $210

DELFT

When Chinese porcelain arrived in the West, Europe was literally dazzled. Nothing of such beauty and brilliance had ever been manufactured there, and the indigenous pottery industries now had to compete with the flood of imports. Majolica had been made in small workshops throughout Holland by potters who were experienced yet open to new techniques. A result of this was delft, a decorated, tin-glazed earthenware, known elsewhere as faience. It first appeared in the early 17th century and the next 120 years were to see the steady development of both technique and quality. Majolica had been mainly multicolored, but delft was nearly all blue and white, imitating Chinese porcelain. Decoration too at first followed Chinese traditions, but later pieces saw innovative themes, such as the peacock jar, with a motif of two peacocks facing a central basket.

The finest period lasted until about 1730, when the seduction of enamel colors and the prettiness of porcelain began to sap the vitality of the medium.

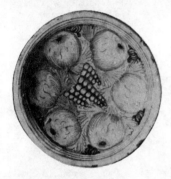

A mid 17th century English delft charger, probably Southwark, 37cm. diam. (Christie's) $920

A Dublin delft blue and white baluster vase, circa 1750, 32cm. high. (Christie's) $1,456

A Bristol delft blue and white barber's bowl, circa 1740, 25.5cm. diam. (Christie's) $1,292

A massive London delft dated polychrome armorial drug jar of swelling form, circa 1656, 36cm. high. (Christie's) $25,855

Early 18th century Dutch Delft blue and white seated Magot, 18cm. high. (Christie's) $1,188

A London delft dated blue and white wet drug jar for S. Cichorei.Sympi with date 1659, 20cm. high. (Christie's) $1,226

177

An English delft polychrome posset pot, either London or Bristol, circa 1695, 24.5cm. wide. (Christie's) $2,359

One of a pair of 18th century Dutch Delft polychrome cows with yellow horns, 21cm. long. (Christie's) $2,453

A Bristol delft blue and white footed bowl, circa 1730, 26.5cm. diam. (Christie's) $2,178

A London delft blue and white Royalist portrait plate, circa 1690, 22cm. diam. (Christie's) $2,541

A Delft mantel garniture, comprising two covered jars and a vase, vase 13in. high. (Christie's) $770

A Lambeth delft blue and white octagonal pill slab, circa 1780, 26cm. high. (Christie's) $3,085

A Bristol delft plate painted in a bright palette with a peacock, circa 1740, 21cm. diam. (Christie's) $1,540

A London delft vase painted in blue24cm. high. (Phillips) $835

A late 17th century Lambeth blue and white delftware dish, 14in. wide. (Dacre, Son & Hartley) $656

DINKY TOYS

The name 'Dinky' has passed into the English language as almost a generic term for model vehicles. Collecting early or even not so early examples is becoming a passion with an increasing number of people, with the major auction houses now devoting entire sales to these.

Dinky toys are something of which almost everyone will have one or two in their attic. Most are worth only a few dollars, though one from the 30's could be worth as much as $800. Generally speaking, if they come with an original box, the value leaps upwards. One of the most sought-after Dinkys is the No. 24 set of motor cars, which includes a Vogue Saloon, Sports Tourer 4-seater and 2-seaters, and will fetch, if boxed, around $8,000.

Ships of the British Navy, set no. 50, complete with box. (Phillips) $354

Rare Gift Set no. 3, comprising a Standard Vanguard, Austin Taxi, Morris Oxford, Rover, Estate Car and a Daimler Ambulance. (Phillips) $1,680

No. 24 Set of Motor Cars, comprising an Ambulance, Limousine, Town Sedan, Vogue Saloon, Super Streamlined Saloon, Sportsman's Coupe, Sports Tourer 4 Seater, Sports Tourer 2 Seater, boxed. (Phillips) $8,850

998 Bristol Britannia Air Liner, Canadian Pacific, boxed. (Phillips) $250

Gift Set no. 4, Racing Cars, comprising a Cooper Bristol, Alfa Romeo, Ferrari, H.W.M. and a Maserati, boxed. (Phillips) $1,200

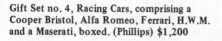

A Willeme Tractor and covered Trailer, boxed. (Phillips) $210

No. 12 Postal Set comprising a Royal Mail Van, Pillar Box, Pillar Box Airmail, Telephone Box, Telegraph Messenger and Postman, boxed. (Phillips) $1,150

299 Post Office Services Gift Set, boxed. (Phillips) $1,000

42 Set Police Hut, Motor Cycle Patrol and Policemen, boxed. (Phillips) $920

934 Leyland Octopus Wagon, yellow and green, boxed. (Phillips) $740

Pre-war No. 64 Set French Factory Avions comprising a Dewoitine, Bloch, Amiot, Potez 662 and a Potez 63, boxed. (Phillips) $3,900

No. 24 Set Motor Cars, comprising an Ambulance, Limousine, Town Sedan, Vogue Saloon, Super Streamlined Saloon, Sportsmans Coupe and 2 Sports Tourers, boxed. (Phillips) $5,300

Rare 675 Ford Sedan Staff Car for U.S. Market. (Phillips) $495

198 Rolls Royce Phantom V, in metallic green and white, boxed. (Phillips) $170

28N Delivery Van, Meccano 1st Type. (Phillips) $2,300

239 Vanwall Racing Car, No. 35, boxed.(Phillips) $195

27Y Studebaker 'Commander', red with tan roof, boxed. (Phillips) $175

280C Delivery Van, Shredded Wheat, 2nd Type. (Phillips) $800

941 Foden 14 ton Tanker, Mobilgas. (Phillips) $1,150

Pre-war No. 68 Set Camouflaged Aeroplanes, comprising an Armstrong Whitworth Whitley Bomber, Frobisher Liner, 3 Hawker Hurricane Fighters, 3 Vickers Supermarine Spitfire Fighters, Armstrong Whitworth Ensign Liner, 2 Bristol Blenheim Bombers and a Fairey Battle Bomber, boxed. (Phillips) $11,500

137 Plymouth Fury Convertible, metallic green, boxed. (Phillips) $195

514 Guy Van, Weetabix, boxed. (Phillips) $2,500

180 Packard Clipper Sedan, orange and grey, boxed. (Phillips) $170

DOLLS

Since earliest times children have played with dolls and some of their roughly made toys turn up on archaeological sites to give mute testimony to distant childhoods. However, the sophisticated dolls which fetch high prices at auction were often never intended to face the rough and tumble of a nursery for they were made to be played with by adult women. The neatly jointed wooden dolls of the 17th and 18th centuries are examples of this. They were treasured by their owners and dressed up in the latest fashions. Many of them had their own trunks full of beautiful costumes.

In the 19th century doll making became big business and bisque headed dolls with rolling eyes and hair that could be combed made their appearance. Queen Victoria was a great collector and spent many hours dressing up her dolls. They were far too precious to be played with by children. It was not until a less rigorous attitude to the young prevailed that doll making became a mass industry and the French and German doll makers dominated the market. In the 20th century there was a great vogue for making dolls in the form of popular heroines like Shirley Temple or Snow White and dolls based on the little princesses Elizabeth and Margaret Rose had a huge vogue.

A bisque figure of a chubby baby, impressed No. 9902, 4½in. high, and a bisque figure of a baby playing with his toes, 5½in. long, impressed Gebruder Heubach. (Christie's) $635

A set of composition dolls representing the Dionne quintruplets with doctor and nurse, 7½in. high, the adults 13in. high, by Madame Alexander. (Christie's) $639

Set of six late 19th century all bisque dolls, German, mounted in candy box, inscribed on cover 'found in the nursery of a ruined old chateau — Verdun, France — 1917', 4in. high. (Robt. W. Skinner Inc.) $650

DOLLS

A cloth character doll, the
head in five sections, 16in.
high, by Kathe Kruse, and
The Katy Kruse dolly book,
published 1927. (Christie's)
$1,745

Simon & Halbig/Kammer &
Reinhardt bisque-headed
doll, 1914-27, 26in. high.
(Hobbs & Chambers)
$789

A bisque headed clockwork
Bebe Premier Pas with kid
upper legs and blonde wig,
17½in. high, by Jules Nicholas
Steiner, circa 1890. (Christie's)
$1,837

A terracotta headed creche figure
modelled as a Turk with moustache
and pigtail, painted wooden hands
and feet, 19in. high. (Christie's)
$610

A pair of advertising dolls
modelled as the 'Bisto Kids',
designed by Will Owen, 11in.
high, circa 1948. (Christie's)
$386

A composition character headed
doll modelled as Lord Kitchener,
in original clothes with Sam
Browne hat and puttees, 19in.
high. (Christie's) $305

A German bisque head doll,
marked 283/297, Max Hand-
werck, 24¾in. high. (Geering
& Colyer) $468

A bisque headed doll's house
doll modelled as a man with
cloth body and bisque hands,
6in. high. (Christie's)
$235

A German bisque head doll,
marked Heubach-Koppelsdorf,
250-4, 25¾in. high. (Geering &
Colyer) $468

DOLLS

A composition mask faced googlie eyed doll, with smiling watermelon mouth, wearing spotted dress, 10½in. high. (Christie's) $610

Early 20th century German bisque bathing belle, resting on one hand, the other raised shielding her eyes, 3½in. high. (Lawrence Fine Art) $587

A composition headed Motschmann type baby doll with dark inset eyes, painted curls and floating hands and feet, 8in. high, circa 1850. (Christie's) $689

A 'Chad Valley' boxed set of Snow White and the Seven Dwarfs in Original clothes, Snow White with painted pressed felt face, jointed velvet body, the blue velvet bodice with pale blue and pink slashed sleeves and short cape, 17in. high, the Dwarfs 9½in. high. (Christie's) $5,291

A composition mask faced googlie eyed doll, with smiling watermelon mouth, wearing pinafore and bonnet, 9in. high. (Christie's) $345

A French bisque headed doll with cork pate, the leather shoes impressed with a number 11, a bee and a Paris Depose, 25in. high. (Ambrose) $2,430

A Hebe bisque headed doll, marks indistinct, with open mouth and upper teeth, sleeping blue eyes and long fair plaited hair, 24in. high. (Lawrence Fine Art) $332

DOLLS

A painted head doll with blue eyes, the felt body in original, clothes, 16in. high, marked Lenci, circa 1930. (Christie's) $202

A bisque headed child doll, marked SFBJ Paris 14, 32in. high, original box marked Bebe Francais. (Christie's) $1,128

A bisque headed character child doll, marked 231 DRMR 248 FANY A2/0M, 14in. high. (Christie's) $3,993

An 18th century group of Italian creche figures, six average height 9in., four average height 11½in., and two at 14½in. (Robt. W. Skinner Inc.) $3,700

A papier mache mask faced doll with turquoise blue eyes, the cloth and wood body in original Central European costume, 15½ in. high, circa 1860. (Christie's) $330

Two all bisque doll's house dolls with fixed blue eyes, blonde wigs and moulded socks and shoes in original national costume, 4in. high. (Christie's) $183

A bisque headed child doll with fixed brown eyes and blonde wig, 10in. high, marked 1079 DEP S&H. (Christie's) $312

185

DOMESTIC EQUIPMENT

One of the best fields for investment is the early mechanical devices put onto the market as labour savers. As improvements were made, the old ones were almost invariably thrown away with the result that, nowadays they have considerable rarity and curiosity value. After a while, it was realised that many of the old gadgets still actually worked. And worked well. Many will swear that their old Victorian coffee mill grinds coffee far better than the brand new electric jobs, that the heavy iron or copper saucepans are far better than their modern counterparts, that bean slicers, apple peelers and cherry stoners add interest to the most mundane of preparatory tasks in the kitchen.

In saying this, I am referring to Victorian appliances. However, it must be said that it is well worth looking out for the now outdated gadgets of the 30's, 40's and 50's. This is a market still in its early stages and with many intriguing contraptions still modestly priced.

Pajot's midwifery forceps, signed Charriere a Paris, late 19th century, 34cm. long. (Christie's) $286

The 'Improved Phantasmagoria Lantern, by Carpenter & Westley, with patent argand solar lamp with a quantity of lantern slides. (Christie's) $369

A 19th century bone saw and three dental elevators. (Christie's) $153

A London Stereoscopic Co. Brewster-pattern stereoscope with brass mounted eye pieces, in fitted rosewood box, 13in. wide. (Christie's) $513

A late 18th century pocket dental scaling kit, with mirror in a shagreen case, 2¼in. wide. (Christie's) $286

A mutoscope in cast iron octagonal shaped case, electrically lit, 22in. high. $822

A Simpson part amputation set, in a fitted mahogany case. $835

A Bonds Ltd./Kinora, pedestal Kinora viewer on moulded wood stand and base inlaid with wood. (Christie's) $1,143

A Baird televisor, No. 204, in typical arched brown painted aluminium case with disc, valve and plaque on front. (Christie's) $1,848

A brass stamp box by W. Avery & Son, 2½in. high. (Christie's) $396

A Pascal's apparatus, unsigned, 14in. wide, with three different shaped glass vessels mounted in brass collars to fit the limb. (Christie's) $811

A late 19th century desk calendar compendium, 3¼in. diam. (Christie's) $270

Rosewood stereo viewer, table top, manufactured by Alex. Becker, N.Y., circa 1859. (Robt. W. Skinner Inc.) $400

An Ive's Kromskop colour stereoscopic viewer, in wood carrying case. (Christie's) $868

Mid 19th century S. Maw, Son & Thompson enema or stomach pump apparatus, English, 12½ x 7½in. $202

DOMESTIC EQUIPMENT

 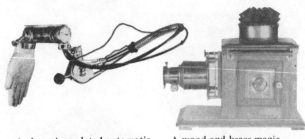 

A cradle-mounted stereographo-scope in black ebonised finish with lens panel, 16in. high. (Christie's) $248

A chromium plated automatic traffic warner, stamped 'Birglow Auto Signal Pat. 375944, Pat. 376564, Reg. design 767816', 42in. long. (Christie's) $198

A wood and brass magic lantern with brass bound lens and chimney with a slide holder and a small quantity of slides in wood box. (Christie's) $277

A set of early Victorian maho-gany jockey scales with ivory plaque De Grave & Co., Makers, London, 39in. wide. (Christie's) $4,329

A Wimshurst pattern plate machine by Philip Harris Ltd., Birmingham, 21.5/8in. wide, and a pair of brass and ebonite discharge forks. (Christie's) $811

A late 18th century 'Ladder Scale', the 1oz. and 2oz. beams stamped De Grave & Co. London, 16.1/8in. wide. (Christie's) $811

A 19th century single cupping set by J. Laundy, with lacquered brass syringe and shaped glass cup, the case 5in. wide. (Christie's) $422

A cast iron sundial by E. T. Hurley, circa 1900, 10¼in. diam. (Robt. W. Skinner Inc.) $425

A 19th century walnut thunder house, the chimney carrying electrical wire, 19.5cm. long. (Christie's) $770

DOOR KNOCKERS

'Rappers', to use their old name, have been popular collectables for many years. Many early ones, in the form of dolphins or lion's head and ring, show Chippendale or Adam influence. Smaller decorative knockers, mostly produced since the 1880's, are now in demand and are made in many forms. Older, well-patinated examples are the most desirable. Look out for a clear registration number on the reverse, as many modern reproductions are made using old moulds.

One of a pair of inlaid bronze mask and ring handles, Warring States/Western Han Dynasty, the masks 9.5cm. wide, the rings 9cm. diam. (Christie's) $86,515

An 18th century wrought-iron door knocker, 10½in. high. $558

William Shakespeare brass door knocker, 6in. high. $35

Harrow School brass door knocker with 'May the fortunes of the house stand' in Latin. $50

A small 20th century brass door knocker depicting the devil. $18

A Victorian heavy bronze door knocker of Regency design, circa 1850, 5in. diam. $85

Robert Burns door knocker in brass, 3½in. high. $18

189

DOORS

Victorian and Edwardian stripped pine and panelled doors are currently much in vogue, and old doors can add much character and security to a house, given the featureless and flimsy nature of their modern counterparts.

Look for unusual doors of all sorts, depending on the image you wish to create. Studded old oak church doors, or even those from a bank vault or prison cell can all be found. Late 19th century doors are among the best quality products and are still quite common.

A late 19th century leaded stained and coloured door window, signed W. J. McPherson, Tremont St., Boston, Mass. (Robt. W. Skinner Inc.) $800

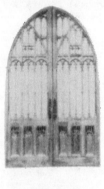

Pair of carved Gothic-style oak doors, 100in. high, 30in. wide. (Robt. W. Skinner Inc.) $1,000

Late 19th century Police cell door, from Bromyard Jail, made by C. Smith, Birmingham. $350

A late 19th century English brass doorway, each door 209 x 77.5cm. (Christie's) $23,925

A pair of Rowley Gallery silvered wood doors, 1920's, 216cm. high. $1,000

Late Victorian Church oak side door with iron fittings. $130

Pair of doors by Jean Dunand for a Normandie liner. $12,250

DOORSTOPS

Why were the Victorians so keen on propping their doors open? Perhaps it was the cult of fresh air but whatever the reason, a vast quality and variety of doorstops survives from that period. Because of the job it had to do, a doorstop must be heavy and the usual material was cast iron, lead or brass in the shape of baskets of fruit, Mr Punches, stout old gentlemen or shire horses. Some doorstops were cast in the likeness of famous people like Queen Victoria or the Duke of Wellington. Even Jumbo, the elephant star of London Zoo, was made into a doorstop after he was sold and exported to America with Barnum and Bailey's circus. He died trying to charge a steam train.

Drawing room doorstops tended to be slightly lighter than those for doors in less elegant parts of the house and were often made of Nailsea glass with air bubbles trapped inside.

Late 19th century cast iron cat doorstop. $60

19th century cast iron lion rampant doorstop. $70

Victorian painted iron stick-stand and doorstop of a boy holding a serpent. (Lots Road) $400

Late 19th century cast iron Mr Punch doorstop. $130

Pair of Georgian brass door stops, the moulded bases with weighted iron insets, 13¾in. high. (Woolley & Wallis) $736

19th century eagle and serpent cast iron doorstop. $260

DOULTON FIGURES

Doulton really started to be noted for figure making when Charles Noke joined the company in 1889. Early examples, however, though finely modelled, were quite drab and did not sell well, so production was suspended until 1912, when he introduced a figure range, one of which, 'Bedtime' (later rechristened 'Darling') found instant favour with the visiting Queen Mary.

The new range featured bolder colors, and a very talented group of designers worked on them. Many are still in production today. Later talents include Margaret Davies, whose work is notable for its meticulous research and attention to detail. Even figures currently still in production can command high prices among collectors, with, for example, the third version of 'St George', by W. K. Harper which was introduced in 1978, fetching $5,000 at auction.

'Pierette' HN644, designed by L. Harradine, issued 1924-38, 7¼in. high. $525

'Balloon Seller' HN583, designed by L. Harradine, issued 1923-49, 9in. high. $220

'Helen' HN1509, designed by L. Harradine, issued 1932-38, 8in. high. $520

'Masquerade' HN599, designed by L. Harradine, issued 1924-49, 6¾in. high. $610

'Old King' HN2134, designed by C. J. Noke, issued 1954, 10¾in. high. $350

'Rosamund' HN1497, designed by L. Harradine, issued 1932-38, 8½in. high. $700

'Mask Seller' HN1361, designed by L. Harradine, issued 1929-38, 8½in. high. $610

'Lady Fayre' HN1265, designed by L. Harradine, issued 1928-38, 5¼in. high. $400

'Mask' HN785, designed by L. Harradine, issued 1926-38, 6¾in. high. $1,000

'Priscilla' HN1340, designed by L. Harradine, issued 1929-49, 8in. high. $240

'Sylvia', HN 1478, designed by L. Harradine, issued 1931-38, 10½in. high. $315

'Wee Willie Winkie' HN2050, designed by M. Davies, issued 1949-53, 5¼in. high. $225

'Stitch In Time' HN2352, designed by M. Nicholl, issued 1966-80, 6¼in. high. $100

'Broken Lance' HN2041, designed by M. Davies, issued 1949-75, 8¾in. high. $315

'Pierette' HN643 designed by L. Harradine, issued 1924-38, 7¼in. high. $610

'Camille' HN1586, designed, by L. Harradine, issued 1933-49, 6½in. high. $315

'Dinky Do' HN1678, designed by L. Harradine, issued 1934, 4¾in. high. $50

'Pantalettes' HN1709, designed by L. Harradine, issued 1935-38, 8in. high. $250

'Verena' HN1835, designed by L. Harradine, issued 1938-49, 8¼in. high. $435

'Polly Peachum' HN550, designed by L. Harradine, issued 1922-49, 6½in. high. $260

'Beggar' HN2175, designed by L. Harradine, issued 1956-72, 6¾in. high. $315 £180

'Bluebeard' HN2105 designed by L. Harradine, issued 1953, 11in. high. $260

'Sibell' HN1695, designed by L. Harradine, issued 1935-49, 6½in. high. $480

'Centurion' HN2726, designed by W. K. Harper, issued 1982-84, 9¼in. high. $110

DRINKING SETS

While some punch sets, for example, date from the 19th century and beyond, the drinking set really became fashionable in the Art Nouveau/Art Deco periods, with such leading designers as Lalique, Daum and Galle. While they were originally intended as largely functional items, in the hands of these craftsmen they could also be highly decorative and can now fetch surprising sums. Like all sets, they are prone to breakage or loss of some of their parts, so complete surviving sets always attract a premium.

A Victorian liqueur set with crimped heart-shaped tray, by Heath & Middleston, Birmingham, 1891, the liqueur bottle 8¼in. high, 12.75oz. free. (Christie's) $480

An Art Deco decanter and glasses, the decanter 22.5cm. high and six liqueur glasses 5cm. high (one glass chipped). (Phillips) $264

An Art Deco glass decanter set, the decanter 20.5cm. high and six octagonal glasses, 6.5cm. high. (Phillips) $774

A Japanese cocktail set decorated in high relief with iris, circa 1900. (Phillips) $1,640

A Schott & Gen 'Jena er Glas' clear glass tea-set, designed by Wm. Wagenfeld, teapot, cover and filter, 11cm. high. (Phillips) $316

A WMF electroplated liqueur set and tray, the decanters 9in. high, the tray 16in. wide, all with stamped marks. (Christie's) $705

Bohemian gold decorated cobalt blue glass punch set, late 19th century, 9½in. high. (Robt. W. Skinner Inc.) $900

A Patriz Huber liqueur set, white metal and glass, stamped with 935 German silver mark and PH, circa 1900, decanter 18.4cm. high. (Christie's) $4,099

A Gabriel Argy-Rousseau pate-de-verre eight-piece liqueur service, the tray 40.1cm. wide. (Christie's) $3,132

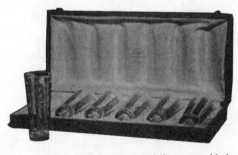

A Lalique oviform clear and frosted glass decanter and stopper, 7in. high, and eight glasses en suite. (Christie's) $288

A set of six Lalique aperitif glasses moulded in clear glass with amethyst tinted panels of Grecian maidens, circa 1930, 9.8cm. high. (Christie's) $1,644

ENAMEL

The star of the British enamels are those made at Battersea's York House for a period of only three years from 1753 to 1756. Not unnaturally, when any of these turn up today they fetch very high prices indeed. Genuine old Battersea has a copper base and looks as if it had been coated with an opaque material similar to glass. However the name Battersea is often misleadingly applied to other enamels which were really made in Wednesbury, South Staffordshire, Bilston or even Czechoslovakia. Old pieces are very pretty and are sometimes decorated with paintings of landscapes or seaside scenes and some of them carry loving messages because they were often given as presents or made as mementoes of certain resorts.

A 19th century Limoges polychrome enamel plaque, in the 16th century style, after Pierre Reymong, 7.1/8 x 5.1/8in. (Christie's) $990

A South German double-ended enamel snuff box of waisted form, circa 1740, 2.5/8in. high. (Christie's) $3,920

A German rectangular enamel snuff box painted in colours with battle scenes from the Seven Years' War, circa 1760, 3in. wide. (Christie's) $5,445

A 19th century French enamel plaque of Eve, signed L. Penet, in ebonised frame, 39 x 27cm. (Christie's) $2,388

Two Staffordshire white enamel tapersticks with gilt metal mounts, circa 1765, one 6.3/8in. and one 6½in. high. (Christie's) $1,866

An Austrian enamelled cigarette case, the cover depicting a Caucasian warrior. (Phillips) $1,050

ENAMEL

A white metal and enamel box with parcel gilt interior, circa 1900, 10.3cm. diam. (Christie's) $861

A George III enamel bottle ticket, Birmingham or South Staffordshire, circa 1770, 3in. long. (Christie's) $264

A South Staffordshire George III enamel bonbonniere, circa 1770, 3in. long. (Christie's) $4,180

One of a pair of late 19th century Viennese silver mounted enamel cornuco-piae, by Hermann Bohm, 8½in. long. (Christie's) $3,036

Two Staffordshire oval enamel portrait plaques, circa 1765, probably Birmingham, each 3¼in. (Christie's) $2,799

An enamel wine funnel, South Staffordshire, circa 1770, 4¼in. long. (Christie's) $1,980

An 18th century Limoges style enamel on copper plate, 7.7/8in. diam. (Robt. W. Skinner Inc.) $600

A Viennese enamel sweetmeat dish with gilt metal mounts, circa 1900, 6.3/8in. high. (Christie's) $1,174

An Austrian enamelled Art Nouveau cigarette case, in the style of Alphonse Mucha, circa 1900. (Phillips) $1,137

ETUIS

An etui sounds like a useful word for crossword puzzle addicts but in fact it was a ladies' companion, a small ornamental case designed to be worn from a chatelaine around the waist or carried in a purse. Etuis contained miniature manicure sets, sewing implements, a snuff spoon, a pencil, a button hook and sometimes a pocketknife – the elegant ladies' Swiss knife kit in fact. They were worn for over 200 years but went out of fashion at the end of the 19th century. Some etuis were very pretty and could be made of gold or hardstone but more commonly of silver, porcelain, ivory or painted enamel.

A German silver gilt mounted white enamel etui, circa 1765, some of the contents with later Dutch control marks, 4in. high.(Christie's) $737

Mid 18th century etui, oval tapered body, fully fitted. $1,000

A George II gold mounted etui, circa 1750, 3¾in. high. (Christie's) $3,139

A Staffordshire enamel etui of upright form, with original gilt metal mounts, circa 1770, 4.1/8in. high. (Christie's) $1,399

George II etui, circa 1745, in green shagreen case. $1,300

A gold etui case, the body chased with flowers and bearing the Royal cypher. (Wellington Salerooms) $8,064

FANS

The folding fan is said to have been invented in Japan around 670 A.D. and introduced first into China and then Europe about the time of Vasco da Gama. Fan sticks were made of ivory, mother of pearl or various woods and covered with paper, parchment, skin, lace or "chicken skin", specially prepared kid skin. They were usually decorated with painting.

The vogue for the folding fan in Europe dates from the 16th century and Elizabeth I is known to have had a good collection. In popularity it supplanted the feather fan which had been used before then. Special conventions were developed for the use of fans and gestures in handling them grew into code signals of an amorous nature.

The Fanmakers' Company was formed in England in 1709 and for a while the importation of foreign fans was prohibited. It was not till the end of the 18th century that the most extravagant and luxurious fans were carried by ladies of fashion and by the 19th century, the fan had become an indispensible fashion accessory.

Fan sticks are often very decorative and made of exotic materials gilded and painted to suit the designs on the leaf. They went through various fashions, growing smaller and then becoming bigger and more flamboyant again. During the Art Nouveau period the shape of the leaves and sticks reflected the artistic style of the time. In the 1920's women carried fans when they went to dances but with the growth in popularity of smoking, this fashion died away. Fan collecting is very popular because it is still possible to find attractive examples at fairly low prices.

An ivory brise fan painted with a lady fishing, 9in., circa 1730. (Christie's) $5,736

A fan, the leaf painted with the return of a hero, the verso with chinoiserie, 10in., French, circa 1760, in glazed case. (Christie's) $3,278

A fan, the leaf painted with a court scene, 10in., circa 1770. (Christie's) $655

A fan, the ivory sticks carved, pierced and gilt with the Altar of Love, 10½in., Italian, circa 1780. (Christie's) $1,346

A French fan with gilded ivory sticks and ivory silk leaf painted with lovers at an altar, circa 1770, 28cm. long. (Phillips) $405

A gilded horn brise fan with pique work, painted with figures on a quay overlooking a bay, circa 1810, 16cm long. (Phillips) $324

A fan with carved, pierced, silvered and gilt mother-of-pearl sticks and the chicken-skin leaf painted and gilded, circa 1760, 30cm. long, probably German. (Phillips) $777

A Chinese fan with carved and pierced shaped sticks of tortoiseshell, mother-of-pearl, stained and unstained ivory and metal filigree with enamel decoration, circa 1840, 28cm. long, in box. (Phillips) $777

A Chinese cabriolet fan with black, pink, silver and gilt lacquer sticks, circa 1830, 28.5cm. long, in original box with label printed in Spanish. (Phillips) $1,053

A fan with carved, pierced, silvered and gilt mother-of-pearl sticks and an 18th century pastiche, signed Donzel, circa 1870, in a shaped, glazed case. (Phillips) $2,268

A 19th century painted fan, the guards inlaid with green enamel, porcelain plaques, semi-precious stones and pearls, probably French, 11¼in. long. (Christie's) $880

A French fan, the carved, pierced and painted ivory sticks decorated with red and green florets, circa 1760, 26cm. long, and a shaped case. (Phillips) $1,053

A Flemish fan with ivory sticks, the guards inlaid with mother-of-pearl and decorated with silver pique, 26.5cm, long. (Phillips) $479

An ivory brise fan painted and lacquered with a classical scene, 8½in., circa 1730. (Christie's) $3,933

A late 18th century Italian fan with pierced ivory sticks, 28cm. long. (Phillips) $535

La Contre Revolution, a printed fan edged with green silk fringe, 11in., French, circa 1790. (Christie's) $901

A French painted pierced ivory brise fan with tortoiseshell guards decorated with silver pique, early 18th century, 21cm. long. (Phillips) $479

A fan, the dark leaf painted with a Biblical scene of figures drinking from a mountain torrent, 10¼in., Italian, circa 1770, in silk covered box. (Christie's) $1,147

A late 18th century fan with carved, pierced and silvered ivory sticks, 24.5cm. long, and a box. (Phillips) $155

An early 19th century fan with carved shaped ivory sticks, the vellum leaf painted with Flora attended by maidens and suitors, 28cm. long. (Phillips) $513

FILM MEMORABILIA

One of the most fascinating and profitable areas of collecting to emerge over recent years is that concerning film memorabilia. It would appear that virtually any artefact connected with the stars of the profession has a marketable value, but if you should chance upon the silk blouse worn by Marilyn Monroe in the film 'Bus Stop' or the red shoes worn by Judy Garland in the 'Wizard of Oz' you really would be into a fortune.

A polychrome film poster, 'Inn of the Sixth Happiness', 20th Century Fox, printed by Stafford & Co. Nottingham, 30 x 40in. (Christie's) $50

Sergio Gargiulo, 'Clark Gable and Vivien Leigh in 'Gone with the Wind', original poster artwork, signed and dated '44, pastel, 16¼ x 12in. (Christie's) $700

A stetson of fawn coloured hatter's plush, accompanied by a letter of authenticity from Gerald A. Fernback stating that 'John Wayne presented . . . his personal stetson when visiting London in February 1951'. (Christie's) $4,000

Metro-Goldwyn-Mayer Studios Tom and Jerry — 'Barbecue Brawl', gouache on full celluloid applied to a water-colour background, 8½ x 11¼in. (Christie's) $1,320

An original Paco Rabanne 'chain mail' dress, accompanied by a letter of authenticity and a film still of Audrey Hepburn wearing it in the 1966 Twentieth Century Fox film 'Two for the Road'. (Christie's) $2,035

Dexter Brown, 'Portrait of Steve McQueen', signed, oil on board, 25½ x 17½in., framed. (Christie's) $1,830

James Dean, '. . . Denn Sie Wissen nicht Was Sie tun (Rebel Without A Cause)' a German polychrome film poster, Warner Bros., printed in Heidelberg, 33 x 23¼in. (Christie's) $150

Ronald Reagan, 'Law and Order' and 'Tropic Zone', two polychrome film posters, Universal productions and Paramount Pictures, both 30 x 40in. (Christie's) $1,425

R. R. Bombe, 'Portrait of Marlene Dietrich', signed, ink inscription dated 15.11.59, watercolour and pencil, 18 x 14in. (Christie's) $185

Cecil Beaton 'Liza, after Delacroix', signed and titled pencil sketch of Audrey Hepburn as Eliza Doolittle in 1964 CBS/Warner film 'My fair lady', 13 x 10in., window mounted, framed and glazed. (Christie's) $900

Two luggage labels each stamped 'S.S. President Roosevelt, Hong Kong to Yokohama, 12 Jun 1964', one inscribed with passenger's details 'Judy Garland', both signed by Judy Garland, signed by Alfred Hitchcock on reverse and annotated with a self-portrait caricature. (Christie's) $325

A 1920's style sleeveless evening dress of black silk chiffon, worn by Betty Grable for publicising the 1940 Twentieth Century Fox film 'Tin Pan Alley'. (Christie's) $120

A photographer's contract comprising a typescript receipt form acknowledging payment and authorising 'Earl S. Moran, . . . to use my photograph for advertising purposes . . . ' inscribed in blue ink with payment details, '$15.00', date 'Los Angeles 26 April '49', and model's name and address, 'Marilyn Monroe, 1301 Nr Harper'. (Christie's) $4,885

A page from an autograph book with manuscript inscription 'Love and Kisses Marilyn Monroe'; with a collection of thirty-two clipped signatures and autographs. (Christie's) $1,320

Charlie Chaplin autographed menu, for the 'Critics' Circle Film Section, Luncheon to Charles Chaplin Esq, Empress Club, W.1., 10.X.52', signed 'Charlie Chaplin'. (Christie's) $110

A 'translucent' evening dress of 'gold' and 'silver' sequins, the bodice with shoe-string straps, the skirt slit to the thigh, worn by Joan Collins as Alexis Colby, 1981. (Christie's) $1,220

Edith Head 'Ginger Rogers in Tender Comrade', signed, charcoal, pencil and coloured crayon costume design, titled by artist and inscribed 'Embroidered organdie', 11¼ x 8¾in. (Christie's) $530

A pair of elaborate costumes of various materials, worn by dancers in the 1978 Universal Studios film 'The Wiz', accompanied by a still showing similar costumes. (Christie's) $325

A rare album containing ninety-four snap-shots of film stars and film studios in Los Angeles, California, 1917-1918, subjects include Charlie Chaplin, Mary Pickford, and various camera-men and directors. (Christie's) $1,300

A one piece running suit of yellow, grey and scarlet 'lycra', and a colour still of Arnold Schwarzenegger wearing the suit in the 1987 Tri Star film 'The Running Man'. (Christie's) $650

A page from an autograph book signed and inscribed 'Rudolph Valentino, London Aug 2 1923', additionally signed by Valentino's wife 'Natacha Valentino'. (Christie's) $400

Ronald Reagan, a single breasted tweed jacket, fully lined, with 'Warner Bros.' woven label, accompanied by a still of Reagan wearing the jacket in the 1947 Warner Brothers film 'Stallion Road'. (Christie's) $1,730

A complete set of eight 'Gone with the Wind' front of house stills; with two promotional programmes and two polychrome film posters. (Christie's) $265

Three unpublished portrait photographs of Peter O'Toole by Bryan Wharton taken in Bagehot St., Dublin, 1976, 10 x 8in. (Christie's) $285

A page from an autograph book with manuscript inscription 'To Marilyn — Love and Kisses Marilyn Monroe'. (Christie's) $1,120

Marilyn Monroe 'Let's Make Love', a polychrome film poster, 20th Century Fox, printed in England, 30 x 40in. (Christie's) $610

An ornate headdress of gilt metal, paper, and fibre and an autographed photograph of autographed photograph of Ava Gardner wearing the headdress in the 1976 Twentieth Century Fox film 'The Blue Bird'. (Christie's) $305

A tailored blouse of pink rose silk, with '20th Century Fox' woven label inside; the blouse reputedly worn by Marilyn Monroe in the 1960 Twentieth Century Fox film 'Let's Make Love'. (Christie's) $4,884

A tiara of simulated diamonds and pearls set in white metal; with a quantity of ornate hair pins, allused to decorate Ava Gardner's hair in her role as the Empress Elizabeth of Austria-Hungary in the 1968 Corona film 'Mayerling'. (Christie's) $610

A painted sign applied with cardboard cut-out letters 'W. C. Fields . . . Poppy', and photomontage portrait of W. C. Fields, advertising the 1936 Paramount Pictures film 'Poppy', 29¾ x 39½in. (Christie's) $160

A U.S.A. Air Corps officer's peak cap with manufacturers details 'Fighter by Bancroft' stamped inside, the cap worn by Clark Gable in the 1949 Metro-Goldwyn-Mayer film 'Command Decision' and a typescript letter from the editor of Picture Show to Mr Browne, congratulating him on his '. . . postcard entry which wins this unique prize of Clark Gable's uniform cap'. (Christie's) $970

An autograph album, containing twenty-five signatures including Glynis Johns, Bela Lugosi, Walt Disney, H.R.H. Edward, Duke of Windsor and Wallis Windsor, Charles Cahplin, Stan Laurel, Oliver Hardy, Bing Crosby, Rex Harrison and others. (Christie's) $1,100

A two piece 'pant suit' of gold lurex reputedly worn by Marilyn Monroe, and given to Jean O'Doul, the wife of Joe Di Maggio's personal manager; accompanied by a copy of a letter from James Gold O'Doul. (Christie's) $2,850

Van Jones, 'Portrait of Grace Kelly', signed, oil on canvas, with inscription 'To Edie, Bucks County Playhouse — from Your Friend Grace Kelly — Dec 25th '49', 18¼ x 14½in. (Christie's) $810

A stand-in model of Boris Karloff as Frankenstein's monster in the 1935 Universal Pictures film 'The Bride of Frankenstein', modelled by Jack Pierce with Karloff's features, the square head with metal clamps circumventing the flattened top. (Christie's) $30,500

FILM STAR POSTCARDS

The most popular period is 1920-39, though stars of the 40's-60's are also in increasing demand. Interestingly, plain-back, postcard size stills of stars fetch virtually as much as actual postcards issued by publishers and film companies. These are known in the trade is Red Letter Cards.

Hand-colored, real photo examples are especially popular with collectors. Condition, as always, is very important. Hand-autographed cards are also worth more. Look out for rarer cards of, for example, 'horror' stars like Karloff and Peter Cushing, also of such performers as James Cagney, Charlie Chaplin, W. C. Fields and most of the Walt Disney stars (including cartoon characters).

It's worth noting, too, that postcards of the old cinemas (often now bingo halls) where these stars appeared can fetch $25-$75, depending on condition and the location of the photograph.

RANDOLPH SCOTT, born 23rd January 1903, debut in 'Sky Bridge' (1931). Pictures include: 'Follow the Fleet', 'The Nevadan Colt 45', 'Sugarfoot'. $3.50

RITA HAYWORTH, real name Margarita Cansino, born 17th October 1919. Pictures include: 'Cover Girl', 'Seperate Tables', 'The Happy Thieves'. $2

RAY MILLAND, real name Reginald Truscott-Jones, born in Neath, Wales, 3rd January 1908. Pictures include: 'Beau Geste', 'Ebb Tide', 'Reap the Wild Wind'. $5

JANE WITHERS, child star. Pictures include: 'Bright Eyes', 'North Star', 'Danger Street'. $5

CHARLES BOYER, born France, 28th August 1899. Pictures include: 'Caravan', 'Fanny', 'Hold back the dawn'. $3.50

FREDDIE BARTHOLOMEW, child star, born London, 28th March 1924, debut in USA in 'David Copperfield' (1935). Pictures include: 'Kidnapped', 'Swiss Family Robinson', 'Little Lord Fauntleroy'. $7

(Border Bygones)

FILM STAR POSTCARDS

HUMPHREY BOGART, one of the most sought after cinema stars, famous as a gangster. $10

MAE WEST, Paramount Pictures No.10. $9

DON AMECHE, pictures include: 'Sins of Man', 'Ramona', 'Alexanders Ragtime Band'. $3.50

GENE RAYMOND, born New York City, 13th August 1908. Pictures include: 'Red Dust', 'Flying Down to Rio', 'Plunder Road'. $3.50

GINGER ROGERS, real name Virginia Katherine McMath, born 16th July 1911. Pictures include: 'Top Hat', 'Swing Time', 'Perfect Strangers'. $5

RUDY VALLEE, born 28th July 1901, real name Hubert Prior Vallee, band leader turned actor. Pictures include: 'Gentlemen Marry Brunettes', 'Man Alive'. $3.50

CLARK GABLE, born 1st February 1901. Pictures include: 'Hell Divers', 'Mutiny on the Bounty', 'Gone with the wind'. $5

RICHARD ARLEN, born 1st September 1900, in Charlottesville, USA, served in British RAF. Pictures include: 'Alice in Wonderland', 'Sea God', 'Grand Canyon'. $5

FRED ASTAIRE, born 10th May 1900, dancer. Pictures include : 'Holiday Inn', 'Ziegfeld Follies', 'Blue Skies'. Won nine Emmy awards in 1958. $7

(Border Bygones)

INGRID BERGMAN, born Sweden, 1917. Pictures include: 'Joan of Arc', 'Casablanca', 'Indiscreet'. $7

VIVIEW LEIGH AND LAURENCE OLIVIER, starred together in Shakesperean works. $9

CLAUDETTE COLBERT, born Paris, 13th September 1907. Pictures include: 'Bride for Sale', 'Secret Fury', 'Texas Lady'. $5

ANNA NEAGLE CBE, actress- producer, real name Marjorie Robertson. Pictures include: 'Nell Gwyn', 'Nurse Edith Cavell', 'Peg of Old Drury', 'A Yank in London'. $5

SHIRLEY TEMPLE, born 23rd April 1929, child star. Pictures include: 'Bright Eyes', 'Wee Willie Winkle', 'Heidi', 'Stowaway', 'Little Princess'. $7

MARGO, real name Maria Castilla, born Mexico, 10th May 1918. Pictures include: 'Lost Horizon', 'Crime without Passion', 'The Leopard Man'.
                $3.50

DAVID NIVEN, born Scotland, 1st March 1910, served in Highland Light Infantry in Malaya, became Colonel. Pictures include: 'Rose Marie', 'Charge of the Light Brigade', 'Guns of Navarone'. $7

ROBERT TAYLOR, born 5th August 1911, Lieutenant in US Navy. Pictures include: 'Ivanhoe', 'Quentin Durward', 'Ambush', TV star in 'The Detectives'. $3.50

MARLENE DIETRICH, real name Maria Magdalene Von Losch, born Berlin, 27th December 1904. Pictures include: 'Dishonoured', 'Blonde Venus', 'Desire'. $12

(Border Bygones)

FIRE IRONS

Before central heating, a blazing hearth was the focal point of a home and the gleaming fire irons used for tending the fire were very much the housewife's pride and joy. They were made of brass, steel, wrought iron, cast iron or copper and fashioned in a wide range of designs. It was necessary to have a shovel, a poker, tongs and a brush and some sets also incorporated a set of bellows for blowing life into reluctant blazes. Then there were also fire dogs for resting the implements on and a fender which gave protection against burning logs or coal tumbling into the room. The Club fender which made its appearance around 1860 is an excellent idea because not only does it form a safety barrier for the fire but it also had little upholstered seats at each corner or all along its front where favoured people could perch near the warmth. In recent years there has been a great rise in popularity of old fashioned, long handled Victorian fire irons, especially the ones made of brass.

There is also a following for "companion sets" of fire-irons hung round a central stem which were made for suburban homes from the 1920's and '30's onwards.

A heavy set of Victorian brass fire irons, 32in. long. $175

An Edwardian brass companion set, 21in. high. $90

Victorian brass barley twist fire irons, 30in. long. $210

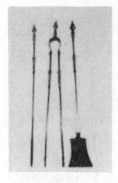

A fine set of Georgian steel fire irons, 32in. long. $350

Four-piece Edwardian brass companion set, 30in. high. $175

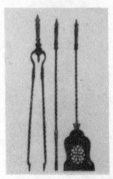

An early set of steel and brass fire irons, 32in. long, circa 1810. £110 $260

FIRE IRONS

A fine pair of brass and enamelled andirons, 26in. high. (Christie's) $3,344

Late Victorian brass companion set, 1880. (British Antique Exporters) $29

A pair of Federal brass andirons and matching fire tools, New York, 1800-25, andirons 20in. high. (Christie's) $1,980

A set of three George III brass fire-irons, 31¼in. long. (Christie's) $775

A set of three George III polished steel fire-irons comprising a poker, a pair of tongs and a pierced shovel with brass vase-pommels, the shovel 30¼in. long. (Christie's) $3,908

A set of three polished steel fire-irons with baluster pommels, 36in. long. (Christie's) $1,144

One of a pair of cast iron foliate andirons, attributed to E. Gimson, circa 1905, 22¼in. high. (Robt. W. Skinner Inc.) $5,500

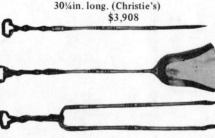

A set of three George III brass fire-irons with shaped ring handles and baluster shafts, 24in. long. (Christie's) $1,960

A pair of brass and iron knife-blade andirons, American, circa 1800, 22¼in. high. (Christie's) $880

212

FLAMBE

Flambe is the name given to a streaky, flame like glaze of a deep blood red color that was devised at the Doulton factory and made its first public appearance to vast acclaim at the St Louis Exhibition of 1904. The technique was discovered by a chemist called Bernard Moore who worked at Doulton's around the end of the 19th century and his glaze was used to stunning effect by artists like Charles Nokes whose flambe elephants are high in collectors' lists of desirables. Flambe is produced by mixing copper oxide and other minerals and allowing fixed amounts of oxygen to enter the kiln at various stages of firing, It is a time consuming and costly business because mistakes were very possible but the trouble proved to be worthwhile because it became so popular with Doulton's customers. Flambe glazes are still being produced.

A Royal Doulton flambe ashtray with elephant heads on the corners, by Moore, 3½in. wide. $190

Pig Dish, 2½in. high x 4½in. long, silver mounted, circa 1927. $525

Two foxes, curled asleep, Model 15, 4in. long. $210

Royal Doulton flambe jardiniere decorated with a desert scene. $490

Monkey, dunce's cap, HN972, 5½in. high. $525

The Dragon, A Royal Doulton flambe figure, 2085, introduced 1973, 7½in. high. $330

Pigeons, two fantail, Model 46, 3¾in. high. $350

Pomegranate, 2¾in. high. $260

A Royal Doulton flambe model of a bulldog, 14.2cm. high. $1,750

FOLEY

The Foley pottery was established in Fenton, Staffordshire in the mid 19th century and was operated from 1903 by E Brain & Co. Its porcelain is noted for the simplicity of its design. That said, in the 1930's work was commissioned from leading contemporary artists such as Graham Sutherland and Laura Knight and is marked with the maker's name and the signature of the artist and decorator. The Foley marks include the brand name Peacock Pottery, with a peacock in a rectangle and Staffordshire knot.

A Foley 'Intarsio' 'Kruger' teapot and cover, designed by Frederick Rhead, modelled as the South African Statesman, 12.7cm. high. (Phillips) $563

Early 20th century Arts & Crafts ceramic umbrella stand, stamped with logo, 'The Foley "Intarsio" England', 27½in. high. (Robt. W. Skinner Inc.) $700

A large Foley Intarsio circular pottery plate painted with sunflowers, 12½in. diam. (Christie's) $224

A Foley Intarsio tapering cylindrical vase with bulbous rim, 8½in. high. (Christie's) $294

A Foley 'Intarsio' tobacco jar and cover, 14.3cm. high, no. 3458, Rd. no. 364386 (SR). (Phillips) $203

A Foley 'Intarsio' earthenware clock case in the form of a miniature longcase clock, circa 1900, 33.8cm. high. (Lawrence Fine Art) $706

A Foley 'Intarsio' earthenware vase of ovoid shape with two handles, England, circa 1900, 26cm. high. (Christie's) $562

214

FUCHI KASHIRA

The Japanese sword is a full-scale work of art, and its accoutrements, such as fuchi kashira (the pommels at the top and bottom of the hilt) are collector's items in their own right. Often these were made and signed by specialist craftsmen and are richly decorated with mythological figures, animals, birds, etc.

Generally speaking, value increases with age and the quality of workmanship. Older ones have often been handed down from father to son as treasured heirlooms, intimately bound up with the family.

A shibuichi migakiji fuchi-kashira, signed Hidekatsu, early 19th century. (Christie's) $880

A 19th century shakudo nanakoji fuchi-kashira, inscribed Ishiguro Masa-yoshi. (Christie's) $968

A 19th century fuchi-kashira, silver takazogan, inscribed Omori Eishu. (Christie's) $2,195

A shakudo nanakoji fuchi-kashira, signed Kondo Mitsuyasu, circa 1800. (Christie's) $1,091

An 18th century shakudo nanakoji gilt rimmed in fuchi-kashira, Soten style. (Christie's) $704

A shibuichi fuchi-kashira, decorated with carp among gilt water-weeds, signed Tomohisa, Mito School, circa 1800. (Christie's) $844

Early 19th century copper fuchi-kashira depicting Raiden among clouds on the kashira, unsigned. (Christie's) $440

A shakudo nanakoji fuchi-kashira, iroe takazogan, reed warblers on branches of blossoming plum, signed Ganshoshi Nagatsune and kao. (Christie's) $739

A 19th century shakudo migakiji fuchi-kashira decorated with Gentoku, signed Yasumasa. (Christie's) $563

A shakudo migakiji fuchi-kashira decorated in taka-zogan with ants and their eggs, 19th century. (Christie's) $563

A 19th century shakudo nanakoji fuchi-kashira, unsigned. depicting a cuckoo in flight. (Christie's) $563

215

FURNITURE

Furniture is more than a collection of utilitarian objects for sitting on, lying on and eating off. It is an expression of the aspirations of the people who use it and the period in which they live. We all need furniture – it is the sort of furniture that we like which is significant. The Egyptians had chairs with rounded legs and ornamented backs; the Romans liked pieces to be heavier and more squat; French furniture during the years before the Revolution was light, curving, elegant and beautifully ornamented – the furniture of the rich and careless. In Britain, furniture has reflected the style of the age from the rough hewn solidity of the Tudor pieces that look as if they were cut by craftsmen from the same oak out of which they made the ships that routed the Armada to the elegance of Regency furniture with spindly legs and basket work chair backs. That was followed by the solemnity of Victorian furniture with bulbous legs on tables and masses of fussy detail on tops of cabinets. The 20th century has seen an enormous change in styles from the fake Mediaevalism of the Arts and Crafts Movement to the chrome and smoked glass styles of the 1970's. Collectors can take their pick of the style of furniture that appeals to them – bergere chairs, papier mache tables decorated with mother of pearl, wardrobes that look as if they are made of panels taken from castle walls or desks with elegant gilding and bayonet legs that look too fragile to carry any weight. The genius of designers like Chippendale, Sheraton, William Morris, Hepplewhite and Pugin can still be appreciated today.

A Regency mahogany canterbury with carrying handle and one division with spindle uprights, 18in. wide. (Christie's)
$4,123

A dining table, the five legs joined by flared stretchers, by Gustav Stickley, circa 1905-1907, 54in. diam. (Robt. W. Skinner Inc.)
$6,800

A Regency oak and parcel gilt sofa, attributed to George Bullock, 61½in. wide. (Christie's)
$106,920

A Sheraton Revival rosewood and marquetry small cylinder desk, 28in. wide. (Dreweatt Neate) $2,232

A George II mahogany card table with folding top, 32¾in. wide. (Christie's) $3,227

A painted and grained pine Empire cupboard, New England, circa 1830, 18¼in. deep. (Robt. W. Skinner Inc.) $900

A Regency mahogany whatnot with two tiers, ring-turned supports and two drawers, 24in. wide. (Christie's) $2,525

A walnut chest-on-stand with moulded quartered top, basically early 18th century, 40in. wide. (Christie's) $2,345

A Sheraton period two tier mahogany dumb waiter, the two tiers with hinged flaps, 37in. high. (Prudential Fine Art) $1,387

A William IV burr-yew davenport with three-quarter spindle gallery and green leather-lined sloping flap, 20½in. wide. (Christie's) $11,228

A Regency mahogany library armchair, the cane filled back and seat with red leather squab cushions. (Christie's) $3,406

A cane-sided plant stand, probably Limbert, circa 1910, 23in. high, the top 16in. sq. (Robt. W. Skinner Inc.) $475

A walnut side table with three drawers on cabriole legs and pad-feet, 30½in. wide. (Christie's) $2,402

A Charles II oak chest-of-drawers with oyster walnut veneered front, 3ft.3in. wide. (Woolley & Wallis) $2,268

Mid 19th century rosewood stool, the padded seat covered in floral needlepoint, 17¼in. wide. (Christie's) $902

Edwardian inlaid mahogany music cabinet with four drawers and open shelf. (Lots Road Chelsea Auction Galleries) $495

Early 20th century wicker arm rocker, 31in. wide. (Robt. W. Skinner Inc.) $200

A George III brass bound mahogany cellaret with a lead-lined interior, 19in. wide. (Christie's) $3,968

Mid Victorian figured walnut davenport with serpentine front and raised stationery box with hinged lid, 21in. wide. (Lalonde Fine Art) $1,650

A George III mahogany breakfront bookcase with two pairs of geometrically glazed doors, 82in. wide. (Christie's) $16,137

A set of Regency mahogany bedside steps with three red leather-lined treads, the top hinged, the middle sliding, previously fitted with a commode, 20½in. wide. (Christie's) $1,645

Late 19th century lacquer cabinet formed in four sections, 216 x 135 x 44cm. (Christie's) $70,400

Late 18th century North Italian walnut and parquetry commode, 50½in. wide. (Christie's) $6,265

A Queen Anne walnut chest-on-stand, the drawers fitted with pierced brass handles, 40in. wide. (Chancellors Hollingsworths') $2,754

A figured walnut inlaid Sutherland table with four turned columns and turned gatelegs with porcelain castors, 35in. wide. (Peter Wilson) $915

A 19th century Italian blue-painted and parcel gilt four-post double bedstead, 71in. wide, 103in. high. (Christie's) $1,996

A George I walnut bureau inlaid with chequered lines, the slant lid enclosing a fitted interior, 41½in. wide. (Christie's) $20,493

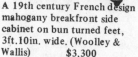

A mid Victorian parcel gilt, painted and sycamore work table with hinged top, 19½in. wide. (Christie's) $1,633

A 19th century French design mahogany breakfront side cabinet on bun turned feet, 3ft.10in. wide. (Woolley & Wallis) $3,300

An early George III mahogany open armchair with padded back and seat upholstered in pink and brown cut velvet. (Christie's) $24,948

GALLE

Perhaps the leading Art Nouveau glass maker was Emile Galle (1846-1904) who also made a great name as a designer of furniture, ceramics and jewelry. Along with his father, he worked at Nancy where he established his glass factory in 1874, turning out a vast number of lamps, vases and tableware decorated with his characteristic flowing designs of foliage, flowers, birds or female figures. He developed his own techniques for making and decorating glass but he was also much influenced by Japanese styles. He exhibited at several Paris Expositions to great acclaim. All his pieces were signed, even the ones made by his collaborators, and he influenced several other glassmakers including the Daum brothers. The Galle factory continued in operation after his death but finally closed in 1931.

A Galle oviform single-handled ewer, the silver mount modelled with stylised flowers, signed, 10¼in. high. (Christie's) $1,066

A Galle double overlay carved blowout vase, the amber glass overlaid with fruiting vines, 27.5cm. high. (Christie's) $7,078

An Emile Galle fruitwood and marquetry table a deux plateaux, 52.5cm. wide. (Christie's) $858

A Galle flask-shaped scent bottle, the neck with a gilt band, rim chip, 12.5cm. high. (Christie's) $570

A Galle double overlay cameo glass lamp, circa 1900, 32.4cm. high. (Christie's) $10,962

A Galle cameo baluster vase, the amber and milky white glass overlaid in purple, carved with fuschia, 16cm. high. (Christie's) $902

A Galle carved and acid etched double-overlay landscape vase, 29cm. high. (Christie's) $8,659

A Galle carved and acid-etched clock, 13cm. high. (Christie's) $4,089

An artistic Galle 'verrerie parlante' vase, engraved Galle expos 1900, 41.5cm. high. (Christie's) $75,504

An enamelled glass jug with stopper, by Galle, decorated with enamelled hearts and a dwarf playing a violin, 20cm. high. (Christie's) $633

A Galle blowout lamp, varying shades of red on an amber ground, signed, circa 1900, 44.5cm. high. (Christie's) $59,508

A tall Galle cameo table lamp, the domed shade and stem overlaid with claret-coloured glass, 63.5cm. high. (Christie's) $12,584

A Galle marqueterie de verre vase, bun foot with body shaped like a crocus bloom, circa 1900, 35cm. high. (Christie's) $13,311

A Galle faience bowl of squat dimpled bulbous shape, 1890 s, 14cm. $435

A Galle mahogany and marquetry two-tier etagere, signed in the marquetry Galle, 59.3cm. wide. (Christie's) $2,662

GAMES

Anyone who was a child in the age before the television will remember evenings passed playing board games or doing jig-saw puzzles. The nostalgia element plays a large part in the enthusiastic collecting of games of which many survive. The jig-saw is a particular favourite, especially those from the 1930's when they were sold by railway companies, steamship lines and many other commercial businesses. The pictures have a period appeal, featuring landscapes or flower filled gardens with white doves on cottage roofs. Try to make sure that all the bits are in the box and that it is in good condition. Other favourite games were Ludo, Snakes and Ladders and card games like Happy Families. There were also general knowledge and word games which offered education as well as amusement. They should be complete and have their dice and shaking boxes where necessary. Even mechanical machines from pier ends are selling well now and 1970's pin ball machines have become collectors' items.

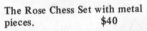

The Rose Chess Set with metal pieces. $40

1950's game of Lotto, complete with cards and counters. $10

1950's Zoo-m-Roo space pinball game. $18

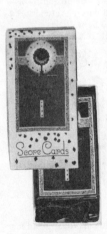

Wireless Whist Score Cards, P840. $7

Oscar, the Film Stars Rise to Fame. $21

Find the Car by Faulkner & Co. Ltd. $5

GAMES

Happy Families by Chad Valley, circa 1910.
$15

Drunken Coachman card game. $10

Sport-a-Crest, Dennis's 'Dainty' Series
N. G829. $5

Tops and Tails Around the World, made in
Austria. $2

Lindy card game. $12

The Cavalry Game. $10

Bussey's Table Croquet game, complete with
balls. $85

History of England card game. $10

GARDEN GNOMES

The idea of 'little people' dates from earliest mythology, and gnomes were said to have guarded the treasures of the inner parts of the Earth. Perhaps it is a subconscious echo of this belief which prompts so many people to populate their gardens with these little figures.

Look out for early gnomes carved out of hardwood or stone. Later 'cast' gnomes with enamelled hats, beards and eyes can still be quite valuable, however, as can some of the handpainted small pottery examples.

1930's garden gnome with red jacket and blue trousers, 12in. high. $18

Early 20th century terracotta garden gnome, 14in. high. $35

An unusual 1940's garden gnome 'spraying the weeds', 7in. high. $50

1960's cast concrete painted gnome with closed eyes. $10

Early 20th century stoneware garden gnome with white enamelled beard. $50

1950's German gnome tying his shoes, A629. $35

1960's cast painted gnome with pipe. $10

A Victorian stoneware garden gnome wearing a pointed red hat and green shorts, 2ft. 3in. high. (Heathcote Ball) $300

Artistic gnome painting a toadstool with spots, 1950's. $35

Sand filled Pebmarsh gnome, circa 1968. $20

(Fred Price)

GLASS

Glass is made primarily from a combination of silicic acid and an alkali, potassium or sodium. Added ingredients make possible the huge variety in glass — for example lead, calcium, metallic oxides or gold. Since the Middle Ages people have been collecting glass and today it is one of the most interesting of the collecting categories.

The Venetian glass making industry dates back to the 11th century and in the 13th century the glassmaking ovens were removed to Murano. It was the German glassmakers who developed the skill of cutting glass which was practised with much success in Bohemia. Ruby glass Bohemian goblets are today highly prized by collectors.

Throughout the centuries and in every country there have been skilled and experimental glassmakers. In the late 19th and early 20th centuries, the Art Nouveau and Deco periods produced artists like Galle, Daum, Tiffany and Lalique whose work changes hands today for astronomical prices. Lalique in particular brought the craft of glass moulding to a high art and he did not only create very expensive objects but also produced utilitarian objects like bottles for perfume manufacturers which made his art accessible for a wide range of people and greatly influenced public taste. Collectors also seek out pewter mounted glass articles produced for the London store Liberty's under the trade name of Tudric.

Glass is essentially a utilitarian material and therefore can be found in many guises — flagons, figurines, plates, beakers, goblets and ewers, chandeliers, vases, perfume bottles and, of course, paper weights. Those made by Baccarat, St. Louis and Clichy are among the most beautiful.

A double eagle historical pint flask, GII-40, bright green, sheared mouth-pontil scar, 1830-38. (Robt. W. Skinner Inc.) $275

A faceted stemmed portrait wine glass, by David Wolff, The Hague, 1780-85, 15.8cm. high. (Christie's) $6,946

A 17th/18th century Spanish amethyst jug, 22.5cm. high. (Christie's) $316

A fine pair of gilt metal and Bohemian glass candlesticks, mid 19th century, 15in. high. (Christie's) $7,832

A baluster toastmaster's glass, the funnel bowl wet on an inverted baluster stem, circa 1710, 12cm. (Christie's) $630

Mid 19th century Bohemian engraved cylindrical beaker with scenes and quotes from The Lord's Prayer, 5½in. high. (Christie's) $550

'Three Dahlias', a Lalique blue opalescent circular bqx and cover of clear and satin finished glass, 20.9cm. diam. (Christie's) $469

'Lys', a Lalique opalescent bowl moulded with four lily flowers, 24cm. diam. (Christie's) $902

A Mount Washington magnum pink dahlia weight, 4¼in. diam. (Christie's) $28,600

A Baccarat double medal cylindrical tumbler with cut foot and sunray base, 10.5cm. high. (Christie's) $1,378

A Lalique frosted glass figure on bronze base, Suzanne, 23cm. high without base. (Christie's) $6,019

An Austrian 'Zwischengold' Armorial tumbler by Johann Mildner, set with a double walled medallion, circa 1794, 12cm. high. (Christie's) $5,760

An early serving bottle, the compressed globular body with a kick-in base, circa 1700, 14.5cm. high. (Christie's) $1,530

Late 19th century two-part cut glass punch bowl, America, 14½in. high, 14¾in. diam. (Robt. W. Skinner Inc.) $900

A Baccarat close millefiori wafer dish, the base with a cane inscribed 'B1848', 10cm. high. (Christie's) $1,533

GLASS

Mid 19th century Bohemian overlay and enamelled casket, the body in opaque white, 5¼in. wide. (Bermondsey) $600

An Almaric Walter pate-de-verre paperweight designed by H. Berge, 8cm. high. (Christie's) $15,334

Mid 19th century cobalt blue blown glass cuspidor, American, 5in. high, 9in. diam. (Robt. W. Skinner Inc.) $250

A Dimple Haig clear glass bottle, decorated with pierced plated mounts depicting Chinese dragons, original stopper, 10½in. high. (Peter Wilson & Co.) $120

Pair of 19th century cut glass lustres, 11½in. high. (Du Mouchelles) $700

A Stourbridge olive-green opaline vase on four gilt feet detailed in white and black enamel, 12¾in. high. (Christie's) $228

An Archimede Seguso 'Compisizione Piume' carafe, circa 1960, 29cm. high. (Christie's) $7,920

A Guild of Handicrafts silver and glass box and cover, designed by C. R. Ashbee, with London hallmarks for 1900, 21cm. high, 16oz. 15dwt. gross weight without cover. (Christie's) $6,894

'Danaides', a Lalique vase moulded with six nude maidens pouring water from urns, 18.3cm. high. (Christie's) $2,525

GLOVES

Not so long ago no lady would be seen out of doors without gloves. With the disappearance of the fashion, they were carefully laid away and now collectors seek them out in second hand clothes shops because gloves are coming back. Some of the earliest gloves to be found date from the 17th and 18th centuries, and they were heavily decorated, fringed and scented, some elbow length and others with slit fingers to show off the wearer's rings. They were worn by both sexes and made of animal skin, embroidered satin, velvet knitted silk, worsted cloth or cotton. Long gloves were secured at the elbow by a ribbon or a plait of horsehair. In Victorian times gloves became more demure, hand stitched of finest suede or leather or made of crocheted silk or cotton. Some of them were fingerless. The dashing leather gloves, often with high stiff gauntlets like aviators' gloves, worn by ladies in the 1930's, are very desirable today and collectors also seek out long black or white suede gloves which were essential wear with evening gowns only forty years ago.

A pair of white kid gloves with deep cuffs of white satin embroidered in silver thread and sequins, mid 17th century. (Christie's) $3,744

A pair of late 19th century American Woodlands Indian gauntlets of brown leather, probably Cree. (Phillips) $672

A pair of gloves of pale cream chamois leather, engraved under the thumb, F. Bull & Co., Jan 4th 1791. (Christie's) $288

Pair of men's kid gloves saide to have belonged to Edward VII. $175

A pair of mid 19th century North American Eastern Woodlands Indian gloves of light brown leather, lined, probably Cree. (Phillips) $235

A lady's glove of white kid, the deep cuff of ivory satin lined with pink silk, early 17th century. (Christie's) $366

GOLDSCHEIDER

It was in 1886 that Friedrich Goldscheider founded his factory in Vienna. After his death in 1897, production continued there under the direction of his widow and brother Alois, until, in 1920, the business was taken over by his two sons Marcel and Walter. In 1927, however, Marcel broke away to form the Vereinigte Ateliers fur Kunst und Keramik.

While such things as vases were produced, the factory is best known for the figures and wall masks which epitomised the Art Nouveau and perhaps even more, the Art Deco styles. The favourite subject was the female form and face, with dress and hairstyles faithfully reflecting those of the period. Dancers abound, in every sense, and, in the more exotic of these, the Egyptian influence is once more in evidence.

A Goldscheider pottery bust of a young woman in the Art Deco style, signed F. Donatello, 23½in. high. (Outhwaite & Litherland) $504

A Goldscheider Art Deco globular lamp base, decorated in white, orange, black and blue with banding, 25cm. high. (Phillips) $243

A Goldscheider terracotta figure of a blackamoor, 23½in. high. (Graves, Son & Pilcher) $1,856

A Goldscheider pottery mask of a girl looking down, Made in Austria, circa 1925, 23cm. high. (Christie's) $473

A Goldscheider pottery figure of a woman wearing a beaded costume, on a black oval base, 18in. high. (Christie's) $2,108

A Goldscheider tin-glazed earthenware wall mask, Wien, Made in Austria, inscribed 8874, 36cm. high. (Christie's) $811

A Goldscheider pottery figure modelled as a naked young lady holding a fan, and trailing a shawl behind, 13¾in. high. (Christie's) $514

A pair of Goldscheider pottery figures of a young girl and a young man, made in Austria, 15in. high. (Christie's) $528

A Goldscheider pottery figure of a dancing girl, designed by Lorenzl, 16in. high. (Christie's) $1,057

A Goldscheider pottery figure, modelled as a sailor holding a girl, 30cm. high. (Christie's) $537

A Goldscheider pottery 'Negro' wall mask, 26.5cm. high. (Phillips) $228

An Art Nouveau Goldscheider pottery figure, modelled as a girl wearing long flowing robes, designed by E. Tell, 65cm. high. (Phillips) $691

'Butterfly Girl', a Goldscheider figure after a model by Lorenzl, 7in. high. (Christie's) $634

A Goldscheider pottery double face wall plaque, the two females in profile, 12in. high. (Christie's) $596

A Goldscheider pottery group after a model by Lorenzl, of a flamenco dancer and a guitar player, 17in. high. (Christie's) $893

GOSS CHINA

Goss china was the first and finest crested china created for the burgeoning tourist trade of Victorian times. It was produced by an enterprising firm called W.H. Goss & Sons — which later became W.H. Goss Ltd. The firm was owned by William Henry Goss, a Londoner born in 1833 who started making Copeland style china in 1858 but in the 1880's he took up the suggestion of his clever son Adolphus and concentrated on producing miniature pieces of china at low prices to be sold to the day trippers who were flocking to every pretty part of the country.

Goss printed towns' crests or coats of arms on each piece made so the buyer had an instant souvenir. By a clever stroke, the crest of any town was only in that town itself so anyone aiming to start a collection — and many did — had to travel all over the country to complete it.

The porcelain made by Goss was ivory colored with simple crests printed on. It was turned out in a vast number of shapes — Roman vases, tombs, shoes, clocks, crosses, lighthouses, replicas of famous buildings and cottages to name only a few. Today the cottages are particularly popular with collectors. Some of them were designed as nightlights so that a candle could glow through the windows and smoke rise from the chimney. They were hardly ever more than six inches long. Goss models of Anne Hathaway's cottage or Robert Burns' cottage at Alloway are particular favourites with collectors. The Goss mark was a goshawk with its wings outstretched and though other potteries copied his pieces, their marks were always different.

Goss Buckland Monachorum Font with Buckland Abbey arms. (Goss & Crested China Ltd) $770

Orknie Craisie by Goss. (Goss & Crested China Ltd) $36

First period figurine 'Ophelia', marked Goss & Peake, dated 1867. (Goss & Crested China Ltd) $2,685

Durham Sanctuary Knocker flower holder wall pocket in brown, by Goss. (Goss & Crested China Ltd) $72

Goss Waterlooville Soldier's Water Bottle, with matching arms. (Goss & Crested China Ltd) $45

Coloured Goss parian bust of Shakespeare from the tomb in Stratford-on-Avon church. (Goss & Crested China Ltd) $152

231

Goss Rhinoceros on oval base. (Goss & Crested China Ltd) $940

Goss eggshell first period cup and saucer, white with violets in relief. (Goss & Crested China Ltd) $179

Second period Goss model of Dutch Sabot. (Goss & Crested China Ltd) $36

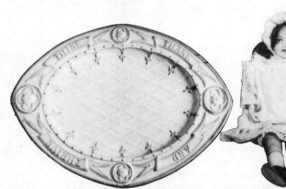

Third period Goss England Flower Girl 'Miss Julia'. (Goss & Crested China Ltd) $376

First period parian 'Think Thank and Thrive' bread plate by Goss, decorated in enamels. (Goss & Crested China Ltd) $448

Goss doll (No.31) child with real hair, glass eyes, china arms and stuffed legs. (Goss & Crested China Ltd) $895

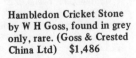

Hambledon Cricket Stone by W H Goss, found in grey only, rare. (Goss & Crested China Ltd) $1,486

Goss three-handled Loving Cup invented by King Henry of Navarre, 38mm. high. (Goss & Crested China Ltd) $20

Goss Old Gateway on Monnow Bridge, white glazed. (Goss & Crested China Ltd) $134

GOSS COTTAGES

The famous Goss factory which started producing china in 1858 started a very popular line in attractive little cottages modelled on the homes of famous people in 1893 and continued making them till 1929. Among the 51 different types they sold were copies of Anne Hathaway's cottage at Stratford on Avon and Robert Burns' home at Alloway.

The cottages were often pastille burners and they sold well because they made attractive and cheap souvenirs. Today they are among the most desirable items in the vast Goss range for collectors who specialise in the products of that enterprising company. The cottages are usually marked with the name W. H. Goss and a goshawk with wings outstretched.

Miss Ellen Terry's Farm near Tenterden in Kent, 70mm. long. $540

Sulgrave Manor, Northamptonshire, 125mm. long. $1,925

Old Market House at Ledbury, 68mm. long. $500

Manx Cottage Nightlight, Isle of Man, 122 mm. long. $280

Shakespeare's Cottage, Stratford-on-Avon, 65mm. long. $130

Wordsworth's home, Dove Cottage, 102mm. long. $700

GOSS COTTAGES

The Goss Oven, orange chimney version, 75mm. long. $375

The Feathers Hotel, Ledbury, 114mm. long. $1,400

Isaac Walton's Birthplace, Shallowford, 86mm. long. $610

Portman Lodge, Bournemouth, open door version, 84mm. long. $610

Ann Hathaway's Cottage, Shottery, 50mm. long. $125

St Nicholas Chapel, Lantern Hill, Ilfracombe, 74mm. high. $280

Thomas Hardy's Birthplace, Dorchester, 100mm. long. $610

Old Maids Cottage, Lee, Devon, 73mm. long. $210

GOSS COTTAGES

The Old Thatched Cottage, Poole, 68mm. long. $700

Charles Dickens' house, Gads Hill, near Rochester. $225

Southampton Tudor House, 83mm. long. $500

First and Last House in England, with annexe, 140mm. long. $1,300

St Catherine's Chapel, Abbotsbury, 87mm. long. $735

John Knox's House at Edinburgh, 102mm. high. $650

Shakespeare's Birthplace, 40mm. long (Late version). $80

Christchurch, Old Court House, 76mm. long. $570

GRAMOPHONE NEEDLE TINS

The collecting of gramophone needle tins developed from the separate hobby of collecting gramophones and phonographs. The tins, which are small, easy to store and cheap to buy, are often found inside the machines or in the lids. They can also sometimes be discovered in boxes of mixed lots at car boot sales or jumble sales. There are also occasional auction sales in London at which needle tins can be bought.

In the early days of gramophones, each needle could be used only once so there was a tremendous demand for them. Because there was no volume control on early gramophones, the tone was set by the needle. Popular tones were medium, loud and extra loud. Needles were sold in boxes of 100 or 200. The boxes were often attractively printed with the trade marks or special designs of the gramophone manufacturer. The principal machine manufacturers and needle producers were HMV, Songster, Columbia, Decca, Embassy and Edison Bell. More information on needle tins can be found from the City of London Phonograph and Gramophone Society which has members in Australia, America, Holland, Germany and the United Kingdom.

Perophone Needles, with the greyhound in green, white and black. **$9**

Judge Brand, Test for fair trial, British tin in pale turquoise. **$5**

Songster Supertone in pale and dark green with Songster in gold. **$9**

Bohin, French tin in yellow and green with a black face. **$10**

Imperial, large shaped tin in orange with black lettering, 250 needles. **$5**

Columbia, an early tin in pale blue and gold, 300 needles. **$7**

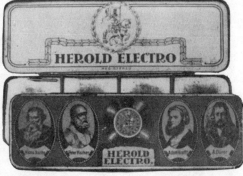

Herold Electro, a large four compartment German tin in red and green. **$60**

Merchantship, a rare large Japanese tin which originally held a wrapped razor blade. **$30**

Herold Tango, square German tin in pale turquoise, one of a series of five. **$10**

GRAMOPHONES

Thomas Alva Edison launched the phonograph in America in 1876 and in 1887 Emile Berliner patented the first gramophone, also in U.S.A. The first machines were jerky because of hand cranked powering but in 1896 the techniques of clockwork mechanisms were worked out and shellac discs replaced the old zinc coated rubber discs. From the time of the First World War, every family wanted a gramophone in the parlour and there were many manufacturers vying for their business. They gave their machines wonderful names like Aeolian, Vocalion, Deccalion and Oranoca. These early machines had big horns, some of which looked very elegant and could be made of brass, painted tin (sometimes decorated with flowers inside), or papier mâché, but as people began to look on the gramophone as a piece of furniture, the horns shrank and were concealed inside the sets which were disguised as cabinets. Collectors also seek out gramophone accessories like record cleaners, needle sharpeners and needle cutters.

A G. & T. double-spring Monarch in oak case, the oak horn 18in. diam., the gramophone circa 1906. (Christie's) $1,232

A horn Pathephone with chequer-strung oak case, horn 22in. diam., (Christie's) $924

A Gramophone Co. mahogany Junior Monarch ('Doric') with single-spring motor, the horn 21½in. diam., circa 1908. (Christie's) $1,001

A Decca Dulcephone horn gramophone with fine tin flower horn. (Onslows) $268

Early HMV wind-up table gramophone with original gilt pleated circular diaphram. (Lawrence Butler & Co.) $820

An HMV Intermediate Monarch gramophone with mahogany case and horn, 1911 (soundbox replaced). (Christie's) $1,158

A Gramophone & Typewriter Ltd. New Style No. 3 gramophone, with 7in. turntable and concert soundbox, circa 1904. (Onslows) $834

An early Kammer & Reinhardt Berliner gramophone with gilt-lined japanned cast iron base. (Christie's) $691

A gramophone with 'The Gramophone Co., Maiden Lane, London, W.C.' label, a 7in. diam. turntable and four single sided E. Berliner's 7in. diam. records, circa 1900-10. (Hobbs & Chambers)$1,600

An HMV Model 203 cabinet gramophone, 5A soundbox and re-entrant tone chamber, the mahogany case with gilt internal fittings. (Christie's) $3,564

An early Kammer & Reinhardt 5in. Berliner Gramophone, with three Berliner records. (Phillips) $2,080

An EMG gramophone of compact Mark 10 design, with papier mache horn, 25in. diam. and approx. 300 classical records. (Christie's) $748

A Gramophone & Typewriter Ltd. Style No. 6 gramophone in panelled oak case and Concert soundbox, travelling arm and brass horn, circa 1901. (Christie's) $1,603

A G. & T. single-spring Monarch gramophone with Morning Glory horn, 24in. diam., circa 1903-04. (Christie's) $492

A Gramophone & Typewriter Ltd. New Style No. 3 gramophone with 7in. turntable, now with Columbia soundbox and brass horn. (Christie's) $1,452

GRUEBY

The Grueby Faience Co was formed in 1897 by William H Grueby in East Boston, MA, initially manufacturing tiles, Della-Robbia style plaques and vases. From 1898 matt glazes of opaque enamel were used in shades of blue, brown, yellow and sometimes red. The most characteristic of these, however is dark green with a veined effect. Vases were hand thrown, some plain, others decorated with geometrical patterns or plant forms in low relief. From 1904 glazed paperweights were made in scarab form. Grueby art pottery usually bears the artist's signature incised and often **GRUEBY POTTERY BOSTON USA** impressed in a circle surrounding lotus blossom motif. Grueby Faience was declared bankrupt in 1908 and though a new company was formed for architectural ware, vase production had ceased entirely by 1913. The tile manufacture was sold in 1919, and finally ceased operation around 1930.

Grueby pottery butterscotch glazed vase, artist's initials W.P. for Wilamina Post, dated 3/12/06, 9in. diam. (Robt. W. Skinner Inc.) $6,500

Grueby pottery two-colour lamp base, Boston, circa 1905, bronze foot signed Gorham Co., 18in. high. (Robt. W. Skinner Inc.) $11,750

A two-colour Grueby pottery vase, artist's initials A.L. for Annie Lingley, circa 1905, 8¼in. diam. (Robt. W. Skinner Inc.) $3,300

A Grueby two-colour pottery vase, circa 1905, 13in. high. (Robt. W. Skinner Inc.) $5,200

Late 19th century Grueby Faience Co. bust of 'Laughing Boy', based on a statue by Donatello, 11in. high. (Robt. W. Skinner Inc.) $1,800

Early 20th century Grueby pottery two-colour vase, Mass., 10¼in. high. (Robt. W. Skinner Inc.) $3,000

HAIR CLIPS

Hair clips or combs were first produced in great numbers in the early 19th century, with the revival of Classical taste. They were often set with paste jewels or inlaid with small silver dots (piqué) or more elaborate gold and silver "posé" inlay. Prince Albert's death in 1861 created a fashion for black clips and combs. Later, silver combs, often with flowing Art Nouveau designs, became popular, while after 1900 erinoid combs were all the rage. A simulated tortoiseshell, this was made by mixing sour milk and formaldehyde!

1950's brown plastic hair clip. $1.50

1950's plastic hair clip with eight imitation pearls. $3.50

Edwardian enamel hair clip. $25

Art Deco red and black plastic hair clip. $35

Edwardian enamel butterfly hair clip. $60

1950's red plastic hair clip. $1.50

Early 19th century bone hair clip. $12

A German horn comb, surmounted by panels of green plique-a-jour enamels amid tendrils set with marcasites, 8.5cm. wide. (Phillips) $136

Edwardian folding hair clip inset with diamonettes. $30

Art Deco hair comb set with brilliants. $5

Tortoiseshell hair clip inset with brilliants, circa 1912. $9

An elaborate Edwardian tortoiseshell hair clip. $18

Edwardian diamonte hair clip mounted in silver. $35

Edwardian mother of pearl hair clip. $9

HANDKERCHIEFS

Fashionable Italians in the Middle Ages were the first to flourish handkerchiefs and they were copied by the well to do in the rest of Europe who before that had found their sleeves perfectly adequate for the purpose of blowing the nose. Early handkerchiefs could be any shape but it was Queen Marie Antoinette of France who thought they should be square and a Royal decree to that effect was actually pronounced in January 1785 — not long before the Queen lost her head at the guillotine.

The handkerchief is not just a utilitarian object, it is a thing of beauty as well. Collectors find good examples in a wide variety of materials ranging from printed gauze to lace edged silk often for very little money. Handkerchiefs printed with pictures, rhymes, verses or comic stories turn up; so do initialled handkerchiefs, beautifully embroidered handkerchiefs and even some painted with scenes from various foreign places brought home as souvenirs.

Early 19th Century printed handkerchief apotheosis of George Washington, England, 26 x 19½in. $1,200

'The Reformers attack on the Old Rotten Tree — of the Foul Nests of our Morants in Danger', handkerchief printed in colour on silk, circa 1830. (Christie's) $316

1930's floral design silk handkerchief in pink, green and white. $25

A large Edward VII silk handkerchief with transfer printed design. $25

'A faithful representation of Her Most Gracious Majesty, Caroline Queen of England in the House of Lords, 1820', a handkerchief on linen, 22in. wide. (Christie's) $576

Copper plate printed handkerchief, England, circa 1800, 18½ x 21in. $875

'A representation of the Manchester Reform Meeting dispersed by the Civil and Military Powers August 16, 1819', handkerchief on linen, 20 x 22in. (Christie's) $504

Souvenir of the Great War with woven silk pictures. $85

A printed George Washington handkerchief, probably England, circa 1800, 12½ x 11½in. $700

Early 19th century printed handkerchief, printed in red on linen, 32 x 25½in. $1,000

HANS COPER

Hans Coper (1920-1981) trained as an engineer in his native Germany, but fled to England in the late '30's. During the war, he met another refugee, Lucie Rie, and went to work in her studio. They started making ceramic buttons, then graduated to domestic ware and in the evenings Coper could experiment with his own designs.

His biggest 'break' came when Basil Spence commissioned two candlesticks from him for Coventry Cathedral.

An early small stoneware bowl by Hans Coper, with undulating rim, circa 1955, 14cm. diam. (Christie's) $7,920

A stoneware goblet vase, by Hans Coper, circa 1952, 15.2cm. high. (Christie's) $5,505

A bottle vase by Hans Coper, oviform body with short cylindrical neck, circa 1958, impressed HC seal, 65.2cm. high, (Christie's) $23,760

A waisted cylindrical stoneware vase by Hans Coper, impressed HC seal, circa 1957, 18.6cm. high. (Christie's) $2,112

A stoneware black bulbous bottle, by Hans Coper, circa 1965, 14.7cm. high. (Christie's) $8,651

A stoneware spherical vase, by Hans Coper, with horizontal flange, 1951, 19cm. high. (Christie's) $11,566

A monumental stoneware 'thistle' vase, by Hans Coper, circa 1965, 57.4cm. high. (Christie's) $44,044

HARDSTONE

This heading covers natural stone such as agate, malachite, lapis lazuli, rock crystal etc which is either carved or turned on a lathe. Eastern examples from all periods are available, often very finely carved, and these can fetch from a few hundred to several thousand dollars, depending on quality and rarity. European carvers, too, worked in the medium. Hardstone carvings can form a very beautiful and worthwhile collection.

One of a pair of Chinese hardstone flowering trees in lacquer jardinieres, 16½in. high. (Christie's) $702

A 19th century reddish-brown agate bust of a male carved in the antique manner, 3½in. high.(Christie's)
$388

A fine pair of gilt metal and malachite candlesticks with vase-shaped nozzles, 6¾in. high. (Christie's)
$2,755

A smoked crystal figure of a hawk, perched on a rocky outcrop, 9in. high. (Lawrence Fine Art)
$303

A rock crystal relief plaque depicting the life of Christ, in the Gothic style, 5¼ x 3½in., mounted in a leather case. (Christie's)
$1,430

A Chinese 20th century carved agate Foo dog in tones of smoky brown, grey and white, 5.3/8in. high. (Robt. W. Skinner Inc.) $650

A Hepple & Co. malachite fish pattern jug, 7in. high. (Anderson & Garland)
$106

244

One of a pair of heavily carved malachite groups of predatory birds, late Qing Dynasty, 20.5cm. high. (Christie's) $1,140

An 18th/19th century lapis lazuli mountain of slender slightly concave cross-section, 26cm. wide. (Christie's) $3,706

A large malachite vase formed as an irregular upright tree trunk issuing from rockwork, late Qing Dynasty, 26cm. high. (Christie's) $683

A malachite flattened baluster vase and cover, late Qing Dynasty, 12cm. high. (Christie's) $285

One of a pair of rock crystal and gilt metal pricket candlesticks, mid 19th century, 11in. high. (Christie's) $3,436

A chalcedony agate group carved as a lady standing holding a scroll, another beside her, late Qing Dynasty, 23cm. high. (Christie's) $498

A green hardstone stele carved with Guanyin astride a caparisonned lion, late Qing Dynasty, 62cm. high. (Christie's) $1,853

A carnelian agate group of two lady Immortals, late Qing Dynasty, 16.5cm. high. (Christie's) $455

A rock crystal vase and cover, the high domed cover with a plain globe finial, late Qing Dynasty, 23.5cm. high. (Christie's) $855

HATS

If you want to get ahead, get a hat! Hats are high fashion and some of the most splendid models can be found in second hand clothes shops for those with the courage to wear them.

Large hats trimmed with feathers which were popular from the late 18th till the early 20th centuries, are difficult to find in good condition because they were so fragile but often feathers alone turn up, dyed in a wide variety of colours and carefully curled. Cloche hats from the 1920's and the elegant little straw hats with eye veils of the 30's and 40's make splendid buys. Victorian silk bonnets can often be found as well as hats trimmed with artificial flowers made of silk or with flourishes of artificial fruit. Men's hats from the past times are bought by both sexes — straw boaters, trilbys and toppers in gleaming plush. Even if you don't want to wear these dashing hats, they can be displayed on bentwood hat or wig stands indoors.

A lady's flat wide-brimmed hat of plaited straw edged with ivory silk ribbon, circa 1770, 14in. diam. (Christie's) $3,000

A large round black hat with pale drab cotton cover bearing a large elaborate badge in wire embroidery of the Bersaglieri. (Christie's) $127

Iroquois beaded velvet cap with floral designs, on black velvet. $435

A Nazi Naval officer's cocked hat with silk lining. (Wallis & Wallis) $192

A 1920's rubber bathing cap. $45

A post-1902 R.N. Flag officer's dark blue peaked cap. (Wallis & Wallis) $352

A silk embroidered linen based nightcap, circa 1600. $5,250

An interesting WW1 steel helmet in the form of a tropical helmet, khaki painted overall. (Wallis & Wallis) $100

An Italian grey-green felt Alpini style hat bearing black embroidered badge of Alpine Artillery. (Christie's) $110

A top hat of brown felt, with black ribbon, by A. Giessen, Delft, circa 1870. (Christie's) $688

A boy's cap of black moleskin with peak of patent leather, circa 1845. (Christie's) $114

A top hat of black beaver, with black silk ribbon, 7in. high, circa 1840. (Christie's) $360

A mourning bonnet of black crepe, circa 1830. (Christie's) $163

A top hat of grey beaver, possibly 1829, labelled M. Strieken, 8in. high. (Christie's) $1,065

A bonnet of black satin trimmed with a large bow and rouleaux, circa 1830. (Christie's) $360

A top hat of grey beaver with narrow ribbon of cream ribbed silk, 5½in. high, circa 1830. (Christie's) $426

A pearl grey bowler hat, made in Italy by Borsalino for Cecil, 112 rue de Richelieu, circa 1800, together with two others and a bowler. (Christie's) $65

A top hat of grey beaver, 7½in. high, circa 1830. (Christie's) $426

HATS

English early 17th century man's neglige cap in white linen worked with gilt chain-stitch. $10,000

A black satin bonnet trimmed with pleating, circa 1880. (Christie's) $26

A child's or young lady's hat of ivory silk quilted with a scale design and trimmed with a rosette of ivory ribbons, circa 1820. (Christie's) $655

A straw bonnet with deep brim, trimmed later with satin with chine silk ribbon and artificial flowers, circa 1830. (Christie's) $340

Moss Bros. grey felt top hat, complete with box. $52

A bonnet of brown striped plaited straw trimmed with brown figured ribbons, edged with a fringe, circa 1850. (Christie's) $65

A 16th century man's embroidered cap embellished with sequins and gold lace trim, England, 8in. high. (Robt. W. Skinner Inc.) $10,000

Dunn & Co. felt bowler hat. $28

A lady's flat wide-brimmed hat of black figured silk laid over plaited straw, circa 1770, 15¼in. diam. (Christie's) $876

HELMETS

Historians now say that the legend about Viking warriors wearing horned helmets is a myth but it is certain that protective helmets for the face and head have been worn by warriors since earliest times and finely wrought helmets and face masks turn up in Greek burial sites and on old Roman camps. The workmanship was of top quality and it is obvious that helmet making was a highly regarded skill. Helmets treasured by collectors range from Cromwellian troopers' helmets to the wartime tin hats worn by air raid wardens. There is a huge range from which to choose and some people can be lucky enough to find one in the trenches of the land fought over during the First World War or on the site of a bygone battle — particularly Border reivers' helmets. Some of the most impressive and elaborate are those made with face guards and manufactured by skilled German helmet makers or by Turkish or Persian manufacturers. The Germans were particularly good at making fearsome masks that struck fear in the hearts of opponents.

A Prussian Infantryman's ersatz (pressed felt) pickelhaube of The 87th Infantry Regt. (Wallis & Wallis) $432

A closed cuirassier's Savoyard type burgonet with raised comb and pointed peak. (Christie's) $1,909

An early 17th century pikeman's pot helmet, formed in two pieces with engraved line decoration and brass rivets. (Wallis & Wallis) $455

A Prussian NCO's lance cap of The 1st Guard Uhlan Regt. (Wallis & Wallis) $1,040

HELMETS

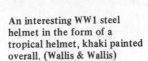

An officer's 1855 pattern shako bearing gilt plate of the 82nd Regiment with VR cypher on the gilt ball, upper lining missing. (Christie's) $728

An interesting WW1 steel helmet in the form of a tropical helmet, khaki painted overall. (Wallis & Wallis) $100

A good other ranks helmet of the 1st Dragoon Guards, brass skull and fittings, brass and white metal helmet plate, red horse hair plume. (Phillips) $810

A Prussian M.1915 Ersatz (Pressed Felt) O.R's Pickelhaube of a Pioneer Battalion. (Wallis & Wallis) $245

A good Spanish Officers shako, fawn cloth, leather peak and headband, simulated leather top. (Wallis & Wallis) $380

A Hesse M. 1915 Infantryman's Pickelhaube, grey painted helmet plate and mounts leather lining and chinstrap. (Wallis & Wallis) $260

Queen's Own Cameron Highlanders: officer's feather bonnet by W. Cater, Pall Mall. (Christie's) $584

A well made modern copy of an English close helmet from a Greenwich armour, of good form and weight. (Wallis & Wallis) $500

A Cabasset circa 1600, formed in one piece with 'pear stalk' finial, plain narrow brim. (Wallis & Wallis) $230

HELMETS

A large round black hat with pale drab cotton cover bearing a large elaborate badge in wire embroidery of the Bersaglieri. (Christie's) $127

An English civil war period pikeman's 'pot', made in two pieces with sunken edges and steel rivetted borders. (Wallis & Wallis) $800

An Italian black velvet fez by Unione Militare, Roma with an embroidered badge surmounted by Fasces. (Christie's) $218

An officer's bearskin cap of the Royal Welsh Fusiliers with fine white metal mounted gilt grenade. (Christie's) $475

A Bavarian M.1915 Uhlan ORs Tschapska, grey painted helmet plate and mounts. (Wallis & Wallis) $315

5th (Northumberland Fusiliers): officer's bearskin cap with regimental gilt grenade, inside is marked H.W. Archer, Esq., 5th Fusiliers. (Christie's) $639

A very rare helmet of an experimental pattern for French Dragoon regiments circa 1900, bearing manufacturer's stamp: B. Franck et ses fils, Aubervilliers. (Christie's) $728

An interesting composite close helmet made up for the Pisan Bridge Festival, the skull from a very rare Milanese armet circa 1440-1450. (Wallis & Wallis) $2,750

A Rifles officer's Astrakhan busby, a tunic with scarlet facings and a composite pouchbelt with a whistle, chin-boss and badge. (Christie's) $435

251

HMS INVINCIBLE ARTEFACTS

HMS Invincible started life in the French Navy in 1744 and was captured by the British Channel Fleet under Anson in 1747 at the Battle of Cape Finisterre. Commissioned into the British Navy, the revolutionary 74-gun Invincible was to have been Admiral Hardy's flagship in the expedition against the French in Canada in 1758. She ran aground on Horsetail Sandbank in the Channel, where, despite attempts to refloat her, she went down on 22 February.

A wooden gun tackle single block with 1¼in. sheave, stamped 'X', 10in. long. (Christie's) $744

A gun cartridge piercing spike with turned beech wood handle, 4in. long, (spike broken). (Christie's) $509

A leather shoe of welt construction, the uppers partially cut away, 9in. long. (Christie's) $1,076

A stoneware jug complete with handle and lipped neck, 9½in. high. (Christie's) $1,468

One of two wicker baskets, one with both handles. (Christie's) $117

One of two cast iron grenades both with wooden fuses, one marked 'X' and one with canvas fuse cover. (Christie's) $1,566

An elm clew block, without pin or sheave, stamped 'XVI', 16in. long. (Christie's) $881

252

A single pulley block with 2¼in. lignum vitae sheave, stamped 'XVIII', 18in. long. (Christie's) $430

Part of a set of parrel tackle comprising two bars of ash or elm, 12in. long, and two trucks, 2¾in. long, and another similar. (Christie's) $391

A sailor's square wooden dinner plate, with fiddle, 11¾ x 11¾in. (Christie's) $1,664

A spirit barrel of approx. 2 gals. capacity, built of fourteen oak staves originally bound with four iron hoops, 17½in. high. (Christie's) $430

A stave built oak save-all or bucket, with wicker binding and pegged oak bottom, and remains of original rope handle, 10¼in. high x 14½in. diam. (Christie's) $352

A 14-second sand glass, the case with turned oak ends, four pine struts and beech packing, 5½in. high. (Christie's) $5,482

An elm clew block with 2in. lignum vitae sheave, stamped 'XVI', 16½in. long. (Christie's) $587

A leather firebucket with stitched sides and bottom, complete with handle, 10in. high, (restored). (Christie's) $1,272

A 32-pounder gun ramrod head stamped '32' and 'I', 6in. diam. (Christie's) $509

HOLD TO LIGHT POSTCARDS

These cards reveal a 'surprise' when held to the light. There are transparencies, which appear 'normal' until held to the light, and cut-outs, which have cut out sections in the form of flames, moons, windows, etc. forming a source of light. Some noted publishers include Hartmann (transparencies), Samuel Cupples (particularly 1904 World's Fair cards) and Meteor Transparencies. Look for Father Christmas cards ($75 plus) and date letter and flame cut-out cards at about $25.

'Behind these naughty children throw a light and you will see them have their bolster fight' $18

'A Happy Christmas', 1905. $12

'A Merry Christmas', Cat hold to light. $12

'Hearty Wishes for Christmas', hold to light card printed in Germany. $10

'A Happy New Year, With Best Wishes', printed in Germany. $9

'A Bright and Happy Christmas', by D.R.G.M. $9

'A Merry Christmas', Windmill hold to light. $10

254

ICONS

An icon is an image or portrait figure, generally one of the sacred personages of the Eastern Church. The subjects are usually Christ, the Virgin, the saints or scenes of religious life and they are always rendered in flat painting in tempera on wood or in very low relief. Sometimes haloes are applied in gold and icons may be studded with precious stones. These religious paintings have been produced by monks of the Orthodox Church since early times and the work was often regarded as an offering towards the discipline of a life of contemplation. Icons are usually set in a flat frame and are often quite small for they were intended to be carried from place to place. The frames themselves can be of great beauty and are often made of precious metal and sometimes also jewelled. An icon set in a triple frame and opening like a screen is called a triptych. They can often be seen set up as objects of worship on church altars. Some icons are of exquisite workmanship and are extremely valuable, especially Russian ones dating from between the 10th and 17th centuries.

A 19th century icon of The Mother of God 'Helper of Those Who Are Lost', 53.5 x 45cm. $1,267

A 19th century Palekh School icon, depicting St. Roman in a wooded landscape, by Ovchinnikov, 17.5 x 11cm. (Phillips) $2,934

The Hodigitria Mother of God, inscribed 'through the hand of Nicholas Lamboudi of Sparta', 15th century, 67 x 47.5cm. $28,512

A Russian icon: The Mother of God Vladimirskaya, Moscow 1861, maker's mark cyrillic I.A., 31 x 27cm. (Lawrence Fine Art) $1,337

Early 17th century icon of St. Onouphrios The Great, signed by E. Lambardos, 55.5 x 36.5cm. $60,192

The Kazan Mother of God, maker's mark of I. A. Alexceev, Moscow, 1908-17, 27.3 x 22.7cm. $1,267

255

A 19th century icon of The Kazan Mother of God, 31 x 26.4cm. $760

An icon of Christ Pantocrator, maker's mark of F.V., Moscow 1830, 32 x 27cm. $1,980

The Virgin Hodigitria, Cretan, 1480-1520, 40.5 x 32.5cm. $7,268

The Mother of God of the Burning Bush, bearing fake assay marks for Moscow, 1908-1917, 71 x 57cm. $5,702

Saint Sergei of Radonejh, maker's mark S.G., Moscow 1908-26, 31 x 27cm. $1,029

An icon of the 'Six Days' (Shestodnev), 19th century, 53 x 44cm. $1,663

An icon of Christ Pantocrator, maker's mark E.U., Moscow, 1899-1908, 22.5 x 17.8cm. $712

A 19th century Russian icon of St. Nicholas the Miracle Worker, maker's mark for N. Dubrovin over 1830, 12½ x 10¾in. (Robt. W. Skinner Inc.) $300

Saint Nicholas, probably Byzantine, early 15th century, shown bust length, 36.5 x 27.5cm. $4,118

INROS

Japanese artistry is shown at its finest in the making of tiny things like netsuke and inros. Inros are slim, rectangular lacquered boxes which were used by men for carrying their family seal, any medicine they needed and their tobacco. These boxes were worn hanging from the belt beside the sword and they were in general use between the 16th and 19th centuries. Most inros were made in three or five sections which slotted neatly together. Cords were threaded through the sides of the box and each cord was secured in place by a bead called the ojime. The knot between the inro and the belt was kept in place by a netsuke, carved in wood or ivory and always in delightful shapes — monkeys, old men, wrestlers, deer, fish — made with wonderful skill and humour.

A 19th century four-case inro with a spherical red glass ojime and a manju netsuke. (Christie's) $6,292

Late 18th/early 19th century four-case nashiji inro, unsigned. (Christie's) $4,114

A 19th century small Roiro two-case inro of fluted fan-shaped form, unsigned. (Christie's) $755

A 19th century four-case Roiro inro with fundame compartments, signed Koma Kyuhaku saku. (Christie's) $4,719

A 19th century bamboo Kodansu inro, signed Toyo and Kao, with a bone ojime attached. (Christie's) $2,516

A 19th century four-case inro decorated in gold taka-makie and inlaid with coral, amber, metal and other materials, 7.2cm. long. (Christie's) $2,431

INSTRUMENTS

There is a huge collecting market for scientific instruments. They range from architects' or surveyors' sets to ships' chronometers and many are appearing on the market now because they have been usurped by electronic gadgets which do the job but do not look nearly as decorative. Microscopes are particularly popular with collectors but they have to be at least early 19th century and made of brass to be worth serious money because later students' microscopes had cast iron bases and struts. Telescopes are much sought after, especially again if brass mounted and collectors long to find long pull-out telescopes dating from the early 19th century which we imagine Nelson raising to his blind eye. There is a huge range of instruments to pick from — theodolites, circumferentors, equatorial dials and graphometers as well as early telephones, typewriters and Morse telegraph keys which were made of brass as well. Some instruments date from early times like a writing duplicator that was in use in the 18th century and was used to copy letters in the days before carbon paper.

A brass transit theodolite by Cooke Troughton & Simms Ltd., London, in mahogany case, 5¼in. wide. (Christie's) $616

An early 19th century lacquered brass and mahogany vacuum pump, 18¾in. long, with an extensive collection of accessories. (Christie's) $8,298

A Country painted globe, New England, circa 1810, 15in. diam., 37in. high. (Robt. W. Skinner Inc.) $5,500

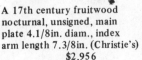

A 17th century fruitwood nocturnal, unsigned, main plate 4.1/8in. diam., index arm length 7.3/8in. (Christie's) $2,956

A pair of early Victorian terrestrial and celestial globes, by Malby & Son, London, dated 1850. (Lacy Scott) $2,227

Late 19th century sectional model of the eye, the plaster body decorated in colours and with glass lenses, 6¾in. high. (Christie's) $541

A 16th/17th century Italian ship's drycard compass, 11cm. diam. (Phillips) $6,200

A small one-day marine chronometer by John Roger Arnold, the dial 64mm. diam. (Christie's) $3,732

An 18th century brass combined analemmatic and inclining dial, signed M:Semah Aboab tot Amsterdam, 185mm. long. (Christie's) $6,600

Late 18th century brass transit instrument, signed Lenoir (Paris), on circular base with three levelling screws, the telescope 53.5cm. long. (Christie's) $3,080

A 19th century brass theodolite, signed by Troughton & Simms, 9½in. high. (Christie's) $811

A lacquered brass compound monocular microscope, by Powell & Lealand, 1901, 49cm. high, in case. (Phillips) $4,650

A gilt brass pedometer, German, possibly Augsburg, circa 1700, 65mm. long. (Christie's) $1,100

A Cary brass sextant with gold scale, numbered 3856, 11¾ x 11¼in. (Lawrence Fine Art) $1,929

A late 19th century oxidized brass surveying aneroid barometer, by Pidduck & Sons, Hanley, 6in. diam. (Christie's) $211

INSTRUMENTS

A 17th century engraved silver and gilt brass geared astronomical dial, signed Ph. Dagoneau, Grenoble, 13.8cm. diam. (Christie's) $5,500

Early 19th century lacquered brass universal equinoctial ring dial, signed Dollond, London, in original fishskin covered case, 9½in. diam. (Christie's) $5,772

An early marine chronometer by John Arnold & Son, with 4½in. circular silvered dial, in mahogany box. (Phillips) $11,600

An ivory diptych dial, with the thrush trademark of Hans Troschel, Nuremburg, dated 1649, 4¼in. long. (Christie's) $2,420

A 19th century brass double-rack action twin cylinder vacuum pump, unsigned, 14in. high. (Christie's) $992

A lacquered brass precision balance, the beam stamped To Weigh/To Grain, No. 5962, with electrical attachments in a glazed mahogany case, 14¾in. wide. (Christie's) $278

A brass cased dip-circle by F. E. Becker & Co., on adjustable stand, 10¾in. high. (Christie's) $528

Early 19th century brass compound monocular microscope, probably English, length of tube 17.3cm. (Christie's) $605

A Betts's portable terrestrial globe arranged so as to fold like an umbrella, 15in. diam. (Christie's) $563

IVORY

Ivory comes from the tusks of the elephant, the hippopotamus or the walrus and it has always been highly prized because it is an ideal material for carving. Different animal tusks provide different colors and qualities of ivory and that of the African elephant is most desirable because it is whiter than the ivory from the tusks of Indian elephants which has a yellowish tinge. The desirability of African Ivory has meant that elephants have had to be protected but smugglers are systematically destroying the herds that used to roam the Continent.

In past times however there was no proscription against the taking of ivory and some magnificent pieces can be found in the shape of figures, boxes, knife handles, combs, buttons, fan sticks, umbrella handles, toilet articles. Sailors on long sea voyages used to spend their spare time carving walrus' horns with intricate patterns and their work is called scrimshaw. Ivory inlaid with designs in precious metals is called Shibayama after a Japanese family who excelled at the work. Unsuspecting buyers are often offered to fake pieces of ivory because plastic can be made to look almost authentic but one test is infallible — plastic melts and ivory does not so a hot needle pressed against the base of a piece will prove authenticity immediately.

A Napoleonic prisoner-of-war period bone-ivory games box, raised on four cabriole legs, 8½in. wide. (Christie's) $1,386

Pair of 19th century carved ivory figures of a swain and his lass, 14cm. high. (Phillips) $1,793

Late 19th century stained ivory group of four children playing beside a drum, 21cm. high. (Christie's) $2,618

IVORY

A 19th century German miniature ivory tankard with silvered metal mounts, 10.5cm. high. (Christie's) $3,674

Late 18th century ivory Kitsune mask, 3.5cm. high. (Christie's) $345

A 19th century carved ivory bust of a bishop in the Gothic style, on silver metal base with lion supports at each corner, 16cm. high. (Phillips) $896

Late 19th century ivory carving of a farmer holding a birdcage, 33cm. high. (Christie's) $2,640

An 18th century ivory work-box of octagonal form, 22.5cm. wide. (Phillips) $684

Late 19th century ivory carving of a hunter, signed Kozan saku, 22cm. high. (Christie's) $792

A pair of curved ivory elephant tusks on ebonised bases, 6ft. high, overall. (Prudential Fine Art) $2,788

Late 19th century boxwood, rootwood and ivory group of doves attending their young, signed Mitsuhiro, 49cm. high. (Christie's) $18,700

An ivory carving of a sennin, eyes inset in dark horn, stylised seal mark, 20.5cm. high. (Christie's) $935

A 19th century ivory okimono of a farmer with a fox and a hare, dressed as humans, 6cm. high. (Christie's) $748

A 19th century ivory mask of a Buaku, signed Ryuraku, 3.8cm. high, (age cracks). (Christie's) $566

A 19th century German carved ivory lidded tankard with caryatid handle, 13¾in. high. (Capes Dunn) $8,055

Late 19th century ivory carving of a scholar, signed Akira, 26cm. high. (Christie's) $704

A pair of Chinese 19th century ivory handscreens with ivory handles hung with ornaments and silk tassels, 13½in. long, contained in a fitted brocade case. (Christie's) $1,870

Late 19th century ivory carving of a kannon, signed Masayuki, 33cm. high, wood stand. (Christie's) $4,114

A 19th century Dieppe ivory tazza, by E. Blard, 17.5cm. high. (Christie's) $2,204

A 19th century Japanese ivory group on wood stand, signed, 8¾in. high. (Capes Dunn) $841

A 19th century Japanese ivory tusk vase, 12in. high, with a lobed wooden base and wood stand, 23in. high overall. (Capes Dunn) $501

JADE

Jade comes in three different types — jadeite which is white with a purple tint or more commonly emerald green. Jadeite is the finest jade that can be found. Nephrite, also green but not so vivid, is a type of jade that has been worked since ancient times and chromoelite is so very dark green that it looks almost black. Jade is mined in Burma, India, Turkestan, Siberia, New Zealand, Silesia and Alaska but strangely not in China although jade is a material highly prized by Chinese people. They imported it from very early times and carved it into a large variety of beautiful objects. It is soft and easy to work and Chinese jade carvers have been perhaps the most skilled in the world. The beauty and intricacy of their work has never been surpassed.

A Mogul dark celadon jade ewer of oval octafoil cross-section, 17th/18th century, 15.5cm. high. (Christie's) $7,840

An early celadon and russet jade burial cicada, Han Dynasty or earlier, 5cm. wide. (Christie's) $570

A celadon lobed hexafoil dish, Northern Song Dynasty, 17.4cm. diam. (Christie's) $8,553

A pale celadon jade model of two mythical birds feeding from a branch of peaches, 6¾in. wide, on wood stand. (Christie's) $3,480

A pale celadon jade tripod libation vessel carved with a single bracket handle, Qianlong seal mark, 13.4cm. high. (Christie's) $6,032

A jade figure of a crouching Buddhistic lion, probably Han/Six Dynasties, 6.8cm. wide. (Christie's) $1,140

JADE

A pale celadon jade figure of a recumbent horse, Yuan Dynasty, 4.6cm. long. (Christie's) $2,143

A jade figure of a recumbent horse, Tang/Song Dynasty, 6.5cm. long. (Christie's) $1,140

A celadon jade brush washer modelled as a pressed hollowed melon, 3in. wide. (Christie's) $986

An 18th century flecked celadon and russet jade box and cover, 8cm. wide, with fitted box. (Christie's) $641

A pale celadon and brown jade vase, 17th/18th century, 12.5cm. high, with wood stand. (Christie's) $7,128

An early celadon jade circular disc, bi, Han Dynasty, 10.7cm. diam., in fitted box.(Christie's) $3,564

An archaic jade pierced circular disc, bi, Zhou Dynasty, 16cm. diam. (Christie's) $1,111

A Longquan celadon yanyan vase, early 14th century, 26.5cm. high. (Christie's) $3,991

A small Longquan celadon jarlet and lotus-moulded cover, 13th/14th century, 7.5cm. high. (Christie's) $1,568

JEWELRY

Of all the artefacts we have inherited from antiquity perhaps jewelry is in greatest supply, thanks to our ancient forebears' obliging custom of burying their dead in company with their valuables! In fact, the durability of precious metals and stones means that plenty of examples exist from all periods.

Jewelry is essentially a fashion accessory and, leaving aside the intrinsic value of the materials, fashion still to a degree dictates what fetches top sums at any time.

To hedge against such vicissitudes, the golden rule when collecting should always be to buy the best you can afford, such as base gold and silver rather than base metal. Very interesting collections can, however, be made out of more unusual items, such as jet, amber, hair brooches or mourning rings. There are possibilities for all tastes and pockets.

Three-stone ring with a total of 3¼ct. claw set in white metal. (Peter Wilson) $2,961

Sapphire and diamond ear-clips, 'Yard', the oval sapphires weighing approx. 5ct. (Robt. W. Skinner Inc.) $5,000

Gold stickpin, set with a large realistically rendered gold 'fly'. (Robt. W. Skinner Inc.) $250

Art Deco diamond bow pin, pave-set with 105 diamonds weighing approx. 3.00ct. and highlighted by calibre cut onyx. (Robt. W. Skinner Inc.) $3,600

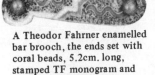

A gold, diamond and plique-a-jour pendant fashioned as a seagull in flight, 7.5cm. wide, probably French. (Phillips) $576

A Theodor Fahrner enamelled bar brooch, the ends set with coral beads, 5.2cm. long, stamped TF monogram and indistinct 925. (Phillips) $360

An Arts & Crafts brooch, possibly Birmingham Guild of Handicrafts, 4cm. diam. (Phillips) $108

A George Hunt enamelled and gemset locket pendant of oval shape, inside is a lock of hair, 8.5cm. long. (Phillips) $1,008

An enamelled and garnet set 'Gothic' brooch, based on a design by A. W. N. Pugin, 4.5cm. across. (Phillips) $504

A Tiffany & Co. two-colour gold, sapphire and moonstone oval brooch, 3.3cm. across. (Phillips) $1,008

A sunray brooch, centring an opal with diamond set cluster and rays, gold set, in Goldsmiths & Silversmiths case. (Woolley & Wallis) $1,490

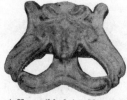

A Kerr gilded Art Nouveau brooch, 6.5cm. across, stamped with maker's mark, Sterling and 1702. (Phillips) $432

A German 'Egyptianesque' plique-a-jour brooch, formed as a scarab, 11cm. wide. (Phillips) $547

A Liberty & Co. gold sapphire and moonstone pendant, probably designed by A. Gaskin, 5cm. long, 15ct. (Phillips) $547

Antique gold and diamond brooch, French hallmarks, designed as a French poodle. (Robt. W. Skinner Inc.) $1,000

Enamelled diamond ring on an 18ct. gold band, English hallmark. (Robt. W. Skinner Inc.) $800

A silver brooch, stamped Georg Jensen 300 and with London import marks for 1965. (Christie's) $117

14ct. gold and diamond ring, the centre oval gold plaque with tiny raised 'fly' encircled in a frame of diamonds. (Robt. W. Skinner Inc.) $850

Cultured pearl and diamond necklace, 'Cartier', a double strand of 86, 9mm. pearls, the diamonds weighing approx. 2.20ct. (Robt. W. Skinner Inc.) $7,000

Art Deco emerald and diamond ring, diamonds weighing a total of approx. 2ct. (Robt. W. Skinner Inc.) $1,100

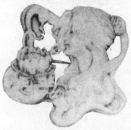

An Unger Brothers Art Nouveau brooch, 5.5cm. across, stamped 925 Sterling fine. (Phillips) $360

A plique-a-jour pin with fresh-water pearls, probably French, circa 1910, marked 800, 1½in. long. (Robt. W. Skinner Inc.) $200

9ct. gold and plique-a-jour Art Nouveau wing brooch in Egyptian style, 4¼in. wide, maker's mark HL conjoined. (Capes Dunn) $547

A Russian diamond, sapphire, ruby and plique-a-jour enamel moth brooch, St. Petersburg maker's mark JV. (Lawrence Fine Art) $16,661

An early George III moss agate and garnet ring on a gold shank with memorial inscription and dated 1765. (Lawrence Fine Art) $514

A 19th century sapphire and diamond frog brooch, set in silver and gold. (Dreweatt Neate) $6,358

An emerald and diamond cluster ring, in a basket mount on a plain gold shank. (Lawrence Fine Art) $1,357

An oval diamond set gold mounted shell cameo brooch, 1¾in. high. (Christie's) $2,860

Zuni silver and turquoise bracelet, openwork silver cuff, 3¼in. diam. (Robt. W. Skinner Inc.) $650

A 19th century oval gold mounted onyx cameo pendant brooch, the frame set with pearls and with black enamel ropework, 2½in. high. (Christie's) $1,650

An old cut diamond and pearl three stone ring, centre stone approx. 1.65ct. (Dreweatt Neate) $3,459

A Murrle Bennett gold wirework oval brooch, with opal matrix and four seed pearls, stamped MB monogram and 15ct. on the pin, circa 1900. (Christie's) $336

A diamond bracelet composed of 17 graduated stones in a half-hoop gold setting. (Morphets) $2,537

JIGSAW PUZZLES

A London map maker invented the first jig-saw puzzle in the 1760's by mounting a map on a sheet of mahogany and cutting it into small pieces with a fine marquetry saw. The reassembling of it was intended to help pupils learn geography. He sold his "dissecting maps" in wooden boxes with sliding lids and his idea was copied by other manufacturers. These early jig-saws were all hand made and quite expensive to buy but their popularity with the public was immediate. Pictures made into puzzles dealt with religious themes or history and mythology. The best known early makers whose work is eagerly sought after by collectors were J. Wallis, W. Darton, J.W. Barfoot, W. Peacock, Dean & Son and J. Betts.

At the end of the 19th century, colored labels showing the finished puzzle were pasted on box lids and they are worth collecting on their own. Mass production techniques and the use of plywood and fret saws meant that it was possible to turn out large numbers of puzzles at a fairly low cost and jig-saws became a craze in the 1920's and 30's before the advent of television. Some of the most famous firms who produced them were Raphael Tuck who made the Zag Zaw; Chad Valley who produced jig-saws for Great Eastern Railway and steamship lines like Cunard and the White Star Line; Frederic Warne who were also the publishers of Peter Rabbit; Victory; Holtsapffel whose puzzles were given the name 'Figure It Out'; Salman; Delta Fine Cut; Huvanco and A.V.N. Jones.

'Ireland' — for teaching youth geography, circa 1820. Unknown, probably William Darton, some replacement pieces and missing necks, 11 x 10in. $215

'Venice', Vera Picture Puzzle, made in France, 1930's, and box, finely cut, with contour cutting and shapes, difficult. Made specially for Truslove & Hansen of London SW1, 9 x 12in. $35

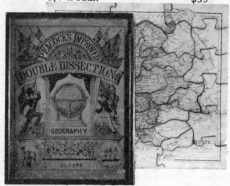

Peacocks Improved 'Double Dissection', Europe on one side, Nursery rhymes on the other. Puzzles cut in sympathy with the map (ie round borders) with large interlocking edge pieces to hold it all together, circa 1895, fine hand-coloured label to whitewood box lid, 11x12in.
$245

(Trench Enterprises)

'Aladdin meets the Sultan's daughter', Huvarco puzzle, 1920's/30's, no box (often Huvarco puzzles were sold ready-made-up and without a box). $45

'De Dame Te Amsterdam', Dutch made puzzle, 1930's. Amateur, but intricately cut (not a manufactured puzzle), difficult, 10 x 13in. $35

'Cunard Liner Berengaria', Chad Valley for Cunard Steam Ship Co., 12 x 16in., with box. $60

'Changing the Guard at Buckingham Palace', Raphael Tuck military puzzle, 1930's distinctive style of cut different to their two styles of zag zaw puzzle (one of which is interlocking, the other push-fit, but both of which include intricate shapes), 15 x 10in., with box. $35

'Washington returning from Fox Hunt', Parker Brothers pastime puzzle and box (USA). 1920-1930's. Finely cut with shapes and colour contoured, a difficult puzzle, 10 x 13in. $50

(Trench Enterprises)

'The History of Joseph and his Brethren', circa 1835. Unknown maker, possibly Edward Wallis. Hand coloured wood blocks, plain mahogany box, lacking original label, 9 x 10in. $350

'The Edge of the Common', Chandos puzzle (F. Hanse), 1920's/30's, 11 x 17in., and box. $70

'King George V loco', Chad Valley for the Great Western Railway Co. 1930's, 8 x 22in. overall, contoured edge, hand coloured photographic print, and box. $80

'Daffodils', Chad Valley 1920's (early Chad Valley cutting style), 14 x 10in. with box. $45

'At Pharaoh's Court', Victory artistic puzzle, 1950's, 14 x 18in. with box. No guide picture is supplied with these puzzles, which include strips of traditional victory shapes amongst the interlocking pieces. $35

(Trench Enterprises)

JUKE BOXES

The upsurge in nostalgia for the Rock 'n' Roll era has made its archetypal symbol, the juke box, into one of the most highly profiled of modern collectables. Collecting, however, does not come cheap, and the costs are not for the faint hearted, with prices starting at around $3,500 and extending well into five figures. The aesthetics have to appeal to you as well — few people are fortunate enough to have space for their own museum, and most collectors share their living rooms, bedrooms and even bathrooms with these large, often gaudy and never unobtrusive items.

One of the bonuses for the collector is that, hopefully, his treasure will be in working order, and may even come ready stocked with discs — an instant nostalgia trip at the touch of a button.

Chantal Meteor, produced England, 1958-1963, 200 selections at 45rpm.
$8,750

Wurlitzer model 1015, produced USA, 1946-1947, 24 selections at 78rpm., plays A sides only. $19,250

Wurlitzer model 2500S, produced USA, 1961, 200 selections at 45rpm.
$3,850

AMI model B, produced USA, 1947-1948, 40 selections at 78rpm. $8,750

AMI Continental 1, produced USA, 1961, 200 selections at 45rpm. $4,900

Wurlitzer model 1400, produced USA, 1951, 48 selections at 78rpm.
$6,125

(The Chicago Sound Co.)

Seeburg Symphonola 148, produced USA, 1948, plays A sides only, 20 selections at 78rpm. $7,875

Wurlitzer model 1800, produced USA, 1955, 104 selections at 45rpm. $6,125

Wurlitzer model 1550, produced USA, 1952-1953, 104 selections at both 78rpm. and 45rpm. $5,250

AMI model I 200, produced USA, 1958, also in England as BAL AMI I 200, 200 selections at 45rpm. $5,250

Wurlitzer model 1050, produced USA, 1973-1974, 100 selections at 45rpm. $8,750

Rock-ola 1428, produced USA, 1948, plays A sides only, 20 selections at 78rpm. $10,500

Mills Empress, produced USA, 1939, plays A sides only, 20 selections at 78rpm. $12,250

AMI model A, produced USA, 1946, 40 selections at 78rpm. $9,625

Wurlitzer model 1100, produced USA, 1947-1949, 24 selections at 78rpm., plays A sides only. $11,900

(The Chicago Sound Co.)

KITCHEN EQUIPMENT

If time could be turned back and the kitchens of Victorian homes could be recreated in their entirety, antique collectors would be in heaven because there is no room more likely to yield treasures than the kitchen. From copper jelly moulds to apple corers, from wire baskets used to store eggs or boil potatoes to huge copper fish steamers, from black leaded ranges to pottery water filters, almost everything in an old kitchen is worth money today. Artistry and care marked the production of each piece, even the stamps used for making embossed butter balls were hand carved with the symbols of roses or thistles. Copper pots were beaten out by hand and when the cook set a rabbit mould it was left to cool in a copper mould in the shape of a crouching rabbit. The price of copper utensils has soared to a tremendous level but there are many other small items which can still be used today and can be picked up for very little. Look for prettily painted tin tea caddies; look for white enamel bread bins with pretty blue lettering; serving spoons with long curved handles; white pottery jelly moulds and wooden draining racks. Also desirable are old fashioned mincers and glass butter churns with a metal fly wheel mounted on the screw top lid. An early 20th century juice extractor with a long handle and a metal bowl for squeezing oranges is worth at least $10. More expensive are knife grinders with large wooden drums and iron crank handles which were turned to sharpen the kitchen knives placed blade down inside.

Plated tin Mouli grater. $9

Victorian enamel slop bucket complete with lid. $35

Victorian blue enamel kettle. $18

A portable plated candle holder, 6in. high, circa 1915. $9

Victorian white enamel jug. $9

Set of three early 20th century tin shredders. $9

274

A late Victorian brass coal box with domed lid and pierced finial, 17in. wide. (Christie's) $551

Late 18th century cast iron bake kettle, original fitted cover with deep flange, 13¼in. deep. (Robt. W. Skinner Inc.) $325

Late 18th century wrought iron broiler, probably Pennsylvania, 20in. long. (Robt. W. Skinner Inc.) $360

Victorian pressed brass bellows, circa 1880. (British Antique Exporters) $33

An attractive butter crock manufactured by The Caledonian Pottery, Rutherglen, 5in. high. $260

Pair of 18th century brass table candlesticks with baluster stems, 11in. high. (Hobbs & Chambers) $172

A mid Victorian black and gilt japanned tole purdonium, with shovel, 12½in. wide. (Christie's) $597

A National currant cleaner by Parnall, Bristol. $85

A Victorian copper oval jelly mold, orb and scepter mark, 5.5in. high. (Woolley & Wallis) $140

Victorian polished steel coal scuttle with a lifting flap and shovel. (Lots Road Galleries) $144

Early 19th century copper coal helmet, also a matching shovel, 17½in. high. (Peter Wilson) $616

A Regency brass tea urn with raised and pierced lid, 13in. high. (Christie's) $225

An early coffee grinder by Parnall. $130

A James I iron fireback. (Russell Baldwin & Bright) $500

A Benham & Froud brass kettle designed by Dr. C. Dresser, on three spiked feet, 24.5cm. high. (Christie's) $473

Victorian brass preserving pan, 1850. (British Antique Exporters) $85

Victorian copper kettle, circa 1850. (British Antique Exporters) $85

An 18th century wrought iron bound salt bucket with swing handle, 7¼in. diam. (Christie's) $203

LABELS

As everyone in advertising knows, it is the label that often sells the goods and they have to be designed as eye-catchers. The designers of some labels made a speciality of turning them into an art and collectors seek out colorful cheese or perfume labels because of that. Perfume labels from the 1920's and '30's are particularly attractive when they were designed in Art Deco styles. The labels on fruit crates are also often very colorful and designed to convey the feeling of country freshness and sunshine. Orange and apple growers in the '40's and '50's would often buy a ready designed label and have it overprinted with the name of their farm or product so the same picture can be found bearing different names. Textile labels are also very appealing though most of them tend to rely on script rather than pictures. Other labels that are eagerly collected are those used for the first appearance of certain items — soap powders for example — or for items which no longer exist or are now packaged in a different way.

Textile label Bayette, registered in South Africa. $5

Columbia Belle Apples, Wenatchee, Washington, 1950's. $2

Raspberryade, Haworth & Sons. $1

Rosey Rapture, Cream Soda. $1

Worm Powder, W. H. Laverack & Son. $1

Haworth's Pineapple Crush. $1

Seltzer Water, Hopkinson & Co. $1

Tic and Nerve Powders, W.K. Harrison. $1

Elixir of Cascara Sagrada, John Baily & Co. $1

Rowntree's Windsor Mixture, 4lb. Base, 1890's. $2

Standard Jamaica Rum, Turnbull, Hawick, 1930's. $2

Yesterday's Paper

LABELS

Textile label Assegai
Fancy Prints, 1930.
$3.50

Rowntree's Ping Pong Biscuits, 1890's. $13

Turnbull's Scotch
Whisky, Hawick,
circa 1930. $2

Habana, Flor de Lopez
Hermanos. $6

Textile label Oubaas, 1930's. $4

Tadcaster Tower,
Lime Juice Cordial.
$1

Sparkling Cherry
Ciderette, non
alcoholic. $1

Soda Water, sparkling
and refreshing. $1

Haworth's Ginger
Ale, Pale Dry. $1

Old Fashioned
Stone Ginger Beer.
$1

Textile label Agrada,
registered in India,
1930's. $3.50

Rowntree's Homoeopathic Cocoa, 1890's. $9

The much improved
Fellon Drink, circa
1900. $3.50

Yesterday's Paper

278

LACQUER

Lacquering dates from around 400 BC, and involved applying up to 40 coats of resin from the Eastern lac tree, each rubbed to achieve a smooth surface. It was applied mainly to previously treated wooden surfaces, but it can also be used on metal, papier mache etc. Lacquerwork became very popular in the 1920's, with such craftsmen as Dunand, Gray and Printz providing beautiful lacquered furniture. Though black is the predominant colour, greens, ochres and yellows can be obtained.

Late 18th/early 19th century lacquer Chinese style fan (uchiwa), 43.7cm. long. (Christie's) $3,436

A red lacquer altar vase carved with eight Buddhist emblems, Qianlong seal mark and of the period, 24.5cm. high. (Christie's) $865

A Gyobu silver rimmed tebako decorated in gold takamakie with flowering peonies, circa 1800, 27.5 x 22.5 x 16.5cm. (Christie's) $6,996

A Momoyama period lacquer Christian shrine (seigan), 49.3cm. high. (Christie's) $101,088

Late 17th century Export lacquer cabinet, 74cm. high, with a fitted 18th century English japanned wood stand, 80cm. high. (Christie's) $6,121

A set of three mid Victorian black and gilt japanned papiermache oval trays, the largest 31in. wide. (Christie's) $1,861

A 19th century Chinese lacquered panel, 33 x 25in. (Dreweatts) $1,680

An early 19th century
Japanese black and gold
lacquer jardiniere, 20½in.
diam. (Christie's)
$2,674

A Korean inlaid black lacquer
hinged rectangular box and
cover, 17th/18th century,
21.8cm. wide. (Christie's)
$2,381

An 18th century Chinese 4½in.
circular red lacquer box.
(Parsons, Welch & Cowell)
$73

A 16th century inlaid black
lacquer four-tiered box and
cover, 27cm. high.
(Christie's) $1,142

A 19th century silver rimmed
fundame tebako, fitted wood
box, 24.2 x 19.1 x 12cm.
(Christie's) $11,368

A red and yellow lacquer six-
tiered square box and cover,
Ming Dynasty, 28.2cm. high.
(Christie's) $2,381

Early 19th century Chinese
Export lacquer picnic box,
15in. wide. (Christie's)
$708

A black and gold lacquer
tray decorated with chinoiserie figures in a landscape,
30in. wide. (Christie's)
$2,675

One of a pair of 19th century
Japanese lacquer picnic baskets, 52cm. high. (Phillips)
$1,453

LADIES UNDERWEAR

The existence of ladies' underwear was first documented in Sumeria around 3,000 BC. About a dozen pairs of monogrammed bloomers purporting to belong to Queen Victoria do turn up every year, and sell for around $500 a piece. Maybe the good lady wore each pair only once, or maybe there's a secret factory somewhere.... Other underwear with personal associations also fetches a premium. A pink mesh bra left by Marilyn Monroe in a London hairdresser's sold at auction for $1,000!

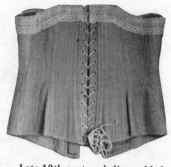

Late 19th century ladies padded corset, edged with lace. $100

Edwardian tie-back petticoat, pleated lace edged, muslin lined and with pocket. $45

Late Victorian nightdress with lace edging. $60

Victorian 'combination' with floral lace edge. $70

Dimety Bustle, with hide and fabric covered steel springs, circa 1880. $210

Edwardian camisole with ribbon and lace inserts.$50

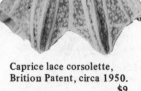

Caprice lace corsolette, Brition Patent, circa 1950. $9

(Kaleidoscope)

LADIES UNDERWEAR

Edwardian Camisole with knitted lace edge and hand stitched buttonholes. $45

Red flannel petticoat with dustcatching hem, circa 1880. $130

Late Victorian high necked corset cover with a lace edge and fabric covered buttons. $20

Late Victorian nightdress with embroidery anglais decoration and lace trimming. $50

1940's pink corset with elasticated waist and chrome fittings. $12

Edwardian combination with fine lace edging. $50

Linen petticoat decorated with embroidery anglais, circa 1912. $14

Victorian open gusset linen 'drawers' with embroidery anglais lace edge. $40

1940's lace edged camisole top. $18

(Kaleidoscope)

LALIQUE

The master of Art Nouveau glass and jewelry making was Rene Lalique (1860-1945). He started his career as a jeweller, using enamel and inlaid glass paste in his lovely creations which expressed the essential forms of Art Nouveau. In 1908 he opened a glass factory at Combs near Paris and turned out large quantities of moulded, pressed and engraved glass. He was especially interested in the technique of sand blasting which he used to create a look of opalescence. In the beginning he was a follower of Emile Galle but later he developed his own style and his greatest success stemmed from the elegant perfume bottles he created from the firm of Coty. He also made table glass, vases and frosted glass figures for car bonnets. The designs with which he embossed his pieces were elegant flowing representations of flowers, birds, fish, animals and female figures. Lalique signed every piece from his factory but after his death the initial R. was omitted from the signature.

'Camargue', a Lalique frosted glass vase, moulded with horses in amber stained cartouches, 28.5cm. high. (Christie's) $4,561

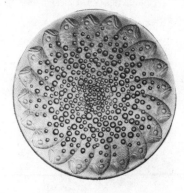

A large Lalique circular, blue opalescent dish, moulded on the underside with carp among bubbles, 35cm. diam. (Christie's) $1,188

A Lalique clear and frosted glass presse-papier, the plaque intaglio moulded with the figure of St. Christopher carrying the infant Christ, 4½in. high. (Christie's) $712

'Oran', a large Lalique opalescent glass vase moulded in relief with flower-heads and foliage, 26cm. high. (Christie's) $7,216

An Art Deco cocktail bar trolley, the bar handle flanked by two inset clear and satin glass panels by Lalique, 88cm. wide. (Christie's) $9,914

A Lalique table lamp, the clear satin finished glass with amber staining, 27.1cm. high. (Christie's) $3,775

'Caudebec', a Lalique vase
with two semi-circular
handles, 14.5cm. high.
(Christie's) $902

'Cote d'Azur Pullman Express',
a Lalique figure, the clear satin
finished glass moulded as a
naked maiden, 16.8cm. high.
(Christie's) $4,404

Lalique amber glass shell
duck ashtray, 2¾in. high.
(Reeds Rains) $186

'Martins Pecheurs', a black
Lalique vase, with impressed
signature R. Lalique, 23.5cm.
high. (Christie's) $8,659

A Lalique square-shaped
clock, Inseparables, the clear
and opalescent glass decorated
with budgerigars, 11cm. high.
(Christie's) $1,584

A Lalique vase, the satin
finished glass moulded
with marguerites, high-
lighted with amber stain-
ing, 20.5cm. high.
(Christie's) $902

'Bacchantes', a Lalique
opalescent glass vase moulded
in relief with naked female
dancing figures, 24.5cm. high.
(Christie's) $13,530

A Lalique glass inkwell.
(Hobbs Parker)
$1,890

'Rampillon', an opalescent
Lalique vase, 12.6cm. high.
(Christie's) $613

LAMPS

Victorian brass lamps with ornate glass bowls and the library lamps with shades like upturned flowers are worth a great deal of money but what are still sometimes overlooked are old brass carbide and Tilley lamps. About 1860 a popular lamp appeared that worked on acetylene. It had a small reservoir of water placed above a container filled with calcium carbide. Artists were always aware of the potential of lamps as objects of beauty but it was not until the arrival of glass workers like Daum, Galle and Tiffany that the art lamp really reached its highest point. These men with Gustav Girschner, Handel, Lalique and Loetz produced some beautiful lamps which fetch astronomical prices today. Tiffany's stained glass lamps decorated with flowers or his tall upstanding versions that look like clusters of lilies sell for thousands of dollars.

A Tiffany Studios enamelled copper electric lamp base, circa 1900, 15in. high. (Robt. W. Skinner Inc.)
$3,700

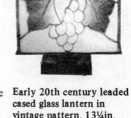

Early 20th century leaded cased glass lantern in vintage pattern, 13¼in. high, 9in. wide. (Robt. W. Skinner Inc.) $450

A 19th century dark blue tinted lacemaker's lamp, 27cm. high. (Christie's) $554

A Tiffany Studios 'lotus' leaded glass and bronze table lamp, 62.5cm. high. (Christie's) $15,048

Rudolph, a robot light fitting, designed by Frank Clewett, 149cm. high. (Christie's) $3,484

A Stilnova painted metal lamp, by Gaetano Scolari, Italy, circa 1959, 67cm. high. (Phillips) $174

A German Art Nouveau silvered pewter nautilus shell desk lamp, stamped M H 20, 27cm. high. (Christie's) $2,692

A Tiffany Studio lamp with green-blue Favrile glass moulded as a scarab, N.Y., circa 1902, 8½in. high. (Robt. W. Skinner Inc.) $3,000

A plated two-branch student's oil lamp with green tinted shades. (Peter Wilson & Co.) $244

A Doulton Flambe figure by Noke, modelled as a seated Buddha, mounted as a lamp, circa 1930, 57.5cm. high. (Christie's) $1,252

'Nymph among the bulrushes', a bronze table lamp cast after a model by Louis Convers, 28.1cm. high. (Christie's) $751

A copper and leaded glass piano lamp, cone-shaped slag glass shade, incised mark 'KK', 13¾in. high. (Robt. W. Skinner Inc.) $400

One of a pair of Tiffany Studios three-light, lily-gold favrile glass and bronze table lamps, 33.2cm. high. (Christie's) $6,336

A Continental porcelain oil lamp base in the form of a white owl with glass eyes, 17½in. high. (Dreweatts) $754

An Almaric Walter pate-de-verre and wrought iron lamp, the amber glass plaque moulded with a peacock, 27cm. high. (Christie's) $3,146

A brass and tole painted table lamp, 20in. high. (Christie's) $330

LAMPSHADES

The 20th century saw not only the introduction of electric lighting, but also a revolution in lighting fixtures. Lampshades have often aspired to works of art in their own right, through the designs of such masters as Lalique, Daum and Galle, while the Tiffany lamp has passed into standard parlance as a generic term. Through the 40's, 50's and 60's too, top designers have incorporated lamp fittings into their ranges, which have made these into the most exciting, practical and beautiful of collectables.

A Galle cameo glass flower form shade, the white body overlaid in deep pink/red/brown, circa 1900, 21.5cm. max. width. $1,237

A Tiffany Studios leaded glass shade, inset with a floral design in deep blue and mauve glass, circa 1900, 46cm. diam. $3,750

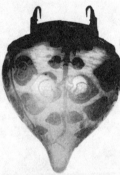

A Le Verre Francais cameo glass hanging lamp shade in the form of a strawberry overlaid in orange and blue, 30.9cm. high. (Christie's) $1,174

A large Daum cameo glass hanging lampshade of shallow domed form, 46cm. diam., signed. (Phillips) $3,024

A pendant lamp shade of shallow bowl shape, signed 'Maxonade Paris', 1ft.6in. diam. (Capes, Dunn & Co.) $231

A cameo glass hanging shade, attributed to Loetz, the mottled pink/white body overlaid in deep red, circa 1900/10, 40cm. max. width. $357

A Lalique opalescent glass hanging shade moulded with swags of fruit, circa 1930, 31cm. diam. $343

LEAD SOLDIERS

Toy maker William Britain launched his invention of hollow cast lead figures on the British toy market in 1893 and for the next sixty odd years until the use of lead in toys was discontinued for health reasons, his firm was first in the field of the production of toy soldiers. When the use of lead was banned, they became collectors' items and now they change hands for staggering sums, especially when it is considered that many of them cost only a penny when they were first bought.

Some of the most desirable are the mounted regiments of the British Army which Britain's introduced in the first year of production and also their sets of foreign regiments like South African Mounted Infantry, a set of which in its original box has sold for $1,000 . Britain's also made less usual sets like Salvation Army bandsmen which sold recently for $2,000.They continued to make toy soldiers up till the time of the Coronation of Queen Elizabeth II in 1953.

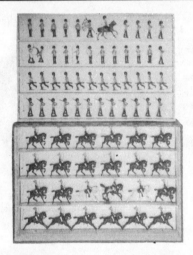

Large display box Set 93, containing Coldstream Guards with mounted officer, four pioneers, thirteen-piece band, two officers, twelve marching, twelve running, two trumpeters, six troopers and fifteen normal troopers, 1938. Britain's. (Phillips)
$11,550

Britains extremely rare display set 131, including cavalrymen, infantrymen, bandsmen, sailors and Camel Corps soldiers, the largest set ever made by Britains. (Phillips)
$17,500

Britains extremely rare Territorials in full dress standing at attention in red uniforms. (Phillips)
$5,103

Britains very rare set 1904, Officers and Men of the U.S. Army Air Corps, four positions, in original green box, 1940. (Phillips) $3,024

German made attractive first grade 52mm. hollowcast British Fusiliers at the slope with mounted officer, 1900. (Phillips) $283

Britains special paint originally from the Poitier-Smith Collection, Royal Horse Guards, 1937. (Phillips) $1,549

Rare set 1629, Lord Strathcona's Horse in original 'Types of the Canadian Forces' box, 1938. (Phillips) $3,402

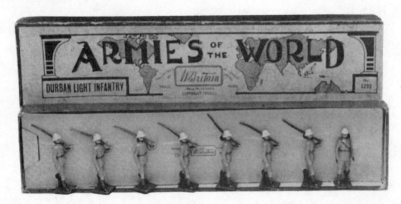

Britains rare set 1293, Durban Light Infantry at the slope, short trousers, unusual paint variation, 1934. (Phillips) $2,457

Britains, unusual set of British Infantry in steel helmets based on the U.S. Marine marching figure, one slight dent, 1940. (Phillips) $2,835

LOUIS WAIN POSTCARDS

Louis Wain (1860-1939) is best known for his illustrations of cats, usually displaying human characteristics. Several hundred of his postcard designs have been identified, and they were used by many publishers. His most famous series is probably the 'Amewsing Write-away' series. In later life Wain became mentally ill, though he continued to work, and his designs became increasingly bizarre. Condition is vital, and cards are generally worth less if the front is written on.

'Off for the Holidays in Style and Comfort', a rare plain black advertising card illustrated by Louis Wain. $60

'Bill Sykes', Tuck oilette card by Louis Wain. $38

'I wish you showers of Good Luck', by the Alphalsa Publishing Co. Ltd. $25

'My word that must have been a German mouse', Tuck's oilette card by Louis Wain. $28

'With best wishes for a Happy Christmas', card with plain back. $25

'Artists in Black and White', calendar postcard No. 5803 by Raphael Tuck. $30

'At Last', 'We Shell', Tuck's oilette card 8819. $30

291

LOVING CUPS

Loving cups usually had two handles and were meant to be given as gifts to mark important events like marriages or betrothals. There were also decorative jugs which were used for the same purpose. In 1930 however the ingenious Charles J. Noke who worked at the Doulton Pottery realised the potential of the symbolism and attractive appearance of loving cups and jugs and started producing them in limited editions to be given as keepsakes and mementoes.

He used slip cast relief jugs which had been made in Staffordshire for many years but decorated them in bright colours and with new themes.

The Wandering Minstrel Loving Cup designed by C. J. Noke & H. Fenton, 5½in. high, issued 1934 in a limited edition of 600. $350

The first one produced was the Master of Foxhounds Presentation Jug which was painted by William Grace and in which the theme of the decoration was continued around the handle. The Regency Coach Jug followed and every year another was introduced into the market including the Dickens Dream Jug, the Shakespeare Jug and Robin Hood and His Merry Men. No more than 1000 of any jug was ever made and each one was numbered and sold with a certificate of authenticity. Some jugs were made to commemorate special historical events like George Washington's Birthday or coronations. Cecil Noke made a loving cup to mark Queen Elizabeth's crowning in 1953 and in 1977 Richard Johnson produced another range of 250 jugs to mark her Silver Jubilee.

George Washington Bicentenary jug designed by C. J. Noke & H. Fenton, 10¾in. high, issued 1932 in a limited edition of 1000, colour variation on handle. $4,375

The Village Blacksmith jug designed by C. J. Noke, 7¾in. high, issued 1936 in a limited edition of 600. $525

LOVING CUPS

The Apothecary Loving Cup designed by C. J. Noke & H. Fenton, 6in. high, issued 1934 in a limited edition of 600.
$480

Treasure Island jug designed by C. J. Noke & H. Fenton, 7½in. high, issued 1934 in a limited edition of 600. $610

William Wordsworth Loving Cup designed by C. J. Noke, 6½in. high, issued 1933 unlimited.
$560

Master of Foxhounds presentation jug designed by C. J. Noke, 13in. high, issued 1930 in a limited edition of 500. $525

Dickens Dream jug designed by C. J. Noke, 10½in. high, issued 1933 in a limited edition of 1000. $610

George Washington Bicentenary jug designed by C. J. Noke & H. Fenton, 10¾in. high, issued 1932 in a limited edition of 1000, variation of handle style.
$2,200

Tower of London jug designed by C. J. Noke & H. Fenton, 9½in. high, issued 1933 in a limited edition of 500. $610

Captain Cook Loving Cup designed by C. J. Noke & H. Fenton, 9½in. high, issued 1933 in a limited edition of 350. $1,400

Sir Francis Drake jug designed by C. J. Noke & H. Fenton, 10½in. high, issued 1933 in a limited edition of 500. $610

293

MATCH CASES

Because early matches were very volatile it was necessary to store them in containers that would restrict any accidental fire for they burst into flame at the slightest knock. By 1827 most friction matches were sold to the public in tin boxes by John Walker of Stockton on Tees and by the 1850's these safety tins were taking a wide variety of different shapes. Some of them were shaped like soldiers, historical figures or animals and as well as being made of tin, they were produced in iron, brass or even precious metals. If the containers were figures, their heads were hinged so that the matches could be placed inside the bodies. There was also a tiny hole in the case into which a single match could be stuck and allowed to burn for the full length of its wooden shaft. This was handy for holding a match steady when melting sealing wax.

Some match cases were made of ceramics or wood and most of them had roughened patches for the striking of the matches. Others had two roughened discs between which the match head could be pulled. Some matches ignited because the ends of them were tipped with chlorate of potash which burned when dipped into sulphuric acid. Contained within their match cases was a small cylinder for carrying the acid.

A Victorian fisherman's creel vesta case, the interior with Essex crystal depicting two trout, by Thos. Johnson, 1882, 5.5cm. long. (Phillips) $3,062

A Victorian enamelled silver vesta case, S. Mordan & Co., London, 1891, 2¼in. high. $527

An early Bryant & May's wax vestas pictorial case, circa 1875. $45

An early Vesta case featuring the Marquis of Lorne by Bryant & May's, London, 1876. $45

An enamelled silver vesta case, S. Mordan & Co., London, 1885, 1½in. high. $527

MATCH STRIKERS

Before matchboxes came into general use, little containers were designed for the holding of matches with strikers on their sides. They were made of wood, bone, glass, papier mache, Tunbridge ware, enamel, stone or china and the striker was always a roughened surface on one side. Many were made by the German firm Conte and Boehme who also made 'fairings' and the strikers were cheap to buy. Many were inscribed with advertising slogans by brewers or mineral water manufacturers and given away by enterprising firms to their customers. Others were printed with lines from funny or suggestive music hall songs of the time. Match strikers went out of use about the time of the First World War but they can be found in jumble sales and junk shops and are generally quite cheap to buy although an example in good condition with an unusual slogan can fetch around $50.

'Mountain Dew' whisky by Robertson Sanderson & Co., Leith, circa 1882. $50

Striker with old 'Good Luck' symbol by Royal Doulton, circa 1905. $70

Stoneware match striker and holder made for Worthingtons, 4in. high, circa 1900. $80

A fine pair of Victorian match strikers entitled 'Cold Hands and Cold Feet'. $220

Porcelain skull match striker, circa 1900. $80

Late 19th century German match holder and striker featuring a boy with his dog. $80

A Doulton Lambeth stoneware ashtray match holder, 'Queen Anne's Mansion'. $50

German cupid match striker and holder, circa 1890. $60

German fairing match striker, circa 1890. **$85**

Ship's striker with hallmarked silver decoration London 1889. **$105**

'Gentleman in Khaki' striker made by McIntyre, circa 1890. **$70**

German match striker 'Penny Please, Sir?', circa 1890. **$130**

Cheerful late 19th century Oriental looking gentleman combined striker/spillholder/ashtray. **$70**

China match striker figurine of a young girl, circa 1890. **$85**

Match holder and striker advertising 'Sir Edward Lee's Old Scotch Whisky', with the slogan 'As supplied to the House of Commons'. **$70**

German match striker in the form of an elephant, circa 1890. **$60**

Doulton Lambeth stoneware match holder and striker for John Dewar & Sons. **$70**

MEDICAL ITEMS

From the comparative safety of the twentieth century, we can look back with a certain morbid fascination and even glee at some of the seeming instruments of torture used by the medical and dental professions of the past. There is an abiding interest in such items and some of them are very finely made and beautifully cased. Apothecary boxes are particularly fascinating and can be quite readily found. Often cased in mahogany, they usually contained a secret compartment for poisons and opiates.

A Pascal's apparatus, unsigned, 14in. wide, with three different shaped glass vessels mounted in brass collars to fit the limb. (Christie's) $811

A wax model of the human head showing the nerves, arteries, veins and muscles, in an ebonised and glazed case, 9¾in. high, by Lehrmittelwerke, Berlin. (Christie's) $302

A 19th century bone saw and three dental elevators. (Christie's) $153

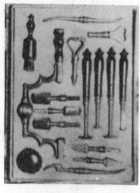

An 18th century set of surgeon's instruments, engraved Ambulance de S M. L'Empereur. (Christie's) $9,882

A 19th century single cupping set by J. Laundy, with lacquered brass syringe and shaped glass cup, the case 5in. wide. (Christie's) $422

A hydraulic tourniquet on octagonal mahogany base, circa 1830, 54cm. high. (Christie's) $605

An apothecary's chest, the mahogany case with recessed brass carrying handle, 10¾in. wide. (Lawrence Fine Art) $771

MEDICAL ITEMS

A late 18th century pocket dental scaling kit, with mirror in a shagreen case, 2¼in. wide. (Christie's) $286

A 19th century cupping set by Weiss, London, with two glass cups in plush lined fitted case, 5½in. long. (Christie's) $432

A Rein & Son 'London Dome' silver plated hearing trumpet, English, circa 1865, 6¾in. long. $430

Late 19th century sectional model of the eye, the plaster body decorated in colours and with glass lenses, 6¾in. high. (Christie's) $541

A 19th century mahogany domestic medicine chest by Fischer & Toller, 9½in. wide. (Christie's) $1,232

Pajot's midwifery forceps, signed Charriere a Paris, late 19th century, 34cm. long. (Christie's) $286

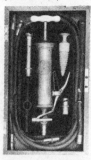

Mid 19th century S. Maw, Son & Thompson enema or stomach pump apparatus, English, 12½ x 7½in. $202

A 19th century amputation saw by Weiss, with anti-clog teeth and ebony handle, 15½in. long. (Christie's) $144

An 18th century decorated baluster two-handled 'leech' jar with cover, approx. 14in. tall. (J. M. Welch & Son) $2,584

MEISSEN

From its inception in 1710, the Meissen pottery produced wares that were sought after by the aristocracy of Europe. The pottery was situated in Meissen, Saxony, and its work was distinguished by sheer elegance and romanticism because pieces were trimmed with posies and bouquets of miniature flowers, realistic looking and exquisitely modelled. During the Napoleonic Wars the demand for Meissen dropped off but in 1849 H.G. Kuhn was appointed Director and the company's fortunes took an upturn. He introduced new models and re-issued 18th century models which had not lost their appeal. The most popular pieces were children and mythological flower bedecked goddesses produced between 1860 and 1890. After 1870 figures of soldiers and people in contemporary costume also appeared. The Meissen mark is a device of crossed swords with dates in some cases. Between 1924 and 1934, a dot was placed between the blades of the swords. Since inception, Meissen fakes have been circulating and some are stamped with the crossed swords.

A large Meissen group of Count Bruhl's tailor on a goat, blue crossed swords and incised numeral marks, circa 1880, 43cm. high. (Christie's) $4,041

A Meissen small cylindrical tankard by Johann G. Horoldt, circa 1728, 10.5cm. high. (Christie's) $28,336

A Meissen kinderbuste, blue crossed swords and incised numeral marks, circa 1880, 25cm. high. (Christie's) $918

A Meissen figure of the Courtesan from the Cries of London series, modelled by J. J. Kandler and P. J. Reinicke, circa 1754, 14cm. high. (Christie's) $2,851

Pair of Meissen Hausmalerei teacups and saucers painted by F. F. Meyer von Pressnitz, circa 1740. (Christie's) $4,958

A Meissen yellow ground quatrefoil coffee-pot and domed cover, blue crossed swords mark, gilder's mark M. to both pieces, circa 1742, 23cm. high. (Christie's) $11,313

A Meissen figure of Dr. Boloardo modelled by J. J. Kandler, circa 1742, 18.5cm. high. (Christie's) $8,553

A Meissen KPM baluster teapot and domed cover, painted by P. E. Schindler, circa 1724, 15cm. wide. (Christie's) $12,474

A Meissen figure of a tailor from the series of craftsmen modelled by J. J. Kandler, circa 1753, 23.5cm. high. (Christie's) $2,656

A Meissen hunting group, blue crossed swords marks and incised X to base, circa 1755, 16cm. high. (Christie's) $1,603

A Meissen deckelpokal, blue crossed swords mark to the base, and gilder's mark c to both pieces, circa 1725, 18cm. high. (Christie's) $13,282

A Meissen group of a Mother and Children modelled by J. J. Kandler and P. Reinicke, circa 1740, 23.5cm. high. (Christie's) $2,673

A Meissen figure of a musician in theatrical costume playing a lute, modelled by J. J. Kandler, circa 1745, 16.5cm. high. (Christie's) $8,910

A Meissen crinoline group of the gout sufferer modelled by J. J. Kandler, circa 1742, 19.5cm. wide. (Christie's) $9,740

A Meissen cylindrical pomade pot and domed cover, painted in the manner of Gottfried Klinger, circa 1745, 15cm. high. (Christie's) $2,851

MENUS

The great hotels of the world and the vast liners that used to carry passengers across the oceans before air travel became usual, attracted customers by the quality and quantity of their food. The preparation of menus was an art form and these lists of delights were treasured by passengers as souvenirs. On the last night of a voyage or holiday it was common for all the people at a certain table to sign their menus as remembrances. The designs of menu cards were elegant and looking at them carries one back to the days of leisurely travel that will never come again. Always at the head of the menu would be the ship's or hotel's logo, often in color. P. & O., Cunard and White Funnel Line all produced lovely menus and some of these turn up in folios or boxes of mixed cards. When they do, if they have been signed by some famous person, the price soars but generally they cost only around $5 each depending on the condition and the attractiveness of the decoration.

M.S. 'Terukuni Maru', N.Y.K. Line, Menu for Monday, 20th March, 1933. $7

M.V. 'Reina Del Pacifico', Dinner Menu for 20th August 1932, a fine Art Deco design. $7

Cunard Breakfast Menu for R.M.S. 'Mauretania', June 12th, 1933. $3.50

Canadian Pacific Dinner Menu, June 7th, 1934. $7

MENUS

P & O Menu for S.S. 'Mongolia', May 18th, 1933, Fancy Dress Ball. $5

Borough of Keighley Mayoral Luncheon, November 29th, 1929. $2

Cunard 'Carte du Jour', R.M.S. 'Mauretania', June 15th, 1933. $5

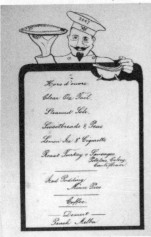

The Walton Walker No. 3847 Ladies Night Programme and Menu, 1926. $12

Cunard Line 'Auld Lang Syne' Menu, R.M.S. 'Mauretania', 1933. $5

Ye Palaontographical Society Menu, 1872, with fine engraving. $14

Yesterday's Paper

MICRO MOSAICS

The art of the mosaic is an ancient one dating back to Classical times and beyond. Though one tends to think of mosaics being mostly of marble, they can be of metal or even of glass. Wonderful glass mosaics were produced in Imperial Russia and by Austrian glass makers in the last century. As their name suggests, micro mosaics are miniature forms of these panels, designed either as simple picture panels, or perhaps incorporated onto a box lid. As with most miniatures, the effect is very fine and delicate.

A micro-mosaic panel of the Colosseum, signed G. Rinaldi, 59 x 77cm. (Phillips) $34,230

Early 19th century circular Roman micro-mosaic decorated in the style of Rafaelli with a finch, the box 3in. diam. (Christie's) $1,730

A 19th century Roman micro-mosaic panel decorated in bright colours with a bunch of flowers, approx. 8in. long. (Christie's) $5,505

A circular tortoiseshell snuff box with detachable cover, the mosaic circa 1820, 2¾in. diam. (Christie's) $1,487

A Roman micro-mosaic panel decorated with Pliny's Doves of Venus, circa 1840, 2.5/8in. long. (Christie's) $1,337

A circular Roman micro-mosaic of a pannier brimming with flowers, circa 1830, the box 2¾in. diam. (Christie's) $2,674

A 19th century Roman rectangular mosaic panel, decorated with a view of the Piazza del Popolo in Rome, 2¾in. long. (Christie's) $1,573

303

MINIATURE BOOKS

Some of the earliest examples are miniature Bibles, made perhaps to aid concealment in times and places where there was religious persecution. All Shakespeare's works have been produced in miniature, and the Victorians reproduced works of prose and poetry in this form. Miniature magazines and newspapers were made either as a novelty or as part of children's toy sets. Often of high quality, they are usually authentic reproductions of the original, and if genuinely old, can be quite valuable.

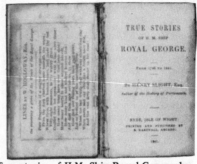

True stories of H.M. Ship Royal George, by Henry Slight, 1841. $45

M.A.P. edited by T. P. O'Connor, September 19th, 1908. $5

Pretty Pets Weekly Magazine, Golden Locks and the Three Bears. $3.50

Pearson's Magazine, 1908, 3in. high. $9

Tales for Tiny People, Cinderella and the Magic Slipper. $3.50

Home Notes, October 15th, 1908, Featuring Handkerchief Toys. $7

The Wooden Post, miniature magazine. $2

MINIATURE PLATES

These were made by most of the major manufacturers such as Doulton, Wedgwood etc. Some were made for dolls' tea sets, others were made as tiny replicas of large plates and designed to be worn as jewelry, mounted on pin brooches (Limoges). They can be transfer printed or hand painted and range in value from $5 to over $200.

Look out for early plates, and good examples of Blue and White. Those with registration marks are scarce.

Mid Victorian embossed miniature meat plate. $14

Wedgwood 'Chaffinch' plate, Windsor Great Park, 1980. $9

Coalport bone china plate with transfer printed pattern, 3in. diam. $14

K. & E. Krautheum Bavarian Porcelain flower design plate, 3¼in. diam. $9

Mavons Ironstone china floral plate, 3in. diam. $45

Staffordshire plate depicting 'the Olde Coach House, Bristol'. $10

Late 19th century Japanese lotus flower miniature plate. $3.50

Limoges transfer printed plate, showing a gallant and his lady, 2in. diam. $20

Green lead glazed plate, circa 1870, 3in. diam. $25

Late 19th century blue and white miniature plate, 3in. diam. $18

Crown Staffordshire bone china plate decorated with a floral spray. $7

19th century pottery plate with blue florally bordered edge, 3¼in. diam. $20

An early 19th century blue and white plate with beaded border, 3¼in. diam. $50

1930's Italian transfer printed plate with gilt border. $5

MINIATURES

The best known miniatures are pieces of dolls' house furniture which are eagerly collected. The best date from Victorian times when dolls' houses were furnished down to the last mat, picture on the wall and leg of mutton on the kitchen table. Some of these tiny pieces were marvels of exactitude and excellent examples of painstaking craftsmanship. It is possible to find tiny lamps with glass globes, baby's prams with wheels that go round, parlour maids in full costume and miniature washing sets complete with potty for beneath the bed. Other miniatures are the apprentice's pieces which every young cabinet maker in the 19th century had to produce before he became a journeyman. They made chests of drawers with inlaid locks or little chairs which were only just big enough for a child to sit in. High prices are also paid for miniature pieces of china which were produced by almost all the major potteries. They were too big for a doll's house and are more like craftsman's miniatures in scale. There are also working scale models of machines in miniature which fetch very high prices.

A miniature upright piano in burr walnut with central inlay, brass candlestick holders and ivory keyboard, 15½in. high. (Christie's) $1,975

A William and Mary walnut oyster veneer and cross-banded chest of small size. (Phillips) $3,280

A tin-plated miniature fire surround and grate with moulded uprights and lintel with pierced slightly bowed basket, 12in. wide. (Christie's) $411

A 19th century miniature wallpapered bandbox, American, 4½in. high. (Robt. W. Skinner Inc.) $325

An Empire mahogany miniature sofa, American, circa 1840, 19in. wide. (Christie's) $1,430

Miniature Victorian wash boiler and dolly in brass. $35

MINIATURES

A 19th century miniature green painted pine blanket chest, American, 9½in. high. (Christie's) $330

A burr-yew wood miniature chest inlaid with lines, on bracket feet, 11in. wide. (Christie's) $4,633

Early 19th century miniature Federal mahogany tilt-top tea table, American, 9in. high. (Christie's) $990

A 19th century miniature Federal mahogany picture mirror, American, 9½in. high. (Christie's)
$1,210

A 17th century miniature oak coffer of panelled construction, probably French, 35 x 21 x 23cm. (Phillips) $1,008

Late 18th/early 19th century miniature Continental painted tall clock case, 17in. high. (Christie's) $550

A miniature Chippendale mahogany desk and bookcase, Rhode Island, 1760-80, 16in. high. (Christie's)
$2,090

Two 19th century miniature painted side chairs, American, 9¾in. and 8¼in. high. (Christie's) $528

A Dutch mahogany and oak miniature clothes press, 21in. wide, 33in. high. (Christie's)
$3,168

An American, 19th century, miniature painted bannister-back armchair, 9½in. high. (Christie's) $495

A 19th century miniature grain painted bowfront chest-of-drawers, American or English, 12in. high. (Christie's) $1,210

A 19th century, American, miniature classical maple fiddleback chair, 10¾in. high, 8¼in. wide. (Christie's) $550

Mid 18th century miniature Chippendale cherrywood chest-of-drawers, 7¾in. high. (Christie's) $1,540

An American, 18th century, miniature Queen Anne maple and pine slant-front desk, with a cherrywood mirror, the desk 11in. high. (Christie's) $3,520

Late 19th century miniature Chippendale walnut slant-front desk, American, 7¼in. high. (Christie's) $1,650

Late 18th century miniature George III mahogany side table, English, 6in. high. (Christie's) $330

A mid Georgian walnut miniature chest, the base with one long drawer on bracket feet, 13½in. wide. (Christie's) $2,141

An American, 19th century, miniature Federal mahogany four-post bedstead with canopy, 15½in. high. (Christie's) $330

MINTON

Thomas Minton was born in 1765 and apprenticed at the Caughley Porcelain Works where he was trained in the art of engraving copper plates for underglaze-blue printed designs. In 1793 he opened his own pottery at Stoke on Trent and his earliest products were earthenwares. A favourite design was Nankeen Temple in the style of the Chinese imports which were flooding into England. Porcelain was added to his output around 1797 and his original china ware pattern book has survived. Minton produced Parian ware, vases in the Sevres style, tableware, tiles, decorated panels and garden ornaments in terracotta and majolica. Many famous artists worked for Minton including T. Allen, who painted vases; T. Kirkby whose speciality was flowers and fruit; H. Mitchell, painter of animals and R. Pilsbury who also painted flowers. Tiles by Walter Crane, Moyr-Smith and E.J. Poynter were much sought after in the Art Nouveau period as were the vases decorated by L.V. Solon.

A Minton Pilgrim vase, painted probably by A. Boullemier after W. S. Coleman, 20cm. high, date code possibly 1873. (Phillips) $434

A Minton figure modelled as a boy in rustic garb, his arm round the neck of a donkey, impressed Minton 196, 20cm. high. (Christie's) $478

One of a pair of Minton majolica vases, twelve-sided oviform shape, date code for 1859 on one vase, 29cm. high. (Christie's) $918

A Minton majolica barrel-shaped garden seat in the Oriental taste, date code for 1873, 50cm. high. (Christie's) $871

A Minton vase, designed by Dr. C. Dresser, U-shaped on four splayed feet, 19.2cm. high. (Christie's) $1,817

A Minton majolica figure of a partially draped putto holding a lyre-shaped viol seated on a conch-shell, impressed Minton 1539 and with date code for 1870, 46.5cm. high. (Christie's) $3,674

MINTON

A Minton pink-ground cabinet cup and saucer, circa 1825. (Christie's) $272

A pair of Minton 'Dresden Scroll' vases and pierced covers in neo-rococo style, 29cm. high. (Phillips) $2,101

A Mintons Kensington Gore pottery moon flask, 34.2cm. high. (Phillips) $555

One of a pair of Minton porcelain dessert plates, one with swallow in flight, signed Leroy, the other with a bird perched on fuchsia branch, 9½in. diam. (Dacre, Son & Hartley) $2,062

A massive Minton 'majolica' peacock after the model by P. Comolera, circa 1875, 153cm. high. (Christie's) $30,800

A Minton porcelain dessert plate, the central pate-sur-pate panel signed L. Solon, circa 1880, 9¼in. wide. (Dacre, Son & Hartley) $495

A Minton white and celadon glazed centrepiece modelled as three putti holding a basket, circa 1868, 26cm. high. (Christie's) $731

A pair of Minton candlestick figures, both in richly decorated costumes and with flowered and striped designs, 22cm. high. (Phillips) $2,769

One of a pair of Minton pedestal form garden seats, naturalistic polychrome colouring on an olive ground, 43cm. high. (Christie's) $3,190

MIRRORS

The earliest mirrors, examples of which have survived in Egyptian tombs, were hand held discs of polished metal and it was not till 1507 that Venetian glassmakers at Murano acquired a monopoly for making mirrors of plain glass backed by an amalgam of mercury and tin. These mirrors tended to distort and spot because the backing soon flaked off but a century later a technique of backing glass with mercury and tinfoil was adopted in England and a factory was started which exported mirrors all over Europe.

When the Duke of Buckingham opened another glass factory at Vauxhall that could make mirrors of large size, a new vogue began and rich people all wanted large mirrors to decorate their homes. They hung them between windows and over chimney pieces and some of them were embellished with beautifully carved frames while others had fine pictures superimposed on top of them. In the 18th century it became the fashion for ladies to give up peering at themselves in tiny hand mirrors and have larger ones on their dressing tables. Swing dressing mirrors and cheval mirrors were produced in large numbers. Each succeeding fashion in furnishing had its equivalent style of mirror ranging from Chippendale gilded pine to Victorian gilt gesso frames and the beaten bronze of the Arts and Crafts period.

A George II walnut and parcel gilt mirror, 52 x 26½in. (Christie's) $21,714

A Dutch marquetry toilet mirror, the solid cylinder enclosing a fitted interior, 21½in. wide. (Christie's) $3,190

A Regency mahogany cheval mirror, the plain frame on reeded uprights, 70½in. high, 32in. wide. (Christie's) $1,156

A Regency carved giltwood and gesso convex girandole, 1.03m. x 59cm. (Phillips) $3,168

A George III giltwood mirror with later oval plate in a tied, out-scrolled rush frame, 39 x 26½in. (Christie's) $6,940

A Regency carved giltwood convex mirror with ribband tied laurel leaf surround, 1.31m. x 78cm. (Phillips) $15,120

An early George III giltwood mirror with later plate, 33½ x 21¼in. (Christie's) $8,530

A Regency satinwood large toilet mirror with oval swing frame, lacking plate, 25½in. wide. (Christie's) $495

One of a pair of giltwood mirrors in the rococo style with cartouche-shaped plates, 35 x 21in. (Christie's) $1,022

A giltwood mirror with rectangular plate in shaped frame, 45½ x 35½in. (Christie's) $4,998

A Chippendale carved giltwood oval marginal wall mirror with contemporary plate and bird crestings, 1.06m. high. (Phillips) $7,200

A George II silver gilt dressing table mirror, by Edward Feline, 1750, 23¾in. high, 62oz. (Christie's) $25,168

A giltwood mirror with later arched shaped bevelled plate with mirrored slip, 54 x 33in. (Christie's) $2,343

A Lalique hand mirror, 'Deux Chevres', 16.20cm. diam., in original fitted case. (Phillips) $1,152

One of a pair of Regency giltwood pier glasses with rectangular plates in leaf moulded frames, 98 x 52½in. (Christie's) $13,959

MODEL BUSES

Many of the finest tin plate toys represented means of transport — trains, ships, cars and buses. They were first powered by clockwork but as the use of it declined, they were driven by friction motors or battery operated electric motors. Both single and double decker buses were made and they often had interesting advertising along their sides. One Bing model made about 1910 of a vehicle belonging to the United Bus Company Ltd carried a large placard advertising the appearance of Harry Lauder at the Tivoli Theatre. American 'Greyhound' buses were produced by Japanese manufacturers in the 1960's and '70's and trolley buses were made by Brimtoy and Betal. Brimtoy's products are particularly good and rival the German equivalents. When the last Paris trolley bus was taken off the road, a clockwork replica model was made by Joustra and sold well. Model buses range in size from one inch to eight feet in length and prices vary according to condition.

F. G. Taylor — UK — Diecast Trolleybus, Post War Example. $70

Wells — UK — Tinplate London Bus, circa 1960's. $110

Modern Toys — Japan 1960, Battery Operated Old Fashioned Tinplate Bus. $125

Russian Novelty Clockwork Bus Track, circa 1960's. $25

Tootsietoy Greyhound Bus (USA), diecast, circa 1940. $85

Joustra — France — 1950's Clockwork Greyhound Tinplate Coach. $110

(Geoff & Linda Price)

French Dinky — 29f Chausson Coach, circa
1956. $130
29d Somua Panhard, circa
1951. $140

Joustra — France — 1950's Ile de France
Tinplate Coach. $165

Maks — Hong Kong — 1960, Copy in Plastic
of the Dinky Coach. $14

TN — Japan 1960's Tinplate Greyhound
Lines Coach. $80

Gamda — Israel, Leyland Worldmaster Diecast
Coach, circa 1950's. $155

Chad Valley — UK — Tinplate Double Deck
Bus — circa 1949. $120

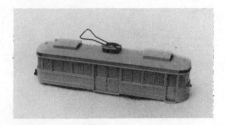

Wiking — Germany — Early Plastic Tramcar —
1950's. $50

Well's Brimtoy — UK — No. 516 Tinplate
Trolleybus, 1950's, Clockwork. $95

(Geoff & Linda Price)

MODEL BUSES

Jye — Spain — 1½ Deck Tinplate Coach,
1950's, Very Rare Model. $110

C.I.J. — France — 1950's Tinplate Coach.
$40

Guntermann — West Germany — 1930's
Tinplate Tram. $260

Japanese 1960's Tinplate Double Deck Bus.
$80

Tipp & Co — Germany — Circa 1950's
Tinplate Bonnetted Coach. $110

Wells Brimtoy Greenline Tinplate Coach,
1950's. $105

Dinky Toys — UK, 1963 Continental Touring
Coach, 1961 School Bus. $140

HJC — Japan — Tinplate 1950's Greyhound.
$105

(Geoff & Linda Price)

MODEL PLANES

The first toy planes made by the Dinky Toy Company were launched on the market in 1934 and given the identification Number 60. The scale used was roughly 1/200. Planes were issued in boxes of six to be sold boxed or singly. Production continued until 1939 when it slowed down and by 1941 came to a standstill because of the lack of raw materials which were needed for the war effort. The original models were made of lead alloy but before 1939 this was replaced by a substitute called Mazak which was an alloy containing aluminium, copper, zinc and some magnesium. Sometimes trace elements that were present made the alloy brittle and cracks appeared. Examine any Dinky toys well because cracks will only get worse. Always store in a cool, dry place out of direct sunlight. The most common model plane produced was the Percival Gull which was produced in many colours but after 1940 the planes were always camouflaged and Spitfires, Hurricanes, Blenheims, Fairey Battles, Armstrong Whitworth Whitleys, Ensigns, Leopard Moths and Vickers Jockys joined the range. Because they were only produced for a short time they are rare and valuable. Boxed sets which are available are The R.A.F. Presentation Set, The Camouflaged Set and The Presentation Set. After the war, Dinky planes were back in production and new ranges were produced in 1946 and in the 50's. Probably the most sought after model to any Dinky collector is number 992 Avro Vulcan. This model of the most famous of the R.A.F. V-Bombers, was produced between 1955 and 1956. The model is quite large and finished in silver. Although it was given the number 992 it carried the number 749.

An original mint and boxed Dinky Vulcan could reasonably be expected to fetch between $1,500 and $2,000 at auction. The original box is extremely rare and adds a great deal to its value.

Lockheed Constellation No. 60C, produced by Meccano France, 1957-63, boxed.
$245

Avro Vulcan No. 992, issued 1955, (not issued in U.K., unknown number released in Canada).
$1,800

British 40-seat Air Liner No. 62X, 1939-41, boxed.
$260

Frobisher Class Air Liner
No. 62, 1939-41, boxed.
$315

Armstrong Whitworth Ensign
Air Liner No. 62P, 1938-41,
boxed. $175

A pre-war Empire Flying Boat
No. 60R, 1937, boxed. $300

Mayo Composite Aircraft
No. 63, 1939-41, boxed.
$525

The first Dinky boxed set,
No. 60, issued in 1934 to
1940. $1,750

Armstrong Whitworth
Whitley No. 62T, Silver,
1937-41, boxed. $260

Douglas Air Liner No. 60T,
(supposed to be a DC3 by
many, but is probably a DC2)
boxed. $280

Flying Fortress No. 62G,
1939-41, boxed. $260

Kings Aeroplane (Envoy)
No. 62K, 1938-41, boxed.
$315

MODEL PLANES

Bristol Britannia No. 998,
1959-65, boxed. $315

JU89 Heavy Bomber, 67A,
1940-41, German markings,
boxed. $350

Nimrod Dinky Comet
(Conversion). $210

A post-war Giant High Speed
Monoplane No. 62Y, R/H Gree.
                    $260

Dinky F-4 U.S.A.F. Phantom,
U.S. Market only. $175

Shetland Flying Boat No. 701,
1947-49, boxed. $1,000

Atlantic Flying Boat, boxed.
                    $525

Camouflaged Whitworth
Ensign Liner No. 68A, 1940-41.
                    $350

Dinky Hurricane, ME109.
                    $70

Camouflaged Frobisher Air
Liner. $385

Dinky Diamond Jubilee
Spitfire, boxed. $175

Pre-war Frog Penguin, unmade
in kits. $35

MODEL SHIPS

During the Napoleonic Wars French prisoners earned money for extra food by various handicrafts and some of the most beautiful were the model ships which they made and sold to local people from stalls set up at the roadsides. The ships were crafted from left over bones, string and straw and embellished with scraps of wood, ivory or metal. Some of them were truly works of art and very accurate models of 100 gun warships like the ones the prisoners had sailed on during hostilities. Examples which have survived are valued at many thousands of dollars. Model ship making has always been a hobby practised by old sailors, some of whom were extremely skilled and managed to imbue their models with their own love of the sea and the ships that sailed on it. Collectors are especially fond of ships under glass and especially of ships in bottles, some of which make it impossible to imagine how they were ever put inside their glass containers.

A 1:100 scale model of a Trouville trawler of circa 1866, built by M. Deveral, Folkestone, 6 x 6½in. (Christie's) $336

Late 19th century possibly builder's model of the fully rigged model of a yawl believed to be the 'Constance' of 1885, built for C. W. Prescott-Westcar by A. Payne & Sons, Southampton and designed by Dixon Kemp, 28 x 35¾in. (Christie's) $6,120

A finely carved 'Dieppe' ivory model three masted man-of-war with spars and rigging, full suit of carved ivory sails, mounted on wood with two ship's boats, 7 x 9in. (Christie's) $994

An exhibition standard 1:75 scale fully planked and rigged model of the French 60 gun man-of-war 'Le Protecteur' of circa 1760, built by P. M. di Gragnano, Naples, 31 x 38in. (Christie's) $7,650

A 20th century American model of the extreme clippership 'Cutty Sark', on a walnut base, fitted in a glass case. (Christie's) **$1,320**

A contemporary early 19th century French prisoner of war bone and horn model man of war reputed to be the French ship of the line 'Redoubtable' of 74 guns, 20½ x 26¾in. (Christie's) **$11,600**

Late 18th century prisoner-of-war carved ivory ship, with rigging and thirty-four gun ports, Europe, 13½in. long. (Robt. W. Skinner Inc.) **$800**

A planked and rigged model of a Royal Naval Cutter built by I. H. Wilkie, Sleaford, 36 x 42in. (Christie's) **$507**

A fully planked and rigged model of a 72-gun man-o'-war, built by P. Rumsey, Bosham, 26 x 37in. (Christie's) **$2,772**

Early 19th century prisoner-of-war bone model of a ship-of-the-line, 7¾in. long. (Christie's) **$3,190**

A 20th century American model of a fishing schooner, 'Kearsar', fitted in a glass case, 33½in. long. (Christie's) $935

Late 19th century carved and painted model of the 'William Tapscot', in a glass and mahogany case, 38in. long. (Christie's) $1,540

A detailed ¼in.:1ft. model of a twelve gun brig of circa 1840 built to the plans of H. A. Underhill by M. J. Gebhard, Tottenham, 36 x 47in. (Christie's) $4,350

A 19th century carved bone model of a frigate, probably French, 16½in. long. (Christie's) $3,080

An early 19th century French prisoner-of-war bone model of a ship-of-the-line, 8½in. long. (Christie's) $2,530

Early 19th century prisoner-of-war bone model of a First Class ship-of-the-line, 21in. long. (Christie's) $9,900

MODEL TRAINS

The first steam locomotive toys were not made in any number until the 1860's although 'Railway Mania' had the world in its grip for twenty years before that. The earliest type of model trains are called 'floor runners' because there were no tracks, which came later. The first great name in toy trains is Theodore Marklin who was attracted to the idea of making clockwork steam trains. He died in 1866 but his widow and sons carried on the business and made it a huge success. In 1891 they exhibited a full railway system at the Leipzig Trade Fair. Other famous trains were made by the Bing company which was founded in Nuremberg in 1863 by two brothers, Adolf and Ignaz Bing. By 1908 it was described as 'the greatest toy factory in the world' and had a pay roll of 3,000 people. Basset-Lowke in Britain and the famous Hornby company also made toy trains which are collectors' pieces today.

A very rare Hornby gauge 0 clockwork model of the Great Indian Peninsula 4-4-2 No. 2 special tank locomotive No. 2711, circa 1937. (Christie's)
$864

A rare Bassett-Lowke gauge 0 (3-rail) electric model of the GWR 2-6-2 'Prairie' tank locomotive No. 6105, in original green and black livery, circa 1937. (Christie's)
$1,748

A rake of three Darsted gauge 0 CIWL Bogie coaches (39cm), including a sleeping car, a dining car and a baggage, all in fine original paintwork, circa 1965. (Christie's)
$1,440

A rare Marklin gauge 0 clockwork model of the 0-4-0 electric locomotive No. RS1020, in original dark green paintwork, with red and black chassis, circa 1927. (Christie's)
$617

A rake of three very rare gauge 1 Central London Railway four wheel passenger coaches, inscribed 'Smoking', by Marklin circa 1903 (one coupling broken). (Christie's)
$11,313

A well restored gauge 0 (3-rail) electric model of the SR 2-6-0 'Mogul' locomotive and six wheel tender No. 897, in original green livery, by Marklin for Bassett-Lowke, circa 1927. (Christie's) $1,440

MODEL TRAINS

A rare Hornby gauge 0 clockwork model
of the DSB 4-4-2 No. 2 special tank locomotive No. 3596, in original maroon livery,
circa 1934. (Christie's)
$720

A rare Bing gauge 1 live steam, spirit fired
model of a German 4-6-2 Pacific Class locomotive and twin-bogie, finished in original
black livery, circa 1927. (Christie's)
$3,497

A Lionel No. 700E gauge 0 (3-rail) electric
model of the New York Central Railway
4-6-4 'Hudson' locomotive and tender No.
5344, in original black livery. (Christie's)
$1,748

A Hornby (3-rail) electric (20v) model of
the LMS4-6-2 locomotive and tender No.
6201 "Princess Elizabeth", in original paintwork, circa 1938. (Christie's)
$1,439

An early and rare gauge 1 hand enamelled
tinplate mainline railway station, by Bing,
circa 1908, 25½ x 9¼in. (Christie's)
$3,086

A rake of three Bing gauge 1 MR four wheel
coaches, including two 1st/3rd coaches and
a brake van, circa 1912. (Christie's)
$206

A Bassett-Lowke gauge 0 (3-rail) electric
model of the SR 2-6-0 'Mogul' locomotive
and tender No. 866, in fine original paintwork, circa 1927. (Christie's)
$1,337

A Hornby gauge 0 (3-rail) electric model
of the SR 4-4-0 No. E420 locomotive and
tender No. 900 'Eton', in original green
paintwork, circa 1937. (Christie's)
$1,131

MODELS

The difference between models and toys is that toys were usually mass produced while models were the individual work of a skilled craftsman. They were usually done as an adult hobby and were not intended as a toy. High prices are paid for miniature working models of steam and traction engines which were often powered by methylated spirits and were marvels of miniaturisation, shining with brass. The German toy makers Bing, Carette and Marklin produced a specialised line of working models of steam trains. Other models were made of moated castles, dolls houses, Noah's Arks complete with animals or Victorian shops, some complete with their scaled down wares. Butchers' shops had ribs of beef, tiled counters and rose cheeked butchers in boaters and striped aprons. One very specialised type of model were the miniature sailing ships made out of pieces of bone by French prisoners of war during the conflict with Napoleon. Models are usually very expensive which is only to be expected considering the hours of work that must have gone into them.

A 1½in. scale model of a spirit-fired Shand-Mason horsedrawn fire engine of 1894. (Phillips) $1,176

A well engineered 3in. scale model of a Suffolk Dredging tractor, built by C. E. Thorn, 27 x 30in. (Christie's) $705

An early 20th century wood model of the 1860 horse-drawn goods wagon owned by Carter Paterson & Co, London and Suburban Express Carriers, 17in. long. (Onslow's) $489

A well engineered 2in. scale model of an Aveling and Porter twin crank compound two speed, four shaft Road Roller, 19½ x 35in. (Christie's) $3,987

A finely engineered model twin cylinder compound undertype stationary steam engine built to the designs of A. H. Greenly, by P. C. Kidner, London, 14½ x 24½in. (Christie's) $2,295

An approx. 4in. scale Foden type twin cylinder overtype two speed steam lorry, built by A. Groves, Watford, 1937 and restored by M. Williams at the British Engineerium, Hove, 1983, 36½ x 88in. (Christie's) $7,650

A 2in. scale model of a single cylinder three shaft two speed Davey-Paxman general purpose agricultural traction engine built by A. R. Dyer & Sons, Wantage, 23½ x 38in. (Christie's) $2,610

A 1½in. scale model of a Burrell single crank compound two speed three shaft general purpose agricultural traction engine, built by J. B. Harris, Solihull, 15½ x 25in. (Christie's) $3,190

An exhibition standard 2in. scale model of the Burrell 5 n.h.p. double crank compound two speed three shaft 'Gold Medal' tractor, engine No. 3846, Registration No. AD7782 'Poussnouk-nouk', built from works drawings by P. Penn-Sayers, Laughton, 19¾ x 27¼in. (Christie's) $10,875

An exhibition standard 3in. scale model of the Savage horse-drawn Electric Light Engine No. 357, built by C. J. Goulding, Newport, 27 x 47in. (Christie's) $4,284

MUSICAL INSTRUMENTS

The need to make music appeared very early in primitive man who thumped away on a drum or blew a simple flute but by the time of the Pharoahs there were some very sophisticated musical instruments including the long golden horns which were found in the tomb of Tutankhamun and which can still be blown to produce a clear note. Percussion, stringed and wind instruments like the serpent, the sackbut, the dulcimer and the cornet were treasured by their owners through the ages and a few have survived today though the earliest and rarest of them are usually in museums or special collections like the one maintained by Edinburgh University in St Cecilia's Hall. Early pianos and harpsichords are especially valuable but perhaps the most cherished of all are early stringed instruments like violins and cellos. Stradivarius and Guarneri violins change hands for very large sums of money.

A classical carved mahogany pianoforte, by James L. Hewitt & Co., Boston, 1820-30, 67in. wide. (Christie's) $1,650

A spinet shaped pianoforte by John C. Hancock, 1779, in a crossbanded mahogany case with figured walnut interior. (Christie's)
$16,720

An English grand pianoforte, by John Broadwood, in mahogany case with sycamore interior on trestle stand, 88 x 38in. (Christie's)
$5,702

An important Steinway parlour concert grand piano, circa 1904, 91in. long, together with a duet stool, 44in. long. (Christie's)
$66,000

MUSICAL INSTRUMENTS

A George III mahogany square piano with ivory keyboard, enamel plaque inscribed 'Longman, Clementi & Comp'y, London, New Patent', 5ft.5in. wide. (Woolley & Wallis) $936

A Classical Revival mahogany inlaid piano-forte, Boston, circa 1825, 72½in. long. (Robt. W. Skinner Inc.) $3,400

A Carillon of twenty-five hemispherical metal bells (glockenspiel), by H. Godden, circa 1810, overall height with stand 55in. (Phillips) $835

A double-manual harpsichord, by Jacob Kirckman, 1761, 91½ x 37in. (Christie's) $123,200

A portable table harmonium in an oak case, by Metzler & Co., circa 1845, 23¼in. wide. (Phillips) $384

An English single manual harpsichord, by Jacob Kirckman, in a mahogany case, 87 x 37in. (Christie's) $24,564

 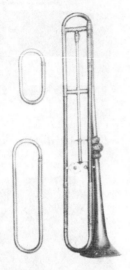  

Mid 17th century Venetian guitar, School of Sellas, length of back 46.6cm., in case. $8,140

A brass slide trumpet by J. A. Kohler, London, circa 1850, in case. $1,221

Early 19th century four or six-keyed ebony flute by Cusson, Valenciennes, in mahogany case. $814

A French pedal harp by Holtzmann, Paris, 5ft.4in. high, circa 1780. $1,302

An Irish harp by John Egan, Dublin, 34¾in. high, circa 1825, in case. $1,628

A presentation set of Union pipes by Robt. Reid, North Shields, 1830. $5,860

A treble viola converted from a Pardessus De Viole, length of body, 34.3cm., in case. $1,139

A cased pair of five-keyed cocuswood flutes by Monzani & Co., London, circa 1815, in mahogany case. $1,709

MUSTARD POTS

Mustard was used as a seasoning for food from pre-Tudor times but the possession of special mustard pots was rare before the end of the 18th century. The earliest pots were of silver made in a drum shape with flowing scroll designs engraved on them.

The late 18th century silversmith Hester Bateman made some very fine ones shaped like vases. Victorian mustard pots were always much larger than the 18th century examples and some are so large that they doubled as marmalade pots. They are the ones which sell for the highest prices.

Bardolph, a Royal Doulton Kingsware mustard pot with silver hallmarked rim, circa 1904, 3in. high. $75

A mustard pot by Eliza Simmance, the handle and body with incised blue leaves, 1875, 2¼in. high. $130

A George III mustard pot, by Samuel Wheatley, 1816, 9.2cm. high. (Lawrence Fine Art) $534

A French mustard pot with clear glass liner, Paris, circa 1825, 3.5oz. (Phillips) $367

Pair of Staffordshire enamel mustard pots with gilt metal mounts, on three pad feet, circa 1770, probably Birmingham, each 5½in. high. (Christie's) $5,443

A C. R. Ashbee silver mustard pot, set with six turquoise cabochons, London hallmarks for 1900, 8cm. high. (Christie's) $1,313

NAPKIN RINGS

Napkin rings are made in many materials from plastic to solid silver, and the value varies accordingly. Numbered sets are more valuable than single rings, and a good bone engraved Georgian numbered set of 12 would easily fetch over $250. Silver examples can be accurately dated from hallmarks and priced accordingly. Personalised rings with monogram or inscription are also desirable. Look out too for ornate rings and those made of ebony inlaid with ivory or mother-of-pearl.

A set of four crocus pattern napkin rings by Clarice Cliff, circa 1930. $260

Pair of late 19th century plated napkin rings with embossed decoration. $18

Pair of early 19th century silver napkin rings with beaded borders. $35

Pair of pewter napkin rings in the Art Nouveau style. $18

Doulton napkin rings issued 1935-39, featuring Sam Weller, Sairey Gamp, Tony Weller, Mr Micawber, Mr Pickwick and Fat Boy. $260 each.

Pair of Victorian silver napkin rings. $35

Pair of 1950's plastic chicken napkin rings. $9

Pair of treen napkin rings with Tunbridgeware decoration. $18

NAPOLEONIC MEMORABILIA

Few figures in history have captured the public imagination like Napoleon, and this is reflected in the wealth of related material that exists in countless different media. Busts and statuettes are prime examples and many documents signed by or relating to the great man are also extant, while his likeness, or sometimes only his famous tricorne, adorn everything from paperweights to carriage clocks and coach panels. Value therefore depends on the rarity or intrinsic value of the piece rather than simply upon his presence!

A rectangular metal mounted frame with oval miniatures of Napoleon and Josephine, signed Derval, 7½in. long. (Christie's) $1,082

A 19th century ivory rotunda with stepped roof and fluted columns framing a statuette of Napoleon, 7in. high, 5½in. diam. (Christie's) $7,576

Napoleon I: Letter signed 'Napoleon', to the Archduke Charles, Compiegne, 24 March 1810, one page, sm. 4to, mounted beside a color printed engraving of Napoleon's head. (Christie's) $3,427

A 19th century brass carriage clock with enamel dial and statuette of Napoleon, 8in. high. (Christie's) $721

After Vauthier: Notables de a France revolutionaire, by E. Bovinet, engravings, 400 x 273mm. (Christie's) $1,082

A Continental biscuit porcelain equestrian group of Napoleon crossing the Alps after the painting by David, mid 19th century, 8in. wide, 10½in. high. (Christie's) $2,164

Napoleon I: Document signed 'Napol', one page, large folio, printed heading the crest, Moscow, 12 October 1812. (Christie's) $1,353

A 19th century French bronze bust of Napoleon, inscribed on the reverse J. Berthoz, 24cm. high. (Christie's) $689

An Empire scarlet morocco leather despatch box with brass hasp backplate, clips and angles, 27in. wide. (Christie's) $7,216

A Continental biscuit porcelain bust inscribed 'Napoleon I', 16½in. high. (Christie's) $2,886

After Jean Baptiste Isabey: Napoleon a Malmaison, by C. L. Lingee and J. Godefroy, mixed method engraving, 637 x 433mm. (Christie's) $505

A bronze equestrian statue of Napoleon issuing instructions from a galloping horse, on a breccia marble base, 10in. wide, 11½in. high. (Christie's) $631

An Empire ormolu toilet mirror, with inscription '. . . taken by a Sergeant of the 11th Lt. Dragoons from Napoleon's Carriage dressing case . . .', 12 x 8in. (Christie's) $1,102

A 19th century bronze bust of Napoleon, signed 'Linedon' on verde antico marble plinth, 18½in. high. (Christie's) $1,713

A 19th century ormolu and porphyry encrier, the pentray centered by a bust of the Emperor with initial N below, 14½in. wide. (Christie's) $2,886

A 19th century French bronze figure of Napoleon, the base inscribed Vela. F. 1867, and on the reverse F. Barbedienne, 28cm. high. (Christie's) $1,361

A 19th century French bronze bust of Napoleon The First, after Ambrogio Colombo, 32cm. high. (Christie's) $998

A 19th century bronze, ormolu and verde antico paperweight mounted with a trophy of Napoleon's hat, sword and scroll, 6in. wide. (Christie's) $1,984

A bronze bust of Napoleon, signed 'Noel Ruffier', 11½in. high. (Christie's) $1,443

After Robert Lefevre: Joseph Napoleon, Roi de Naples et de Sicile, by L. C. Rouolle, colored mixed method engraving, 436 x 324mm. (Christie's) $396

A 19th century French bronze statue of Napoleon on Horseback, on rouge marble base, 61cm. high. (Christie's) $2,755

Pellerin & Co., Publishers: Genie; Musique de la Garde Republicane; Fanfare de Dragons; Hussards; Chasseurs; and Musique de Hussards, colored engravings, 373 x 265mm. (Christie's) $144

After Cornillet: Napoleon au Palais des Tuileries; and Napoleon assis, after F. Flameng, 304 x 210mm. (Christie's) $505

A 19th century bronze group of Napoleon and a French soldier, 6½in. wide, 7in. high. (Christie's) $631

A 19th century bronze bust of Napoleon signed 'Noel R', on spreading verde antico marble plinth, 6½in. high. (Christie's) $216

NAPOLEONIC MEMORABILIA

An Empire ormolu mounted mahogany fauteuil de bureau with revolving circular seat covered in ochre leather, 21½in. diam. (Christie's) $99,220

Early 19th century circular tortoiseshell box, the cover painted with Napoleon on horseback, 3in. diam. (Christie's) $541

A trooper's helmet of the French Cuirassiers (Second Empire) with chin-chain, mane and tuft, 18in. high. (Christie's) $1,804

A 19th century bronze bust of Napoleon as First Consul, 36cm. high. (Christie's) $635

Napoleon I: Document signed 'Nap', granting a pardon to Jean-Marie Merle, who had been sentened to 5 years hard labour in 1805 for desertion, one page, oblong folio, 395 x 505mm.. (Christie's) $1,984

An ivory statuette of Frederick the Great on eight-sided base carved with relief portraits of ladies, 7¼in. high. (Christie's) $4,690

Napoleon I: Endorsement signed 'N', 26 May, 1813, one page, folio, printed heading of Ministere de la Guerre, Bureau de la Gendarmerie. (Christie's) $631

One of two early 19th century French shallow circular boxes, possibly Grenoble, 3½in. diam. (Christie's) $270

Early 19th century marquetry coach panel inlaid in shaded woods with Napoleon on horseback, 27¾ x 19½in. (Christie's) $1,262

NETSUKE

The traditional Japanese kimono had no pockets so any possessions had to be carried around in little purses or boxes swinging from the belt, which was a sash called the obi. The cords which attached the purses to the obi were held in place by a netsuke (pronounced netsky). The simplest netsuke were wooden toggles but adroit Japanese craftsmen soon seized the opportunity of turning the toggle into an object of beauty by carving it into the shape of birds, animals, flowers or people. It became a matter of pride to own a fine netsuke and by the end of the 18th century the elaboration of the carving reached a peak with many famous artists specialising in netsuke alone.

Netsuke were made out of wood, ivory, bone, rhino, buffalo or stag horn, jade, jet, turtle shell, amber or more rarely metal. The subjects were innumerable ranging from characters in Japanese folk tales and representations of traditional craftsmen to eroticism which was a popular subject.

A large number of the over 3000 craftsmen known to have made netsuke lived around Osaka, Nagoya, Kyoto and Edo but the popularity of their wares declined after 1868 when Japan was opened up to the West and foreign style clothes with pockets began being worn. The popularity of netsuke with tourists however meant a rebirth in the craft and vast numbers of them − though of inferior quality to earlier netsuke − have been exported to America and Europe or sold to visitors in Japan itself.

Early 19th century lacquered wood netsuke of Tososei, unsigned, 6.3cm. high. (Christie's) $1,580

An ivory netsuke of a seated kirin, signed Yoshimasa, circa 1800, 10.5cm. high. (Christie's) $44,616

An 18th century ivory netsuke of a dog and awabi shell, signed Tomotada, 3.5cm. high. (Christie's) $12,083

An ivory netsuke of a Daruma doll, signed Mitsuhiro and kao (1810-75), 4cm. high. (Christie's) $4,089

A 19th century ivory netsuke of Songoku the magical monkey, signed Mitsuhiro, 5.2cm. high. (Christie's) $13,013

An 18th century ivory netsuke of an Amagatsu doll, signed Masanao (of Kyoto), 5.5cm. high. (Christie's) $48,334

A 20th century ivory netsuke, Boyasha Sonjiro, signed Nasatoshi, 5 cm. high. (Christie's) $6,692

An ivory netsuke of a grazing deer, unsigned, circa 1800, 6.2cm. high. (Christie's) $4,833

An 18th century ivory netsuke of Shoki and Oni, unsigned, 7.7cm. high. (Christie's) $2,974

A 19th century cloudy amber netsuke of Fukurokuju, 6.3cm. high. (Christie's) $1,301

Early 18th century wood netsuke of a bitch and puppies, signed Matsuda Sukenaga, 6.8cm. long. (Christie's) $1,673

A boxwood netsuke of Daruma, signed Sansho (1871-1936), 4.3cm. high. (Christie's) $7,807

A 19th century boxwood netsuke of a large snake holding a rat in its jaws, signed Masanori, 5cm. wide. (Christie's) $2,992

Late 18th century wood netsuke of Roshi seated on a mule (seal netsuke), 7cm. high. (Christie's) $1,766

An ivory seal netsuke carved as a well-known foreigner who came to Nagasaki, signed Mitsumasa, circa 1880, 4.8cm. high. (Christie's) $792

A 19th century Hirado ware netsuke of Gama Sennin, impressed signature Masakazu, 8.1cm. high. (Christie's) $1,022

An 18th century ivory netsuke of a grazing horse, unsigned, 7cm. high. (Christie's) $3,346

A 20th century ivory netsuke of Ryujin, signed Masatoshi, 9.2cm. high. (Christie's) $6,506

A 19th century metal netsuke of a Kendo mask, signed Nagayasu saku, 3.8cm. high. (Christie's) $3,718

Early 19th century wood netsuke of an ostler trying to shoe a horse, 4.8cm. long. (Christie's) $2,416

A 20th century stag-antler netsuke of an owl, signed Masatoshi, 4.5cm. high. (Christie's) $5,948

A wood netsuke of a dog with one foot on a clam shell, Kyoto School, circa 1780, 3.4cm. high. (Christie's) $1,936

Late 18th century ivory netsuke of Moso and bamboo shoot, signed Awataguchi, 8.4cm. high. (Christie's) $5,205

A 19th century wood netsuke of three human skulls, signed Yoshiharu, 5.3cm. wide. (Christie's) $2,602

OILIANA

The awkward sounding name of "Oiliana" has been coined to describe anything connected with the oil business from oil cans to advertising signs. From the beginning of the century when motoring first began, the oil companies were extremely astute at self advertisement and missed no opportunity of pushing their name into the public eye. Collectors can find, in particular, oil cans which were used on every service station before the invention of self pouring cans, bearing the names of Shell, Castrol and Mobiloil as well as B.P. and the lesser known Pratts. Most sought after are the ones made for Shell and Castrol, especially the High Performance Oil containers and Aeroshell and Castrol R. Another pourer used for Oil Power is also collectable. Some cans were just the old style re-painted and a subsequent style, which persisted till the 1950's, can be seen in the quarter and half pint pourers. The old enamel signs used by the Shell Oil Company on their service stations are very highly regarded by collectors.

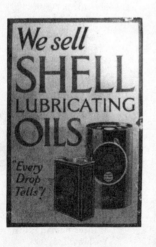

R.O.P. Russian Oil Products oil can and grease tin. $70

Shell Oil half pint pourer. $25

Gamage's Motor Oil, one gallon tin. $175

Lobitos High Quality Motor Oil bottle, Ireland. $20

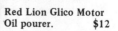

Red Lion Glico Motor Oil pourer. $12

Shell Lubricating Oil tin, late 40's. $25

(Mike Smith's Motoring Past)

338

OILIANA

Esso 'Put a Tiger in Your Tank', sign. $80

Pratt's Motor Oil tin sign, 'Do You Need Oil?' $55

Castrol Motor Oil cut out counter display card. $55

Coolie Motor Oil tin from Lagos, Nigeria. $60

Carburol Additive dispenser. $40

Shell Lubricating Oils enamel sign. $350

National Benzole open/closed sign. $150

Glico oil can, one gallon. $55

Fina Oil bottles. $18   each

(Mike Smith's Motoring Past)

OILIANA

Castrol Motor Oil guides.
$10   each

Set of three Castrol Motor
Oil pourers, half pint, pint,
one gallon, 1966. $55

BP 'Buy from the Pump'
enamel sign, 18 x 12in. $90

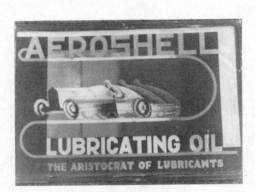

Castrol Motorcycle Oil tin.
$25

Aeroshell Lubricant Oil tin
sign. $600

Redex Upper Cylinder
Lubricant dispenser. $175

Shell Motor Oil cans, 1930's.
Small $50
Large $40

Castrol Motor Oil tin cut out
display sign. $175

Cross Country Motor Oil
pourer, USA. $50

(Mike Smith's Motoring Past)

OINTMENT POTS

In the days when medicine was less advanced than it is today, sick people were prepared to try almost anything to become well and newspapers were full of advertisements promising miraculous cures if such and such a medicine or ointment was used. Quack medicine dealers made fortunes with their potions and the bottles and jars which can be found in rubbish dumps today make fascinating collections. Often they carried labels listing the cures they would effect and the claims were astonishing. The ingredients contained in the ointments were not listed because they were often ineffectual or, at worst, harmful. When legislation was passed making it necessary for ingredients to be listed — and even later when advertising claims had to be upheld — the day of the spurious patent medicine was over. Some early ointments were sold in attractive jars ranging from Delft ones of the 16th century to glazed pottery ones of the Victorians. They are cheap to buy and easy to display as well as being interesting and colourful.

'Professor" Holloway's Ointment was sold world-wide because of brilliant promotion. (Over £26,000 per annum was spent on advertising in 1850). Holloway became very rich and a great philanthropist with an estate valued at 15 million pounds on his death in 1883.   Non pictorial pots $12   Pictorial pots $5

The propriety ointment with the longest history — Singleton's Eye Ointment, on sale from late 1700's until 1949, was based on a recipe 'invented' by Dr. Thomas Johnson in 1596. The pots contained a thin layer of ointment, covered by parchment and later foil, which was designed to be held against the eye. Early pots were bulky with a large pedestal foot and unglazed examples are extremely rare. From 1780-1825 they were signed Fulgham, from 1826-1858 they were signed Green, then reverted to Singleton.
          Early examples $45   19th & 20th examples $2

Brown's Herbal ointment, later Nature's, inscribed 'In all pulmonary complaints, soreness of the chest and lungs, sore throat, neuralgia, rheumatism, croup in children, severe pains in the stomach, spinal diseases, epilepsy or fits, affections of the heart and liver, for corrupt sores of long standing such as ulcers and tumours of a scrofulous character'. Hence 'cure-alls'.
          Small 1¾in. high. $9   Large 2¾in. high. $25

OINTMENT POTS

Cook's Carbolic Jelly, Nottingham, 1.1/8in. high. $70

Small bluish glaze pot with dark blue decoration, circa 1700. $155

Handall's Celebrated Ointment, Plymouth. $45

Sands' Ointment, 1½in. high. $60

An early bluish glaze pot with dark blue decoration, circa 1780. $95

Grandfather's Ointment. $55

Clarke's Miraculous Salve 'Best Application For . . . , 2.5/8in. high. $14

'Poor Man's Friend', by Dr. Giles Roberts, on sale from late 1700's, to early 1900's, 1.5/16in. high, by courtesy of Bridport Museum. $70

Moonseed Ointment, The Great Household Remedy, Swindon, 2in. high. $45

No Name Ointment, Birmingham. $35

'Delescot', bluish tin glaze pot, Duke St., London, 1749. $260

Isola 'The Bishop's Balm', 1¼in. high. $140

OINTMENT POTS

Pinkish tin glaze ointment pot, possibly 17th century, 1.1/8in. tall. $80

An early bluish glaze ointment pot with dark blue decoration, circa 1730. $125

Mrs. Croft's Ointment, West Hanley, near Chesterfield. $25

Sturton's Poor Man's Cerate, Peterborough. $55

Bluish grey glaze ointment pot, circa 1730, 1.5/8in. high. $45

The Egyptian Salve, Wolverhampton, based on a recipe first recorded in the Ebers Papyrus in 1500 B.C., 1½in. high. $14

Tibbald's Blood Tonic pot, Taunton, complete with its advert, 1¼in. high. $45

'Poor Man's Friend', sold by Beach & Barnicott, Bridport, circa 1840, 1¾in. high. $25

Boots 'Confection of Senna' pot with attractive fern decoration, 3¼in. high. $18

Clarke's Miraculous Salve, Lincoln, 'For the Cure of . . . , 1½in. high. $7

Waller & Son, bluish tin glaze pot, Guildford, Surrey, late 18th century. $260

Machin's Infallible Pearl Ointment, Dudley. $35

PAPIER MACHE

Papier mâché was invented by the French and was popular from the early 19th century to the High Victorian period. It was usually coated in lacquer, which was decorated with painting or even mother of pearl inlay, and the greatest craftsmen in the medium were probably Jennens and Bettridge, whose work is now very sought after. Many items were made, from trinket boxes to decorative pieces of furniture.

A Russian papier mache box realistically painted with a scene of two fishermen on a riverbank, signed and dated, 19 x 17.5cm.
(Phillips) $423

A Regency scarlet and gilt japanned papier-mache tray, with impressed mark 'Clay King St/Covt. Garden', 20¼in. wide. (Christie's)
$8,995

A Victorian papier-mache baluster vase with flared rim painted with two oval panels, 13½in. high. (Lawrence Fine Art)
$210

A 19th century papier-mache tray with shaped edge and a design of flowers by Evans. (Lots Road Galleries)
$417

One of a pair of mid Victorian black, gold japanned papier-mache spill vases, 8in. wide. (Christie's) $471

A mid Victorian black, gilt and mother-of-pearl japanned papier-mache table-bureau, 14¾in. wide. (Christie's)
$1,258

An early Victorian black and gilt japanned papier-mache card box with lifting lid, 11¼in. wide. (Christie's)
$550

PARIAN

Parian is slightly translucent, silky textured, matt white porcelain which looks a little like marble but which can be molded to produce figures and reproductions of sculpture. Most of the porcelain manufacturers produced lines in Parian ware and these ranged from Wedgwood to Belleek. It was particularly effective in making small figures of Greek goddesses.

It first appeared about 1840 when two firms, Minton and Copeland and Garrett recognised the possibility of making Parian statuary and this idea was also adopted by Wedgwood in 1848. They all turned out slightly less than lifesize models of Classical figures and sold them as adornments for modern homes where they were used as decorations in conservatories and halls. Later, when the technique of manufacture was refined, Parian was used for the manufacture of tableware and ornaments.

A large Parian group entitled 'Detected', signed R.J. Morris, 41cm. high. (Dee & Atkinson) $284

Coloured Parian bust of The Beautiful Duchess, who was Georgiana, Duchess of Devonshire. (Goss & Crested China Ltd.) $2,250

A Sam Alcock & Co Parian seated portrait figure of Wellington with joined hands and crossed legs, 28cm. high. (Phillips) $498

A Copeland Parian group, entitled 'Go To Sleep', impressed Art Union of London, J. Durham Sc 1862, 26in. high overall. (Anderson & Garland) $525

Kirk Braddon Cross in brown washed parian. $140 £82 Unusually, the white parian example is more valuable. (Goss & Crested China Ltd) $325

Parian bust of Lord Palmerston on socle base and fluted column, 335mm. high. (Goss & Crested China Ltd.) $270

A Parian bust of Wellington wearing military uniform, 14in. high. (Christie's) $234

A Minton Parian group of Ariadne and the Panther on rectangular base, year cypher for 1867, 13.7in. high. (Woolley & Wallis) $390

A Goss Parian bust of Queen Victoria, for Mortlock's of Oxford Street, 236mm. high. (Phillips) $400

A coloured Parian group modelled as a young girl on rockwork, entitled 'You can't read', 12¼in. high, possibly by Robinson & Leadbetter. (Christie's) $222

A Parian standing female figure, probably Belleek but unmarked, 36.5cm. high. (Lawrence Fine Art) $159

One of a pair of glazed Parian figure brackets, allegorical figures in rock-like niches, 9½in. high. (Capes, Dunn & Co.) $163

A Minton parian figure of Dorothea, after John Bell, 13¾in. high, registration tablet for 1872. (Parsons, Welch & Cowell) $323

A Parian figural group of sleeping children 'Le Nid', circa 1875, signed 'Croisy', 15in. high. (Robt. W. Skinner Inc.) $750

An 18th century French biscuit group modelled as a bearded god attended by two cupids, 40cm. high. (Christie's) $1,069

PATCH BOXES

Up until the 19th century smallpox was a scourge that attacked all classes of society and even if patients were fortunate enough to survive an attack, they were often left with pock marked faces. To conceal the scars, fashionable women in the 18th century began wearing tiny patches, either round or shaped like hearts and stars, on their faces. The fashion proved to be so becoming that even women who were not victims of smallpox took to wearing patches. The little patches themselves were kept in special boxes made of papier mache, silver or painted enamel from Battersea, Bilston, Birmingham or South Staffordshire where they were manufactured by fusing glass onto copper and painting the decoration on by hand. The box was then fired at a very high temperature. After the disappearance of patches from a well to do lady's toilette, the boxes continued to be used for snuff, nutmeg or to hold little sponges soaked in aromatic vinegar which was used like smelling salts.

A Staffordshire portrait patch box, the lid with 'Marquis of Wellington', circa 1813, 4cm. $525

Early 19th century oval Staffordshire patch box, 3.5cm. $435

A Staffordshire patch box of oval form, lid mirror lined, 4cm. $1,300

A South Staffordshire oval enamel patch box, transfer-printed and painted on the cover with Bristol Hot Wells, circa 1800, 1¾in. long. (Christie's) $544

A Staffordshire small oval combined patchbox and nutmeg grater, with gilt metal mounts, circa 1765, 1.7/8in. long. (Christie's) $629

Late 18th century oval Staffordshire patch box, the lid printed with a view of Buckingham Palace, 4cm. $525

A Bilston enamel combined bonbonniere and patch box, 5cm. high. (Lawrence Fine Art) $1,116

A George III enamel patch box, South Staffordshire, circa 1770, 1.5/8in. wide. (Christie's) $2,420

A Bilston patch box of circular form, circa 1775, 1¾in. diam., slight damage. $1,010

PEWTER

Pewter is an alloy based on tin with the addition of other metals which may be lead, brass or copper. It is thought to have been made by the Romans but was most popular in Britain during Elizabethen times when it was employed for church vessels, domestic purposes and civic functions. Pewter began to be used for church vessels in the early Middle Ages when it replaced wood for the chalices. Until the 15th century it was customary to bury a pewter chalice with the priest. Pewter chalices, flagons, alms dishes and collecting plates can still be found in many church vaults. Generally speaking pewter was a makeshift substitute for silver and it was worked in the same patterns and styles as the more precious metal. Some pewter, particularly from Germany, was intricately decorated and cast in relief but such items are rare and pewter is generally spare and workmanlike in design. Artists continue to work in pewter and it appears very successfully in Liberty's Tudric and Clutha designs for serving flagons.

A lighthouse coffee pot, by G. Richardson, Boston, 1818-28, 10½in. high. (Christie's) $330

A WMF electroplated pewter drinking set with shaped rectangular tray, circa 1900, tray 48 x 34cm. (Christie's) $946

A flask with a threaded cap, by James Weekes, N.Y., 1820-43, marked with Laughlin touch, 7in. high. (Christie's) $495

A 19th century pewter leech jar, the pierced lid with carrying handle, 7in. high. (Christie's) $382

A WMF rectangular shaped pewter mirror, 14in. high, stamped marks. (Christie's) $691

A tapering cylindrical mug, by Frederick Bassett, N.Y., 1761-80, marked with Montgomery touch, 4½in. high. (Christie's) $935

A Liberty pewter and Clutha glass bowl on stand, designed by Archibald Knox, stamped Tudric 0276, circa 1900, 16.3cm. high. (Christie's) $656

A rectangular pewter-rimmed kobako, unsigned, circa 1800, 9.3 x 8.3cm. (Christie's) $1,320

Late 18th century porringer, New England, 4½in. diam. (Christie's) $264

A pewter circular plate, marked on base with 'Love' touch, Laughlin 868, Phila., circa 1750-1800, 8½in. diam. (Christie's) $286

A Jugendstil polished pewter triptych mirror in the style of P. Huber, 32.2 x 53.4cm. (Christie's) $626

A Kayersinn pewter jardiniere, stamped Kayersinn 4093, 29.8cm. high. (Christie's) $375

A tankard with S scroll handle, by Parks Boyd, Phila., 1795-1819, marked with Laughlin touch 546, 7½in. high. (Christie's) $2,090

A Liberty & Co. 'Tudric' pewter box and cover, designed by Archibald Knox, 11.9cm. high. (Christie's) $380

A covered pitcher of baluster form, by Thos. D. and S. Boardman, 1830-50, marked with Laughlin touch 435, 10in. high. (Christie's) $330

PHONOGRAPHS

The first phonograph was invented in America in 1876 by Thomas Alva Edison and ten years later the gramophone was patented by Emile Berliner. Originally Berliner's machine played zinc coated rubber discs and the sound was very jerky because it was hand cranked. However 1900 the clockwork mechanism was more sophisticated and the first shellac discs had appeared. Most of the machines on sale then had large horns usually made of brass but occasionally of papier mache or painted tin which looked very pretty. Machines produced by firms like The Gramophone Co, G and T, or H. M. V. had attractive names like Aeolian, Vocalion, Deccalion and Oranoca. It was fashionable to have a gramophone in the parlour and soon, to make the machines merge more with household furniture, the horns were removed and gramophones were encased in neat cabinets with the loudspeakers inside. As well as old gramophones and phonographs, collectors also look for gramophone needles, record cleaners and needle sharpeners.

An Edison Fireside phonograph, Model A No. 25426, the K reproducer, crane and 36 two-minute and four-minute wax cylinders in cartons. (Christie's) $748

An Edison Diamond disc phonograph in walnut case of Louis XV design, 50in. high, and 46 Edison discs. (Christie's) $1,188

An Edison Home phonograph, Model A No. H104435, with B reproducer, crane 42in. long, and 25 cylinders. (Christie's) $693

An Edison Amerola 1A phonograph, No. SM 950 in mahogany case with two-minute and four-minute traversing mandrel mechanism, 49in. high. (Christie's) $1,782

An early Edison electric phonograph mechanism, in oak case with glass cover, with rear part of a Bettini carrier arm (lacks Edison carrier arm, Bettini reproducer and horn). (Christie's) $1,960

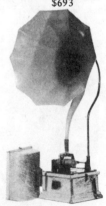

An Edison Fireside phonograph, Model A No. 31916, now with Diamond B reproducer, Model R and Model K reproducers with adapter ring. (Christie's) $646

An Edison Bell 'Commercial' electric phonograph, No. 21164, the motor in oak base with accessories drawer. (Christie's) $1,336

An Edison Home phonograph, early Model A, with automatic reproducer, and modern brass witch's hat horn. (Christie's) $427

An Edison concert phonograph with Bettini spider diaphragm, American, circa 1902. $2,059

An Edison Diamond Disc phonograph, Chippendale Laboratory Model (C19) No. SM 106640, 51½in. high, with nineteen discs. (Christie's) $748

An Edison spring motor phonograph with Bettini Type D reproducer, American, circa 1903. $1,552

An Edison Fireside combination type phonograph, Model B No. 89443, with four minute gearing. (Onslows) $700

An Edison Red Gem phonograph, Model D No. 316478D, with K combination reproducer, maroon fireside octagonal horn and crane. (Onslows) $491

An Edison Standard phonograph, Model C No. 660275, with combination gear and Bettini reproducer. (Onslows) $357

An Edison Triumph phonograph, Model A No. 45259, in 'New Style' green oak case, with 14in. witch's hat horn. (Christie's) $770

PHOTOGRAPHIC ITEMS

Enlargers, dryers, darkroom lamps, viewers, cutters, tripods are all pieces of photographic equipment that display excellent workmanship and ingenuity of manufacture. In the same field are early stereoscopes of which the Brewster was the most popular in its Victorian hey-day. They were made for viewing daguerrotypes and the ones mounted on pedestals sell for anything between $200 and $2,000. Another unusual piece of photographic equipment is the cinematograph and a wealth of both apparatus and film can still be found. However a problem with early films is that they are highly inflammable, so take care. Pathescope, a French firm, pioneered the home movie and their cameras and old films as well as amateur films may provide wonderful documentary material for the years between the wars. Projectors are considered to be not very desirable by collectors because early Bioscopes are very unwieldy, however there are a few projectors that weigh slightly less and they include the Lumiere Brothers Cinematographe camera/projector which sells for around $5,000.

Kodak glass and celluloid store sign, 37 x 15in., in black frame, circa 1910, with 'Kodaks' in 8in. gold recessed letter on black background. (Robt. W. Skinner Inc.) $475

A 35mm. Globuscope 360° Panoramic camera No. 1094 with a Globuscope 25mm. f 3.5 - 22 lens with pouch case, film case and film resin all in maker's box. (Christie's) $1,623

A Kodak 27 x 13in enamelled street sign with both sides in white lettering stating 'All "Kodak" Supplies', circa 1920's. (Christie's) $73

An early brass mounted 35mm. hand-cranked cinematograph projector with R.R. lens, 15in. high. (Christie's) $1,755

An Arthur Branscombe, 'King Kodak. A topical burlesque in two acts', a play apparently written during 1892. (Christie's) $353

A brass reproduction Petzval-Type daguerreotype camera, signed Voigtlander & Sohn in Wien, no. 084, circa 1956, 12¼in. long. (Christie's) $2,530

A metal Kodak store sign, triangular with heavy metal bracket, 'Developing Printing Enlarging'. (Robt. W. Skinner Inc.) $85

PHOTOGRAPHS

One of the most revolutionary inventions was the camera which made it possible to record history at the flick of a switch. After George Eastman invented his Kodak camera in the 1880's, the door was thrown open to ordinary people to take their own photographs — a challenge which they grasped eagerly. There are two schools of photography collecting. Firstly, specialists seek out photographs taken by the famous names of the art — William Henry Fox Talbot, Julia Margaret Cameron, Roger Fenton, Robert Adamson and David Octavius Hill, Matthew Brady and the Rev. Charles Dodgson (Lewis Carroll). Prices paid for their plates are however very high and the more modest collector seeks out the work of less famous people. Views of distant places are well regarded, especially scenes of Indian hill stations during the British Raj or places that have been radically changed by events. Another popular area is photographs of British towns and slum scenes or pictures of ordinary people working at their jobs, particularly agricultural labourers in the days before mechanisation.

Cecil Beaton — H.R.H. Princess Margaret — One of thirty-three gelatin silver prints, 1950's. (Christie's) $685

Bill Brandt — Children of Sheffield — Gelatin silver print, image size 12 x 10½in., 1930's, printed 1980's. (Christie's) $548

Burmese portraits, architecture and topography — thirty-four albumen prints, approx. 8 x 11in., 1880's. (Christie's) $881

Guglielmo Pluschow — Nude studies — Two albumen prints, each approx. 8¾ x 6½in., circa 1900. (Christie's) $391

Count Zichy — A quantity of photographs, majority gelatin silver prints, including advertising and fashion photographs. (Christie's) $627

F. M. Sutcliffe — A bit of news (at Robin Hoods Bay) — Toned gelatin silver print 8 x 6½in., 1880's. (Christie's) $685

Bill Brandt — Tic-Tac men at Ascot races — Gelatin silver print, image size 11¼ x 10¼in. 1930's, printed 1980's. (Christie's) $783

Man Ray — R. Rosselini, H. Langlois (Cinematheque Paris), Jean Renoir — Gelatin silver print, 7 x 9½in., titled in pencil and with photographer's ink credit stamp 'Man Ray — Paris', 1940's. (Christie's) $490

Bill Brandt — Cocktails in a Surrey garden — Gelatin silver print, image size 12¼ x 10½in., 1930's, printed 1980's. (Christie's) $744

Herbert G. Ponting — The Potter at his Wheel, Japan — Brown-toned gelatin silver print, 13¼ x 19in., 1902-5. (Christie's) $548

Marville (S...pont) — Reclining nude — Albumen print, 5¾ x 7¾in. mounted on card, 1850's/60's. (Christie's) $489

Baron Wilhelm von Gloeden, attributed to — Three little boys and Young boy seated — Two albumen prints, 1900. (Christie's) $587

Robert Doisneau — Hell — Gelatin silver print, 15¼ x 12 in. pencil signature and number '28961' on reverse, 1950's. (Christie's) $1,273

Anthony Osmond-Evans — Portrait of Mother Theresa — R-type colour print, 20 x 16in., signed by photographer, November 1987. (Christie's) $352

Anon — Russian trader being served tea — Albumen print, 9½ x 7¼in., mounted on card, 1860's. (Christie's) $587

PHOTOGRAPHS

William Henry Fox Talbot —
The Fruit Sellers — Calotype,
7¼ x 9in. numbered 'LA 300'
in ink on reverse, 1842.
(Christie's) $8,330

Joseph Cundall — Highlanders
— Albumen print, 9 x 7¼in.
arched top, mounted on card.
1856. (Christie's) $391

Cecil Beaton — Andy Warhol
and Candy Darling — Gelatin
silver print, 7½ x 8¾in.,
photographer's credit stamp
on reverse, 1969. (Christie's)
$392

Anon — Everyday life in
London — One of fifty-eight
gelatin silver prints, each
approx. 15¾ x 19½in., 1950's.
(Christie's) $548

Robert Frank — Mother and
child — Gelatin silver print,
9 x 13½in., 1950's. (Christie's)
$3,133

Willy Prager — Girl on beach
— Gelatin silver print,
9½ x 7in. photographer's ink
credit stamp and number
'3223' on reverse, 1920s/30s.
(Christie's) $391

M. F. Moresby, J. Robertson
and others — Rio de Janeiro,
Sydney, Auckland and the
Crimea — Part album of approx.
eighty-nine photographs and
five composite panoramas,
1858. (Christie's) $8,224

John Thomson — Street Life
in London — Text by Adolphe
Smith, with thirty-seven
woodburytypes, approx.
4¼ x 3¼in., printed borders
and titles, 1878. (Christie's)
$3,132

Bill Brandt — Coach party,
Royal Hunt Cup Day, Ascot
— Mammoth gelatin silver
print, 24 x 28¼in., mounted
on board, printed early
1970's. (Christie's) $352

PIANOLA ROLLS

Pianola rolls could be made either by a special machine attached to a piano (thus recording an actual performance) or they could be produced mechanically. Most early examples are of classical or religious music, but the ones to look out for are those of swing or honky-tonk music produced in the 1920's. The wrappings of pianola rolls are often very elaborate and ornate, and when you consider that these can often still be picked up for a dollar or two, we're talking real value for money.

Harrods Ltd., 'Badinage', by Victor Herbert, 1911. $9

Keith Prowse & Co., 'I'm bringing a red, red rose', from 'Whoopee', by W. Donaldson, duty stamp, 1916. $10

Universal music Roll, 'Gliding', a fox trot by P. L. Grant, 1900. $12

The Boston Music Co. Ltd., 'The Rosery', by Nevin, with duty stamp, 1895. $5

The Brixton Music Roll Exchange 'Italian Concerto'. $5

Meloto, 'Pleasant Memories', by Godiana, 1902. $5

Aeolian Company Ltd., 'Hearts and Flowers', 1898. $3.50

The British Autoplayer Company Ltd., 'Valse Caprice', 1890. $7

Meloto Song Roll 'I know a lovely garden', played by Cyril Westbury, 1899. $5

Aeolian Company Ltd., 'Oh Mr Rubinstein', 1898. $3.50

PICTURE FRAMES

Picture frames can often be more valuable than the picture they enclose. Prices as high as $7,500 can be paid for carved and gilded frames dating from the time of Louis XIV and for Italian 18th century "Salvator Rosa" frames. Dutch tortoiseshell frames of the 17th century are in the same price bracket. Old frames are snapped up by collectors who want elegant mounts for their paintings and drawings. Frames which might have been sold for firewood a few years ago are today soaring into the four figure bracket. Among the favourites are heavy gilt Victorian frames, bamboo and cane frames (providing they are old) and frames made of unusual woods like maple or burr elm which were fairly common in Victorian times. Padded velvet frames that were used to mount watercolour paintings of flowers are very popular provided they are not too faded or threadbare. Smaller frames are also making high prices. These include Victorian, Art Nouveau and Art Deco silver photograph frames. It is important to make sure that the silver is not worn away by over-enthusiastic cleaning.

An embossed and pierced shaped silver photograph frame, London, 1900, 8in. high. (Dacre, Son & Hartley) $270

A WMF plated figural easel-backed mirror, stamped maker's marks, 37cm. high. (Phillips) $870

One of a pair of early George III white painted and gilded picture frames attributed to Wm. Vile and John Cobb, 75 x 59in. (Christie's) $40,176

A Liberty silver and enamel picture frame, designed by Archibald Knox, with Birmingham hallmarks for 1904, 21.2cm. high. (Christie's) $5,909

An Art Nouveau silver photograph frame, stamped maker's marks W.N. and Chester hallmarks for 1903, 22.3cm. high. (Christie's) $450

One of a pair of carved and pierced sandalwood picture frames with Japanese folded silk and paper pictures, 19½ x 14in. (Edgar Horn) $310

An Art Nouveau silver picture frame, 35cm. high, marked WN and for Chester 1903. (Phillips) $518

A Wm. Hutton & Sons Arts & Crafts silver picture frame, London hallmarks for 1903, 20cm. high. (Christie's) $2,272

A Wm. Hutton & Sons Arts & Crafts silver picture frame, London hallmarks for 1903, 20cm. high. (Christie's) $2,187

An Edwardian Art Nouveau silver and enamel photograph frame, Wm. Hutton & Sons Ltd., London, 1904, 10.25in. high, also an Elkington & Co. vase, Birmingham, 1906. (Reeds Rains) $1,162

A Liberty & Co. silver and enamelled picture frame, 19 x 14.50cm., with Art Nouveau hinged support, hallmarked L. & Co., Birmingham, 1899. (Phillips) $2,664

An Art Nouveau photograph frame, maker's marks W.N. and Chester hallmarks for 1903, 31cm. high. (Christie's) $3,048

A Ramsden & Carr silver picture frame, with London hallmarks for 1900, 15.5cm. high. (Christie's) $1,425

An Art Nouveau silver picture frame, 28cm. high, marked SB, Birmingham, 1903. (Phillips) $374

A late Victorian oblong photograph frame, by Wm. Comyns, London, 1904, 6¾in. high. (Christie's) $230

PIN CUSHIONS

Needlewomen always need a safe place to stick their needles and pins so pin cushions have been available for centuries but it was the Victorians with their passion for prettifying everything that turned them into things of beauty.

Pincushions can be found in many sizes and an enormous variety of shapes, covered with silk, satin, velvet or coarser fabrics, trimmed with lace and ribbon or decorated with embroidery. Some pincushions are inserted like pads inside silver, metal or wooden shoes, boots, birds, hedgehogs, pigs, coaches or dolls. Others are trimmed with intricate beadwork and embroidered with encouraging mottos. They look prettiest when stuck all over with close packed pins, many of them with coloured heads.

Victorian plated pig pin cushion, 4in. long. $35

Late Victorian pin cushion on an ebonised base. $7

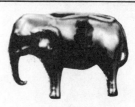

Late 19th century plated pin cushion in the form of an elephant. $18

Plated brass pin cushion in the form of a sow, circa 1895. $35

Heart shaped pin cushion inscribed Merry Christmas and Argyll & Sutherland Highlanders. $70

White metal shoe pin cushion, circa 1900. $25

Victorian horse's hoof pin cushion with plated mounts. $25

Bone pin cushion 'Chrystal Palace, London 1851'. $45

Victorian bead work pin cushion. $45

PLASTER

Plaster, being inexpensive and easily mouldable, is ideally suited to the mass production of the cheap and sometimes nasty seaside souvenir type ornaments. There are, however some very collectable items to be found in the middle range of stylised and colorful Art deco figures of the 30's. The works of notable sculptor Richard Garbe, often depicting women in flowing robes and with streaming hair, are definitely top of the range. Whatever the subject, these pieces are always worked in a gentle and evocative style.

An English plaster panel, in oak frame carved 'Speed with the light-foot winds to run', 42.2 x 37.7cm. (Christie's) $168

A Richard Garbe green-tinted plaster figure of a naked seated maiden, 1928, 104cm. high. (Christie's) $1,074

A pair of Regency polychrome plaster figures of Chinese figures in court dress with nodding heads, 13¾in. high. (Christie's) $17,028

A Richard Garbe plaster figure of a naked maiden, 1912, 99cm. high. (Christie's) $660

A 19th century tinted plaster bust of a gentleman, after Houdon, 70cm. high. (Christie's) $827

A James Woolford plaster figure modelled as a diving mermaid with a dolphin, circa 1930, 59cm. high. (Christie's) $315

A 19th century painted plaster wall bracket, in the form of a winged cherub issuing from acanthus leaves, 51cm. (Osmond Tricks) $86

An early 19th century French plaster bust of a young officer, cast from a model by F. Leclercq, 51cm. high. (Christie's) $1,861

Pair of painted plaster book-ends, each modelled as a bowl of fruit, 8¾in. high. (Christie's) $277

A plaster bust of George II, his hair dressed with laurels. (Christie's) $707

A late 19th century English polychrome plaster bust of Florence Nightingale, by T Woolner, 1874, 58.5cm. high. (Christie's) $706

A Richard Garbe plaster figure of a naked kneeling maiden with streaming hair and flowing drapery, 102cm. high. (Christie's) $1,239

A late 19th century French original plaster half length portrait of Mme. La Baronne Cecile Demarcay, signed J. B. Carpeaux, 80cm. high. (Christie's) $29,392

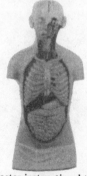

A late 19th century French plaster bust of 'L'Espiegle', signed on the shoulder J. B. Carpeaux, 51cm. high. (Christie's) $2,571

A plaster portrait bust of The Hon. Mrs Maryanna Marten by Augustus John, 24in. high. (Woolley & Wallis) $1,353

A plaster instructional torso coloured and numbered and arranged so as to dismantle for display purposes, 33in. high. (Christie's) $918

PLASTIC

Plastic arguably came of age as a decorative material in the Art Deco period, when a multitude of different items, often in strikingly geometrical forms and dazzling colors were fashioned from it. Many of these now fetch enormous sums, but items from the 50's too are becoming increasingly popular and are still affordable. 50's plastic jewellery, handbags, radios etc. are recognisable often by their highly stylised design and their softer, pastel color tones.

Early 1960's silver blue plastic robot with red flashing eyes and three different sonic sounds. $85

1950's green plastic salt and pepper. $5

Pair of pale blue plastic egg cups, 1950's. $2

1950's green plastic perpetual calendar with Venetian scene. $9

1950's green plastic modermistic powder bowl, 5in. diam. $10

1950's pink plastic swan ornament. $9

1960's Vidor portable plastic radio. $38

(Border Bygones)

362

PLATES

There are as many different kinds of plates as there are different potteries and porcelain factories. Plates can make a fascinating collection an look well displayed on walls or in glass fronted cupboards. Some collectors stick to the same or matching colours or similar themes in decoration. Before embarking on a serious search for plates, it is essential to buy a good book on china marks and one of the best for English porcelain is Geoffrey Godden's "Encyclopaedia of English Porcelain Manufacturers". A point to bear in mind is that any plate bearing the mark "Bone China" or "Made in England" suggests the date of manufacture is in the 20th century. The word "England" added to a mark implies that it is post 1891 because in that year the McKinley Tariff Act imposed place of origin on a mark. The words Trade Mark were added after 1862 and a pattern mark or number indicates a date no earlier than 1810. The Royal Arms were incorporated in marks after 1800.

One of a pair of pearlware plates and a creamware plate, one 9¾in. diam., 1810-30. (Christie's) $286

Doulton crackleglaze plate with shaped edge. $27

A Longton Hall strawberry leaf moulded plate, circa 1755, 23cm. diam. (Christie's) $3,448

A Castelli small plate, painted with a putto in flight holding a book, 17cm. diam. (Phillips) $802

One of two 19th century slip-decorated Redware plates, American, 11¼in. and 12in. diam. (Christie's) $385

Doulton 'Make Me Laugh' rack plate, Behind the Painted Masque Limited Edition Series, 9in. diam., 1982. (Abridge Auctions) $18

A Rouen shaped circular plate painted in a famille verte palette, circa 1740, 25cm. diam. (Christie's) $1,948

One of a pair of pearlware plates, each octagonal painted with swags of lemons with brown leaves, 1810-20, 7¾in. diam. (Christie's) $198

A Coalport cabinet plate, signed by F.H. Chivers, with ripened fruit on an earthy ground, 10½in. across. (Christie's) $529

A Bow circular plate painted in famille rose with a Chinese lady, probably Lan Ts'ai Ho, 22.5cm. diam. (Phillips) $1,586

Doulton 'Short Headed Salmon' rack plate, signed by J. Birbeck, 9½in. diam., circa 1913. (Abridge Auctions) $105

A Coalport porcelain dessert plate from the service presented by Queen Victoria to the Emperor of Russia in 1845, 10in. wide.   (Dacre, Son & Hartley) $2,557

A Maw & Co. circular pottery charger painted in a ruby red lustre with winged mythical beast, 13½in. diam. (Christie's) $382

A London delft blue and white Royalist portrait plate, circa 1690, 22cm. diam. (Christie's) $2,541

A Barr, Flight & Barr plate, decorated probably in London and in the manner of the Baxter workshop, 23.5cm. diam. (Phillips) $501

One of a pair of pierced Imari plates, 8in. diam.. (R. K. Lucas & Son) $159

Doulton octagonal plate painted with white pate-sur-pate flowers on a brown ground, by Eliza Simmance, 1878, 10in. diameter. (Abridge Auctions) $195

A Russian Imperial porcelain dinner plate, 23.5cm. diam., cypher mark of Nicholas I in blue. (Phillips) $668

One of a pair of Caughley plates from the Donegal Service, painted at Chamberlain's factory, circa 1793, 21cm. diam. (Christie's) $1,724

Doulton 'At the Cheshire Cheese' Dr Johnson Series rack plaque, 13in. diam., circa 1909. (Abridge Auctions) $57

Late 17th century Arita blue and white charger. (Christie's) $2,805

Doulton 'Gibson Girl' rack plate, by Charles Dana Gibson, circa 1901. (Abridge Auctions) $60

A Chinese famille verte plate, Kangxi, circa 1725, 9¼in. diam. (Woolley & Wallis) $672

A Castelli armorial plate from the Grue workshop, 25cm. diam. (Phillips) $9,168

POMANDERS

Pomanders are really first cousins to vinaigrettes and, like them, date from the time when personal hygiene and laundry care were not all they are now. The most basic pomander was probably an orange stuck with cloves, but like most other Good Ideas, they became more and more sophisticated, coming complete with hook, made from such attractive materials as silver and ceramics, and beautifully decorated. It's interesting to note that they are enjoying quite a revival today!

A silver pomander with eight compartments, circa 1700, 2in. high. (Christie's)
$4,452

Early 18th century German silver pear-shaped pomander in three threaded sections, 2.5/8in. high. (Christie's)
$798

A German spherical pomander, 6.4cm. high, 17th century, 80gr. $2,200

Early 18th century German silver pomander with entwined foliage stem, 2in. high. (Christie's) $272

Early 18th century silver gilt pomander of threaded acorn shape, 2½in. high. (Christie's)
$1,052

A silver gilt pomander, the six-hinged segments engraved with flowers and foliate sprays, circa 1600, probably German, 1¾in. high. (Christie's)
$4,950

Early 18th century German silver pear-shaped pomander with perforated interior, 2½in. high. (Christie's)
$816

PORTRAIT MINIATURES

Before the invention of the camera people gave their loved ones portraits of themselves painted in miniature as remembrances. With the development of the Empire, when many young men went abroad, the trade of the miniaturist expanded greatly for the travellers wanted to take pictures of loved ones with them. One of the finest miniaturists was Nicholas Hilliard who worked at the time of Queen Elizabeth I, but his clientele was confined to the very rich and well born. Later, the practice of having a miniature done spread to the emergent middle class and watering places like Bath, Tunbridge Wells or Cheltenham supported colonies of miniaturists. Many of them were women but the most famous were Richard Cosway, Henry Spicer, Horace Hone, Richard Crosse, Ozias Humphrey, Jeremiah Meyer, Charles Bestland and George Engleheart. The best miniatures were painted with watercolor on ivory which gave a flesh like glow to the skin and an opaque color to the clothes.

Richard Gibson, a gentleman facing right in armour and white linen collar, on vellum, gilt metal frame with reeded border, oval 2¼in. high. (Christie's) $2,494

Captain and Mrs. Wm. Croome, by G. Engleheart, both signed and dated 1811 and 1812, later gold frames, ovals, 3¼in. high. (Christie's) $8,316

Thomas Flatman, a nobleman called John Maitland, 2nd Earl and Duke of Lauderdale, on vellum, signed with initial, oval 2.1/8in. high. (Christie's) $7,128

John Smart, a miniature of Peter Johnston, signed with initials and dated 1803, gold frame, oval 3½in. high. (Christie's) $10,692

Aldani, a miniature of a gentleman seated on a stone wall, signed, gilt metal frame, rectangular 3.1/8in. high. (Christie's) $1,782

William Grimaldi, a portrait of a child seated beside a tree with a blue finch on his hand, signed, gold frame, oval 2¾in. high. (Christie's) $6,237

367

PORTRAIT MINIATURES

Andrew Plimer, an officer in scarlet uniform with blue facings and silver lace, gold frame, oval 3in. (Christie's) $3,207

John Smart, a miniature of Miss Elizabeth Cottingham of County Clare, signed and dated 1777, gold frame, oval 2in. high. (Christie's) $10,335

James Green, a gentleman possibly the Rt. Hon. Edward Ellice, gold frame, oval 3.1/8in. high. (Christie's) $981

Philip Jean, a gentleman in blue coat with gold buttons, gold frame, oval 2.5/8in. high. (Christie's) $715

David Des Granges, a miniature of a lady in black dress with lace border and white lace collar, on vellum, oval 2.3/8in. high. (Christie's) $8,019

Studio of Richard Gibson, a gentleman believed to be Sir John Germaine, on vellum, oval 3.1/8in. high. (Christie's) $1,782

George Place, a miniature of an officer of the Weymouth Vol. Artillery, gilt metal frame, oval 4¾in. high. (Christie's) $5,346

John Smart, Jane Palmer in ermine-bordered pale blue surcoat, signed with initials and dated 1777, gold frame, oval 1¾in. high. (Christie's) $7,128

John Comerford, Capt. James Hughes in the blue uniform of The 18th Dragoons (Hussars), signed and dated 1807, oval 3in. high. (Christie's) $2,138

Cartology is the name given to the collecting of postcards and it is a vast field because since postcards first appeared in Austria in 1869, people have been sending them to each other across the entire world in their millions.

The postcard boom began in Britain in 1870 and early ones were designed to take the address on one side and the message and illustration on the other. These cards came complete with a half penny stamp and were seized on as the ideal way of keeping in touch with friends at a low cost. It was not till 1894 that cards were produced for use with an adhesive stamp and in 1902 the vogue for pretty postcards really took off when an Act of Parliament was passed allowing the message and address to be written on the same side. Collectors usually pick a special theme for their collections – and the world is their oyster because there are postcards on every possible subject. Some people collect views of their home towns; others like pin-up pictures of favourite stars; many specialise in cards depicting transport; others in naughty seaside cards like the ones drawn by Donald McGill. Among the most valuable cards are those with moving parts which sell for between $10 and $20 each and cards by manufacturers C. W. Faulkner and Tucks Record Cards are always popular. Shell Aviation cards can go as high as $50 each but the majority sell for lower prices unless they are signed by a celebrity like the card that had the extra bonus of a little sketch by Picasso. It sold for $1,000.

'Three dogs', German Art card, T.S.N. Series No. 1281. $3.50

Art card of a cat by Louis Wain, published by J. Salmon, Sevenoaks. $26

Embossed chrome lithographic art postcard of a cat, by P. F. Series 7072, France. $5

'I've quite come out of my shell here', a mechanical novelty card by E.T.W. Dennis. $14

Boots Cash Chemists 'English Birds', Series 29 'Pigeons'. $5

Art study of two horses by R. Trache, German A.H. Series 464. $5

HUMOROUS

'I saw you first' , German embossed chromo lithograph, 1905. $5

'I didn't want to do it', Valentines Series, 1914. $2

'Patriots', from Raphael Tuck's 'Some' Clothes Series. $3.50

'How can we play 'Husbands and wives' when we're both girls? Women are doing all the men's jobs nowadays!', Donald McGill card published by Inter-Art Comique Series No. 2703. $5

'Summer girls and some are not' by J. L. Biggar, published by E.T.W. Dennis & Sons Ltd. $2

'The voyage was glorious but..' (the spasms!!! - pencilled in), 'Write away' card by Bamforths, 1912. $3.50

'We'se out Sportin', Raphael Tuck's Oilette Card No. 9092. $5

'Oh! You silly girl!' (Police interest). $3.50

'For tampering with His Majesty's Males', from the 'Witty' Series by Bamforth. $20

HUMOROUS

'Things aren't what they used to be' by G. E. Studdy, 'Bonzo' Series card by Valentines. $7

Leslie Lester Ltd., 1950's comic card, 'now all Henry wants to do is stay home every night and play with my pussy'. $1

'A trifle bald perhaps but Oh! Boy! I'm strong with the hens' Alpha Series, 'Smile Messengers'. $2

'Another puzzle for the Post Office. Bill: But I dunno the bloke's address. 'Arry: Can't yer write and arsk him for it?' The Humor of Life as seen by Phil May Series 6075. $7

'I'm frightened of nothing — but this put the wind up me at Wembley!!' 'Felix' the film cat comic card No. 4889. $9

Unusual comic card with Transvestite interest, 'It must be nice to be a girl, my heart it beats like mad, the feeling I've got through wearing these, is the nicest I ever had'. $12

'I'm the new housemaid, won't the Master be pleased!', comic card printed in Saxony. $2

'Everybody's doing it! This is what a sailor did!' comic card circa 1905. $3.50

'Oh, lor! Fancy 'avin' a pain in that!' 'Early' Donald McGill card (1907), published by E. S. card No. 2085. $7

'Greetings from the Territorial Camp, Barrow in Furness'. $10

'Lights Out', Camp Silhouette No. 10, photochrom. $18

Cut-out postcard, put string through white dots at corner of eyes. $35

'Heroes All', Titanic memorial postcard, April 14th, 1912. $55

The Alpha postcard 'Broadcasting', produced in Saxony. $7

Chamomile (Anthemis Nobilis), Tucks gramophone record postcard, 'Many Happy Returns of the Day'. $10

'Chin Chin Chinaman, Strikee Matchee on him Patchee' $10

Wreck of the G.E.R. Cromer to London Express at Colchester, July 12th, 1913. $90

'Herzliche Gruesse aus Nurnberg', model postcard, 1918. $90

POSTERS

Posters were meant to go on walls and they had to put their message across at the blink of an eye. The best of them display a high standard of artwork and printing and many famous artists have been connected with the poster since they first became massively popular at the end of the 19th century. Prices paid for old posters today range from a few dollars to many thousands and rarity, style, content and artist all play a part in determining the cost. Toulouse Lautrec is perhaps the most famous of the poster artists and the ones he drew for the Moulin Rouge have been so often reproduced and copied that they have become almost cliches. Another much copied poster artist is Alphonse Mucha who designed the publicity material for Sarah Bernhardt for six years. Cassandre was a highly regarded poster artist in the first half of the 20th century and it was he who designed the magnificent poster for the liner Normandie looking at it bow on. One of Cassandre's contemporaries was Pierre Fix-Masseau who did wonderful posters for French State Railways. The creation and collection of posters goes on today and anyone who had the presence of mind to collect one Andy Warhol did for the RCA Colour Scanner in 1968 has a valuable property on their hands. Posters have been produced promoting everything from cigarettes to circuses, from films to motor cars and most valuable are lithographs printed on silk which have kept their richness of color for unfortunately many old posters fade with time. There is a monthly magazine called "The Poster" for aficionados.

La Revue Des Folies Bergere, by Jules Alexandre Grun, lithograph in colours, 1905, printed by Ch. Verneau, Paris, 1246 x 880mm. (Christie's) $225

Chemin De Fer, Martigny-Orsieres, by Albert Muret, lithograph in colours, 1913, on wove paper, printed by Sonor, 1000 x 700mm. (Christie's) $525

Summer; Spring; Autumn; Winter, by Alphonse Mucha, lithograph in colours, 1896, on wove paper, 1040 x 530mm. (Christie's) $10,200

Pierre Stephen, lithograph in colours, on wove paper, printed by Bauduin, Paris, 1538 x 1175mm. (Christie's) $630

Ein Rausch In Rot, Maskenball Wilder Mann, by C.M.I., lithograph in colours, 1928, on wove paper, 920 x 612mm. (Christie's) $225

Camp Romain, Vin Rouge, Rose, Blanc, by L. Gadoud, lithograph in colours, on wove paper, 1600 x 1200mm. (Christie's) $240

Laren, Tentoonstelling 1916, Hotel Hamdorff, Zunki Joska, by Willy Sluiter, lithograph in colours, printed by Senefelder, Amsterdam, 1086 x 778mm. (Christie's) $420

For Real Comfort, New Statendam, Holland-America Line, by Adolphe Mouron Cassandre, lithograph in colours, 1928, 1050 x 806mm. (Christie's) $1,500

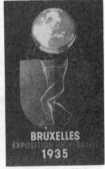

Rhum Charleston, by Leon D'Ylem, lithograph in colours, published by Vercassou, Paris, 1982 x 1275mm. (Christie's) $112

Steinhardt, Unter Den Linden, by Hans Lindenstaedt, lithograph in colours, 1912, on wove paper, 710 x 945mm. (Christie's) $450

Bruxelles, Exposition Universelle, 1935, by Marfurt, lithograph in colours, printed by Les Creations, Publicitaires, Bruxelles, 1000 x 620mm. (Christie's) $105

Etoile Du Nord, by Adolphe Mouron Cassandre, lithograph in colours, on wove paper, 1048 x 752mm. (Christie's) $1,275

Alcazar Royal, by Adolphe Crespin and Edouard Duych, lithograph in colours, 1894, 1010 x 775mm. (Christie's) $420

David Hockney at the Tate Gallery, lithograph in colour, 1980, on wove paper, signed in pencil, 760 x 505mm. (Christie's) $67

Pousset Spatenbrau, by Jean Carlu, lithograph in colours, on wove paper, printed by J. E. Goosens, Lille, 795 x 508mm. (Christie's) $330

S. V. U. Manes, 150 Vystava, Clenska, lithograph in colours, 1929, printed by Melantrich Praha, Smichov, 1250 x 950mm. (Christie's) $180

'Lenin's Push Into The Business Generation', by K. Poliarkova and R. Mozchaeva, lithograph in colours, 965 x 650mm. (Christie's) $142

L'Oiseau Bleu, by Adolphe Mouron Cassandre, lithograph in colours, 1929, on wove paper, 996 x 616mm. (Christie's) $1,170

Peugeot, by Rene Vincent, lithograph in colours, printed by Draeger, 1170 x 1540mm. (Christie's) $1,200

Poster, 'Dolomiten Ski-Schule Val Gardena (Grodental) m.1300-2200'. (Onslows) $110

Opera, Bal Des Petits Lits Blancs, L'Intran, by Marie Laurencin, lithograph in colours, 1931, 1600 x 1196mm. (Christie's) $1,500

G. Marconi, Le Maitre De La Radio, by Paul Colin, lithograph in colours, printed by Bedos & Cie, Paris, 1578 x 1130mm. (Christie's) $330

Soiree De Paris, Spectacles, Choregraphiques et Drama-tiques, by Marie Laurencin, lithograph in colours, signed in pencil and dated 1924, 796 x 578mm. (Christie's) $255

POSTERS

Jane Renouardt, by Pierre
Stephen, lithograph in colours,
printed by M. Picard, Paris,
1538 x 1175mm. (Christie's)
$150

Raden Van Arbeid, by R. N.
Roland Holst, lithograph in
colours, on wove paper,
1084 x 794mm. (Christie's)
$600

Job, by Alphonse Mucha,
lithograph in colours, 1898,
on wove paper, printed by F.
Champenoise, Paris, 1500 x
1010mm. (Christie's)
$5,250

Wilhelm Mozer Munchen-Nord
Adalbertstr, by Ludwig
Hohlwein, lithograph in
colours, 1909, on wove paper,
1250 x 911mm. (Christie's)
$270

XXVI Ausstellung Secession,
by Ferdinand Andri, lithograph in colours, circa 1904,
on wove paper, 920 x 602mm.
(Christie's) $13,050

Raphael Tuck, Celebrated
Posters No. 1501, Ogden's
Guinea Gold Cigarettes and
another. (Christie's)
$47

Exposition Des Peintres Litho-
graphes, by Fernand Louis
Gottlob, lithograph in colours,
1899, printed by Lemercier,
Paris, 1195 x 790mm.
(Christie's) $450

G. B. Borsalino Fu Lazzaro &
C, by Marcello Dudovich,
lithograph in colours, 1932,
printed by R. Questura,
Milano, 1390 x 1000mm.
(Christie's) $375

Nord Express, by Adolphe
Mouron Cassandre, lithograph
in colours, 1927, on wove
paper, 1048 x 752mm.
(Christie's) $1,950

POT LIDS

In the 19th century one of the most common containers for a myriad different items ranging from hair dressing to anchovy paste was a circular shallow ceramic pot with a loose fitting lid that rested on a slight lip around the top of the pot. One of the most prolific manufacturers of these pots was F. & R. Pratt and Co of Fenton in Staffordshire. They made pots for more than 300 different outlets and the manufacturers who bought their wares filled the pots with such diverse things as ointment or jam. The way their wares were distinguished for the public was by brightly colored lids which were transfer printed and designed to catch the eye. It is those lids that collectors seek out today. The most popular designs ranged from portraits of Queen Victoria and other popular heroes of the day to pretty landscapes or rural scenes. Pot lid collectors look for them in rubbish dumps and the value is dictated by the condition and rarity of the lid.

A Gay Dog. (Phillips) $1,914

The Kingfisher, early issue, the reverse stamped '6' or '9'. (Phillips) $1,653

Bears Reading Newspapers. (Phillips) $3,654

Pegwell Bay, S. Banger, Shrimp Sauce Manufacturer. (Phillips) $522

Sebastopol. (Phillips) $191

Exhibition Buildings 1851, large, figures omitted, white surround. (Phillips) $1,740

A Prattware pot lid depicting Wellington seated, 5in. diam. $220

Medium small lid depicting bear hunting. $1,000

A Prattware pot lid depicting Strathfieldsay, 5in. diam. $150

A pot lid, 'England's Pride', black background and beaded border, 4¼in. diam. $275

Belle Vue Tavern (with cart). (Phillips) $1,218

Victorian pot lid titled 'The Fair', 4in. diam. $65

Pot lid 'Our Home', one of only two known examples. $4,500

The 'Garden Terrace', a medium small lid. $525

Small pot lid with purple lined border, 'The Bride'. $435

A large pot lid with marbled border, 'The Late Duke of Wellington'. $210

A medium pot lid with chain border 'Embarking for the East'. $175

A medium pot lid with laurel leaf border, 'The Allied Generals'. $250

A large pot lid with double line border and title, 'Napirima Trinidad'. $260

Pot lid by Mayer Bros., circa 1850, 12.7cm. diam. $4,750

A pot lid, 'The Buffalo Hunt'. $1,750

POWDER FLASKS

In the days of muskets and barrel loading guns, men carried their gunpowder in flasks attached to their belts. One of the most common materials for those flasks was horn which could be elaborately engraved and decorated with foliage or scrolls. One of these horn flasks today can cost several hundreds of dollars but less valuable are flasks of metal like the ones made by Batty, Hawkins, Ames, Dixon or the American Flask and Cap Company. They were turned out in large numbers and are still fairly plentiful. Most were decorated in some way; a few were fluted while others carried carved coats of arms, basket weave patterns or engraved battle scenes. Old Colonial powder horns were often decorated by the owners themselves and carved with personal mottos and devices.

A good embossed copper powder flask (R. 355) 8in., graduated nozzle stamped G. & J. W. Hawksley. (Wallis & Wallis) $90

A powder horn circa 1800, brass circular base plate engraved with the device of the Percy Tenantry, 13½in. long. (Wallis & Wallis) $135

An embossed copper powder flask (R.535), 8in. embossed with panel of geometric and foliate ornament, patent brass top stamped James Dixon & Sons. (Wallis & Wallis) $87

An 18th century Persian all steel powder flask, of swollen boat or swan form. (Wallis & Wallis) $107

A good scarce Japanese cow horn powder flask, 5½in. very well made and polished, turned ivory spout and collar emanate from fluted horn tehenkanemono. (Wallis & Wallis) $160

An engraved rifle horn with carved horntip powder measure, Midwest, dated 1843, in cartouche, 4½in. long. (Robt. W. Skinner Inc.) $1,200

A good 18th/19th century Transylvanian stag horn powder flask, 6in. decorated overall with geometric devices. (Wallis & Wallis) $175

A brass mounted Continental lanthorn powder flask, fixed baluster turned nozzle swivels on knuckle joint for cut off. (Wallis & Wallis) $150

A 17th/18th century Persian Circassian walnut powder flask, 6in., sprung steel lever charger with shaped top. (Wallis & Wallis) $400

PREISS FIGURES

Art Deco found one of its most vivid expressions in the bronze and ivory, or chryselephantine, figures of F. Preiss. Virtually nothing is known about Preiss, save that he was probably born in Vienna, his forename may be Friedrich and he flourished in the late 20's and 30's. His work was closely copied by one Professor Otto Poerzl, working out of Coburg, so closely copied in fact that there is speculation that they may be one and the same.

Preiss modelled classical and modern nudes – and the Olympic figures, lithe and vibrant, glorifying the body beautiful and so much in tune with the spirit of the 1936 Olympics and the Nazi preoccupation with the physical prowess of the Aryan master race that suspicion has abounded that Preiss was an adherent of the movement.

What is in no doubt is that the present popularity of Preiss figures has meant that they fetch phenomenal sums at auction. A negative effect is the appearance of very clever reproductions – caveat emptor!

A painted bronze and ivory figure, 'Hoop Girl', 20.50cm. high, inscribed F. Preiss. (Phillips) $1,872

Kneeling girl with clock, a bronze and ivory figure cast after a model by F. Preiss, 54.4cm. high. (Christie's) $14,071

Art Deco bronze and ivory figurine of a young woman on a jetty holding a canoe paddle. (Biddle & Webb) $3,586

Mandolin Player, a bronze and ivory figure cast and carved from a model by F. Preiss, signed, 59cm. high. (Christie's) $31,395

'Bat Dancer', a bronze and ivory figure cast and carved from a model by F. Preiss, 23.5cm. high. (Christie's) $5,412

Flute Player, a bronze and ivory figure cast and carved from a model by F. Preiss, 48.5cm. high. (Christie's) $28,090

PREISS FIGURES

'Torch Dancer', a bronze and ivory figure cast and carved from a model by F. Preiss, 41.5cm. high. (Christie's) $6,314

'Con Brio', a bronze and ivory figure cast and carved from a model by F. Preiss, 29cm. high. (Christie's) $9,020

A painted bronze and ivory figure, 'Champagne Dancer', 41.50cm. high, inscribed on bronze F. Preiss. (Phillips) $3,600

'Sunshade Girl', a gilt bronze and ivory figure cast and carved from a model by F. Preiss, 20.2cm. high. (Christie's) $2,035

An Art Deco green onyx mantel clock with ivory figures carved after a model by F. Preiss, 25.2cm. high. (Christie's) $2,349

A painted bronze and ivory figure, 'Sonny Boy', 20.50cm. high, inscribed F. Preiss. (Phillips) $2,160

'Russian Dancer', a bronze and ivory figure cast and carved after a model by F. Preiss, 32.4cm. high. (Christie's) $5,051

An Art Deco bronze and ivory figurine of a young bather reclining on a large rock. (Biddle & Webb) $7,498

'Nude', an ivory figure carved after a model by F. Preiss, on a green marble base, 43.9cm. high. (Christie's) $12,528

QUILTS

The tradition of quilting thrived in the homesteads of America at the time of the first settlers when women used to meet together and hold quilting parties. The reason for their industry was to provide warm bedding for their families but some of the quilts they made were very beautiful and traditional patterns were handed down from mother to daughter through the generations. They were made from two thicknesses of cloth with a layer of padding between. The padding was often teased out sheep's wool taken from the scraps that were found sticking to trees or hedges. Quilts were stitched by hand with minute stitches using scraps of any materials that were available, favourite old dresses or cast off clothes. Each piece was stiffened at the back with paper. The women often used old letters or pages from household account books for this purpose and so it is often possible to date old quilts which can be extremely valuable. Some are so precious and fragile that the owners have them framed and glazed.

Early 19th century red and blue patchwork Calamanco coverlet, America, 108 x 100in. (Robt. W. Skinner Inc.) $1,200

Mid 19th century crib quilt, the red, yellow and green calico patches arranged in the 'Star of Bethlehem' pattern, 28in. square. (Robt. W. Skinner Inc.) $400

A wool bed rug, worked with a darning stitch in a tree-of-life pattern on a natural wool foundation, dated 1773, 84 x 85in. (Christie's) $11,000

An appliqued album quilt, cross stitch name in corner 'Miss Lydia Emeline Keller, 1867', :American, 84 x 86in. (Robt. W. Skinner Inc.) $2,100

A cotton and wool Jacquard coverlet, New York State, 1816, the field of double rose and flower medallions. (Robt. W. Skinner Inc.) $425

An Amish patchwork quilt, Pennsylvania, early 20th century, in shades of red, green, blue, purple and black arranged in "Sunshine and Shadow" pattern, 83 x 85in. (Robt. W. Skinner Inc.) $1,400

A patchwork cover of log cabin design worked with brightly coloured pieces of mainly floral printed cottons and worsted, 2.1m. x 2.04m. (Phillips) $299

A pieced and quilted cotton coverlet, American, late 19th century, worked in Triple Irish Chain pattern, 82 x 84in. (Christie's) $880

Patchwork quilt, America, 19th century, the red, green and yellow cotton patches arranged in the 'New York Beauty' pattern, 90 x 90in. (Robt. W. Skinner Inc.) $1,500

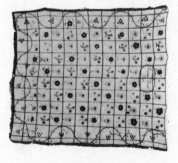

An embroidered blanket, probably New York, 'Lucretia Brush(?) Busti, 1831', large blue and white check, 6ft.4in. x 7ft.4in. (Robt. W. Skinner Inc.) $5,800

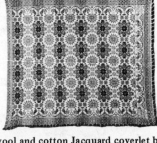

An appliqued and stuffed cotton coverlet, American, late 19th century, worked in Basket of Flowers pattern, 80 x 86in. (Christie's) $2,860

A wool and cotton Jacquard coverlet by S. B. Musselman, Milford, Bucks County, Pennsylvania, 1840, fringed on three sides (minor staining), 102 x 82in. (Christie's) $2,640

A patchwork quilt, Penn., signed and dated in ink on the back, 'Phebeann H. Salem's(?) Presented by her Mother 1848', 8ft.11in. x 9ft. (Robt. W. Skinner Inc.) $1,900

An Amish pieced and quilted cotton coverlet, probably Pennsylvania, early 20th century, of Joseph's Coat of Many Colours pattern, 89 x 89in. (Christie's) $1,210

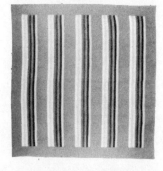

An appliqued and quilted cotton coverlet, Pennsylvania, late 19th/early 20th century, with four spreadwing eagles centering a sunburst design, 67 x 72in. (Christie's) $286

A Mennonite pierced cotton quilt, Lancaster County, Pennsylvania, late 19th/early 20th century, a variant of the "Rainbow" pattern, 84 x 88in. (Robt. W. Skinner Inc.) $1,600

RACKETANA

Primitive bat and ball games date from earliest times, but unlike real tennis which goes back at least to medieval times, lawn tennis, table tennis, badminton and squash did not emerge as formalised sports until the second half of the nineteenth century.

Modern lawn tennis rackets date from around 1880 and were nearly always strung with gut, though experiments were made with a vellum face. Vellum battledores from the early game of battledore and shuttlecock (which developed into badminton in the 1860's or 1870's) can sometimes be found, but the shuttlecocks are very rare indeed.

These battledores were often cut down for table tennis in the 1890's until John Jaques & Son produced their own under the registered title "Ping-Pong"—representing the "ping" on the table and the "pong" on the hollow battledore. Wooden bats, with a variety of coverings or none at all, first appeared around 1900.

Original ink drawing found in a family album and dated 1901. $45

Box of Gardiner's lawn tennis balls (unused), 1920's. $85

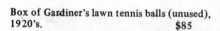

Table tennis battledore with single vellum sheet in bamboo frame, circa 1900, made by J. R. Mally. $85

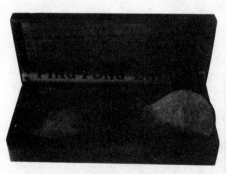

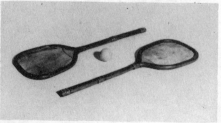

De Luxe 'Ping-Pong or Gossima' set in wooden box, by J. Jaques & Son, circa 1900. $350

A pair of very rare table tennis battledores with single vellum sheet in bamboo frame, circa 1900. $175

RACKETANA

Very high quality lawn tennis racket by Slazenger, circa 1895 and showing the flat-topped head characteristic of the period. $350

Handsome multiple press in solid mahogany and with brass fittings, circa 1910. $175

1930's lop sided real tennis racket. $130 £7

Squash racket by T. H. Prosser & Sons, circa 1900. $175

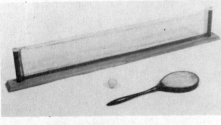

Unusual free-standing table tennis net produced by Grays of Cambridge, circa 1900, with the idea of avoiding damage to the edge of the table. $50

Miniature lawn tennis game made in Germany, circa 1900. $85

An early 20th century lawn tennis racket. $85 £50

A 1930's 'Vitiv' badminton racket with decorations characteristic of the period. $50

The only known surviving example of Pouch Ball, an American variant of table tennis, circa 1900. $350

(The Gurney Collection)

Huge shuttlecock, made in India circa 1840, and designed for the game of battledore and shuttlecock in the garden. $210

Table tennis bat, circa 1900, delicately cut out in fretwork. $85

Miniature battledore and shuttlecock set, the battledores faced with vellum and only 8in. overall. $130

Very large vellum battledore, 23in. overall, for the game of battledore and shuttlecock, circa '1890. $130

Silver-mounted table tennis bat with high quality Art Nouveau decoration and hallmarked for Birmingham, 1901. $610

Very fine label for a French table tennis set, showing a tournament scene, circa 1900. $210

Tinted 1920's photograph by H. Jetter, showing an unusual backhand. $70

(The Gurney Collection)

Fine 'fish-tail' lawn tennis racket, circa 1920.
$175

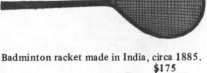

Badminton racket made in India, circa 1885.
$175

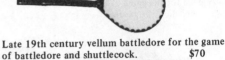

Miniature 19th century racket, for tennis-on-a-table. $130

Late 19th century vellum battledore for the game of battledore and shuttlecock. $70

Unusual 1930's table badminton set with miniature rackets strung with silk. $85

Victorian table tennis set with a fine illustration of domestic play. $175

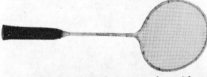

Very rare American badminton racket with steel shaft and head and wire stringing, circa 1925.
$175

Late nineteenth century vellum battledore for the game of battledore and shuttlecock.
$105

'Ping-Pong — The Great Tennis Game for the Table', by Parker Bros., Salem, U.S.A., circa 1900. $350

(The Gurney Collection)

ROBOTS

The last country to enter the toy making market was Japan. In the pre-war period their toys were regarded as cheap rubbish but today they dominate the market and ninety per cent of the output is theirs. They began making tin plate toys in the 1950's but the big break through came in the 1960's when they began producing battery operated, or occasionally clockwork powered, space men and moving models of robots. Very few of the robots to be found did not originate in Japan. They were based on Robby the Robot from the 1950's film "Forbidden Planet" and they can walk, shoot, talk, give off flashes of light and whirl round. It was robots in particular that caught the public imagination and collecting them has grown into an art form. A pure robot must not have a human face behind its plastic dome. Originally of tin plate, they have been replaced by plastic and these are not quite so highly regarded or valuable.

Attacking Martian, battery operated, moveable legs, chest opens to reveal flashing guns, with box, by Horikawa (mk. 6), Japanese, 1960's, 23cm. high. (Christie's)$1,009

Sparky Robot, clockwork mechanism, moveable legs and sparking eyes, with box, by Yoshiya, Japanese, 1950's, 19.5cm. high. (Christie's) $562

Answer-Game, battery operated immobile, executes simple mathematics, flashing eyes, by Ichida (mk. 3), Japanese, 1960's, 35.5cm. high. (Christie's) $2,494

Gear Robot, battery operated, moveable legs with coloured wheel rotating chest and flashing head, possibly by Horikawa, Japanese, 1960's, 22.5cm. high. (Christie's) $622

Busy Cart Robot, battery operated, pushing and lifting a wheelbarrow, with box, by Horikawa (mk. 6), Japanese, 1960's/1970's, 30cm. high. (Christie's) $1,187

Ultraman, clockwork mechanism, moveable arms and legs, with box, by Bullmark (mk. 5), Japanese, 1960's, 23cm. high. (Christie's) $355

Sparky Jim, battery operated with remote control, moveable legs and flashing eyes, Japanese, 1950's, 19.5cm. high. (Christie's)$1,247

Nando, the mechanism activated by air pressure through remote control, moveable legs and head, with box, by Opset, Italian, circa 1948, 13cm. high. (Christie's)$2,197

Astoman, clockwork mechanism, moveable arms and legs, by Nomura (mk. 1), Japanese, 1960's, 23.5cm. high. (Christie's)$1,067

Space Explorer, battery operated box transforms into Robot, revealing '3-D' television screen, with box, by Yonezawa (mk. 2), Japanese, 1960's, 29.5cm. high. (Christie's) $2,434

Mr. Robot, clockwork mechanism and battery activated, with box, by Alps, Japanese, 1950's, 20cm. high. (Christie's) $1,602

Dyno Robot, battery operated, moveable legs, opening mask to reveal a flashing red dinosaur's head, with box, by Horikawa, Japanese, 1960's, 28.5cm. high. (Christie's) $770

Confectionary Dispenser, battery operated, with coinslot, transparent chest showing sweets, Italian, late 1960's, 139cm. high. (Christie's) $2,257

Giant Robot, battery operated, moveable legs, chest opening to reveal flashing gun, possibly by Horikawa, Japanese, 1960's, 41cm. high. (Christie's) $1,187

Talking Robot, battery powered, mobile, speaks four different messages, with box, by Yonezawa (mk. 2), Japanese, 1950's, 28cm. high. (Christie's) $1,542

One of the most booming areas of the collecting world is rock 'n roll memorabilia which ranges from anything connected with the Beatles to the platform stage boots of Elton John. No rock 'n roll star worth his or her salt will throw anything away ever again now that fans are prepared to pay huge prices for an old jacket worn by Jimi Hendrix and a hat that touched the head of Paul McCartney. Anything connected with the early stars, no matter how tenuous the connection, is worth money. Fan photographs sell well, so do promotional dresses issued to usherettes at Beatles concerts but if the photographs are signed by the stars themselves and if the usherette managed to persuade the Beatles to scrawl their signatures on her skirt, then you are talking real money. Musical instruments played on by the Beatles, an early record by Elvis Presley before he hit the big time, even plastic musical boxes with statuettes of Elvis on them sell for large sums and show no signs of losing their value.

A receipt from 'Mannys Musical Instruments Store' in New York, signed on the reverse 'Love Jimi Hendrix' in black ballpoint pen, c.1969. (Phillips) $588

An R.I.A.A. presentation gold disc presented to Tito Jackson for the Jacksons LP 'Triumph', c.1980. (Phillips) $1,384

A good set of all four Beatles autographs in blue ballpoint pen, individually mounted beneath a colour photo from the 'Sgt. Pepper' session, 37cm. x 36.5cm., c.1967. (Phillips) $1,124

Rolling Stones - A set of autographs (incl. Brian Jones) on a sheet of headed notepaper from the 'Westbridge House Hotel' in Pontefract Yorkshire, 30cm. x 21cm. (Phillips) $692

A good 9 x 8in. black and white photograph of the 'Blues Brothers' signed on the front by John Belushi and Dan Aykroyd, 33cm. x 31cm. (Phillips) $484

A handwritten letter from John Lennon to a fan, the letter written in blue/black ink pen on white notepaper, 10in. x 8in. (Phillips) $1,124

Cher - A leather and simulated 'leopard-skin' pillbox hat made by 'Carlotta by Carlos Roncancio' signed 'Cher'. (Phillips) $726

Two unused Apple mirrors, incorporating the Apple logo surrounded by a black border. (Phillips) $484

'Bad' twelve inch single signed on the front cover 'Michael Jackson' in black felt-tip pen. (Phillips) $294

An R.I.A.A. presentation platinum disc presented to Sting for the LP 'Nothing But the Sun', c.1987. (Phillips) $1,730

Elvis Presley's outstanding white one piece stage suit decorated with gilt studs in a 'shooting star' design all over the costume, with letter of authenticity from the suit's designer Bill Belew. (Phillips) $44,980

E.L.O. - A rare Australian double platinum award for the LPs 'A New World Record' and 'Out of the Blue'. c. February 1978, 67cm. x 49cm. (Phillips) $380

A copy of a single page of sheet music for the song 'I Am the Walrus' signed 'Love John Lennon' in black ink, c.1979. (Phillips) $1,297

E.L.O. - A red satin promotional jacket for the 1979 LP 'Discovery'. The E.L.O. logo and the word 'Discovery' colourfully embroidered on the back. (Phillips) $121

B.P.I. presentation silver disc for the LP 'Hollies Live Hits' presented to 'Polydor Ltd.' c.1977. (Phillips) $415

A telegram from Ringo Starr to a Dutch newspaper dated 4 June 1964 explaining 'Very sorry I couldn't come to Holland hope to see all my Dutch fans on the next trip - Ringo Starr'. (Phillips) $3,114

Sex Pistols - A set of six original streamers used to promote the LP 'Great Rock and Roll Swindle', designed by Jamie Reid, each 15cm. x 71cm. (Phillips) $86

John Lennon - One page of handwritten lyrics 'Instant Karma' c.1970, the last two verses and chorus of the song in black felt-tip pen on card. (Phillips) $7,958

Elvis Presley - An American in house platinum disc for the 1977 LP 'Moody Blue'. The award mounted above a plaque. (Phillips) $1,903

A Yamaha FG-110 acoustic guitar with nylon strings, once the property of Paul McCartney, circa late 1960s, sold with a letter confirming authenticity from the vendor. (Phillips) $4,152

A large print of an oil painting by June Kelly of Elvis signed and dedicated on the front by Elvis 'Billy beautiful pal Elvis Presley', 58cm. x 48cm. (Phillips) $1,211

The Beatles - 'Yesterday and Today' 'butcher sleeve' peeled, (Capitol T2553 mono) with record enclosed, very good condition. (Phillips) $553

Elvis Presley's 'Russian Double Eagle' gold coloured metal belt, intricately meshed with two eagle head fasteners. (Phillips) $4,498

Sex Pistols - A promotional poster depicting the withdrawn artwork for the single 'Holidays in the Sun', 81cm. x 82cm., c.1977. (Phillips) $224

Old England 'Flower Power' wristwatch. The watch face coloured gold and bright pink in a 'Flower Power' design, by Richard Loftus. (Phillips) $432

Al Jackson/Booker T and the MGs - A mounted bronze trophy award presented by Memphis Music Awards, 1972, 17cm. high. (Phillips) $484

A cheque from 'Lennon Productions Ltd.' to the 'Freedom Fund' for the sum of 1000 Pounds, signed by Lennon in blue ballpoint pen and dated August 10th, 1971. (Phillips) $2,595

An original sketch by John Lennon executed in black felt-tip pen headed 'Love from John and Yoko' above a self portrait of John Lennon and Yoko Ono signed and dated 'John Lennon 1969'. 22cm. x 17cm. (Phillips) $2,076

A handwritten song order in Lennon's hand for the track listing for the album 'Sgt. Peppers Lonely Hearts Club Band' in black ballpoint pen, 20cm. x 25cm. (Phillips) $1,384

John Lennon and George Harrison - A black and white photographic print taken during the lecture given by the Maharishi in August 1967, 68cm. x 58cm. (Phillips) $121

'The Beatles' (white album) PCS7067/8 No.0532377 signed by all four Beatles in full on the rear inside cover in blue felt-tip pen. (Phillips) $1,384

An 8 x10in. black and white photograph of The Who performing on 'Ready, Steady, Go' signed by all four members with doodles by Keith Moon. (Phillips) $328

Bruce Springsteen - One page of handwritten lyrics for the song 'I Got the Fever', with 'Idea 4' written at the top of the page, in ballpoint pen, c.1972. (Phillips) $3,460

RUGS

Oriental rugs performed a dual role — they were spread on floors or divans but also hung on the walls like pictures. They were highly prized and looked on as family securities, only to be sold when times were hard. Some of the ones that turn up are very ancient indeed and all were hand knotted so the larger ones represent years of painstaking work which is reflected in the high prices paid for them by collectors. Other well regarded rugs are those designed for Morris & Co at the end of the 19th century. They were woven with the interlacing foliate designs popularised by William Morris and many of them were designed by Morris himself or by John Henry Dearle. Earlier in the century there was a vogue for needlework rugs, many of which only lasted if hung on walls. Those which have survived fetch extremely good prices. Another interesting type of rug are those made during the Art Deco period with angular lines and angles in the design. They were revolutionary in their time and are still eye catching today.

Mid 19th century Bordjalou Kazak rug, 5ft. x 6ft.7in. (Robt. W. Skinner Inc.) $5,100

A hand-knotted woollen rug, the design possibly by A. Knox, with Celtic motif in pink and blue on a white ground, 153.5 x 86cm. (Christie's) $527

Marion Dorn, an abstract small carpet woven in khaki and pale blue green, 8ft. x 4ft. 2in. (Lawrence Fine Art) $783

Late 19th century Kazak prayer rug, Southwest Caucasus, 5ft.10in. x 3ft. 4in. (Robt. W. Skinner Inc.) $1,300

A Kazak Karatchoph rug, the tomato red field woven with a cream octagon within diced spandrels, dated 1862, 4ft.5in. x 4ft.9in. (Lawrence Fine Art) $12,139

An antique East Anatolian part cotton and metal thread Prayer Kilim, 7ft. 2in. x 4ft.7in. (Christie's) $1,633

RUSKIN POTTERY

The Ruskin Pottery of West Smethwick, near Birmingham, was started by William Howson Taylor in 1898 and thrived until his death in 1935. He named his pottery after John Ruskin, who he much admired, and it was famous for the beautiful afterglaze on earthenware which Taylor was able to produce. Unfortunately only he knew the secret of those glazes and before he died he destroyed his worknotes. The products of the Ruskin Pottery are very varied ranging from bowls, vases and eggcups to hatpins. Various marks were employed usually incorporating the name Taylor or Ruskin and a device of a pair of scissors which was scratched or painted on the base. Some pieces were dated.

A Ruskin high-fired transmutation glazed vase, 1911, 38cm. high. (Christie's)
$594

A Ruskin flambe vase, mallet-shaped with blue and red speckled glaze, 1909, 17.4cm. high. (Christie's)
$236

A large Ruskin high fired transmutation glaze vase and matching circular stepped stand, England, circa 1930, 36cm. high including stand. (Christie's)
$346

A Ruskin high fired shaped cylindrical vase, 1925, 23.6cm. high. (Christie's)
$600

A large Ruskin low-fired crystalline glaze vase of swollen cylindrical shape, England, 1926, 41.5cm. high. (Christie's)
$283

A Ruskin high fired transmutation glaze vase, England, 1933, 21cm. high. (Christie's)
$283

SAMPLERS

From the early 18th century young girls of leisured families were set to make a sampler when they were around ten years old as a sort of "apprentice piece" to show their developing skill as needlewomen. The samplers were designed to display the various stitches which the girl could execute and they were laid out in stylised form incorporating the letters of the alphabet, the maker's name and age, sometimes the place where it was made and a stitched representation of the owner's home. Occasionally lines from hymns or edifying mottos were also included. Samplers have a refreshing simplicity and appeal and are often treasured as relics of a particular family. The custom of making samplers ended around the time of the First World War though in recent years needlework sampler kits are being produced again.

Late 18th century framed needlework sampler, by Charlotte Richardson 13 years, Dec. 1786, American, 17 x 20in. (Robt. W. Skinner Inc.) $1,500

A needlework sampler 'Susannah Styles finished this work in the 10 years of her age 1800', worked in silk yarns on wool ground, 13in. square. (Robt. W. Skinner Inc.) $1,000

Sampler with alphabet verse and figures of plants and birds, dated 1824, 17 x 13in. (Lots Road Chelsea Auction Galleries) $501

A needlework sampler by Mary Ann Cash, 1801, the linen ground worked in coloured silks, 37 x 30cm. (Phillips) $356

A 17th century needlwork sampler by Anna Stone, the linen ground worked in pink, green and blue silk threads, 41 x 19cm. (Phillips) $1,176

Needlework sampler, 'Betsey Stevens, her sampler wrought in 10th year of her age AD 1796', silk yarns on linen, 15 x 16in. (Robt. W. Skinner Inc.) $3,000

397

Needlework sampler, silk yarns worked on ivory linen ground fabric, by 'Harriatt Shoveller, 1799', England, 12½ x 17in. (Robt. W. Skinner Inc.) $1,600

Framed needlework pictorial sampler, inscribed 'Harroit Hoyle, Aged 21, 1834', 24 x 24in. (Robt. W. Skinner Inc.) $2,200

Needlework spot sampler, Germany, 1759, vivid polychrome silk yarns on natural linen fabric, 12 x 21½in. (Robt. W. Skinner Inc.) $2,500

Needlework sampler, 'Sally Butman her work in the 11th year of her age, 1801', Marblehead, Mass., 10.3/8 x 12½in. (Robt. W. Skinner Inc.) $15,000

Needlework sampler, England, dated 1826, silk yarns in a variety of stitches on natural linen ground, 13 x 15½in. (Robt. W. Skinner Inc.) $700

A needlework picture, by Mary Fentun, dated 1789, 21¼ x 16½in. (Christie's) $2,860

An early 19th century needlework sampler by S. Parker, aged 14 years 1817, 37 x 32cm. (Phillips) $862

An early 19th century needlework sampler, by Elizabeth Campling, aged 12 years, the linen ground embroidered in silks, 31.5 x 34.5cm. (Phillips) $338

A nicely worked needlework sampler, by Sarah Iesson, the linen ground embroidered in silks, 33 x 21cm. (Phillips) $708

Late 18th century needlework sampler, worked in silk yarns of gold, light blue, red, brown, ivory and black on natural linen, 7 x 10½in. (Robt. W. Skinner Inc.) $3,300

A needlework sampler worked in silk yarns on natural coloured linen, 'Susanah Cadmore, 1805', 12½ x 13¼in. (Robt. W. Skinner Inc.) $500

A sampler 'Wrought by Harriot Wethrell May Aged 10 years, Plymouth Massachusetts, June 10th 1830', 16¼ x 16½in. (Robt. W. Skinner Inc.) $1,900

Late 18th century Spanish needlework sampler with silk embroidered stylised floral and geometric designs, 15½ x 18½in. (Robt. W. Skinner Inc.) $300

A needlework family record, silk yarns in shades of blue, green, pale peach, ivory and black on natural linen ground fabric, 18¼ x 14½in. (Robt. W. Skinner Inc.) $900

A needlework sampler, by 'Sarah Pell, Febrery 21, 1830', wool yarns on white wool fabric, 12½ x 16in. (Robt. W. Skinner Inc.) $850

An early 19th century needlework sampler by Elizabeth Bushby, March 6, aged 10 years, 1822, 45 x 42cm. (Phillips) $523

Framed needlework pictorial verse sampler, by Eliza. A. Machett, New York, March 22, 1828, 16½ x 16in. (Robt. W. Skinner Inc.) $500

Needlework sampler, by 'Elizabeth Tonnecliff, her work done in 1791', silk yarns, 16 x 20¼in. (Robt. W. Skinner Inc.) $8,700

SARDINE DISHES

In Victorian and Edwardian times people sat down to large afternoon teas and one of their favourite snacks was tinned sardines. Refined families did not like the idea of a vulgar tin appearing on their tea table so they devised the practice of having the maid put the sardine tin in a pretty box which was specially made for the purpose. The boxes were manufactured by most major British potteries and in large numbers in Czechoslovakia. They were sometimes decorated with flowers or fruit but most commonly with fish. Though most of the boxes were made of pottery with pottery lids some were made of porcelain or cut glass and a few had silver lids. Fine examples of sardine boxes from Spode or Minton can fetch as much as $750 today.

Pottery bamboo design sardine box with woven pattern on lid, made in Alloa, Scotland by Waverley. $125

Fluted porcelain sardine box decorated with violets and gilding with a finely painted fish. $115

Gilded porcelain sardine box with water weed pattern, English, unmarked. $105

Cut glass sardine box with silver plated stand and lid, unmarked. $175

Czechoslovakian porcelain sardine box with a green marbleized effect and a good painted fish. $280

English porcelain sardine box with a finely painted fish with red fins, complete with silver plated stand and fork. $245

Apricot glaze sardine box marked Flos Maron, with pierced silver plated stand. $245

Fluted white porcelain sardine box with a finely painted fish, marked with an eagle, on plated stand. $435

Gilded pottery sardine box with woven sides and decorated lid embellished with water lilies and reeds, unmarked, probably English. $125

SEALS

Seals were used for closing letters and were symbols of authenticity, like a personal signature because they nearly always incorporated the owner's initials or family crest. They could be worn hanging from a watch chain or as a ring. Larger seals were kept in a writing desk. These desk seals from the 17th and 18th centuries were shaped like mushrooms with wooden handles and a carved silver seal set in the end of the stem. More sophisticated examples were slimmed down and had the handles decorated with semi-precious or precious stones.

A Tiffany sterling silver sealing wax set, N.Y., circa 1891-1902, 8½in. sq., wt.approx. 20 troy oz. (Robt. W. Skinner Inc.)
$800

Fob seals were great favourites with the well-to-do business men from the Victorian and Edwardian eras. They were made of gold, silver or silver gilt, had ornate handles and were sometimes studded with gems. A cluster of fob seals was the mark of a great nob in the mid 18th century.

Seals are still worn as signet rings and have been used for that purpose since Roman times. Designs are very varied. As well as coats of arms or initials, there are self portraits, pictures of favourite deities in the case of the Romans, or symbols of clubs and affiliations. A large number of Masonic signet rings can be found.

A gold mounted bloodstone table seal, the stem formed as a hand, 1830, 3.5/8in. high. (Christie's)
$1,982

A two-colour gold and hardstone articulated triple desk seal by Faberge, St. Petersburg, 1908-17, 9.1cm.
$5,224

A 19th century Swiss gold musical seal with chased foliage handle. (Christie's)
$1,573

An early 19th century English three-colour gold fob seal, 5.3cm. $652

A gold desk seal with handle modelled in ivory as a hand clasping a baton with bloodstone or cornelian seal ends, circa 1830, 2¾in. long. (Christie's) $2,557

A two-colour gold and amethyst table seal, the citrine matrix with crest and initials, circa 1830, 2¾in. high. (Christie's)
$1,900

401

Mid 18th century English gold fob seal, with pierced scroll handle, 2.7cm.
$261

Early 19th century Swiss gold musical fob seal with central winder, 4.2cm. high.
$870

Late 18th century English gold double-sided swivel fob seal of oval form, 5.3cm. $652

Early 19th century English gold fob seal of large size, oval with reeded and fluted mount, 5cm. $696

Early 19th century Swiss gold and enamel musical fob seal, 4.2cm.
$1,174

An English gold fob seal of oblong form, with plain foiled citrine matrix, 4cm., circa 1835. $369

Early 19th century English gold fob seal with plain oblong bloodstone matrix, 3.8cm. $478

A gold double-sided swivel fob seal with scrolled wirework mount in the form of two serpents, 5cm., circa 1810. $1,654

An English gold fob seal with armorial-engraved oblong citrine matrix, 4.1cm., circa 1835.
$435

SEVRES

The prestigious Sevres pottery was started at Vincennes by King Louis XV of France in 1756 and from the beginning its products were of exquisite quality and style. In 1876 the factory removed to St Cloud where there is today a fine museum which displays some of the beautiful things made there since the pottery's inception.

Sevres technicians were always eager to experiment with formulae and pastes and they were able to devise a kaolin based paste which closely resembled the ancient and secret Chinese formula. They also produced a silicate paste which made it possible to provide a magnificent range of colors for decoration of the pieces. Some of the very best artists in France worked for Sevres over the years. The sculptor Rodin was one of their modellers and so was A. Leonard who made lovely unglazed figures.

One of two Sevres two-handled feuille-de-choux seaux a bouteille, with painter's marks of Tardy and Tandart, 26cm. wide. (Christie's) $1,837

One of a pair of late 19th century Sevres pattern royal blue-ground oviform vases and fixed covers with gilt bronze mounts, 42cm. high. (Christie's) $1,116

A Sevres rose pompadour square tray, blue interlaced L marks enclosing the date letter E for 1757 and painter's mark of Noel, 14.5cm. sq. (Christie's) $6,492

A Sevres bleu nouveau baluster milk jug, blue interlaced L mark enclosing the date letter q for 1769, and painter's mark B, 12cm. high. (Christie's) $613

A pair of Sevres-pattern bleu-celeste ground ormolu mounted baluster vases, circa 1860, 60cm. high. (Christie's) $3,110

A Sevres sucrier and cover interlaced L's enclosing date letter s for 1771 and mark possibly of Mereaud, 11.5cm. high. (Christie's) $2,262

SEVRES

A Sevres hop-trellis fluted cup and saucer, circa 1765. (Christie's)　$475

A Sevres bust of Napoleon as First Consul, dated 1802, 29cm. high. (Christie's) $1,093

Late 19th century Sevres pattern gilt bronze mounted two-handled centrepiece, 27.5cm. wide. (Christie's) $998

A Sevres hard-paste green-ground soup tureen and cover, gilt interlaced L marks and HP mark of Prevost, circa 1785, 30cm. wide. (Christie's) $1,584

A Sevres-pattern porcelain and ormolu mounted mantel clock, imitation interlaced L and initial marks, circa 1880, 61.5cm. high. (Christie's) $3,732

A Sevres hard-paste cup and saucer, blue crowned interlaced L mark enclosing date letter U for 1773. (Christie's) $554

A Sevres ornithological circular sugar bowl and cover, blue interlaced L marks enclosing the date letter U for 1773 and painter's mark of Evans, 11.5cm. high. (Christie's)　$766

A Sevres white biscuit group of Le Valet de Chien modelled by Blondeau after Oudry, circa 1776, 30.5cm. long.(Christie's) $1,749

A Sevres plate, 23.5cm. diam., LL mark enclosing date letters EE for 1782, painter's marks for Capelle and probably Huny. (Phillips)　$6,847

SEWING BOXES

Sewing tables, workboxes, bobbin and reel stands are very well worth collecting and some were made in richly polished wood by expert craftsmen, or papier mache, often ornamented with painted flowers and mother of pearl. Sewing chairs and early sewing machines are valuable but the collector with less money can concentrate on the boxes of mixed items that often turn up at auction and contain unexpected treasures like lengths of silk in period wrappers, old cotton reels, ladies' companion sets, wooden mushrooms for darning socks, thimbles, old packets of needles and pins or chatelaines, needle cases, lace bobbins, lacemakers' cushions, embroidery frames, tambour hooks, netting tools and pin cushions. Some of the needle cases were made of Mauchline ware, Tunbridge ware, Fern ware, tortoiseshell, ivory, wood or even gold and silver. All the small things associated with needlework are being avidly collected since the uprise in home crafts and today's needlewomen take pleasure in using the tools that were used by their grandmothers and great grandmothers.

An early 19th century veneered Anglo-Indian Colonial rectangular sarcophagus shape workbox, 14in. wide. (Woolley & Wallis) $2,970

Mid 19th century chinoiserie decorated lacquer sewing box, containing ivory implements, China, 14½in. wide. (Robt. W. Skinner Inc.) $550

An Indian fruitwood, ivory and micro-mosaic workbox with mirror-backed interior, 18in. wide. (Christie's) $1,996

A Victorian brass and velvet 'perambulator' sewing box, possibly America, circa 1880, 7½in. long. (Robt. W. Skinner Inc.) $400

An early 19th century French satinwood workbox, 12 x 35.5 x 26cm. (Phillips) $2,492

A 17th century needlework casket, the front and side panels of raised and stuffed stumpwork, England, 10¾in. wide. (Robt. W. Skinner Inc.) $2,600

A 19th century miniature stencilled sewing box, American, 10in. high, 14in. wide. (Christie's) $286

A William & Mary oyster walnut veneered lacemaker's box with brass escutcheon, 21in. long. (Woolley & Wallis) $1,360

Early Victorian Macassar ebony veneered sarcophagus-shaped workbox inlaid with mother-of-pearl, 12in. wide. (Woolley & Wallis) $486

SEWING MACHINES

As early as 1845 an American machinist called Elias Howe invented the first sewing machine and in the years that followed they were produced in an enormous variety of sizes and shapes by different manufacturers but it was the Singer Sewing Machine Company that took the lion's share of the market. By 1890 they turned out ten million machines which were so good that many of them are still useable today. The sewing machines that are valued by collectors are those with immaculate paint and decoration, for many were covered with elegant gilded scrollwork that makes them decorative objects. Early machines to look out for apart from Singer's are the Imperial Sewing Co of Birmingham; the Howe Sewing Machine Co; those imported from Germany by J. Collier and Son of Clapham Road, London; Wright and Mann of Ipswich and the small chain stitch machines sold by James Weir of Soho Square which were pirated copies of earlier machines made in Canada by Charles Raymond.

Late 19th century oak and iron sewing machine. $85

A Grover & Baker hand sewing machine, serial no. 441414, brass disc and gilt lining, on mahogany base, circa 1873. (Phillips) $1,840

A Grover & Baker hand-sewing machine, the brass Patent plaque with patents to 1863. (Christie's) $1,584

Small chain-stitch machine, made in Germany, imported by Leigh & Crawford, Holborn, London, circa 1888. $140

A European sewing machine by The Coventry Machinists Co. Ltd., with hand wheel for bobbin winding. $1,750

'Howe' lock-stitch machine with rubber belt drive and hand-painted floral and filt decorations, Howe Sewing Machine Co. circa 1876. $260

SHAKER

This simple, sturdy furniture was produced in the late 18th and early 19th century by the Shaker sect in New England and New York State, originally for use by community members. Later, however, chair-making in particular developed into quite an industry supplying neighbouring towns. The pieces were painted (usually dark red) but undecorated. Most typical items are rocking chairs and slat back chairs designed to be hung on a wall rail. Production declined after 1860.

A Shaker splint sewing basket, probably Enfield, Connecticut, 19th century, 15½in. diam. (Christie's) $880

Early 19th century Shaker pine commode with hinged slant lid opening to reveal a shelf interior, 18in. wide. (Robt. W. Skinner Inc.)
$4,500

A Shaker miniature lidded pail with strap handle and two fingers, 2.3/8in. high. (Christie's) $550

A 19th century Shaker cherry hanging cupboard, 24in. wide.
$3,500

Shaker maple tilter ladder-back sidechair with rush seat, circa 1875, 39½in. high. (Robt. W. Skinner Inc.)
$600

Early 19th century unfinished Shaker needlework sampler on natural linen, 8½ x 10¼in.
$1,300

19th century three-tier Shaker spool rack, 7½in. high.
$1,300

Painted staved wooden cheese/butter box, possibly Shaker, circa 1830, 6½in. diam. (Robt. W. Skinner Inc.) $475

Shaker butternut sewing box, the drawers with ebonised diamond escutcheon and turned ivory pull, New England, circa 1820, 7½in. wide. (Robt. W. Skinner Inc.) $7,750

A 19th century oval putty grained Shaker box, America, 5.7/8in. long. (Robt. W. Skinner Inc.) $3,300

Shaker birch chest-of-drawers, probably New England, circa 1840, 38½in. wide. (Robt. W. Skinner Inc.) $1,100

A Shaker painted pine and poplar cupboard, possibly N.Y., circa 1830, 28in. wide, 86¾in. high. (Robt. W. Skinner Inc.) $3,500

American 19th century Shaker cherry drop-leaf table. $3,500

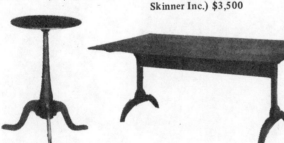
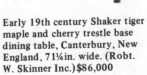

Early 19th century Shaker cherrywood stand, 60cm. high. $13,000

Early 19th century Shaker tiger maple and cherry trestle base dining table, Canterbury, New England, 71¼in. wide. (Robt. W. Skinner Inc.) $86,000

Early 19th century Shaker pine and maple work table, probably New England, 36in. high. (Robt. W. Skinner Inc.) $2,000

SHAVING CREAM POT LIDS

Shaving cream was sold in ceramic pots with decorated lids during the 19th and early 20th centuries. Some of the lids bore the names of famous hotels, distinguished barbers, or chemists like Boots, while others bore pictures of sporting events. Racing or cricket were particular favourites. They were made by the big potteries of the time and the fancier ones usually came from Doulton. The lids sell today for between $10 and $500 each depending on the condition and quality of the decoration. Lids with coloured scenes sell for the most. One or two were printed with recommendations from famous people and several claimed to be used by Prince Albert. The retailing of shaving cream in those attractive pots ended around 1920.

Army & Navy Toilet Club, The United Service Shaving Cream. $45

Violet Shaving Cream, Prepared by C. & J. Montgomery of Belfast, a rare Irish lid. $45

S. Maw, Son & Thompson, Ambrosial Shaving Cream, Perfumed with Almonds, small size. $45

Dale's Almond Shaving Cream, Prepared by John T. Dale, Stirling, Scotland. $45

Erasmic Shaving Cream, lid complete with matching pot. $45

Muire Bouquet Shaving Cream, 'Does not dry on the skin', the French name had sales appeal.
$60

Fred Diemer, Superior Shaving Cream, an old lid from the City of London. $30

Henri Freres, Creme D'Amandes, Ambrosial, a French style lid with an attractive trade mark. $60

John Gosnell & Co. Ambrosial Shaving Cream, an early lid.
$85

Low, Son & Haydon, Almond
Shaving Cream, Strand, London.
$55

Blondeay & Cie, Premier
Vinolia Shaving Cream for
Sensitive Skins, circa 1920.
$45

Boots Creme D'Amande for
Shaving, probably the most
common shaving cream lid.
$14

Professor Browne's
Luxuriant Shaving Cream,
Fenchurch Street, London.
$45

Carter's Imperial Shaving
Cream, an unusual lid with
white lettering in a black
background. $70

H. Osborne, Cream of
Almonds, Byram Toilet Club,
Huddersfield. $30

Ch. Jaschke's Shaving Cream,
Regent St., London, decorated
with a gold band. $35

Roger & Gallet, Creme de
Savon, a French lid and pot
printed in green. $25

Spratt's Perfect Shaving Cream
a small London lid complete
with directions. $35

F. S. Cleaver's Saponaceous
Shaving Cream, from the
'Inventor of the Celebrated
Honey Soap', London.$70

Creme de Savon, by F. Millot
of Paris, a plain but rare
French lid. $35

Gay & Sons Celebrated
Shaving Cream, London.
$60

SHAVING MUGS

Before electric razors there was a great ritual involved in the act of shaving and men mixed up their lather in big shaving mugs which were often decorated with pictures or inscribed with the owner's name. Most of the mugs were made of pottery but richer people often owned them in silver or porcelain. There were also a few mugs made of brass or copper. Some of the rarer mugs had jutting out lips for water, soap, a brush and the razor and they were called four in ones; there were also three in ones but the majority were simply large mugs like big beakers. French shaving mugs were always taller and thinner than those used in England. Shaving mugs can often be picked up quite cheaply but care should be taken not to buy reproductions. Genuine old mugs feel heavy to the hand and have worn bases. Don't buy mugs that are chipped even if they are old. Among the rarest shaving mugs are crested ones made by the Goss pottery which can sell for around $100 each.

Swan shaped shaving mug with gilt edging, circa 1900. $55

Goss shaving mug with colour transfer of 'The Gibbet Cross, Minehead'. $70

Pearl lustre shaving mug, on four scroll feet, bearing the crest of New Brighton. $35

Large, late 19th century, shaving mug with floral decoration and gilt edging. $45

Tall French shaving mug known as a brush vase with gilt and floral decoration, circa 1890. $70

Large, late 19th century, shaving mug with floral decoration and unusual double handle. $70

Torquay Ware shaving mug in brown and cream bearing the motto 'Better do one thing, Than dream all things!' $55

Three in one shaving mug with a place for water, the soap and a brush, circa 1900. $55

An interesting signed shaving mug, G. Wiegand, with floral decoration. $80

Victorian shaving mug with hand-painted floral decoration and gilt edging. $70

Large late 19th century bowl shaped shaving mug with floral decoration and shaped handle. $45

Late Victorian shaving mug decorated with floral sprays. $35

Personalised shaving mug in white with gold lettering, 'Thomas Ricks, Maskelyne, Pontypool, 1908'. $85

Late Victorian pewter shaving mug with embossed floral decoration. $95

Souvenir Coronation shaving mug for H.M. King George VI and Queen Elizabeth. $45

Heavy Victorian plain white shaving mug. $35

'Glimpses of the East', a multi-coloured shaving mug, circa 1920's. $45

Late Victorian shaving mug with fine floral decoration and dark blue frieze. $60

Elegantly shaped white shaving mug decorated with pink floral sprays. $35

Elegantly shaped white shaving mug decorated with pink floral sprays. $35

Souvenir Coronation shaving mug for George V and Queen Mary. $45

SHELLS

Among the favourite souvenirs of distant places for travellers in the last century were exotic shells. They treasured the beautiful abalone or mother of pearl shell, the Queen Conch and the magnificent Nautilus. Rare examples like Conus Gloriamarus changed hands for considerable sums even in Victorian times and today will cost a collector several hundred dollars. Some people restrict their collections to only one type of shell and try to find it in various sizes which records its growth development. Victorians were great lovers of all kinds of shells and ladies set mirrors and made shell pictures out of the small, prettily coloured ones found on British beaches. There was also jewellery made of shells. Another type of shell that makes an interesting collection are examples of shell money for shells were used as coinage among tribes in America, Asia, Africa and Australia. The commonest type was the cowrie shell which is abundant in the Indian Ocean and was used as money in Bengal, Western Africa and New Guinea where it was tied in lengths of 40 or 100.

Early 20th century shell art picture frame. $70

Late 19th century Barbadian pair of sailor's Valentine shell pictures, 9in. wide. $717

Early 20th century shell art pin cushion in the form of an anchor. $35

A fine golden cowrie shell from the Fiji Islands. $525

Shell art jewellery box with wooden lining. $50

The infernal harp shell from the Fringing Reef, Mauritius. $260

A Solomon Islands shell ornament, Kap Kap, the tridacna clam shell base with turtle shell disc attached, 11.7cm. diam. (Phillips) $691

A replica of an example of scrimshaw presented to Queen Victoria on the launching of 'The Great Britain', 21.5cm. long. $1,400

One of three 19th century shell pictures in octagonal wooden frames, 11in. wide. (Lots Road Chelsea Auction Galleries) $480

SHIPS FIGUREHEADS

Ships' figureheads were originally designed to strike terror into the hearts of opponents—imagine the dragon prows of Viking longships materialising through the mists! Later, they adopted a gentler image, often comprising well-endowed female figures and seen rather as good luck mascots, though some fierce-looking birds and animals did perpetuate the aggressive aspect. When ships were broken up, figureheads were often kept for sentimental reasons or transferred to new craft, which is probably why so many survive today.

A 19th century painted and carved pine eagle, possibly taken from the stern of a ship, America, 28in. long. (Robt. W. Skinner Inc.) $1,900

A carved and painted figure of Victory, American, circa 1880, 69½in. high. (Robt. W. Skinner Inc.) $4,000

Early 19th century carved and polychrome figurehead, New England, 23in. high. (Robt. W. Skinner Inc.) $3,500

A 19th century English carved oak ship's figurehead, carved in the form of a lion's head, 109cm. high. $829

A carved and painted ship's head figure, modelled as a partially clad mermaid, 38in. high. (Christie's) $1,320

A 19th century carved and polychrome allegorical figure, America, 52in. high. (Robt. W. Skinner Inc.) $5,500

English 19th century carved and polychromed ship's figurehead, the bearded figure wearing a toga, 188cm. high. $3,509

414

SHOP SIGNS

In days gone by shops could be identified from a distance by the signs that hung outside them. During early times when a large proportion of the population could not read, these signs were necessary and they became traditionally associated with certain retailers — the barber's shop had its blood stained bandage wound round a long pole; the chemist its mortar and pestle; the wine merchant its bush; the shoemaker a fine top boot; the pawnbroker his three gilded balls. Today, the signs that have survived are very valuable and there is a strong collecting interest in them. Particular favourites are the wooden blackamoors and Red Indians that used to stand outside tobacconists' shops. Occasionally figures of soldiers were used. There was a shop in Perth that was guarded by a man sized figure of a Highlander in full kilted dress with a huge black busby on his head. When he came up for auction recently he sold for several thousand dollars.

Early 20th century American carved and painted trade sign, 39¼in. high. (Christie's) $550

A carved and painted counter top cigar store Punch figure, by Chas. Henkel, Vermont, 1870, 26in. high. (Christie's) $19,800

Late 19th century moulded iron and zinc jeweller's trade sign, America. (Robt. W. Skinner Inc.) $600

An American 19th century painted iron trade sign, 40in. high, 15in. wide. (Christie's) $2,640

Late 19th/early 20th century painted and gilded tin and wrought-iron wall mounted trade sign, American or English, 42½in. high, 39in. wide. (Christie's) $4,180

A moulded zinc polychrome tobacconist figure, Wm. Demuth, N.Y., circa 1890, 67½in. high without base. (Robt. W. Skinner Inc.) $11,000

SIGNED PHOTOGRAPHS

During the boom years of the cinema, fans of particular stars wrote to Hollywood in their millions asking for signed photographs of their idols. The studios did not disappoint them and employed Press Officers to despatch photographs in return but in most cases the signatures were forged by the officers themselves. This means that a signed photograph of Clark Gable may not be so valuable as it seems − the signature is probably not his and because of his huge popularity, there will be thousands of others around. Even signed photographs of famous politicians like Churchill are not necessarily genuine because some employed writing machines to forge their signatures but modern techniques have made it easier to detect these. The most valuable signed photographs are those with a history. If it can be proved that a picture was signed by the person who sat for the photograph, the price escalates. Personal dedications or individual comments added to the signature help in this. It is safest to look for signed photographs of people who would not be products of a studio publicity machine − a signed picture of Picasso or Virginia Woolf is likely to be genuine and could be worth around $250. Even more valuable are portraits of people who were alive in the early years of photographic portraiture − Tchaikovsky and Queen Victoria for example. Signed pictures of them sell for at least $1,500. Collectors especially value signed pictures of. Royalty and of the Presidents of the United States (where the writing machine problem does crop up). Certain photographic portraitists can elevate the price of a picture − a Karsh for example will fetch a high price.

'Sincerely', Jean Kent. $3.50

Edward G. Robinson, Picturegoer Series 658. $25

George Robey as Falstaff. $9

'Yours sincerely', Billie Burke. $3.50

Lauren Bacall, 20th Century Fox. $25

'Best wishes', Peggy Cummins, Ealing Studios. $9

Robert Browning (John Wilson)
$1,000

Sir E. H. Shackleton
(John Wilson) $435

Signed photograph of Bernard Law
Montgomery with Eisenhower.
(John Wilson) $210

Robert E. Lee (John Wilson)
$2,100

SIGNED PHOTOGRAPHS

A good head and shoulders portrait photograph signed and inscribed 'Sincerely Gary Cooper', 9 x 7in. (Christie's) $225

Rita Hayworth and Maureen O'Hara, two good portrait photographs, each signed and inscribed by subject 'To Teresa', both 14 x 11in. (Christie's) $240

A good head and shoulders portrait photograph with manuscript inscription 'To Rose Marie Betts with kindest regards Gary Cooper 1938', 14 x 11in. (Christie's) $142

A half-length portrait photograph signed and inscribed 'To Phyllis from Clark Gable', 9½ x 7¾in. (Christie's) $305

A head and shoulders portrait photograph signed 'Sincerely Boris Karloff', 7 x 5in; with a rare half-length publicity photograph of Lon Chaney in the role of 'The Wolf Man' 1940. (Christie's) $400

A collection of ten publicity photographs, each signed and inscribed 'To Phyllis . . . ' subjects include Grace Kelly, Ingrid Bergman, Mel Ferrer, Ava Gardner, Gene Kelly, Robert Taylor, Lana Turner, Stewart Granger, largest 10 x 8in. (Christie's) $485

A good half-length publicity photograph, signed and inscribed 'To Betty from Ronald Reagan', 7 x 5in. (Christie's) $445

A good head and shoulders portrait photograph, with manuscript inscription 'To Hazel Betts Cordially Carole Lombard', 14 x 11in. (Christie's) $284

A good head and shoulders portrait photograph by Laszlo Willinger, with photographer's ink credit on reverse, and manuscript inscription 'Best wishes always to Hazel Betts, Clark Gable', 13 x 11in. (Christie's) $200

SIGNED PHOTOGRAPHS

A good head and shoulders portrait photograph, signed and inscribed 'Sincerely Spencer Tracy', 7 x 5in. (Christie's) $85

A good head and shoulders portrait photograph signed and inscribed, with a contract comprising a typescript agreement between Hal E. Roach studios and Marjorie Whiteis. (Christie's) $1,830

Two unpublished portrait photographs of Elia Kazan by Bryan Wharton, both taken in London, 1978, each 10 x 7in. (Christie's) $120

A good head and shoulders portrait photograph, signed and inscribed 'To Theresa with sincere good wishes Basil Rathbone', 13¾ x 10¾in. (Christie's) $245

A good head and shoulders portrait photograph of John Garfield in flying jacket, signed and inscribed 'For Victory, Edgar Johnny Garfield', 10 x 8in. (Christie's) $90

Tyrone Power and Robert Taylor, two good head and shoulders portrait photographs each signed and inscribed by subjects 'To Rose Marie Betts . . .', both 14 x 11in. (Christie's) $205

Errol Flynn and Olivia De Havilland, two good head and shoulders portrait photographs, by Elmer Fyer, each with photographer's blindstamp, signed and inscribed by subjects 'To Hazel Betts . . .' both 14 x 11in. (Christie's) $260

A good full-length portrait photograph of Charlie Chaplin in his famous tramp guise, signed and inscribed 'With best wishes, Sincerely Charlie Chaplin', 7 x 5¼in.; and a half-length publicity photograph. (Christie's)   Two $570

A good half-length portrait photograph of Susan Hayward signed and inscribed 'To Milton — much love Susan', 12¾ x 9¾in., with portrait photographs of Yvonne De Carlo, and Jayne Mansfield. (Christie's) $650

SIGNED PHOTOGRAPHS

Marilyn Monroe signed autograph from an album page.
(Vennett Smith) $1,300

Louis Bleriot (John Wilson)
$220

Louis Pasteur (John Wilson)
$1,300

Ulysses S. Grant (John Wilson)
$2,100

Bernard Law Montgomery
(John Wilson) $130

Charles de Gaulle
(John Wilson) $700

Sir Winston Spencer Churchill,
with Montgomery.
(John Wilson) $2,200

Rudyard Kipling (John Wilson) $960

Walt Whitman (John Wilson)
$960

Haakon VII (and family)
(John Wilson) $350

Noel Coward (John Wilson) $150

SILHOUETTES

Before the era of photography, if you couldn't afford a portrait, you might sit for a silhouettist. These little black and white likenesses are named after Etienne de Silhouette, a French politician who, it seems, believed in cutting everything down to essentials. They first appeared around 1750, and were done either freehand or by tracing the shadow of a profile on a piece of black paper. Later, more sophisticated techniques developed. The art flourished too among amateurs, and was regarded as quite a drawing-room accomplishment.

Augustin Edouart, a full length group silhouette of the Lambe family, Hogarth frame, 12in. high. (Christie's)
$1,514

A silhouette of a young woman in original gold leaf frame, America, circa 1830, image 7¼ x 5in. (Robt. W. Skinner Inc.)
$3,115

A full-length profile of William, 1st Marquess of Lansdowne by Wm. Hamlet the elder, inscribed and dated 1785 on the reverse, 8¾in. rectangular.
$1,730

A full-length profile of Wm. Pitt, by Wm. Wellings, signed and dated 1781, rectangular 10½in.
$4,620

A coloured profile of Lieut. Robert Conry by Charles or John Buncombe, circa 1810, oval 3¼in. $805

A lady by J. Thomason, circa 1795, in profile to sinister, painted on plaster, oval 8.6cm. $610

A coloured profile of an officer of the Life Guards called Nunn Davie, by C. Buncombe, circa 1795, oval 4¾in. $1,575

SILHOUETTES

A bronzed profile of a lady by John Field, signed Miers and Field, circa 1810, 5.7cm. oval. $1,730

A bronzed profile of an officer of the Light Dragoons called George Baker by John Field, circa 1810, oval 3in. $1,120

Miss Mary Ann Lovell as a child, by W. Phelps, 1786, painted on plaster, oval 8.5cm. $1,640

A full-length profile of a young lady of the Gosset Family, circa 1780, rectangular 11½in. $3,750

A young lady by J. Thomason, in profile to dexter, painted on plaster, circa 1790, oval 8.5cm. $575

A full-length profile of John, Earl of St. Vincent, by Wm. Wellings, signed and dated 1783, oval 11¼in. $5,000

A lady, in profile to dexter, painted on plaster, circa 1795, oval 4in. $385

Isaac Taylor III, a family conversation group, silhouette painted on glass, 12.5/8in. high. (Christie's) $1,540

A gentleman by J. Thomason, inscribed 1797 on the reverse, oval 12.7cm., with verre eglomise border. $575

A rectangular silhouette on paper by John Buncombe, of Catherine Reynolds of Newport, circa 1785, 90 x 70mm. (Phillips) $226

A rectangular conversation piece by Wm. Welling, of a husband and wife taking tea, signed and dated 1874, 280 x 380mm. (Phillips) $4,832

A gentleman standing full-length profile, by Augustin Edouart, cut-out on card, signed and dated 1836, 10¾in. high. (Christie's) $495

A full-length profile of a family group, by Augustin Edouart, signed and dated 1825, cut-outs on card, 13in. high. (Christie's) $1,573

Pair of early 20th century silhouettes, 'The Bull Fighters', by Wilhelm Hunt Diederich, 9½ x 13in. (Robt. W. Skinner Inc.) $450

An oval black silhouette by John Buncombe, of a lady, circa 1800, 95mm. high. (Phillips) $143

Pair of early 19th century bronzed silhouettes by F. Frith, signed and dated 1844, 10½ x 8½in. (Parsons, Welch & Cowell) $512

A gentleman profile to left, by John Miers, on plaster, oval 3½in. high. (Christie's) $131

SILK POSTCARDS

Though some English, Spanish and other examples exist, most hand-embroidered and woven silk postcards are of French origin. These cards were popular with soldiers in France during the First World War, who sent them home to their sweethearts. Few, however were posted *as* postcards, and most were enclosed in envelopes to protect them. Some were made in the form of envelopes, with a scented card, silk handkerchief or printed card insert for a private message. Such inserts usually add about $2 to the value. Most sought after are those of Regimental badges, year dates and scenes. Value can range from $5 for a simple flower to $350 for a T. Stevens 'personality' of the day. Condition is all-important. Being so delicate, silk postcards are very prone to 'foxing' (brown patches caused by damp). Even the most beautiful cards are of little value if damaged or badly foxed.

'Bonne Annee', silk greeting card by La Rosa. $5

Embroidered silk card 'Yours for ever', with enclosed card 'Tell her that I love her', by Fabrication Francaise. $5

'Cartel de Toros', by Alcana, Madrid. $5

'Home Sweet Home', by W. H. Grant, Coventry, postally used in 1915. $35

'United we stand', French envelope type, by Fabrication Francaise, Paris. $7

Woven silk card, 'Flames', Albert, 1914, by E. Deffrene.
                                    $25

'To my dear mother from your loving son', by J. S., Paris, 1915. $10

'To my dear wife', envelope type by Visa, Paris. $5

Envelope type with patriotic flags by T.M.T., with insert card 'I'm thinking of you'. $10

Embroidered silk card 'Good Luck', with silk ribbon. $9

A.S.C. (Army Service Corps) with Regimental badge by J. J. Saint. $14

'From your soldier boy', with woven butter-fly, envelope type by M. M., Paris. $9 £5

'Good Luck' card with a felt cat and applied scrap. $3.50

'To my dear sister', envelope type with pat-riotic flag by H. S. $9

SPORTING STONEWARE

Stoneware is basically earthenware baked at a higher temperature, making it very tough and able to withstand decoration by polishing, staining, cutting into the ware itself or even through the glaze to the body (sgraffiato). Sporting stoneware was produced principally by Doulton, and comprises a range of mugs and jugs with relief figures of famous sportsmen. They were first introduced in 1880 and the figures are the work of John Broad, perhaps the best known being his W. G. Grace jug.

A silver mounted cycling jug and two beakers, circa 1900, the jug 8in. high, the beakers 4¾in. high. $315

A golfing jug, sprigged in white with the panels of 'The Lost Ball', 'Putting' and 'Driving', impressed Lambeth mark, circa 1880, 20cm. high. $490

A waisted mug applied with moulded white figures of a bowler, wicket keeper and a batsman, circa 1900, 6in. high. $210

A cricketing jug, the moulded relief figures against the buff saltglaze ground within stylised floral borders outlined in white slip and coloured in blue and green, circa 1900, 9¼in. high. $300

A silver mounted sporting tyg, circa 1900, 6in. high, the silver rim maker's mark H. W., Sheffield. $280

A cricketer's mug applied with moulded white figures of a bowler, wicket keeper and a batsman, circa 1880, 15.5cm. high. $210

A cricketing tyg, impressed registration mark and dated 1884, 6¼in. high. $420

A mug with applied moulded golfing vignettes of 'The Drive', and 'The Lost Ball', circa 1900, 5in. high. $400

A beaker with relief white figures of a shot putter, a runner and a long-jumper, the silver rim hallmarked 1900, 5in. high. $105

A cycling mug with three applied white figures inscribed 'Military', 'Road' and 'Path', circa 1900, 4¾in. high. $150

A cycling jug with three white vignettes, inscribed 'Military', 'Road' and 'Path', circa 1900, 7¼in. high. $210

A sporting jug with three moulded white vignettes, a man running, men playing football and a man putting the shot, circa 1900, 8in. high. $155

A cricket jug with applied vignettes of a bowler, wicket keeper and a batsman, circa 1900, 7in. high. $280

A rugby football jug with vignettes of two men kicking a ball, a scrummage and two of the men running with a ball, 1883, 7½in. high. $225

A cricket mug with three applied figures of batsmen in high relief, registration mark of 1880, 5¼in. high. $245

A golfing jug with three applied white vignettes of 'The Lost Ball', 'Putting' and 'Driving', circa 1900, 7¾in. high. $455

STAFFORDSHIRE FIGURES

Devotees of Arnold Bennett's novels about the Five Towns will be aware of the names Fenton, Longton, Hanley, Burslem, Tunstall and Burmantofts — Bennett left one out — which were the centre of the great pottery industry of the 19th century. It was there that Staffordshire figures were produced in their thousands and bought with eagerness to adorn chest tops and mantlepieces in homes all over the country. At one time there were over 400 factories going full blast in the area around Stoke on Trent to satisfy the demand.

Staffordshire figures were unsophisticated in their modelling and cast in the shape of popular heroes or characters from stories, plays and poetry. There was an especially popular line in politicians and heroes like Wellington and Nelson. They were press moulded and decorated in underglaze blue and black with touches of color in overglaze enamel and gilding. Early examples have closed bases or a small hole in the base while 20th century pieces are usually slip cast in Plaster of Paris moulds and are open ended.

A group of Napoleon III and Empress Eugenie, the oval base named in gilt moulded capitals, circa 1854, 12in. high. (Christie's) $238

A pair of Staffordshire pugilist figures modelled as the boxers Mollineux and Cribb, circa 1810, 22cm. high. (Christie's) $2,729

A figure of The Tichborne Claimant, holding a bird on his left hand, a rifle at his side, 14in. high. (Christie's) $406

A Staffordshire pearlware sailor Toby jug, circa 1800, 29.5cm. high. (Christie's) $1,270

A pair of Staffordshire pearlware figures of Mansion House dwarfs, after the Derby porcelain originals, 15cm. and 17cm. high. (Phillips) $2,254

A 19th century Staffordshire pottery portrait figure of the Rev. John Wesley, 7in. high. (Reeds Rains) $116

A Staffordshire group of children, entitled 'Scuffle', 19cm. high. (Phillips) $412

A group modelled as Hercules wrestling with a bull, circa 1810, 5½in. high. (Christie's) $1,266

An Obadiah Sherratt group of Polito's menagerie, circa 1830, 29.5cm. high. (Christie's) $21,546

A jardiniere modelled as a rectangular plant holder of wooden slats, impressed Brown, Westhead Moore, 33cm. high. (Christie's) $2,392

One of a pair of late 18th century Staffordshire pottery cow creamers, 6¼in. long. (Dacre, Son & Hartley) $2,304

Early 19th century Staffordshire bust of John Wesley mounted on a marbleised pedestal base, 11½in. high. (Robt. W. Skinner Inc.) $175

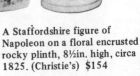

A pair of early Staffordshire figures of Whieldon type, depicting a sailor and a soldier, 15cm. and 15.5cm. high. (Phillips) $7,682

Pair of mid 19th century Staffordshire pottery equestrian groups of the Prince and Princess of Wales, 7½in. high. (Reeds Rains) $279

A Staffordshire figure of Napoleon on a floral encrusted rocky plinth, 8½in. high, circa 1825. (Christie's) $154

STAFFORDSHIRE FIGURES

One of a pair of early 19th century Staffordshire pottery figures of putti, 6in. high. (Reeds Rains) $201

A Staffordshire group of a sheep and a lamb standing calmly together on a shaped rectangular base, 10cm. high. (Phillips) $616

A 19th century Staffordshire pottery portrait figure of Wm, Shakespeare, 9in. high. (Reeds Rains) $139

A Staffordshire Phrenology bust by L. N. Fowler, late 19th century, 30cm. high. (Christie's) $1,058

A pair of figures of the Prince of Wales and Prince Alfred, circa 1858, 10¾in. high. (Christie's) $387

A Staffordshire figure of James Blomfield Rush, circa 1850, 10in. high. (Christie's) $1,626

A Staffordshire erotic figure of a barmaid, circa 1820, 19cm. high. (Phillips) $1,369

A pair of Staffordshire figures of a gardener and companion of Ralph Wood type, circa 1780, 19.5cm. high. (Christie's) $4,356

A figure of George Parr, holding a cricket ball in his right hand, circa 1865, 14in. high. (Christie's) $819

STAINED GLASS WINDOWS

Throughout the ages, stained glass, first produced by the Egyptians, has been one of the loveliest ways of adorning any building. It is interesting to note that, despite modern technology, it has been virtually impossible to improve upon the quality and beauty of medieval cathedral glass, where even the flaws hold the light and enhance the effect.

The Art Deco period saw stained glass translated into modern settings, and the Tiffany lamps of the 20's are among the loveliest examples of this.

Edwardian stained glass window with diamond shape centre, 18in. wide. $55

A stained glass panel with scene of mediaeval punishment, 18¾ x 15in. (Capes Dunn & Co.)
$2,337

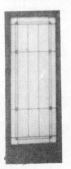

Two early 20th century prairie school style leaded glass windows, 20½ x 53½in. and five smaller, 18 x 18¾in. (Robt. W. Skinner Inc.)
$1,100

A late 19th century leaded stained and coloured glass window, signed W. J. McPherson, Tremont St., Boston, Mass. (Robt. W. Skinner Inc.) $800

Tiffany glass mosaic panel, entitled 'Truth', New York, 1898, 87½ x 44¼in. (Robt. W. Skinner Inc) $10,000

Flemish 16th century grisaille and yellow-stained glass roundel, 24.46cm. square. (Sotheby's) $1,425

One of a pair of Gruber leaded glass doors, 1920's, 180cm. wide. (Sotheby's)$3,300

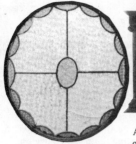

Art Deco style stained glass door roundel, 1930's. $55

A set of four late 18th or early 19th century English painted glass panels of female allegories of Justice, Faith, Hope and Charity, probably by Thos. Jarvis, after Sir J. Reynolds, each panel 72 x 40cm. (Christie's) $3,490

One of a pair of 18th century English oval stained glass armorial panels, 46 x 34.5cm. (Christie's) $734

A large 19th century English stained glass panel showing a lady in Renaissance costume at the prie-dieu, 100 x 55cm. (Christie's) $826

An Art Deco leaded stained glass panel by Jacques Gruber, 70.2cm. wide, 50.3cm. high. (Christie's) $5,772

A large rectangular glass panel by John Hutton, sand blasted and wheel engraved with Perseus before the Three Graces, 206.5 x 97cm. (Christie's) $2,706

A leaded and stained glass panel by George Walton, after a design by Charles Rennie Mackintosh, 133.6cm. high, 91.4cm. wide. (Christie's) $1,082

A 17th century French rectangular stained glass panel centred with an oval of the martyrdom of St. Stephen, 46.5 x 59cm. (Christie's) $918

A large 19th century English stained glass panel of Mary Queen of Scots, 151 x 80cm. (Christie's) $1,837

STANDS

This universal expression covers anything upon which items can be hung, propped, leant or draped. There are umbrella stands, candlestands, reading stands, music stands, plant stands, wig stands, hat stands, coat stands, kettle stands, boot stands, shaving stands... stands for every sort of item you can imagine. The Victorians were great lovers of stands and some of the ones they dreamed up seem to create more clutter than they tidied away. Particularly interesting to collectors are elaborately carved coat and hat stands made in the shape of trees with life size bears trying to climb up. Coats and hats were hung on the tree's branches. More appealing are china umbrella stands, many of them by potteries like Doulton or in Chinese porcelain. Boot stands are often found with scrapers and brushes for cleaning dirty shoes set in at the sides. Music stands were often lyre shaped and very elegant, especially the ones dating from the Georgian period.

An Art Nouveau oak hall stand with circular mirror, stylish hooks and embossed copper panels, 36in. wide. (Lots Road Chelsea Auction Galleries) $567

Regency dark mahogany small fly press with two small drawers to the front, on squat circular feet. (G. A. Key) $875

An Italian walnut pedestal with shaped rectangular top on a bombe support, 50¼in. high. (Christie's) $2,020

A Regency brass and rosewood etagere with four rectangular trays, 16½in. wide, 39½in. high. (Christie's) $13,783

A cane-sided plant stand, probably Limbert, circa 1910, 23in. high, the top 16in. sq. (Robt. W. Skinner Inc.) $475

A magazine stand with cutouts, Michigan, 1910, 20in. wide. (Robt. W. Skinner Inc.) $700

STANDS

An Edwardian mahogany and inlaid pedestal jardiniere with liner. (J. M. Welch & Son) $380

A set of George III mahogany library steps with moulded handrail and leather-lined treads, 104in. high. (Christie's) $6,891

A rosewood grained one-drawer poplar stand, American, circa 1830, top 21 x 16in. (Robt. W. Skinner Inc.) $6,250

A black and gold-painted umbrella stand with scrolling foliate sides, 32in. wide. (Christie's) $902

A Regency mahogany teapoy with folding top enclosing a divided interior, 26¾in. wide. (Christie's) $9,768

Early 20th century Mission oak magazine stand with cut out arched sides, 49in. high. (Robt. W. Skinner Inc.) $500

A Federal tiger maple candle-stand, New England, circa 1810, top 17 x 17½in. (Robt. W. Skinner Inc.) $1,300

A marquetry panelled oak smoking rack, possibly Stickley Bros., Michigan, circa 1910, style no. 264-100, 22in. high, 24in. wide. (Robt. W. Skinner Inc.) $130

A mid Victorian black and mother-of-pearl japanned papier-mache music stand, 17¾in. diam. (Christie's) $613

435

One of a pair of walnut torcheres with lobed tray-tops and hexagonal shaped shafts, 10in. wide, 30½in. high. (Christie's)
$1,156

Painted Tramp art stand with drawers, possibly New York, 1820-40, 17½in. wide. (Robt. W. Skinner Inc.)
$300

Chippendale cherry candle-stand, the shaped top with ovolo corners, circa 1780, 26in. high. (Robt. W. Skinner Inc.)
$2,500

A Chippendale style mahogany urn table, 25in. high. (Christie's) $646

An early 18th century Italian carved giltwood stand with a simulated green marble top, 1.10m. high. (Phillips)
$1,200

A George II grained pine pedestal, 53¼in. high. (Christie's)
$10,081

Gustav Stickley inlaid tiger maple open music stand, circa 1904, no. 670, signed with Eastwood label, 39in. high. (Robt. W. Skinner Inc.)
$7,250

A pair of late 18th century Italian parcel gilt and green painted torcheres, 69½in. high. (Christie's)
$7,810

A Victorian mahogany folio stand with brass ratcheted adjustable open slatted slopes, 76cm. high. (Phillips)
$2,550

STEREOSCOPIC CARDS

Stereoscopes were a Victorian invention, and viewers came in various forms, such as 'hand-held' or 'cabinet table'. When the cards are inserted a three-dimensional image appears. Special cameras were produced to take two simultaneous images at different angles and thus create the effect.

Stereoscopic cards were produced in large numbers and could be bought over the counter. 'One-off' rare cards of unusual subjects taken by local photographers can be very valuable indeed.

The 'New Woman' comic stereoscopic photo-print card, circa 1895. $3.50

Rare advertising stereoscopic card, Nestles Swiss Milk Chocolate with 'Indian Rhinoceros Jim', 1890's. $45

Three hunters - Stereoscopic daguerreotype, hand-tinted, gilt-painted, 1850's. (Christie's) $2,937

Rotary Photo Company No. 31450A, real photo stereoscopic card of Mr Oscar Asche. $5

Excelsior stereoscopic tours card, published by Mr E. Wright, Burnley. 'State coach and horses after the explosion at Calle Mayor, Madrid', 1890's. $35

Stereoscopic card No. 12030, published by B. W. Kilburn, 1897. 'Russian torpedo boat with its crew, Moscow, Russia.' $20

Stereoscopic card No. 12188, published by B. W. Kilburn, Littleton, N.H., copyright 1897, 'Russian Homes'. $14

STICKLEY

Gustav Stickley was the eldest of six brothers, including L. & J. G. and G. & A., all of whom were active as U.S. furniture manufacturers in the early 20th century. Gustav trained as a stone-mason, but became best known for his chair designs, mainly in the American Colonial style. The brothers' business relationships were obviously complicated: L. & J. G. left Gustav's factory in 1900 to found their own, then bought it in 1916 following his bankruptcy. The Stickley Manufacturing Co, formed then, is still active today.

An early Gustav Stickley settle with arched slats, 1901-03, 60in. wide. (Robt. W. Skinner Inc.) $27,000

A copper and amber glass lantern, style no. 324, by Gustav Stickley, circa 1906, 15in. high, globe 5¼in. diam. (Robt. W. Skinner Inc.) $7,500

A Gustav Stickley round slat-sided waste basket, no. 94, circa 1907, 14in. diam. (Robt. W. Skinner Inc.) $1,200

A Gustav Stickley slat-sided folio stand, no. 551, 1902-03, 40½in. high, 29½in. wide. (Robt. W. Skinner Inc.) $3,000

An inlaid oak three-panelled screen, designed by Harvey Ellis for Gustav Stickley, circa 1903-04, 66¾in. high, each panel 20in. wide. (Robt. W. Skinner Inc.) $18,000

A Gustav Stickley bent arm spindle Morris chair, circa 1907, with spring cushion seat. (Robt. W. Skinner Inc.) $1,300

A Gustav Stickley nine-drawer tall chest, no. 913, circa 1907, 36in. wide, 50in. high. (Robt. W. Skinner Inc.) $4,000

Gustav Stickley oak table lamp with wicker shade, circa 1910, 22in. high, 18in. diam. (Robt. W. Skinner Inc.) $1,100

A Gustav Stickley hall mirror, style no. 66, circa 1905-06, 28in. high, 36in. wide. (Robt. W. Skinner Inc.) $1,200

A leather upholstered dining chair, no. 355, by Gustav Stickley, circa 1910, 33¼in. high. (Robt. W. Skinner Inc.) $950

A Gustav Stickley oak 'Eastwood' chair with original rope support for seat, circa 1902. (Robt. W. Skinner Inc.) $28,000

A hammered copper chamberstick, by Gustav Stickley, circa 1913, 9¼in. high. (Robt. W. Skinner Inc.) $700

A Gustav Stickley table with twelve Grueby tiles, 1902-03, 23¾in. wide. (Robt. W. Skinner Inc.) $49,000

A Gustav Stickley two-door bookcase with keyed tenons, no. 716, 42½in. high. (Robt. W. Skinner Inc.) $2,500

A drink stand, by L. & J. G. Stickley, no. 587, circa 1912, 16in. sq. (Robt. W. Skinner Inc.) $650

A Gustav Stickley slat-sided cube chair, no. 331, circa 1910, 25¼in. wide. (Robt. W. Skinner Inc.) $5,250

SYPHONS

The fashion for taking soda water or seltzer in spirits and wine started in the early 19th century and in order to make sure that the liquid was aerated, it had to be kept under pressure. There were some early patents, both French and English, for soda water bottles and they had wonderful names like Gazateur and Seltzogene. A few were liable to explode and therefore the bottles were encased in basket weave or wire net to prevent shards of glass injuring people. The classic soda syphon shape was devised in the late 19th century and the tops were of tin or pewter. Later they were porcelain lined and chrome plated before the advent of modern plastic tops. A few early syphons had porcelain bodies and some were made of colored glass — pink, green, blue, yellow, brown or amber.

An early Sparklets wire-bound soda syphon. $18

Blue glass soda syphon inscribed Job. Wragg Ltd., with acid etching on front, dated 1902. $20

Greenock Apothe-caries & Lawsons Ltd. soda syphon, circa 1902. $10

Spaco Ltd., blue glass soda syphon with silver plated top. $20

Faceted clear glass syphon by Wrights of Walkery, 31cm. high. $28

One shot, basket covered, Sparklets type syphon, 32cm. high. $14

Amber glass writhened syphon by Parker Bros. of Drighlington, 31cm. high. $45

Table syphon by J. Burgess, 12in. tall. $10

TAPESTRIES

Tapestry dates from ancient times, but remained principally an amateur occupation in Europe (with the Bayeux as perhaps the supreme example) until the 14th century, when major centres developed at Arras, Tournai and Brussels in Belgium and the Beauvais and Gobelins factories in France. Medieval tapestries were often used as portable draught screens. From the 16th century such leading painters as Raphael were commissioned to design them.

A 17th century Brussels verdure tapestry, depicting a dog and animal beside a river, framed by trees and foliage, 2.92 x 2.46m. (Phillips) $5,184

An 18th century Gobelins tapestry woven in wools and silks with two Chinamen in a landscape, 9ft.6in. x 5ft. 4½in. (Christie's) $9,979

Early 18th century Brussels tapestry woven in silk and wool with the family of Darius prostrate before Alexander the Great, 13ft.9in. x 22ft.7in. (Christie's) $6,998

Early 18th century Brussels tapestry woven in wool and silk depicting Neptune, 13ft 10in. x 10ft.4in.(Christie's) $4,665

A 16th century Dutch tapestry woven in silks and wools with Christ and the woman caught in adultery, 7ft.10in. x 6ft.7in. (Christie's) $18,662

A 17th century Brussels tapestry depicting a boar hunt, 9ft. x 6ft.1in. (Christie's) $5,702

Late 16th century Flemish Verdure tapestry woven with various scenes in a forest, 8ft. 5in. x 21ft.11in. (Christie's) $24,883

TAPESTRIES

A 17th century Brussels tapestry woven in silks and wools, 10ft.11in. x 10ft.6in. (Christie's) $8,553

A 17th century Brussels tapestry woven in well preserved wools and silks, 8ft. x 11ft.2in. (Christie's) $14,256

A late 17th century Brussels tapestry in well preserved silks and wools, 9ft.8in. x 7ft.10in. (Christie's) $19,245

Mid 18th century Brussels tapestry woven in silk and wool with Jupiter and his eagle receiving thunderbolts from Vulcan, 13ft.1in. x 8ft. 4in. (Christie's)$5,909

A 17th century Spanish or Italian tapestry woven in muted colours, 94 x 99in. (Christie's) $6,577

An Aubusson tapestry woven with lovers and sheep in a rustic landscape, 7ft.6in. x 4ft.8in. (Christie's) $3,576

A 17th century Flemish Verdure tapestry woven with a dog beneath a tree in a pond by a forest clearing with a palace beyond, 8ft.5in. x 9ft.7in. (Christie's) $3,421

An 18th century Louis XV Beauvais tapestry from the Tenture des Verdures Fines, woven in silk and wool, 8ft. 7in. x 6ft.1in. (Christie's) $5,702

A late 17th century Flemish Verdure tapestry with a shepherd and shepherdess in a forest with their flock, 9ft. 3in. x 8ft.7in. (Christie's) $4,561

TASSIE MEDALLIONS

There are two famous Tassies — James who lived between 1735-99 and his nephew William who was born in 1777 and died in 1860. Both of them were skilled makers of medallions and the senior Tassie was the man who made the famous copy of the Portland Vase. James Tassie was born at Pollokshaws, Glasgow, and settled in London where he set up a thriving business making cameo portraits of the distinguished people of the day. The cameos were made of decorated glassware with the relief in ceramic paste and the results were astonishingly lifelike. Everybody who was anybody wanted to sit for Tassie. His nephew William succeeded him in the business and was as successful and as skilled as his uncle. There are some excellent examples of Tassie ware in the British Museum.

Hugh, 1st Duke of Northumberland, K.G., signed with a 'T', inscribed and dated 1780, on black ground. (Christie's) $1,230

William Pitt, by Tassie probably after Flaxman, on blue ground. (Christie's) $2,835

Major M. Macalister of the Glengarry Fencibles, signed Tassie F, inscribed and dated 1796, on blue ground. (Christie's) $1,510

William, 1st Earl of Mansfield, signed Tassie F, dated 1779, on blue ground. (Christie's) $1,700

Philip Dormer Stanhope, 4th Earl of Chesterfield, by Tassie after Gosset, integral white paste ground. (Christie's) $1,100

Admiral Lord Duncan, signed Tassie F, inscribed and dated 1797, on green ground. (Christie's) $1,410

443

TAXIDERMY

Stuffed animals and birds are not to everyone's taste but the best examples really deserve to be regarded as works of art. The stuffed animal or bird must be set in a mobile, lifelike manner in a suitable background with details of its natural habitat. Condition is very important because taxidermy specimens are very liable to attack from moths and beetles.

The art of taxidermy thrived during the Victorian period when there was an enormous demand for it. Sportsmen sent fish, foxes, badgers, stags' heads and even the heads of buffalo, lions and tigers for stuffing and mounting. In drawing rooms there were enormous glass cases full of colorful birds perched on flowering trees or set pieces with partridges and pheasants striding through tufts of heather. So great was the demand that most towns had their resident taxidermist and some of them were very skilled indeed. Mostly they put labels at the back of the cases or else signed their work in some way — Peter Spicer of Leamington left a signed pebble on the floor of his cases. Only top quality items in good condition sell for large sums of money today.

Osprey by Grant of Devizes, circa 1880. $435

Grey Squirrel by H. Bryant of Wellingborough, circa 1910. $130

Shelduck by T. E. Gunn of Norwich, circa 1890. $190

(The Enchanted Aviary)

Otter (taxidermist not known), 1919. $410

Fox by J. Hutchings of Aberystwyth, circa 1900. $520

African Grey Parrot in oval dome (removed for the photo) by W. Lowne of Yarmouth, circa 1900. $220

Black-headed Gull by E. C. Saunders of Yarmouth, circa 1910. $165

Canada Goose by W. Hine of Southport, circa 1920. $520

TAXIDERMY

3 Bream by J. Cooper of London in bowed case, 1912. $1,650

Green Woodpecker by E. C. Saunders of Yarmouth, circa 1910. $165

Pheasant (partly white) by J. Gardner of Oxford Street, London, circa 1880. $165

Badger by J. Gardner of Oxford Street, London, circa 1880. $260

Cuckoo & Wryneck by T. E. Gunn of Norwich, circa 1900. $190 £110

Pair of Nightjars with two chicks by J. Cooper of London, circa 1890. $300

(The Enchanted Aviary)

446

TEA CADDIES

The word "caddie" comes from the Malay "kati" which means a measure of tea, around one and a quarter pounds. It was imported into the English language when tea began to be brought to this country in ship loads to cater to the new upper class taste for drinking it but it was very expensive, working out at about $20 a pound. For that reason people who bought small amounts of the precious leaf did not want to waste a single shred and they stored their tea in special little chests or boxes with locks to prevent pilfering. The earliest and most pedestrian caddies were made of pottery or porcelain but when it became the fashion for the tea to be carried into the drawing room along with the tea things for the lady of the house to dispense into the tea pot herself, caddies of gold or silver and more commonly fine woods began to appear. Chippendale, Sheraton and all the fashionable cabinet makers of the day produced caddies to match the styles of their furniture and they were ornamented with brass, ormolu, tortoiseshell, coloured straw or paperwork and inlaid with exotic woods. Some of them are very beautiful and the finest examples have moved into the top bracket of collectables. However there are cheaper ones still to be found, especially those made of painted tin with hinged upper lids which Victorian housewives kept on their kitchen shelves.

A Regency shaped tortoiseshell tea caddy, on bun feet. (Hetheringtons Nationwide) $704

An early 19th century blond tortoiseshell tea chest, the hinged lid reveals two lidded compartments with silver plated knobs, 7in. long. (Woolley & Wallis) $429

A George III satinwood, rosewood and fruitwood tea caddy, the crossbanded lid with a silver plaque with initials J. E. R., 12¾in. wide. (Christie's) $1,676

A two-compartment Tunbridge-ware tea caddy. (David Lay) $250

A George III satinwood, marquetry and painted octangular tea caddy with hinged top, 6½in. wide. (Christie's) $957

A Regency tortoiseshell tea caddy with gilt metal lion handles, 12½in. wide. (Christie's) $660

A Regency tortoiseshell veneered rectangular tea chest with wire inlay, 7in. long. (Woolley & Wallis) $445

A George III treen (applewood) tea caddy formed as a large apple with hinged cover and ebonised stem, 6in. high. (Christie's) $4,653

Early 19th century painted tin tea caddy, America, 5¼in. wide, 5in. high. (Robt. W. Skinner Inc.) $500

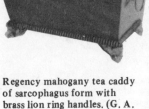

Regency mahogany tea caddy of sarcophagus form with brass lion ring handles. (G. A. Key) $264

A Regency burr walnut and mahogany two division tea caddy with glass mixing bowl. (Hobbs Parker) $504

A George III laburnum tea caddy with a divided interior, on bracket feet, 10in. wide. (Christie's) $1,180

A Meissen tea caddy with domed shoulder, circa 1755, 10.5cm. high. (Christie's) $623

A Leeds creamware tea canister of octagonal shape, 12.5cm. high, incised no. 25. (Phillips) $2,087

A Berlin Reliefzierrat rectangular indented tea caddy and cover, painted in colours with putti playing on clouds, circa 1700, 14.5cm. high. (Christie's) $4,114

Late 18th century Whieldon pattern square shaped pottery tea caddy, 4in. high. (Reeds Rains) $259

A pair of South Staffordshire opaque tea caddies for Bohea and Green, circa 1760, about 13.5cm. high. (Christie's) $7,088

A Meissen rectangular tea caddy and cover, circa 1735, in fitted case, 11cm. high. (Christie's) $3,456

A Meissen rectangular tea caddy and cover painted in Silbermalerei with chinoiserie figures, circa 1740, 13.5cm. high. (Christie's) $4,713

A Lowestoft blue and white arched rectangular tea caddy, blue crescent mark, circa 1775, 10cm. high. (Christie's) $243

A Lowestoft blue and white rectangular octagonal tea caddy, circa 1765, 13cm. high. (Christie's) $1,686

TEAPOTS

Because the first tea came into Britain from China, the practice of pouring it out of a special china pot accompanied it and the early teapots resemble those used by the Chinese, with the same sort of decorations and swinging handles of cane across the top of the lid. Europe's china manufacturers recognised the opportunity of appealing to customers with well designed and prettily decorated tea pots and some of those which survive are exquisite, especially by Meissen, Wedgwood, Derby, Rockingham and other high class manufacturers. Some stuck to Chinese style decorations but others were a riot of pretty flowers and elegant gilding. In the late 19th century novelty teapots began to appear, some in the shape of animals. Minton produced one like an elephant in the 1870's. Others were in the shape of people with one arm acting as the spout and the other as the handle. Every artistic period has produced its characteristic teapots. Clarice Cliff's angular versions are the epitome of the Jazz Age and more recent teapots often return to Chinese or Japanese styles like the ones made by potter Lucie Rie.

A black basalt tea kettle and cover, circa 1800, 23.5cm. high, (base cracked, rim to cover repaired). (Christie's) $359

A Worcester blue-scale globular teapot and cover, blue square seal mark, circa 1770, 14.5cm. high. (Christie's) $766

A stoneware teapot and cover by Lucie Rie, covered in a matt manganese glaze, circa 1958, 15cm. high. (Christie's) $469

A stoneware teapot by Shoji Hamada, the cut sided body with short spout and arched handle, 18.7cm. high. (Christie's) $1,496

A Frankfurt Faience teapot and cover, painted in a bright blue with Chinese style figures, 13.5cm. high. (Phillips) $1,670

A Bottger rectangular teapot and cover painted in Schwarzlot enriched in gilding by I. Preissler, circa 1720, 15cm. high. (Christie's) $60,214

450

A Worcester faceted teapot, cover and stand, circa 1765, 14cm. high. (Christie's) $1,452

A pearlware cylindrical teapot and cover, applied with figures of Lord Rodney and Plenty, circa 1785, 13cm. high. (Christie's) $653

A Capodimonte oviform teapot with scroll handle and spout, blue fleur-de-lys mark, circa 1750, 14.5cm. wide. (Christie's) $1,188

A Linthorpe teapot, the design attributed to Dr. C. Dresser, 21.3cm. high. (Christie's) $172

A Minton majolica-ware teapot and cover in the form of a Chinese actor holding a mask, 14cm. high, impressed Mintons, model no. 1838, date code for 1874. (Phillips) $660

An unglazed stoneware teapot and cover by Michael Cardew, with bound cane handle, circa 1950, 17.8cm. high. (Christie's) $844

A Rockingham Cadogan teapot, of peach shape, 4½in. high, impressed Brameld. (Dreweatt Neate) $103

A Vincennes bleu lapis conical teapot, blue interlaced L marks and painter's mark of Thevenet, circa 1753, 11cm. high. (Christie's) $1,742

A Minton majolica-ware teapot and cover in the form of a monkey, 15.5cm. high, impressed Mintons, model no. 1844, date code for 1876. (Phillips) $1,023

A Wedgwood Whieldon pineapple teapot and cover, 10cm. high. (Phillips) $1,386

A Capodimonte oviform teapot with scroll handle and spout, blue fleur-de-lys mark, circa 1750, 14.5cm. wide. (Christie's) $1,188

A Wedgwood creamware globular teapot and cover, painted in the manner of David Rhodes, circa 1768, 15cm. high. (Christie's) $2,913

A Staffordshire creamware oviform 'pebble-dash' teapot and cover of Whieldon type, circa 1760, 13cm. high. (Christie's) $18,150

Sir Roger de Coverley Series teapot, 5in. high, circa 1911, depicting Sir Roger in the garden. $100

An 18th century Worcester porcelain teapot, the domed lid with flower finial, 6in. high. (Hobbs & Chambers) $207

A stoneware teapot with cane handle by Bernard Leach, circa 1920, 17.2cm. high. (Christie's) $1,080

An 18th/19th century Kakiemon type mokkogata teapot with shallow domed cover and arch-shaped handle, 19cm. long. (Christie's) $1,248

A black glazed terracotta teapot and cover, printed in yellow and decorated in enamels and gilt, 16cm. high. (Phillips) $80

TEDDY BEARS

Some of the prices paid in auction for Teddy Bears have caused eyebrows to be raised in astonishment. A good Steiff bear can easily command over $1,000 and the world record is now $90,000. The two words 'good' and 'Steiff' make a great difference. The history of the Teddy bear only goes back to 1902 when keen hunter President Theodore Roosevelt was shown in a political cartoon refusing to shoot a cuddly little baby bear. An American toy maker called Morris Michtom made a cuddly toy bear and asked permission to call it after Theodore so the Teddy bear was born and soon every child except the very poor had one. The most famous Teddy bears were made in Germany by a crippled dressmaker called Margarete Steiff who saw a copy of the Roosevelt cartoon. Her bears were not as endearing as Michtom's because they had humped backs, long arms and long noses but they caught the popular market and Miss Steiff marked them with a distinctive button stapled into one of their ears which give collectors a guideline to the authenticity of their bears.

A pale plush covered teddy bear with brown glass eyes, cut muzzle and reinforced felt feet, 22in. high. (Christie's) $374

An early gold plush tumbling teddy bear, the body of wood and cardboard, containing a key-wind mechanism, 9in. high. (Lawrence Fine Art) $97

A honey plush covered teddy bear with boot button eyes, wide apart ears, 13½in. high, with Steiff button in ear (one pad moth eaten). (Christie's) $831

A golden plush covered teddy bear with pronounced hump, pointed snout and with Steiff button in ear, 29in. high. (Christie's) $4,719

Alfonzo — a very rare short red plush teddy bear, with button eyes, excelsior stuffing and felt pads, dressed as a Russian, 13in. high, with Steiff button. (Christie's) $19,600

A silver plush covered teddy bear with button eyes and felt pads, 14in. high, with Steiff button. (Christie's) $1,039

A pale golden plush covered teddy bear with embroidered snout and slight hump, 15½in. high, with Steiff button. (Christie's) $1,337

A plush covered polar bear with button eyes, felt pads and joints at hips, 16in. long, with Steiff button, circa 1913. (Christie's) $727

A golden plush covered teddy bear in the form of a child's muff, 15in. high. (Christie's) $290

A musical teddy bear with swivelling head operated via his tail, 43cm. high. (David Lay) $360

A plush covered pull-along bear mounted on a wheeled frame, 23in. long, with raised letters, Steiff button, circa 1920. (Christie's) $790

A clockwork somersaulting teddy bear dressing in gold felt jacket, blue trouser and white vest, by Bing of Nuremberg, 9in. high. (Christie's) $943

A gold plush teddy bear, with metal Steiff disc in left ear, German, circa 1907, 25in. high. (Hobbs & Chambers) $3,200

A long cinnamon plush cover, teddy bear with large button eyes, central face seam, wide set ears, 21in. high, circa 1905, probably Steiff. (Christie's) $2,910

A golden plush covered teddy bear with boot button eyes, cut muzzle, hump and elongated limbs, with Steiff button in left ear, 19in. high. (Christie's) $871

TELEPHONES

"Mr Watson, come here, I want you," was the first complete sentence ever spoken over a telephone in June 1875 by Alexander Graham Bell in Boston, USA. Although attempts to invent a speaking machine had been going on for at least twenty years, notably by a German inventor called Professor Philip Reis Friedrichsdorf, Bell was the first to utilise continuous current in his application. His name is in the record books today by a lucky chance for another inventor Professor Elisha Gray, filed his own patent for a similar appliance only a few hours after Bell's. It took prolonged litigation before Bell's claim triumphed. In 1878 the first telephone switchboard for commercial operation was opened at Newhaven, Connecticut, and from that day, the world took to the speaking machine with alacrity.

Many of the oldest telephones that can be found today are of the Ericsson type which was used in Sweden, Denmark, France, Germany and Britain. They look magnificent with polished mahogany or walnut stands and brass fittings. There is also a vogue among collectors for finding old fashioned telephones like the light French ones that have been much copied in reproduction and the ones that were wall mounted with a speaker at face level. Interior decorators and theatrical or television companies are always on the look out for period telephones and a particular favourite is the phone on a stand with a hook at the side for the earpiece which was in common use in a number of homes before the Second World War. The slightly later heavy black or white phones with weighted bases look well too in modern homes.

Supplied by the G.P.O., year of manufacture 1920's. $175

Manufactured by L. M. Ericsson (England), supplied by National Telephone Co., and later by G.P.O. This is a magneto instrument, years of manufacture 1890-1920. $435

Supplied by Grammont, Paris, year of manufacture 1924. $260

The main part of this telephone was made in Germany, but the handset was made in Britain, supplied by The British Home and Office Telephone Co., London. These telephones were in use in the Ritz Hotel, London, in the 1930's and 40's. $175

Supplied and manufactured by The British L. M. Ericsson Manufacturing Co., Beeston, Notts, these instruments were used in large offices, hotels and houses. This particular phone was part of an 18 station intercom system, year of manufacture 1926. $225

Supplied by Franco-Radio Telephoné, Paris, year of manufacture, 1940's. This is a magneto instrument. $175

Supplied by Association des Ouvriers en Instruments de Precision, Paris, this is a magneto instrument. $210

British supplied and manufactured by Gent & Co. Ltd., Leicester, now part of the Chloride Gent Group. This telephone is part of an intercom system, year of manufacture 1920's and 1930's. $175

Supplied and manufactured by G. E. C., Coventry, year of manufacture 1910—mid 1920's. These instruments were used in small hotels, offices and country houses. This telephone was part of a five station intercom system. $175

TERRACOTTA

Terracotta is a fired clay, principally associated with sculpture, and terracotta figurines were common in Greek and Roman times. The art was revived during the Renaissance, when the Della Robbia family in Venice specialised in enamelled terracotta Madonnas. In the eighteenth century France became a leading centre of production, with such superb craftsmen as Houdon and Pajou (to whom we are indebted for the portrait sculpture of many leading figures of the day) and Clodion, who modelled mythological figures.

A 19th century terracotta garden ornament, probably France, 25½in. diam., 25½in. high. (Robt. W. Skinner Inc.) $750

A late 18th century French terracotta bust of a man wearing The Order of St. Esprit, in the style of Pajou, 20in. high. (Christie's) $2,811

A set of three black glazed terracotta jugs of graduated size, printed in yellow with portraits and vases of enamelled flowers. (Phillips) $160

A French terracotta bust of an 18th century lady with dressed hair, 16in. high. (Christie's) $2,505

A pair of Regency painted terracotta figures modelled as Chinese ladies, 8½in. and 8in. high. (Christie's) $366

A French terracotta bust of an 18th century boy, 18in. high. (Christie's) $3,288 .

A pair of 19th century Continental terracotta figures of a peasant girl and a boy, 90cm. and 91cm. high. (Phillips) $2,700

457

TERRACOTTA

A Cypriot terracotta chariot drawn by two horses, 7th-6th century B.C., 13cm. long. (Phillips) $656

A terracotta figure of Eros, 4th-3rd century B.C., Boetia, 7.5cm. high. (Phillips) $426

A Cypro-geometric bowl raised on three looped supports, circa 1700 B.C., 15cm. high. (Phillips) $1,230

A 19th century French group of Bacchus and a Bacchante, cast from a model by Clodion, 33cm. high. (Christie's) $734

A 19th century French terracotta bust of a little girl, attributed to Houdon, 39cm. high. (Christie's) $1,837

A Cypriot terracotta equestrian figure, slight traces of red and black pigment, 7th-6th century B.C., 11.5cm. high. (Phillips) $311

A Cypriot terracotta equestrian figure, 7th-6th century B.C., 15cm. high. (Phillips) $360

A pair of 19th century French terracotta busts of 'L'Espiegle' and 'Le Printemps', signed J.-Bte-Carpeaux, 48cm. and 55cm. high. (Christie's) $5,143

A terracotta figure of Eros, naked except for a drape across the shoulders, Boetia, 4th-3rd century B.C., 7cm. high. (Phillips) $328

TEXTILES

Textiles are a vast subject and provide a fascinating insight into life down the ages, since they are intimately connected with dress and domestic life. Hair and wool were in use from prehistoric times, while linen, derived from flax, was also an early discovery, declining only when cotton became more widespread. The silks and satins of the East were always sought after—the former being of such importance that the ancient trade route from China to the Mediterranean was known simply as the Silk Road. Today, few textile sales are without rich examples of Oriental cloths.

The subject covers not only the materials themselves, but also the arts connected with them which flourished at various times, such as beadwork, tapestry, needlework, stumpwork, quilting, samplers, embroidery and lace making—the list is endless. Now, of course, the use of synthetic fabrics have greatly extended the textile industry's range, though it remains to be seen whether they will become the collectables of the future.

A 19th century Rescht cover of red worsted decorated with multi-coloured insertions and applique, 2.24 x 1.45m., fringed, lined. (Phillips) $672

A mid 19th century needlework picture by Ann Wright, designed with a tablet showing 'The Given Chap. of Exodus', The Ten Commandments, Moses and Aaron, 46.50 x 31.50cm. (Phillips) $1,596

A rectangular cushion worked with metal thread strapwork and foliage on a green silk velvet ground, 26in. (Christie's) $233

A mid 18th century gros et petit point arched firescreen panel worked in coloured wools with a garden scene of musicians, 87.50 x 67cm. (Phillips) $806

Late 18th century needlework pocketbook, silk yarns worked in a variant of the Queen stitch, probably New England, 4¾ x 4in. (Robt. W. Skinner Inc.) $550

A mid 19th century Japanese fukusa, of blue silk with embroidered, applied and couched silks in pastel shades, 78 x 66cm. (Phillips) $745

TEXTILES

Late 19th century Soumak bag face, S. Caucasus, (minor wear), 1ft.7in. x 1ft.6in. (Robt. W. Skinner Inc.) $650

One of a pair of 17th century needlework stumpwork pictures, England, 5¼ x 4¼in. (Robt. W. Skinner Inc.) $2,300

A Chinese needlework picture, the ivory silk ground embroidered in shades of blue, brown, ochre and ivory, 36cm. square. (Phillips) $286

A late 19th century Chinese k'o-ssu picture of fighting warriors on horseback and on foot, with companion, 1m. x 0.25m. (Phillips) $656

Needlework picture, 'Shepherdess of the Alps', N.Y., 1800, 12½ x 15¼in. (Robt. W. Skinner Inc.) $1,800

A late 19th century Chinese k'o-ssu cover, the centre worked in pastel silks on a gold thread ground, 1.84 x 1.44m., lined. (Phillips) $1,771

Late 18th century silk embroidered picture, New England, 21 x 19in. (Robt. W. Skinner Inc.) $3,500

A 17th century Turkish bocha, the linen ground embroidered in shades of red, blue, yellow and green silks, 1.10 x 1.04m. (Phillips) $1,260

An Arts & Crafts linen cover embroidered in red and ivory linen, 1.46 x 1.58m. (Phillips) $453

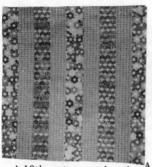

A 19th century patchwork coverlet worked in plain and printed cottons, 2.80 x 2.60m. (Phillips) $291

A late 18th century oval silk-work picture depicting a country lass gathering wheat-sheafs in her apron, 34 x 28cm. (Phillips) $806

A late 18th century Benares cover of red silk gauze woven in gold thread with a central shaped medallion, 1.08 x 1.14m. (Phillips) $297

A 19th century Chinese coverlet of crimson silk, lined and fringed, 2.32 x 2.14m. (Phillips) $288

A shaped panel of 19th century Chinese silk, the blue ground embroidered with coloured silks in pekin knot and satin stitch, 2.08m. high, joined. (Phillips) $648

A late 18th century embroidered picture, the ivory silk ground worked mainly in satin stitches, 65 x 70.50cm. (Phillips) $604

A silk embroidered picture, Mass., 1807, worked in silk yarns on ivory silk satin ground fabric, 8 x 8½in. (Robt. W. Skinner Inc.) $2,200

A late 19th century Japanese wall hanging of K'o-ssu woven in pastel coloured silks and gold thread, 3.04 x 1.80m. (Phillips) $3,240

An Oriental panel, the fuchsia ground worked in coloured silk threads with butterflies, flowers and Oriental figures, 2.60 x 2.40m. (Phillips) $972

THERMOMETERS

The first thermometer was invented by Galileo who lived at the end of the 16th and beginning of the 17th centuries. His thermometer was a simple glass tube ending in a bulb and the open end immersed in water. He noticed when the water was heated, it rose up the tube which could be calibrated. The most common thermometer in use for many years after that was a simple tube with red liquid in it and mercury in the bulb. Galileo's invention could not only be used in assessing the degree of fever in sick people or measuring the weather but it helps with jobs like brewing, cooking, hatching chickens, gardening and photography. Today the old fashioned thermometer is gradually going out of use as electronic devices and heat reactive pads are being introduced but there are thousands of old ones around and collectors are snapping them up fast.

Red Indian plastic novelty spirit thermometer. $5

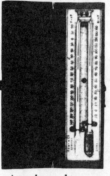

An oak cased thermometer with ivory dial engraved 'Kemp & Co. Ltd., Bombay', 4¾in. long circa 1850 $175

Brass cased incubator mercury thermometer with inbuilt hook. $9

Duckham's Oils enamel sign. $140

An early 19th century mahogany wheel barometer and thermometer signed J. Watkins, London, (Christie's) $1,650

Late 19th century brass framed thermometer, 10in. high. $12

A 19th century wheel barometer and thermometer inscribed Zuccani, London. (Parsons, Welch & Cowell) $651

Stephens Inks enamel sign. $130

TILES

Dutch tiles were among the finest made in the 16th and 17th centuries and they exported them all over the world. They were often blue and white and the patterns were sometimes copied from Chinese ceramics. Early Dutch tiles were often large, about twelve inches square, and they were often laid on floors or around fireplaces. There is an ancient synagogue in Cochin, South India, with a floor laid entirely in 16th century Dutch blue and white tiles.

In the 19th century tiles became very popular for many different types of decoration and they were not only put around hearths and on floors but set into toilet tables and cupboard tops, built into bathrooms, made into kettle stands and cheese stands or simply framed. Minton's were one of the first companies to start making tiles around 1830 and other ceramic manufacturers followed their lead. Because they were washable and cheerful looking tile-panel pictures were often used in shops, especially butcher's shops or dairies, and in hospitals especially in children's wards where they were made into nursery rhyme pictures. Artists like William de Morgan realised the artistic possibility of the tile and made many beautiful ones based on Persian Iznik designs.

Four of a set of twenty-five late 18th century English tinglaze tiles. (Woolley & Wallis)   Twenty-five $493

A Wedgwood pottery tile picture by W. Nunn, 46 x 77cm. $1,310

A set of four Continental ceramic tiles, square, each depicting industrial and artisan subjects in the purist style, 10½in. sq., printed marks, each painted with Cocrah. (Christie's) $1,167

Bristol delft polychrome tile, circa 1760, 13cm. square, slightly chipped. $350

Liverpool delft tile printed in black with a garden scene, circa 1760. $175

A Safavid tile panel with a figure of Sagittarius surrounded by palmettes, 4ft. 1in. x 2ft.10in. (Christie's) $14,877

A large early 20th century Doulton decorative tile picture of Little Jack Horner. $7,000

Late 19th century Mettlach tile picture, signed C. Warth, 16¾in. high. $187

A Castelli rectangular plaque painted with Pan being comforted after the musical contest with Apollo seated, circa 1725, 28cm. square. (Christie's) $1,458

A De Morgan tile panel, comprising three tiles, 1882-8, 51 x 20.6cm. $875

A Doulton terracotta tile picture by George Tinworth, moulded and carved in low relief with Samson, circa 1880, 8½in. x 8½in. $525

TITANIC MEMORABILIA

The fate of the 'Titanic' has fired the imagination of each succeeding generation, and interest in what seems likely to become one of the great legendary tragedies of our times continues unabating. The recent seabed pictures of her hulk have only served to increase this fascination, which is reflected in the prices paid for almost any object connected in some way with the great liner.

The fact that each item usually has a romantic story attached to it of course adds to its attraction and value.

A napkin ring belonging to a survivor and carried by her on the voyage recently sold for $750, while letters sent by passengers can still command up to four figures.

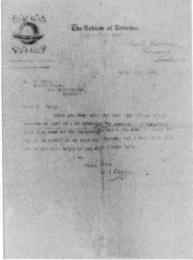

A typed letter to Mr R Penny from W. T. Stead, dated 9 April 1912, on The Review of Reviews writing paper. (Onslow's) $1,467

Titanic Leaving Southampton, glossy monochrome postcard, published by Nautical Photo Agency, N.W.7. (Onslow's) $228

White Star Royal Mail Steamer Titanic, artist drawn, pre-sinking colour postcard, postmarked 1st August 1912, State Series, Liverpool. (Onslow's) $228

'The Iceberg', a contemporary bromide photograph with ink inscription, 'Iceberg taken by Capt. Wood S.S. Etonian 12 April 1912 in 41° 56N 49° 51W S.S. Titanic Struck 14 April and sank in three hours', 200 x 255mm. (Onslow's) $374

TITANIC MEMORABILIA

White Star Line Olympic and Titanic Smoke Room, a monochrome postcard to Master
Tom Richmond, 14 Lennox Road, Crookston, Paisley, Lothian, postmarked Queenstown
3.45pm 11 April. (Onslow's) $2,445

A bronze Carpathia medal awarded to
R. S. C. Cowan, the captain, in recognition of
gallant and heroic services, from the survivors
of the S. S. 'Titanic'. (Onslow's) $1,059

Launch of White Star Royal Mail Triple-Screw
Steamer Titanic at Belfast, Wednesday, 31
May 1911, at 12.15pm, a printed card admis-
sion ticket in two portions, each numbered
1246, overall size 84 x 136mm. (Onslow's)
                                         $1,793

The new White Star liner 'Titanic', artist
drawn pre sinking photographic postcard,
Real Photos Series. (Onslow's) $2,600

S.S. Titanic, the cast brass nameplate from
Lifeboat No. 12, 322mm. long x 39mm.
wide. (Onslow's) $9,128

White Star Line Triple-Screw R.M.S. Olympic and Titanic 45,000 tons each, The Largest
Steamers in the World, a colour postcard from R. Phillips to Mr. Wm. Squires, 4
Northfield Cottages, Ilfracombe, Devonshire, postmarked Queenstown 5.45pm 11 April.
(Onslow's) $3,260

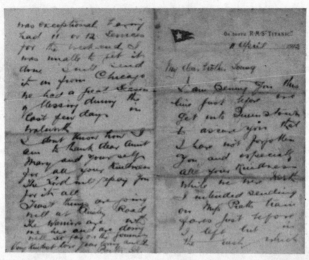

On board R.M.S. 'Titanic', an autographed letter on official writing paper signed by Pastor John Harper, 11th April 1912, (Onslow's) $6,200

"My Dear Brother Young, I am penning you this line just before we get in to Queenstown to assure you that I have not forgotten you and especially all your kindness while we were North. I intended sending on Mrs Pratt's train fares just before I left but in the rush which was exceptional having had 11 or 12 services for the week-end I was unable to get it done. I will send it on from Chicago. We had a great season of blessing during the last few days in Walworth. I don't know how I am to thank dear Aunt Mary and yourself for all your kindness the Lord will repay you for it all. Trust things are going well at Paisley Road. The warriors are with me here and are doing well so far on the journey. Very kindest love your loving auld Pastor J.H."

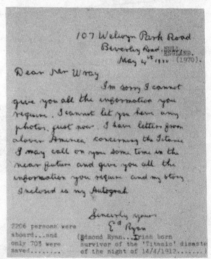

"While on a visit to Paris I met my friend who wishes me to write a few words on *Titanic* disaster, on 14 April 1912 just before midnight came the awful crash. Which was so unexpected officers and crew did not know what to do, boats launched and not nearly filled and terrible to relate not saving one-third of the passengers aboard including the crew and was caused through absolute carelessness. I did not see my husband again after he put me in lifeboat No.11. I saw the *Titanic* gradually disappearing also eight distress markers she sent up heard the explosions and then disappear under the water taking hundreds of souls with her. We had neither lights, water or provisions in our boat, it was intensely cold and scarcely anyone properly clothed in the early dawn we could see the ice field and we were simply in the midst of enormous icebergs we were picked up by S.S. *Carpathia* about 6.00 a.m. I cannot speak too highly of her captain officers crew and passengers. F. Angle a survivor 15 Oct. 1913"

A contemporary account written by Mrs F. Angle of the disaster dated 15 October 1913, on two sheets. (Onslow's) $978

Edward Ryan was a small child on board the *Titanic*, his father Patrick was a victim in the disaster and his grandfather Thomas Ryan with assistance from Thomas Scanlon MP brought a claim against The Oceanic Steam Navigation Company, owners of The White Star Line, of negligence and were awarded a judgement of £100.

A letter from Edward Ryan to Mr W. Ray, 4th May 1920. (Onslow's) $75

TOBACCO JARS

The first criterion for the tobacco jar is that it should not absorb moisture from the tobacco and allow it to dry out. Many early ones were made from lead, and, since this was an easily damaged and reusable material, very few have survived. In the 17th and 18th centuries, lead was superceded by lead or foil-lined wood and later, in the 19th century, by glazed earthenware.

Shapes were many and varied: the larger, barrel shaped jars were most often used by tobacconists to store their stock.

Paddy tobacco jar by Doulton, 5½in. high, issued 1938-41. $450

Doulton Burslem Morrisian Ware tobacco jar and cover decorated with a band of dancing girls, 5½in. high. $80

A stoneware Martin Bros. bird tobacco jar and cover, dated 1903, 28cm. high. (Christie's) $4,354

Royal Doulton Sung tobacco jar and cover of hexagonal form, 6¼in. high, circa 1930. $225

A waisted jar and cover painted with rings of white flowers, c.m.l. & c., date letter for 1907, 6½in. high. $180

A Foley 'Intarsio' tobacco jar and cover, 14.3cm. high, no. 3458, Rd. no. 364386 (SR). (Phillips) $203

Nightwatchman Series tobacco jar, 5½in. high, circa 1909, by Noke, depicting a watchman carrying a pike. $72

Royal Doulton Kingsware tobacco jar decorated in relief with a gentleman smoking, 8¼in. high. $75

A Liberty & Co. 'Tudric' pewter tobacco box and cover, designed by Archibald Knox, 11.9cm. high. (Christie's) $380

A treen barrel-form tobacco canister, the lift-off cover set with a wine bottle and two glasses, 7in. high. (Christie's) $330

Double Foxes (one curled), a Royal Doulton Kingsware tobacco jar with silver hall-marked rim, circa 1912, 7½in. high. $427

Old Charley tobacco jar by Doulton, 5½in. high, issued 1938-1941. $420

A Martin Bros. stoneware tobacco jar and cover, modelled as a grotesque grinning cat, 1885, 22cm. high. (Christie's) $10,962

A tobacco jar and cover, the body with incised brown glazed cows frolicking amongst incised green foliage, r.m. & e., circa 1895, 6½in. high. $240

A Bretby tobacco jar and cover, inscribed 'Nicotiank', 16.5cm. high. (Phillips) $94

A tobacco jar decorated with applied blue and white beads, r.m., impressed date for 1888, 4¼in. high. $27

TOBACCO SILKS

These were issued in the early part of this century by various cigarette companies such as Godfrey Phillips (BDV brand) and Kensitas (Flags series). They can vary from cigarette card size through postcard to cabinet and large size. They were issued with a protective wrapper and this should be still intact — in fact, to be of value, they should really be in mint condition. Smaller ones are usually kept in albums, but the larger sizes, when framed, can make attractive wall decorations.

B.D.V. Cigarettes, Regimental Colours, 14th The Kings Hussars. $5

B.D.V. War Leaders, General Cadorna. $9

B.D.V. Victoria Cross Heroes, Lieut. General Sir Douglas Haig, K.C.B. $10

B.D.V. Celebrities, King of Roumania. $7

War Leaders, B.D.V. Lord Kitchener. $7

B.D.V. Celebrities, Princess Mary. $18

B.D.V. British Admirals, Admiral Sir John R. Jellicoe, 1916. $7

TOBACCO SILKS

B.D.V. Celebrities, David Lloyd George. $14

B.D.V. War Leaders and Celebrities, the New Coalition Cabinet, Mr Balfour, Admiralty. $7

Old Masters Set 5, Auguste Strobel. $2

B.D.V. Old Masters, The Blue Boy, cabinet size. $28

B.D.V. Regimental Colours, Prince of Wales, North Staffordshire. $5

B.D.V. Old Masters, Bacchante, cabinet size. $32

Great War Leaders and Warships, B.D.V., Rear Admiral Bernard Currey. $7

Flags series B.D.V., the Allied Flags. $10

B.D.V. Great Leaders and Warships, Admiral Sir George Neville. $7

TOLEWARE

Toleware is essentially painted tin, and is akin to bargeware inasmuch as the original purpose was to make basic, functional items such as coffee pots more decorative. As in so many cases, however, what started as something relatively simple became much more sophisticated. Some toleware items, such as coalscuttles became very florid and ornate and worthy of a place in the most elegant drawing room. These can now fetch many hundreds of dollars at auction.

A 19th century French oval toleware tray, the maroon ground heightened in gilt with foliate and military trophies, 26in. wide. (Christie's) $539

A mid Victorian black and gilt japanned tole purdonium, with shovel, 12½in. wide. (Christie's) $597

A mid Victorian black and gilt japanned tole hubble-bubble, with metal label of Lowe, London, 10½in. high. (Christie's) $346

A Victorian tole workbox, the glazed octangular lid decorated with a winter scene, 19½in. wide. (Christie's) $1,331

Decorated tin coffee pot, possibly Maine, circa 1830, 8½in. high. $875

A Regency black japanned tole coal box on cabochon feet, 24in. wide. (Christie's) $629

Late 19th century American Toleware painted and stencilled chocolate pot, 8½in. high. (Christie's) $1,100

TRADE CARDS

Trade cards were given away by travelling salesmen and sometimes presented to customers by storeholders. They advertise all manner of goods from sewing items to musical instruments and 'quack' cures, and reflect the humour and freedom of the advertising of Victorian times.

The quality of artwork on some is surprising, and some well-known artists were probably involved in their design. Technically, too, they reflect the best of the age in terms of chromolithographic printing and pictorial excellence.

Look out for good clean examples with colorful, pictorial fronts and printed details of the product on the back. Unusually shaped cards are also prized. Sometimes these cards turn up in scrap albums and even inside books, and they do represent a worthwhile investment.

Hagan's Magnolia Balm, 'For beautifying the complexion', presented by J. W. Robinson, Druggist and Chemist, Southbridge, Mass. $5

'Now dollies, if you be good we'll have Bromangelon for dessert. Nothing but the addition of hot water required'. $3.50

Kendall Mfg. Co., French Laundry, 'To protect yourself from the evil effect of using soap made from impure materials', Providence, R.I. $5

'Compliments of Fechheimer's Shoe Department, 102 W. Fifth Street. Admiration'. $7

Prize Lincoln Buck Wilton, 'Compliments of the Domestic Sewing Machine Co. $10

J. & P. Coats' Thread, 'I say Sissy! the umbrella that boy has got was certainly not sewed with Coats colored thread'. $7

TRADE CARDS

Hires' Rootbeer, 'An uninvited guest', the Charles E. Hires Co., 11-119 Arch Street, Philadelphia. $9

Brown's Iron Bitters, 'A certain cure for diseases. Beware of imitations'. $5

'A flat Dutch cabbage', E. F. Harmeyer, Walnut Street, Cincinnati, Ohio, Agricultural Implements. $7

'Perfumed with Austen's Forest Flower Cologne', W. J. Austen & Co., Oswego, N.Y. $7

Sailing ship trade card for Vouwie Bros, 'Forest City Baking Powder, absolutely pure' $20

'Agers Dry Hop Yeast is the best in use', Dole & Merrill Mfrs., Boston, New York. $5

Hoyt's German Cologne, 'Fragrant and lasting', E. W. Hoyt, Lowell, Mass. $9

'The White is the Sewing Machine of the Day', by C.H. Burdick, Boxo, Brookfield, New York. $18

'Balls Health Preserving Corset is the best in the world', Walter H. Tarr, Cincinnati, Ohio. $7

TRADE CARDS

Presented by Household Sewing Machine Co., Providence, R.I., T. S. Arnold, Agent. $14

'King of the Blood', D. Ransom, Son & Co., Proprietors, Buffalo, New York, 'Read the testimonials'. $7

Willimantic Six Cord Thread, 'The best, so good, so smooth, so strong, so free'. $9

Lautz Bros. & Co., Master Soap, Buffalo, New York. $7

The Allenburys' Clock, 'This clock can be used to inform the mother as to the hour for giving baby his next bottle.' $20

'For Tomato Catsup, E. F. Harmeyer, 227 Walnut Street, Cincinnati, Ohio, Agricultural Implements'. $5

Beatty's Organs, Beatty's Piano's, Washington, New Jersey, 'The largest piano and organ establishment on the globe'. $9

'Use Tarrant's Seltzer Aperient, to regulate the stomach, the liver, the bowels'. $7

Warren & Wing, New England Agents, Tremont Street, Boston, Household Sewing Machine Co. $14

TRADE CARDS

Austen's Forest Flower Cologne, 'The most fashionable and lasting perfume of the day'. $5

'A good angels visit, Scovill's Sarsaparilla and Stillingia or Blood and Liver Syrup.' $10

'Dran Pa oo ought to put on one of Carters Backache Plasters', Carter Medicine Co., New York. $3.50

J. G. White, 'Harness, Trunks and Bags, Carriage Trimming', Sign Big Trunk, Cooperstown. $5

A large scrap type trade card by Hoeninghausen's Central Tea Store, Detroit, Michigan. $9

'Dr White's Cough Drops are the best, they are in truth a veritable delicacy'. $7

Industrial Insurance, Metropolitan Life Insurance Co., Central Block, Lewiston, Me. $5

Horsfords Acid Phosphate, 'For mental and physical exhaustion, Dyspepsia'. $5

John English & Co. 'Imperial diamond drilled eyed needles', patent Great Britain, 1863. $5

TRAYS

When it became fashionable to drink tea in the afternoon, butlers or maids were required to carry a loaded tea tray into the drawing room every day. In the 18th and early 19th century the trays that were used were more often made of wood and could be the work of a fashionable cabinet maker like Chippendale or Vile who made trays with high lattice work sides out of mahogany. Hepplewhite and Sheraton trays were often made of mahogany too, oval shaped and decorated with a stylised shell in the middle. The handles were often brass scrolls. Victorian trays were far more flights of fancy because they preferred them to be bright and colorful — sometimes made of enamel painted all over with roses, japanned metal or papier mache set with mother of pearl. Returning travellers often brought home engraved trays of brass from India or Burma and in the 1920's tin trays decorated with bold Art Deco designs made their appearance.

A 19th century large papier mache tray with raised rim, 30½ x 22in. (Lawrence Fine Art) $2,472

A late 19th century enamelled pub tray Dunville's Whisky. $70

A papier-mache tray of rounded rectangular form, gilt painted with flowering plants on a black ground, 30in. wide., circa 1840 $645

An 19th century oval papier mache tray, centrally decorated after Morland, 30in. wide. (Dreweatts) $1,276

A Regency mahogany two-handled rectangular wine tray, on melon feet, 13½ x 9¾in. (Geering & Colyer) $910

18th century metal tray decorated with a bird, urn and floral displays. $340

A 19th century Japanese black and gold lacquer tray, 23.5in. wide. (Woolley & Wallis) $1,935

A mid Victorian black and gilt japanned papier-mache tray of waved and shaped rectangular form, 23¾ x 31in. (Christie's) $2,055

1930's oak tray with moulded edge. $14

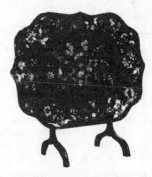

A Regency scarlet and gold papier-mache tray with everted gallery, 30in. wide. (Christie's) $660

'Coca Cola' advertising tip tray, round, America, circa 1905. (Robt. W. Skinner Inc.) $200

A papier-mache tray fixed to a folding wooden stand, 31½in. (Lawrence Fine Arts) $2,700

An inlaid waiter with an everted brim, on four cast feet, by Tiffany & Co., 1878-91, 9½in. diam., gross weight 10oz. (Christie's) $19,800

'Clysmic' advertising tip tray, oval, copy reads 'Clysmic, King of Table Waters' (Robt. W. Skinner Inc.) $50

Late 19th century silver mounted shibayama inlaid lacquer tray, signed Yasuaki, 24cm. diam. (Christie's) $2,805

19th century papier-mache tray, stamped Clay, London, with cricketing scene.(Phillips) $1,300

Victorian mahogany butler's tray on stand, 1860. $260

A painted tray by Duncan Grant, circa 1920, 35.3cm. diam. $875

VANITY FAIR CARICATURES

The society magazine *'Vanity Fair'* was published in London from 1869 till 1914. It did not survive the Great War perhaps because of the decimation of its clientele. It carried news of the society functions, the Royal family, satire, fashion but, most notably, it carried cartoons, not always flattering, of eminent society figures of the day. These cartoons were colored lithographs and they were also sold to the public as colored prints made from the original plates. Copies that can be found today are valuable because the plates are no longer available.

The cartoons are of very fine quality, measuring approximately seven inches by twelve in most cases and a short, witty biography of the subject which was always added must be included for the cartoon to have its full value. They were published in a numbered series but those that are most highly regarded are the rarer ones and those in pristine condition. A number of well known artists contributed caricatures to Vanity Fair including Phil May and the famous Spy.

Sir Henry Drummond Wolff, 'Consular Chaplains', September 5th, 1874. $35

Mr Alexander J. Beresford-Hope, M.P., 'Batavian grace', September 10th, 1870. $45

Prince George Frederick Ernest Albert, K.G.,
'Our Sailor Prince', May 24th, 1890. $70

Mr Henry Fawcett, M.P., 'A radical leader',
21st December 1872. $45

The Right Honourable Sir William Robert
Seymour Vesey Fitzgerald, G.C.S.I., Bombay,
May 2nd, 1874. $60

Sir Thomas Salter Pyne, C.S.I., Afghan Engineering, February 15th, 1900. $55

The Duke of Sutherland, 'Simple and unassuming, he is the very Duke of Dukes', July 9th, 1870. $45

Sir Roderick Impey Murchison, 'A faithful friend, an eminent servant, and the best possible of Presidents', November 26th, 1870. $60

Brigadier-General Sir Evelyn Wood, K.C.B., V.C., 'The Flying Column', November 15th, 1879. $60

Lord Lytton, 'The best specimen now extant of the utterly immovable politician', October 29th, 1870. $35

VETERINARY ITEMS

Like medical items for humans, veterinary instruments of the past hold an immediate fascination; many an animal lover will shudder with relief that their pet will no longer be subjected to such horrors. Vets too may be relieved, for many old instruments are fairly primitive, such as a device for dehorning bulls, which weighed all of 28 lbs!

It's interesting to note those which have stood the test of time, and also to note old cures and potions.

Veterinary First Aid and Minor Operations for Farmers. $25

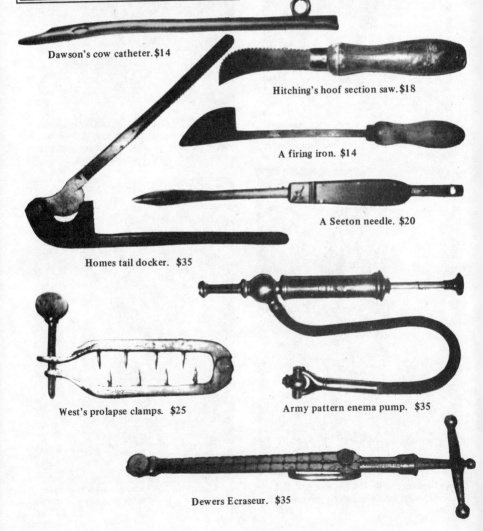

Dawson's cow catheter. $14

Hitching's hoof section saw. $18

A firing iron. $14

A Seeton needle. $20

Homes tail docker. $35

West's prolapse clamps. $25

Army pattern enema pump. $35

Dewers Ecraseur. $35

482

VINAIGRETTES

When they ventured abroad Tudor ladies carried pomanders up to their noses to ward off evil smells and prevent them breathing in noxious air. The pomander was often only a dried orange stuck with cloves and the vinaigrette was its more sophisticated descendant and carried by ladies of Victorian times.

They were little boxes made of gold, silver, pinchbeck, glass or porcelain and one side was a pierced grill. Inside was kept a small piece of sponge or wadding soaked in aromatic oils or vinegar which were thought to ward off disease when sniffed and bring back consciousness to swimming heads. In the filthy steets of big cities, a sniff at the vinaigrette must often have been a necessity.

Vinaigrettes were made to look as ornamental as possible and some were studded with precious or semiprecious stones. They could be worn like brooches or chatelaines suspended by a chain while others were carried inside a muff or purse. Vinaigrettes by Nathaniel Mills are particularly desirable especially the ones with embossed views on the lid.

A gold and enamel mounted nephrite vinaigrette, probably 19th century, 3¼in. high. (Christie's) $1,321

A 19th century Chinese Export oblong vinaigrette with engine-turned base, by Khecheong of Canton, circa 1850. (Phillips) $178

A George III articulated fish vinaigrette, 7.25cm. long, by Samuel Pemberton, Birmingham, 1817. (Phillips) $598

An oblong 'castle-top' vinaigrette chased with a view of Litchfield Cathedral, by N. Mills, 1843-4. (Christie's) $1,652

A silver gilt engine turned vinaigrette, by Nathaniel Mills, Birmingham, 1825, 1¾in. long. (Christie's) $580

A William IV vinaigrette, the cover chased in relief with a ruined building, by Taylor & Perry, Birmingham, 1835. (Phillips) $800

A Victorian oblong silver-gilt castle-top vinaigrette, with a view of a large church, Yapp & Woodward, Birmingham 1844. (Christie's) $544

An attractive late Victorian vinaigrette, the cover set with turquoise and incised with a name in Persian script, by William Summers, 1888. (Phillips) $147

A George IV rectangular purse shaped silver vinaigrette, by Clark & Smith, Birmingham, 1824, 1.25in. long. (Woolley & Wallis) $159

A large silver gilt castletop vinaigrette, the hinged cover chased with a view of Warwick Castle, by Nathaniel Mills, Birmingham, 1839, 1¾in. long. (Christie's) $1,452

An early 19th century gold engine-turned rectangular vinaigrette, 3 x 2.2cm unmarked, circa 1830. (Phillips) $935

A Victorian shaped oval gilt-lined vinaigrette, the lid depicting a river scene with tree-lined banks and buildings, Nathaniel Mills, Birmingham 1846, 1½in. (Christie's) $471

A silver gilt vinaigrette, the cover repousse and chased with four pheasants in a wooded landscape, by Ledsam, Vale & Wheeler, Birmingham, 1829, 1¾in. long. (Christie's) $1,089

A parcel gilt vinaigrette, the cover repousse and chased with a man in 17th century dress, by Nathaniel Mills, Birmingham, 1835(?), 1¾in. long. (Christie's) $907

A small oblong gold vinaigrette, the cover with a winged putto holding a butterfly. (Christie's) $1,416

A silver gilt vinaigrette with engine turned sides and base, London, 1829, maker's initials A.D. possibly for Allen Dominy, 1.5/8in. long. (Christie's) $635

VINAIGRETTES

An oblong silver gilt castle-top vinaigrette chased with a view of Westminster Abbey, by Taylor & Perry, Birmingham, 1839. (Christie's) $712

An oblong silver castletop vinaigrette chased with a view of Abbotsford House, by N. Mills, Birmingham, 1837. (Christie's) $541

A Victorian rectangular vinaigrette, the cover chased with a view of York Minster, by Joseph Willmore, 1842, 4cm. wide. (Christie's) $422

Victorian shaped rectangular vinaigrette, by Yapp & Woodward, 1848, 3.5cm. wide. (Christie's) $195

A silver gilt vinaigrette of scallop shape, by Matthew Linwood, Birmingham, 1802. (Christie's) $398

Silver gilt cushion-shaped vinaigrette, by John Shaw, circa 1810, 3.2cm. wide. (Christie's) $195

An oblong silver gilt vinaigrette with pierced foliage panel on the cover, by J. Bettridge, Birmingham, 1827. (Christie's) $213

An unusual, silver gilt vinaigrette chased as a crown, by Joseph Willmore, Birmingham, 1820, with suspension ring. (Christie's) $1,069

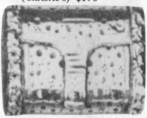

A George III vinaigrette in the form of a purse, by John Shaw, Birmingham 1819, 2.8cm. (Lawrence Fine Art) $172

A large oblong silver castle-top vinaigrette chased with St. Paul's Cathedral on matted ground, by N. Mills, Birmingham, 1842, 4.8cm. long. (Christie's) $1,025

A George IV silver gilt rectangular vinaigrette, with maker's marks of T. & S. Pemberton, Birmingham, 1821, 3.4cm. (Lawrence Fine Art) $100

An oblong silver castletop vinaigrette chased with a view of Kenilworth Castle, by Nathaniel Mills, Birmingham, 1839. (Christie's) $455

VIOLINS

A violin case by W. E. Hill & Sons, London.   *$8,791*

The 'cradle' of the modern violin was Cremona in Italy where, in the 16th century Andrea Amati developed the design which became the standard for the instrument we know today. His grandson Nicolo was the family's greatest craftsman. The founders of the other great Cremona violin-making families, Guarneri and Stradivari, studied under him and, with their sons, continued to make outstanding violins, violas and cellos. Violins by these masters will now fetch untold sums at auction, though it is interesting to note that there are more 'Strads' in the U.S. alone than were ever produced by the family!

A viola by Giuseppe Lucci, length of back 16½in., in a case lined in green velvet by Gewa. (Phillips) $3,795

A violin by Antonio Capela, 1972, length of back 14in., in shaped case. (Phillips) $198

A violin by William Glenister, 1904, length of back 14. 1/16in., with a bow. (Phillips) $1,567

A violin by Vincenzo Sannino, 1910, length of back 14.1/16in, with a shaped case and cover. (Phillips) $10,725

A violin by Joannes Gagliano of Naples, circa 1790, length of back 14in., in case. (Phillips) $9,308

A violin by Lorenzo Arcangioli of Florence, circa 1840, length of back 13.7/8in. (Phillips) $6,930

A violin by Salomon of Reims, 1746, length of back 14. 13/16in., in an oblong, velvet-lined and fitted case. (Phillips)
$2,970

A Florentine violin, circa 1770, bearing the label Lorenzo and Tommaso Carcassi, anno 1773, length of back 14in. (Phillips)
$9,075

An English violin, bearing the label of G. Pyne, Maker London, 1888, 14.1/8in. long, with bow. (Phillips)
$2,880

A viola, by B. Banks of Salisbury, circa 1770, length of back 15.3/8in., in a shaped and lined velvet case. (Phillips)
$9,308

A violin by J. A. Chanot, 1899, length of back 14.1/8in., with a silver mounted bow, in case. (Phillips)
$5,728

A violin by Wm. E. Hill & Sons, London, 1904, length of back 14in., in a mahogany case. (Phillips)
$8,055

A violoncello by Wm. Forster, London, circa 1784, 29in. long, in wood case. (Phillips)
$6,720

A violin by Carolus F. Landulphus, 1766, length of back 13. 15/16in., with a silver mounted bow, in an oak case. (Phillips)
$57,280

A Neapolitan violon-cello, circa 1750, attributed to G. Gagliano, 29.7/16in. long, with a silver mounted bow and cover. (Phillips) $58,800

A viola by F. Gagliano in Naples, 14½in. long, upper bouts 7.1/8in. long, lower bouts 9in. (Phillips) $17,600

A violoncello, circa 1750, of the Tyro-lesse School, label-led Carlo Tunon, 1732, 29.3/16in. long, in wood case. (Phillips) $7,056

A violin by J. N. Leclerc, circa 1770, 14in. long, with two bows, in case. (Phillips) $2,520

A violin by Alfred Vincent, dated 1922, 13.14/16in. long, in a shaped case, by E. Withers. (Phillips) $3,024

A violin by Dom Nicolo Amati of Bologna, 1714, 14.1/16in. long, in case. (Phillips) $15,120

A viola, circa 1830, of the Kennedy School, 15.5/16in. long, with two bows, in an oblong case. (Phillips) $2,436

A violin attributed to R. Cuthbert, 1676, 13.7/8in. long, in case. (Phillips) $1,310

WALKING STICKS

From the shepherd's crook to the masher's whangee cane, the walking stick has had a variety of functions and perhaps the least of them was helping to support the halt and the lame. The fashionable man about town in the 17th and 18th centuries always carried his walking stick with him when he went out for a stroll. In old prints dandies can be seen leaning negligently on their sticks and it is obvious that there's nothing wrong with their legs. These fashion accessories were made of cane, rosewood, fruitwood, ebony, ash, ivory, bone, shark's vertebrae or rhinotail. Sometimes the handles were carved from ivory or hardstone or else made of precious materials like gold or silver. From time to time sticks turn up which have a watch, a telescope or a drinking flask attached to them and a few sticks concealed a sword with the slender steel blade attached to the handle and concealed down the middle of the shaft. Often sword sticks were carried by travellers to foreign parts and today they would be regarded as an offensive weapon, making anyone who carried such a stick liable to arrest.

More workaday sticks are those which were country made — often a length of wood cut from a hedge and adroitly carved by a rural artist. The handles of those rough sticks were often carved in the shape of animal heads. Shepherd's crooks were an opportunity for local artistry to be displayed and the handles were cleverly carved from horn. Today in rural districts there are still competitions at fairs to find the best carved crook. Other collectable sticks include comic ones such as were used by music hall comedians, especially the curling blackthorn stick that was one of the trademarks of Harry Lauder and, of course, Charlie Chaplin's cane which recently sold for thousands.

A Kloster Veilsdorf cane handle, formed as a bearded old man, circa 1770, 7.5cm. high.(Christie's) $810

Late 19th century Uncle Sam animated ivory cane, America, 35in. long. (Robt. W. Skinner Inc.) $1,400

Top of the handle of a captain's 'going ashore' cane. $20,000

A rare Meissen cane handle in the shape of Joseph Frohlich lying on top of a barrel, 1743, 13.5cm. $8,750

A Bow spirally moulded cane handle of tapering form, circa 1750, 5.5cm. high. (Christie's) $1,942

A French vari-coloured gold and enamel mounted parasol handle, with Paris restricted gold warranty mark in use from 1838, 3¼in. long. (Christie's)$2,877

WALL MASKS

In the 1930's wall plaques were very fashionable. They could be made of glass, brass, wood, pottery, plaster or porcelain but it was the plaster ones that were most common especially the three flying ducks which became a cartoonists' joke when portraying middle class homes. Today the ducks are making a comeback and they are snapped up by collectors. Cheap plaster plaques were given away as prizes by fairground operators and so were carved wooden plaques showing interior scenes. Slightly more exclusive were pressed brass plaques featuring "Olde Worlde" scenes like stage coaches in inn yards and monks roistering around refectory tables. The upper end of the plaque market include Clarice Cliff's hand painted ones which sell for high prices today and some very attractive plaques were produced by Minton, Imari and Wedgwood. Goldscheider and Newport made plaques in the form of stylised masks as did Doulton whose mask of a woman's face in green celadon by Charles Noke is one of the most expensive that can be found today.

A Royal Doulton face mask, 'Jester', probably HN1630, 28.5cm. long, c.m.1. & c., date code for 1937. (Abridge Auction) $200

A Goldscheider tin-glazed earthenware wall mask, Wien, Made in Austria, inscribed 8874, 36cm. high. (Christie's) $811

A Royal Doulton 'Grey Friar' wall mask, 7¼in. high. circa 1940-41. (Abridge Auction) $525

A Goldscheider pottery double face wall plaque, the two females in profile, 12in. high. (Christie's) $596

Glazed Florence Goss wall vase, with radiating hair and feathers, 120mm. high. (Goss & Crested China Ltd) $435

A Lenci pottery wall plaque in the form of a young woman's head, wearing a colourful scarf, dated 1937, 29.5cm. (Bearne's) $619

WAR POSTERS

War posters were an essential part of the propaganda of both sides from the First World War onwards. Perhaps the most familiar posters from that time, and certainly the most frequently reproduced, are the recruiting posters. Few will be unfamiliar with the classic 'Kitchener Needs You' or 'Women of Britain say "Go!"' signs which resulted from the decimation of the regular British Expeditionary Force in 1914.

Second World War posters were aimed also at the home-based civilian war effort, with major artists making their contribution. 'Careless talk costs lives' and 'She's not so dumb' reflect the constant preoccupation with security. The US and Germany also issued propagandist and recruiting posters, the German ones dating from World War Two often emphasising, in dark grey tones, the dour, "iron-hard" quality of the German forces.

Strictly Between These Four Walls Careless Talk Costs Lives, poster by Fougasse. (Onslow's) $147

Come Into The Ranks and Fight For Your King and Country, poster by W. H. Caffyn, double royal. (Onslow's) $51

Holidays By The Sea Take Care of Minefields, poster by Chan, double crown; and one other. (Onslow's)
Two $77

Join The Regular Air Force A Career With Adventure, poster by Winslade, double royal. (Onslow's) $112

Daddy, What Did You Do In The Great War?, poster by Savile Lumley, double crown. (Onslow's) $536

Women Of Britain Say Go, poster by E. V. Kealey, double crown. (Onslow's)
$294

WAR POSTERS

Take The Road To Victory
Join The W.A.A.F., poster by
Foss, double crown. (Onslow's)
$60

Everyone Should Do His Bit
Enlist Now, poster by Baron
Low, double crown, (Onslow's)
$190

Every Woman Not Doing Vital
Work is Needed Now, poster
by Winslade, double crown.
(Onslow's) $103

To Make the World a Decent Place to Live In,
Third Liberty Loan, 92 x 142cm. (Onslow's)
$80

They Kept the Sea Lanes Open, Invest in
the Victory Liberty Loan, 74 x 100cm.
(Onslow's) $80

Halt the Hun, Buy U.S. Government Bonds, double crown.
(Onslow's)
$70 £40

U.S.A. Bonds, Third Liberty
Loan Campaign, Boy Scouts
of America, double crown.
(Onslow's) $225

Teufel Hunden, German
nickname for U.S. Marines,
double crown. (Onslow's)
$42

WATCH STANDS

Since man began carrying a watch around 400 years ago there have been stands on which to hang them at night or when they were not being worn but most of the very early ones have long ago disappeared or are in the show cases of museums. The sort of watch stand that most frequently turns up today dates from the 19th century and is a single pillar type made of wood, brass, agate or marble. The better ones had a pivot which allowed the watch to be tilted for more convenient viewing.

More expensive are well head watch stands which consisted of two pillars joined at the top by a bar from which the watch could be suspended. Another two-pillar design had a pivoted holder and sometimes a short central pillar on which there might be a mirror or a cushion. Frequently plain two-pillar stands had a little dish for holding rings, studs and trinkets.

Even more unusual were "triangular prismatic watchstands" which were made of hard wood, often beautifully inlaid, with a small door at the back which gave access to a velvet lined interior. Some of them had front and back panels and the watch was held safely inside when travelling.

Travelling watch stands were made to several designs and often had a souvenir type decoration. Some had hinged lids which were fitted with a stud or hook and the watch could be hung from them so that it nestled in its dished backing. These custom made stands often had locks decorated with ivory, bone or brass.

A mahogany and rosewood watch stand on inverted bun feet, 6½in. high. $175

German porcelain watch holder entitled 'Sedan'. $350

19th century German watch holder entitled 'Gravelotte'. $350

A Doulton Punch and Judy watch stand with a bright blue glaze, circa 1905, 11½in. high. $1,125

20th century American ebony and ivory watch stand, 6¼in. high. $350

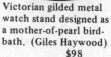

Victorian gilded metal watch stand designed as a mother-of-pearl bird-bath. (Giles Haywood) $98

WAX MODELS

The Egyptians were already modelling in beeswax and the fluency and adaptability of the medium has appealed to artists down the ages. Wax models are frail, though, and few early examples have survived. Wax miniatures were particularly popular in the 18th and 19th centuries, and notable craftsmen included Percy of Dublin, Isaac Gossett, Mountstephen and Ball-Hughes, who in the 19th century developed his own hardening process.

A pair of Victorian wax reliefs of Queen Victoria and Prince Albert, in mahogany frame, 6 x 8½in. (Christie's) $187

A shoulder-waxed-composition doll, German, circa 1880, 16in. high, right arm loose. $260

A group of late 18th century cream-coloured wax bust-length profile medallions, each 2¼in. high.(Christie's) $622

A shoulder-waxed-composition doll with blonde mohair plaited wig, German, circa 1880, 18in. high. $443

An American 19th century arrangement of various wax fruits on a wooden pedestal base, under a glass dome, 21in. high. (Robt. W. Skinner Inc.) $475

A pair of poured wax portrait dolls, modelled as Edward VII and Queen Alexandra, 21in. high, by Pierotti. (Christie's) $1,837

One of a pair of glazed waxed octagonal reliefs of Robt. Adam after Tassie, 6 x 4½in. (Christie's) $1,331

WEDGWOOD

The Wedgwood Pottery was first established at Burslem in 1759 by Josiah Wedgwood but it moved to Etruria in 1769. It was famed for its green glazed wares, cream coloured wares, black basalt, jasper and cane ware. Parian busts, marketed as Carrara busts, appeared in 1848 and the company also successfully experimented in lithography which gave an imitation of oil painting on pottery. Good quality bone china was produced at Etruria between 1812 and 1829 but after the last date the company concentrated on traditional earthenware until 1878 when the making of bone china recommenced. The advertising at that time said, "We intend to produce articles of the highest quality...". Wedgwood bone china was decorated by some notable artists including Thomas Allen, Therese Lessore, A. and L. Powell and K. Murray. Wedgwood enjoyed great commercial success in the early 20th century with their "Fairyland Lustre". Earthenware production continued at the same time and their transfer printed tiles, majolica ware and pottery decorated with printed landscapes was hugely popular.

A Wedgwood caneware custard cup and cover with rope twist handle, 7.5cm. high. (Phillips) $1,040

A Wedgwood blue and white jasper bulb pot and cover, impressed mark and V, circa 1785, 24cm. high.(Christie's) $1,840

A Wedgwood garden seat of rounded hexagonal shape, impressed Wedgwood, 46cm. high. (Christie's) $1,355

A 19th century Wedgwood jasper model of the Portland Vase, 10½in. high. (Reeds Rains) $792

A Wedgwood black basalt encaustic decorated vase, painted in red and enriched in white with a lady and attendants, late 18th century, 24cm. high. (Christie's) $2,217

A large Wedgwood black basalt pot pourri vase and cover with loop handles, 12in. high. (Parsons, Welch & Cowell) $784

495

WEDGWOOD

A Wedgwood majolica-ware 'Kate Greenaway' jardiniere, modelled as a lady's straw bonnet, 16.5cm., impressed Wedgwood and moulded registration mark. (Phillips) $379

A Wedgwood blue and white jasper cylindrical teapot and cover, circa 1790, 10.5cm. high. (Christie's) $847

A Wedgwood three-colour jasper dice-pattern cylindrical jardiniere, 9cm. high, and a stand, circa 1790. (Christie's) $1,439

A Wedgwood caneware oviform jug and cover, 22cm. high, and a saucer dish, circa 1815. (Christie's) $931

Pair of Wedgwood black basalt encaustic decorated oviform two-handled vases and one cover, circa 1800, 37.5cm. high. (Christie's) $5,702

A Wedgwood vase designed by Keith Murray, 16.5cm. high. (Christie's) $121

A rare and important Wedgwood Sydney Cove medallion, titled below Etruria 1789, the reverse impressed, 5.7cm. overall diam. (Phillips) $27,600

An Art Deco Wedgwood animal figure, modelled as a fallow deer, designed by J. Skeaping, 21.5cm. high. (Phillips) $230

A Wedgwood Fairyland lustre black-ground small globular jar and cover, circa 1925, 8.5cm. high. (Christie's) $2,359

WEIGHTS

Weights come in many shapes and sizes and were produced for such diverse users as apothecaries, jewellers, greengrocers etc. Complete sets are worth more than single weights. After a weight was cast, a lead insert would be put in and trimmed to the exact weight before official stamping. Weights for commercial purposes had to be periodically checked and impress stamped, and these markings can make a weight much more interesting.

A set of Apothecary Weights in a bakelite box by W. & J. George & Becker Ltd. $35

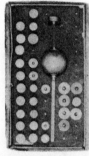

An early hydrometer with float and thirty brass weights, English, 1750-80, 7½in. long. $525

A pair of W. & T. Avery snuff scales, to weigh 1lb., class B. No. A189 with brass pans, together with a set of 5 weights. (Osmond Tricks) $210

A cased set of Jacobus Listingh coin weights, Dutch, dated 1659, 3½ x 6¼in., in leather slip case. $5,250

A set of brass Troy Weights from ¼oz. – 2oz. $35

An 18th century Dutch rectangular wooden box containing an iron and brass balance, together with weights, 25cm. long. $4,800

Great Western Railway solid iron balance weight. $18

WOOD, RALPH

The Wood family of Burslem are famous to collectors because of their high quality pottery figures made by two, if not by three, generations of Ralph Woods. Ralph Wood Senior, who died in 1772, and his brother Aaron developed an individual style for their productions which they passed onto their respective sons. Ralph's son, also named Ralph lived betwen 1748 and 1795, and worked as a potter of model figures in Burslem with his cousin Enoch (died 1840). Their products were particularly noted for delicate coloring. Ralph Wood III succeeded his father Ralph but died at the early age of 27 in 1801. Some earthenware figures that bear the name mark Ra Wood may have been his handiwork as may also be porcelain examples. Enoch Wood started his own factory in 1784 and in 1790 went into partnership with James Caldwell, making tableware marked Wood & Caldwell which was shipped to America in vast quantities.

A Ralph Wood Toby jug of conventional type, circa 1770, 25.5cm. high. (Christie's) $2,692

A Ralph Wood figure of a recumbent ram, on an oval green rockwork base moulded with foliage, circa 1770, 18.5cm. wide. (Christie's) $3,801

A Ralph Wood group of the Vicar and Moses of conventional type, circa 1770, 21.5cm. high. (Christie's) $643

A Staffordshire creamware group of St. George and the Dragon of conventional Ralph Wood type, circa 1780, 28.5cm. high. (Christie's) $3,630

A pair of Staffordshire figures of a gardener and companion of Ralph Wood type, circa 1780, 19.5cm. high. (Christie's) $4,356

A Ralph Wood Bacchus mask jug, circa 1775, 23.5cm. high.(Christie's) $545

WORCESTER

Porcelain has been produced in the city of Worcester from 1751 to the present day. The first period up till 1774 is called the Dr Wall period when soft paste porcelain was made at Warmstry House on the banks of the Severn. In 1783 Thomas Flight purchased the works, and well designed and decorated porcelain as well as many blue and white pieces were produced. They made dessert ware and comports in glazed porcelain supported by Parian figures and their Limoges ware was exhibited at the Paris International Exhibition of 1855. In 1862 the company was renamed the Worcester Royal Porcelain Company with Richard William Binns as Art Director and Edward Phillips in charge of production. Their products were of very high quality, and the firm is best known for the heavily jewelled decoration of the table services and for the high quality painting and gilding. They also produced figures in ivory paste with bright glazes and enamelled decorations. The birds made by Dorothy Doughty are especially famous.

A Royal Worcester 'ivory' mermaid and nautilus centre-piece, decorated by Callow-hill, circa 1878. (Christie's) $1,399

A Worcester plate from The Duke of Gloucester Service, gold crescent mark, circa 1775, 22.5cm. diam. (Christie's) $23,595

Royal Worcester vase and cover painted by Ricketts, 11in. high. (Reeds Rains) $713

A Worcester, Flight, Barr & Barr, urn-shaped two-handled vase and cover, circa 1820, 46cm. high. (Christie's) $2,376

A Worcester blue and white bottle and a basin transfer-printed with The Pinecone and Foliage pattern, circa 1775, bottle 22cm. high, basin 27.5cm. diam. (Christie's) $1,439

A Royal Worcester reticulated oviform vase by George Owen, pattern no. 1969, gilt marks and date code for 1912, 17cm. high. (Christie's) $2,799

499

A large 'bow' vase, signed
John Stinton, 30.5 cm. high,
shape no. 1428, date code
for 1908. (Phillips)
$4,342

A pair of Royal Worcester
figures modelled as a lady
and gentleman, 14in. high,
circa 1887. (Christie's)
$1,480

A Grainger's Worcester
pedestal ewer with a painted
scene of swans, signed
indistinctly, 10in. high.
(Hetheringtons Nationwide)
$858

An ovoid vase, the body well
painted with two Highland
cattle, signed H. Stinton,
21cm. high, shape no. 1762,
date code for 1910. (Phillips)
$1,107

Royal Worcester Hadley-
style footed vase, designed
as a jardiniere, 1906, 5in.
high. (Giles Haywood)
$458

A Royal Worcester porcelain
jug (ice tusk), circa 1884,
approx. 12in. tall. (G. A. Key)
$548

Worcester porcelain jug, the
blush ivory ground with hand-
painted floral sprigs, circa
1902, 7in. high. (G. A. Key)
$346

One of a pair of Grainger Worcester
mugs with single spur handles,
titled below painted panels,
'Drawing Cover' and 'The Death',
11.5cm. high. (Phillips)
$12,606

A Dr. Wall Worcester quart
mug with strap handle,
circa 1770, 6.1/8in. high.
(Robt. W. Skinner Inc.)
$275

WRISTWATCHES

The first watches were made with only one hand and were carried in the fob pocket of the trouser waistband, moving to the waistcoat in the 19th century. The invention of the wrist watch did not take place till the 20th century.

Early watches had a lever and cylinder escapement and were made by Mudge, Tompion, Graham, Quare, Frodsham, Breguet, Leroux, Barraud and Ellicott. When wrist watches appeared a multitude of makers adopted the idea but the one which is most sought after is the Rolex, especially slim rectangular ones made in the 1930's. The Rolex Prince was produced in stainless steel, gold, silver or striped gold and the case was curved for the wrist. The movement was of nickel silver. The Rolex Oyster first appeared in 1927 and for sheer reliability has become a by-word. Ladies' Rolex Oysters fetch about half the price of those for men which can go for around $2,000 for an automatic. Among women's watches the most desirable are Art Deco diamond set models by Patek Philippe and Vacheron & Constantin.

A circular Swiss gold gent's wristwatch with chronograph, by Universal, Geneve, the signed movement jewelled to the centre, 36mm. diam. (Phillips)
$2,618

An early platinum and gold Cartier Santos gent's wristwatch, the movement signed Cartier, with roman numerals and blued steel hands, 25mm. long. (Phillips)
$11,220

A circular Swiss gold automatic gent's wristwatch, by International Watch Co., with centre seconds and baton numerals, 34mm. diam. (Phillips)
$374

A gentleman's wristwatch in heavy metal circular case, inscribed Audemars Piguet and Co., Geneve, 34mm. diam. (Christie's)
$790

A rectangular 18ct. gold gent's wristwatch, the movement with silvered dial signed for J. W. Benson, London, 1937, 39mm. long. (Phillips)
$524

A Swiss two colour gold circular gent's wristwatch, by Supra, with gilt Roman numerals and subsidiary seconds, 27mm. diam. (Phillips) $304

WRISTWATCHES

A hexagonal Swiss gold wrist-watch, by Rolex, the movement with engraved silvered dial and blued hands, 31mm. long. (Phillips) $524

A Swiss gold hexagonal gent's wristwatch, by Cartier, the signed dial with Roman numerals, 31mm. long. (Phillips) $2,197

A Swiss gold circular gent's wristwatch, by Vacheron and Constantin, the signed sil-vered dial with subsidiary seconds, 28mm. diam. (Phillips) $2,704

An 18ct. gold rectangular wristwatch signed Vacheron & Constantin, Geneve, with monometallic balance, jew-elled to the centre with 17 jewels, 32mm. x 25mm. (Christie's) $1,443

An 18ct. gold Cartier wrist-watch, the white and grey enamelled dial numbered 1-24, the plated movement signed Bouch-Girod, 33mm. diameter. (Christie's) $2,887

A stylish square gold wrist-watch inscribed Patek Philippe, Geneve, the plated movement adjusted to five positions, 26mm. square. (Christie's) $2,117

A Swiss gold circular gent's wristwatch, by Patek Philippe, the signed dial with baton numerals and subsidiary seconds, 34mm. diam. (Phillips) $2,281

A circular half hunter cased Swiss gold gent's wristwatch, by Rolex, the front with enamel numerals opened by a button at the VI position, 31mm. diam. (Phillips) $1,496

A fine and rare split second wrist chronograph, signed Patek Philippe & Co., Geneva, the nickel 25-jewel movement with mono-metallic balance. (Christie's) $93,500

WRISTWATCHES

A steel oyster perpetual bubble back gent's wristwatch, by Rolex, the signed silvered dial with Arabic numerals, (Phillips) $676

A lady's Swiss gold wristwatch, by Corum, the case in the form of a Rolls-Royce radiator, with 'R.R.' badge and 'Spirit of Ecstasy' mascot, 28mm. long. (Phillips) $1,156

An 18ct. gold circular wristwatch, the movement signed Russells Limited, the signed enamel dial with subsidiary seconds, London 1926, 33mm. diam. (Phillips) $473

A Swiss two colour gold Rolex Prince wristwatch, the signed silvered dial with Arabic numerals and subsidiary seconds below, 42mm. long. (Phillips) $4,394

A rare 18ct. gold split-second chronograph wristwatch in circular case, the signed movement with monometallic balance, jewelled to the centre with 20 jewels. (Christie's) $3,657

A rectangular Dunhill wristwatch in yellow metal case, the white enamel dial with mottled brown centre, 33mm. x 28mm. (Christie's) $423

A Swiss gold cushion shaped gent's wristwatch, by Longines, the signed dial marked for Alex Scott, Glasgow with subsidiary seconds, 31mm. long. (Phillips) $574

An 18ct. gold Cartier Panta calendar wristwatch, with quartz movement, heavy brick-link gold bracelet and invisible deployant Cartier clasp - 26mm. x 35mm. (Christie's) $8,085

A rectangular Swiss white gold lady's wristwatch by Baume & Mercier, Geneve, the bezel set with thirty-six diamonds, 28mm. long. (Phillips) $1,533

ZEPPELIN MEMORABILIA

The Zeppelin was invented by Count von Zeppelin around 1900, and the term strictly applies only to the German airships of the First World War period. Memorabilia is not common but does exist in such forms as bookends made from Zeppelin timber and items jettisoned from, for example, the crippled German L33 as it struggled unsuccessfully to reach Germany after a bombing raid on London in 1916. (It crashed and was scuttled by its crew.)

'Zeppelin' a white metal cigarette and match holder, 22.8cm. long. (Christie's) **$267**

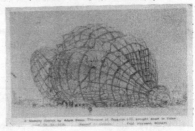

A Memory Sketch by Adam Eruce Thomson of Zeppelin L33, brought down in Essex, September 23rd, 1916. **$18**

Count Zeppelin in his airship Zeppelin III, postcard by Cook & Sons (Soap) 1908. **$15**

A Tipp R101 tinplate Zeppelin, German, circa 1930, 25½in. long. **$1,750**

"Zepp" Charm, made out of framework of Zeppelin, brought down in Essex, September, 1916. **$14**

An Imperial German World War I Zeppelin crew badge (Army). (Wallis & Wallis) **$470**

Commemorative serviette for the R101 Zeppelin, 5th October 1930. **$60**

Index

INDEX

INDEX

INDEX

Glico 339
Globes 258, 260
Globuscope 352
Gloves 228
Gnomes 224
Godden, H. 327
Godiana 356
Goldscheider 229, 230, 490
Goldsmiths & Silversmiths 267
Golfing jugs & mugs 427, 428
Gone with the Wind 203, 206
Goodall & Son, Chas. 42
Gorham Co. 83, 239
Gosnell, John & Co 409
Goss & Peake 231
Goss China 231, 232
Goss Cottages 233-235
Goss, Florence 490
Gottlob, Fernand Louis 376
Goulding, C. J. 325
GPO 455
Grable, Betty 204
Grafton 166
Grammont, Paris 455
Gramophone & Typewriter Ltd 238
Gramophone Needle Tins 236
Gramophones 237, 238
Grand Jubilee Volume of Little Folks 113
Grand Libellule 95
Granger, Stewart 418
Grant of Devizes 444
Grant, Duncan 478
Grant, P.L. 356
Grant, Ulysses S. 420
Grant, W.H. 425
Gray, T. 107
Grays of Cambridge 386
Great Expectations 73
Great Western Railway Co. 271, 497
Green Woodpecker 446
Green, James 368
Greenaway, Kate 98
Greenline Coach 315
Greenly, A. H. 325
Greenock Apothecaries & Lawsons Ltd 440
Grenades 252
Grey Squirrel 444
Greyhound Coach 313, 315
Greyhound Lines Coach 314
Grimaldi, William 367
Grindlay, Capt. Robert M.G. 73
Grose, J. & Co. 95
Grover & Baker 406
Groves, A. 325
Gruber, Jacques 432
Grueby 239
Grun, Jules Alexandre 373
Guitar 328
Gulliver's Travels 113
Gun cartridge 252
Gun tackle block 252
Gunn, T.E. 444, 446
Guntermann 315
Gyobu 279
Gyokumin 158

H.L. 268
Haakon VII 421
Hagan's Magnolia Balm 473
Hagenauer 104, 125
Hague, The 54
Hair Clips 240
Halford, F.M. 72
Hall stand 434
Hamada, Shoji 450
Hamlet, Wm. 422
Hampston & Prince 176
Han Dynasty 102, 264, 265
Hancock, John C. 326
Handall's Celebrated Ointment 342
Handkerchiefs 241, 242
Handwerck, Max 183
Hannell's 20
Hans Anderson's Fairy Tales 113
Hans Coper 243

Hardstone 244, 245
Hardy, Oliver 207
Hardy, Thomas 234
Harmeyer, E.F. 474, 475
Harmonium 327
Harp shell 413
Harper, Pastor John 467
Harper, W.K. 194
Harps 328
Harpsichord 327
Harradine, L. 192-194
Harris, J. B. 325
Harris, Philip 188
Harrison, George 394
Harrison, Rex 207
Harrods Ltd 356
Harrow School 189
Harry Peck's 21
Hart & Co. 87
Hase, Henry 45
Hassall, John 113
Hathaway, Ann 234
Hats 246-248
Hawksley, G. & J.W. 379
Haynes & Jeffy's 55
Hayward, Susan 419
Hayworth, Rita 208, 418
HC 243
Heath & Middleston 185
Heath Robinson, G. & Birch, J. Ltd 116
Helmets 249-251
Hendrix, Jimi 391
Henry VIII 33
Hepburn, Audrey 203, 204
Hepburn, Katherine 69
Hepple & Co. 244
Herold Electro 236
Herold Tango 236
Heubach, Gebruder 182
Heubach-Koppelsdorf 183
Hewitt, James L. & Co. 326
Hidekatsu 215
Hignetts 126-129, 136
Hilderscheimer, S. 26
Hill, R. & J. 135
Hill, W.E. & Sons 486
Hill, Wm. E. & Sons 487
Hilliard & Thomason 88
Hine, W. 445
Hires, Charles E. Co. 474
Hirschfield, Nathaniel, J. 39
Hitchcock, Alfred 204
HMS Invincible Artefacts 252, 253
HMV 237, 238
Hockney, David 374
Hoeninghausen's Central Tea Store 476
Hohlwein, Ludwig 376
Hold to Light Postcards 254
Hollies, The 392
Holloway's Ointment 341
Holme 85
Holst, R.N. Roland 376
Holtzmann 328
Hopi 16, 17
Horikawa 389, 390
Homby 322, 323
Hornet, The 151
Horoldt, Johann, G. 299
Horsfords Acid Phosphate 476
Hotspur Book for Boys 114
Houdon 458
Houghton-Butcher Mfg. Co. 92
Household Sewing Machine Co. 475
Howard & Sons 108
Howe Sewing Machine Co. 406
Howett 94
Hoyle, Harriot 398
Hoyt, E.W. 474
Huber, P. 349
Huber, Patriz 196
Hudson 323
Hukin & Heath 137
Humerous Postcards 370, 371
Humidor 161
Hunt, George 266

Hunt, Wilhelm 424
Huntley & Palmers 61, 62
Huny 404
Hurley, E.T. 188
Hurricane 318
Hutchings, J. 445
Hutton, John 433
Hutton, Wm. & Sons Arts & Crafts 358
Huvarco 270
HW, Sheffield 427
Hydrometer 497

I.A. 255
Iceberg, The 465
Ichida 389
Icons 255, 256
Iesson, Sarah 398
Ihagee 91
Ile de France Tinplate Coach 314
Ilex Mill Co. Ltd 65
Imari 365
Infants Magazine 113
Inglis, R.W. 48
Inros 257
Instruments 258-260
International Watch Co. 501
Ishiguro Masayoshi 215
Isola 'The Bishop's Balm' 342
Italian Directoire 107
Ivalek 167
Ive's Kromskop 187
Ivory 261-263

J.D. 54
J.V. 268
Jackson, A.E. 114
Jackson, Al 384
Jackson, Michael 392
Jackson, Tito 391
Jacob & Co., W.R. 61, 62
Jacquet-Droz 36
Jade 264, 265
Jaques, J. & Son 385
Jarvis, Thos. 433
Jaschke's Ch. 410
Jean, Philip 368
Jensen, Georg 267
Jentsch & Meerz 18
Jervis Art 121
Jetter, H. 387
Jewelry 266-268
Jigsaw Puzzles 269-271
John, Augustus 31, 361
Johnnie Walker 82
Johns, Glynis 207
Johnson, Thomas, Dr. 341
Johnson, Thos. 294
Jones, George & Sons 109
Joustra 313
Joyce, Richard 120
JP 170
JU89 Heavy Bomber 318
Judge Brand 236
Juke Boxes 272-273
Jye 315

Kakiemon 24, 112, 452
Kammer & Reinhardt 238
Kandler, J.J. 300
Kandler, J.J. and Reinicke, P.J. 299
Kangxi 365
Kap Kap 413
Karloff, Boris 207, 418
Kauba, C. 84
Kayersinn 349
Kazak 395
Kazan, Elia 419
Kealey, E. V. 491
Kearsar 321
Kelly, Grace 207, 418
Kelly, June 393
Kemp & Co. Ltd 462
Kemp, Dixon 319
Kendall Mfg. Co. 473
Kennedy School 488

508

INDEX

INDEX

INDEX